Best wishes
Graham

ABOUT THE AUTHOR

Graham Majin worked as a broadcast journalist and senior producer for more than twenty years — fourteen at BBC News. His inside knowledge gives him a unique insight into how journalists think and how news is produced. He is the author of magazine articles, academic papers and book chapters which explore how the concept of Journalistic Truth is understood differently by audiences, journalists and academics and how it evolves over time. *Truthophobia* is his first, full-length book on journalism. He enjoys walking, cycling and trying to play jazz saxophone. He lives in Dorset on the sunny south coast of England.

Independent Publishing Network *publishers*
71-75 Shelton Street, London, WC2H 97Q, UK

First published in Great Britain by
Independent Publishing Network in 2023

Paperback: ISBN   978-1-80352-475-7

www.truthophobia.net

TRUTHOPHOBIA: How the Boomers Broke Journalism

The Story of the Death of Impartial and Objective News

Graham Majin PhD

For

Harry, George & Annabelle,
Mum, Dad, Cyril, Gerald and all the Old Gang.

"It makes all the difference in the world whether we put Truth in the first place or in the second place."
— Richard Whately.

"The young have exalted notions, because they have not been humbled by life or learned its necessary limitations... All their mistakes are in the direction of doing things excessively and vehemently. They overdo everything; they love too much, hate too much, and the same with everything else." — Aristotle.

"Our brains are designed for tribal life, for getting along with a select group of others (Us), and for fighting off everyone else (Them)."
— Joshua Greene

"It is very difficult to see one's own most cherished ideas in perspective, as parts of a changing and, perhaps, absurd tradition." — Paul Feyerabend.

"The most dangerous man to any government is the man who is able to think things out for himself, without regard to the prevailing superstitions and taboos. Almost inevitably he comes to the conclusion that the government he lives under is dishonest, insane, and intolerable." — H.L. Mencken.

"Those who can make you believe absurdities can make you commit atrocities" — Voltaire.

Contents

PART THREE
How the Boomers Broke Journalism

Acknowledgments

This book grew out of my doctoral thesis, so first I would like to thank my PhD supervisors Professor Tim Luckhurst and Dr. Ben Cocking. As a distinguished historian of journalism, Tim's insights have been a particular inspiration to me in writing this book. Thanks also to my examiners Professors Richard Whatmore and David Welch for their thought-provoking comments and generous praise. I am grateful to my colleagues at Bournemouth University for their friendship and for intellectual nourishment. Thanks especially to Dr. Catalin Brylla for discussions about cognitive psychology and philosophy and to Dr. Henry Loeser for sharing his memories of the US in the late 1960s and early 1970s. I am immensely grateful to Douglas Falconer for proof-reading the manuscript and for advice about structure and narrative. Thanks to the poet and novelist Dr. Chris Greenhalgh for permission to quote from *The Cool End of Red*. Thanks to the radio presenter and author Ray Clark for sharing his recollections about music radio during the 1960s. Thanks also to Jasper Bouverie, Tim Knight and Grant Pollard for numerous thought-provoking conversations about ideology, culture and science, and to Grant for advice with the cover design and for photography.

I would like to thank the BBC's former North America Editor Jon Sopel who gave his time generously and responded patiently to my questions. My criticisms are aimed at Narrative Led News in general, not at Jon himself. Thanks also to the distinguished scholar of journalism Gaye Tuchman for responding to my email enquiries. Again, my quarrel is with the logic and coherence of Tuchmanism, not with Professor Tuchman — it is for the reader to judge where truth lies. Thanks also to Doctors Justin Schlosberg and Tim Hayward for sharing their experiences of being criticized in a BBC documentary about misinformation. To Karen Plumbley-Jones I owe more than I can express here, but thank you especially for being inspiring, and for

i

intelligent conversation while rambling round the shire. Finally, although many of the insights and ideas in this book have come from other people, the views expressed are my own, therefore responsibility for any deficiencies or errors rests solely with me.

What is a Boomer?

Defining Boomers is tricky. Demographic analysis reveals different baby booms at slightly different times in the US, the UK and elsewhere. There were, in fact, two distinct booms within the boomer generational cohort. This is significant because older boomers became role models for younger boomers. The most striking example of this is perhaps the Beatles, most of whom were born in 1940, and who became icons for those born around ten years later. The phenomenon of a huge cohort of young people learning from other, slightly older, young people and forming a coherent generational tribe, is central to understanding the Boomer Ideology. In many ways, the first wave of Boomers (what anthropologists refer to as "prestigious individuals") displaced the traditional role of adults and became ideological parents to the second wave. The resulting "vortex of immaturity" is one of the themes of this book.

For those who crave neat demographic boundaries and labels, an extensive technical literature of generational analysis is available. Christopher Winship and David Harding's *A Mechanism-Based Approach to the Identification of Age–Period–Cohort Models* (Sociological Methods & Research. 2008; 36, 3) is a good place to start. If pushed, I would suggest 1940-1955 as being the core natal years for Boomers. Those born after 1960 are Generation X — they are post-Boomers. For those who argue that people born between 1955 and 1960 are Boomers, I would say they are at best BINOs — Boomers in name only. They arrived after the party was over. As a rule of thumb therefore, I consider Boomers to be people who were teenagers, or young adults, during the 1960s. But demographics are a distraction. It is the ideology and worldview of the Boomers that concerns us here, not demographics. We are trying to understand the Boomers, not define them.

Introduction

The Boomer Version of History

Journalism and Truth

W e need information. Like food and water, it is essential for our survival. However, not all information is equally useful. Good information must be strategic — it must be relevant to our current needs. It must also be accurate and complete. The ability to distinguish between good and bad information is a basic human skill, like the ability to distinguish between good and bad food. Making a decision based on inaccurate or incomplete information can be very dangerous. In everyday conversation we say that good, nourishing information is 'true'. The bad stuff we refer to as 'untrue'. Some information we obtain from our own direct experience of the world. For example, we don't need much help to find out if it's raining, we can just look out of the window.

But we can't check everything ourselves. Instead, we rely on other people to supply us with information. The testimony we receive from others gives us, effectively, more eyes to see with and more ears to hear with. Their testimony helps us learn from their experiences, successes and failures. However, this is where things start to get interesting. How can we be certain that the testimony provided by other people is true? The answer is simple. We can't. Every time we believe what other people tell us, we expose ourselves to the danger that they may be wrong, or willfully trying to deceive, or manipulate us. The uncomfortable truth is that other people's interests and desires do not always align with our own. It will sometimes be advantageous, and therefore tempting, for them to mislead us, and for us to mislead them. Fortunately, human beings have also evolved tools to detect unreliable information and lying. The human capacity for doubt and skepticism is an epistemic defense mechanism. Without it we would all be gullible fools, unable to distinguish good information from bad. Therefore, as the evolutionary psychologist Dan Sperber explains, "the abilities for overt intentional communication and epistemic vigilance must have evolved together."[1]

Journalism is a particular form of testimony. Our need for journalism reflects our basic, psycho-cognitive need for good, relevant, truthful information. We use journalism as a mouse uses its whiskers. It helps us navigate. It helps us build a picture of the world, sniff out opportunities and avoid dangers. As the journalist Ben Bagdikian put it, "News is the peripheral nervous system of the body politic, sensing the total environment and selecting which sights and sounds shall be transmitted to the public."[2]

Thus, journalism has an intimate relationship with truth. Using the language of philosophy, we can say that news is defined by its epistemic purpose. Journalism must aspire to tell the truth, or at least we must believe it does, otherwise it cannot qualify as journalism. Fictional storytelling is not journalism. Propaganda is not journalism. The outward shape of journalism may change over time, but its core, epistemic purpose cannot or it would cease to be journalism. However, although its fundamental relationship with truth cannot change, journalism is not a fixed thing. Different journalisms evolve in different places and at different times to serve the needs of society and the dominant ideology of the age. It follows therefore, that when there are two competing ideologies, we can expect to see two competing journalisms. This is precisely what we see in the early 2020s – Official Journalism and Unofficial Journalism, two genres that are incompatible with one another and mutually hostile.

This book is an attempt to explain where we are and how we got here. It tells the story of how journalism has changed over time and how it continues to change. It will argue that many of the controversies surrounding journalism, fake news and truth come from the fact that we live at a time of ideological flux. Consequently, there is disagreement about which journalism is the right journalism, disagreement about what is true and disagreement about how we understand truth.

Challenging the Boomer Version of History

There are two major obstacles that prevent us seeing exactly where we are and how we got here. The first is that the Boomer generation changed how the concept of 'truth' is understood. The old, common-sense, folk understanding of 'truth' came under relentless assault from Boomer scholars and intellectuals who were 'truthophobic' — profoundly hostile to the way their parents and grandparents understood the words 'reality', 'truth' and 'knowledge'. It may sound strange to hear that the concept of 'truth' can change. But this is because we use the word 'truth' to describe many different things in many different contexts. This equivocal, imprecise use of language causes a great deal of mischief. It will be helpful therefore to bear in mind that what concerns us in this book is 'Journalistic Truth' – a technical kind of truth. It will also be useful to think of truth as 'legitimate knowledge' – beliefs that are widely accepted by a particular group or society. The study of knowledge, truth and reality is referred to by philosophers as epistemology. The first barrier to understanding the problems of contemporary journalism is therefore epistemic. More on this later.

The second barrier to understanding where we are and what's going on, is that the Boomer generation rewrote the history of journalism to make it conform to their values and worldview. From the 1970s onwards, revisionist histories of journalism began to appear in which the concept of truth was stripped-out and replaced by sociological and political perspectives. The Boomers labelled the old way of understanding journalism the 'Whig Interpretation of History'. The phrase was first used by the British historian Herbert Butterfield in 1931 who used it to refer to a narrative constructed by writers who were, "Protestant, progressive, and Whig, and the very model of the nineteenth-century gentleman." It was a narrative, he claimed, that tended to "produce a story which is the ratification if not the glorification of the present."[3]

The American journalism scholar James Carey, writing in 1974, drew on Butterfield's analysis and complained that although traditional histories were not inaccurate, they were not responsive to the needs of the Boomer generation. The problem, he said "is not that the Whig interpretation was wrong or failed to teach us anything, but it is moribund."[4] Carey did not challenge the established facts of journalism history, however he did seek to rearrange them into a new, Boomer-friendly narrative. The old narrative, he said, "is exhausted, it has done its intellectual work." Numerous scholars on both sides of the Atlantic followed Carey's lead, unleashing a torrent of fashionable revisionism. For example, in 1978 the American academic Roy Atwood enthusiastically urged historians to "initiate revision" and proclaimed that the "frameworks within which the history of journalism has been viewed must be turned upside down and inside out."[5]

In the same year, an influential book was published that promised to challenge "many commonly held assumptions about the role of the press". In it, the British historian George Boyce wrote a chapter in which he "reappraised" the view that journalism's role was to create informed voters by providing them with truthful news. Boyce ridiculed the concept that journalism was the "Fourth Estate" — an essential part of Liberal Democracy. "The whole idea of the Fourth Estate" Boyce said, "was a myth". Victorian journalists, he argued, were really only driven by greed and vanity. They wanted to make as much profit as possible and elevate their status in the social hierarchy. To achieve this, they camouflaged their true motives by claiming they were searching for truth, helping to create an informed electorate and protecting democracy. Boyce's truthophobic conclusion was that all this was nonsense — the Victorians had "invented a political myth."[6]

A chapter in the same book by the academic Philip Elliot went further. He ridiculed the "cherished beliefs" of newspapermen. Drawing on philosophical relativism, he mocked the possibility that journalists could supply truthful information. It was impossible, he argued, because there was no such thing as truth. Using this circular, truthophobic reasoning he criticized the, "myth of neutral information — that the codes and practices of professional journalism will lead to the production of neutral, unbiased facts about the world." Elliot mocked journalists who aspired to be impartial describing them as "intellectual eunuchs". He singled out the British communist writer Claud Cockburn for praise because he was a "committed radical journalist". Elliot ended his chapter with a suitably truthophobic Cockburn quote, "The humbug and hypocrisy of the press begin only when newspapers pretend to be 'impartial' or 'servants of the public'. And this only becomes dangerous as well as laughable when the public is fool enough to believe it."[7]

Another truthophobic contributor to the book, Anthony Smith, poked fun at what he described as Victorian journalism's naïve, childlike faith in the power of shorthand. There was no such thing as truthful, honest journalism, he claimed — it was an illusion created by shorthand,

> "The advent of shorthand which transformed the business of reporting into a kind of science... A fully competent shorthand reporter seemed to have acquired an almost supernatural power... it seemed at first that reporting was capable of providing a true mirror of reality."

Smith concluded that, like a drowning man in a leaking life jacket, the old journalism could no longer support itself with "scanty and fraying intellectual equipment". The Boomer way of knowing was now dominant — impartial Victorian Liberal Journalism was dead, "The clarity of purpose which absorbed and concentrated the energies of English journalism at its peak a century ago has gone and will never return."[8]

During the 1970s and 1980s, these views became the accepted orthodoxy in academia. For example, in 1988 the Boomer academics James Curran and Jean Seaton produced a popular, highly influential textbook described as a "classic and authoritative introduction to the history, sociology, theory and politics of the media in Britain."[9] Following Roy Atwood and other Boomer intellectuals, Curran and Seaton boasted their mission was not to explore the history of journalism, but to "stand it on its head". Copying the now-fashionable formula, they dismissed pre-Boomer scholarship as the "Whig History of Journalism" which they referred to as a "political mythology". Instead of the old mythology, Curran and Seaton constructed a new one — the Boomer History of Journalism. This revisionist narrative was a ratification and glorification of the values, assumptions and prejudices of the Boomer generation. For example, it assumed that journalism ought to be a force for social change, not a source of truthful information. Using the vocabulary of Boomer campus activism of the 1960s and 1970s, Curran and Seaton explained that during the Victorian era, "insurgent journalism" sustained a "radical sub-culture" and that there was widespread "militancy within the radical press" fueled by an "activist working class". In keeping with the new Boomer Interpretation of History, the concept of truth is barely mentioned by Curran and Seaton. When it does appear, it is dismissed as an "abstract and elevated principle" which "may seem a little incongruous to contemporary ears".

The Boomer Interpretation of History stood history on its head by reversing cause and effect. Boomer historians argued that Victorian Liberal Journalism was not profitable because the public wanted to read impartial, truthful news. Instead they argued the public was persuaded to want impartial, truthful news because it was profitable. This is like arguing that grocery stores are not profitable because people want to eat, but that people are tricked into wanting to eat to make grocery stores profitable. To make the Boomer Interpretation of History sound less implausible, Boomer scholars concealed the real reason why Victorian Liberal Journalism was successful in the first place. The concept of truth was airbrushed out of the picture altogether.

Another popular history of journalism, written by the Boomer historian Kevin Williams, explained that journalism became popular during the Victorian era, not because it valued impartial truth-seeking, but because it,

> "Articulated the tastes and interests of the bourgeoisie… The newspapers' exposition of middle-class values was also motivated by straightforward commercial considerations… The commercial interests of the press became increasing tied up with the rapidly expanding, better off and better educated, middle classes."[10]

This highlights a major failing of the Boomer Interpretation of History, namely that it lacks any genuine explanatory power. It is a description masquerading as an explanation. For example, if we take William's sentences and substitute the phrase "Boomer generation" for "middle class", then we get the equally valid, but equally trite, observation that during the last third of the 20th Century, the media articulated the "tastes and interests" of the Boomer generation, and that the media's,

"Exposition of the values of the Boomer generation was motivated by straightforward commercial considerations… The commercial interests of the media became increasing tied up with the rapidly expanding, better off and better educated, Boomer generation."

All this tells us is that journalism, like any other commercial product, will respond to demand from powerful, wealthy groups. People, in other words, get the journalism they want. What the Boomer version of history doesn't explain is what sort of journalism did the Victorians want, and why did they want it? The answer is they wanted truthful journalism because they wanted to live in a Liberal Democracy, and they believed truthful journalism was essential to help them realize their hopes and ambitions. What the Boomer Interpretation of History really tells us therefore is, not what the Victorians believed, but what Boomer historians believed.

The ideology of Victorian Liberalism preached thrift, hard work, self-reliance, self-control and individual responsibility. In a tough, Darwinian world, people were seen as rational individuals who needed truthful journalism to help them make good decisions and compete in the race of life. The Boomer generation despised this ideology and rejected it. It was, they believed, no longer relevant. What they wanted was a more idealistic and Utopian approach to life. They rejected their parents' and grandparents' assumptions about reality and human nature, and demanded an ethical-political form of journalism that would help change the world, not merely describe it. The Boomer Interpretation of History was therefore not innocent. Its truthophobia was motivated by the Boomer's desire to discredit the values of Victorian Liberalism and legitimize their own. To make history conform to their own worldview, the Boomers rewrote it.

The Boomer version of the history, in other words, was not constructed in a vacuum. It should be seen in the context of broader currents of

Boomer intellectual thought. For example, in 1975 the Boomer philosopher, artist and activist Henry Flynt published a book in which he preached a doctrine of "cognitive nihilism" — the need to erase all traces of Victorian Liberal thought and epistemology as a necessary prelude to transforming society and creating a Boomer-friendly future. Flynt's number one target was the old, common-sense understanding of truth which, he said, was being used by the older generation to crush the Boomer's dreams and deny them political, economic and cultural power. Flynt explained,

> "The important consequence of my philosophy is the rejection of truth as an intellectual modality... In rejecting truth, I advocated in its place intellectual activities which have an objective value independent of truth."[11]

Flynt wanted to see a world in which dreams, longings and shared generational desires would change the world and liberate people from the oppression and alienation of everyday life. Even impossible things, he said, would become possible if the old concepts of reality and truth were destroyed,

> "I cannot exercise my freedom to walk through walls until the whole cognitive orientation of the modern era is restructured throughout. The project of restructuring the modern cognitive orientation is a vast one. The natural sciences must certainly be dismantled... Someday we will realize that we were always free to walk through walls. But we could not exercise this freedom because we structured the whole situation, and the evidence, in an enslaving way."[12]

This, he assured his readers, was a radical epistemic and Utopian vision, not madness,

> "There may be only a hair's-breadth of difference between the state I propose and mental incompetence or death — but still, there is all of a hair's breadth. I magnify this hair's-breadth many times, and use it as a lever to overturn civilization."[13]

Flynt said the Boomers were on the verge of something human beings had never achieved before. They were about to create Utopia. It was a stage of development he referred to as the "third level" of politics,

"The third level of politics has to do with the Utopian aspect of modern political ideologies, the aspect which calls not only for society to change, but to change for the better. Typical third-level political goals are the abolition of war, the abolition of the oligarchic structure of society, and the abolition of economic institutions which value human lives in terms of money. In all of human history, society has never changed on this third level."[14]

Cognitive nihilism, the urge to utterly destroy Victorian Liberalism and start over, was a major theme of Boomer culture. For example, in 1970, the *Madison Kaleidoscope*, a Boomer Underground newspaper, mocked the idea of gently reforming the old order. Radical change, it shouted,

"Must start with genuine revolution, with a complete transformation of all the conditions of social life. The present generation must destroy blindly, indiscriminately, everything that exists, thinking only 'as fast as possible, as much as possible'".[15]

The distinguishing feature of Boomer histories of journalism was epistemic nihilism. The concept of Journalistic Truth was banished to the margins of intellectual discussion. The key challenge for Boomer historians was to write about news, while avoiding the concept of truth. It was a delicate enterprise — like trying to write about clocks while denying the concept of time. The legacy of this is that today, most people's understanding of the history of journalism is the product of the revisionist text books produced by the Boomers during the 1970s, 1980s and 1990s. Like cement, the Boomer Interpretation of History has hardened. In the 2020s, its truthophobic narrative, is accepted uncritically as fact and rarely questioned.

Three Journalistic Goals:
Aletheia, Arete and *Nomisma*

What this book attempts to do is to restore epistemology to our understanding of journalism. However, challenging a well-established narrative is not easy. The consensus does not welcome deviance. For example, the American political scientist Bruce Gilley, who in 2017 questioned the Boomer version of colonial history, found himself accused of gross ignorance. However, as Gilley pointed out, those who criticized him started with the assumption that the Boomer version was correct, and that any departure from it must therefore be wrong. As Gilley put it, "the so-called "errors" of my article are not errors at all, but rather are self-referential appeals by anti-colonial scholars to the scholarship of other anti-colonial scholars". The rot he said was, "very deep indeed. Nothing short of a complete rewriting of almost everything published in the last half century about colonialism will allow us to recover something like an authentic history of that period". Gilley had discovered how difficult it is to challenge a well-entrenched narrative.[16]

In order to put the concept of truth back into our understanding of journalism, it will be helpful to think of three different goals that can motivate journalists:

1. Journalists can honestly try to tell the truth as best they can. I will use the old Greek word *aletheia* (pronounced al-ee-thia) to refer to this goal of truth seeking and truth telling.

2. Journalists can try to make the world a better, fairer place and help bring about social justice. This might involve encouraging people to do what is ethically-politically right and discouraging them from doing what is ethically-politically wrong. I will use the Greek word *arete* to refer to this goal of seeking to bring about change to make the world a better place.

3. Journalists can try to make money by giving audiences whatever they want and whatever they will pay for. Here the goal is to maximize revenue by creating popular content. I will use the word *nomisma* to refer to this goal of seeking commercial success and market dominance.

In the real world, these goals overlap. For example, *aletheia* and *arete* are fundamentally different motives and are often incompatible with one another. However, they might not always be incompatible. It will sometimes be ethically-politically useful to tell people the whole truth. Similarly, *nomisma*, the goal of being commercially successful, usually complements both the goals of *aletheia* and *arete*. Journalists who want to promote social justice will also want their journalism to be popular. Nor are these the only possible motives in play. Journalists are human beings; they will also want to impress people, please their employers and boost their reputations and careers. What follows then, can be thought of as an epistemic history of contemporary journalism, one that rejects truthophobia and acknowledges the existence of the relationship between journalism and truth. What you are about to read is therefore a long-overdue corrective to the canon of doctrine that has dominated since the 1970s. For those schooled in Boomer media theory, and raised within the dominant intellectual paradigm of the late 20th Century, this book may feel unfamiliar and uncomfortable. I ask only that readers approach what follows with an open mind.

PART ONE

THE BOOMERS
AND
THEIR IDEOLOGY

Chapter 1

Prologue.
The Beatles v Fat
Man Johnson

"Legends of the slaughter of a destructive monster are to be found all over the world. The thought underlying them all is that the monster slain is preternatural and hostile to mankind."

E. S. Hartland, The Legend of Perseus

Fat Man Johnson entered the first-class compartment and placed his bowler hat, rolled umbrella and briefcase on the luggage rack. He sat, unfurled his copy of the *Financial Times* and then paused to inspect his fellow travelers. A look of disapproval spread across his face, as if he had detected an unpleasant odor. In front of him were four young men. They were sharply dressed, wearing the latest, fashionably-cut suits. They had mop-top hair styles. One of them winked at Johnson, smiled and tried to strike up a conversation. Johnson glowered and tried hard to ignore them.

Suddenly, Johnson noticed the window was open; cold air and noise were pouring in. He stood, closed the window and returned to his paper. The young men are prickled. "Do you mind if we have it open?" one of them asks. "Yes I do" Johnson snaps. "Yes, but there's four of us, and we'd like it open, if it's all the same to you," says another. Johnson points out that he is a regular traveler and argues, "I suppose I have some rights!" "So do we!" retorts one of the youngsters with spirit. Johnson refuses to compromise and retreats behind his newspaper.

One of the young men produces a transistor radio and switches it on. Jangly pop music blares from its speaker. "We'll have that thing off as well" says Johnson and he leans forward to switch it off. Its owner protests, but Johnson overwhelms him with fast talking, an authoritative manner, and a superior knowledge of transport bylaws. "An elementary knowledge of the Railway Act's Subsection B & C's blue appendage would tell you I'm perfectly within my rights."* He smiles a nasty, smug smile. One of the young men tries an appeal based on the principles of socialism and collectivism, "Yeah, but we want to hear it, and there's more of us than you. We're a community, like a majority vote. Up the workers and all that stuff!" Johnson suggests a different solution, "Then I suggest you take that damned thing into the corridor, or some other part of the train where you obviously belong." One of the young men leans slowly towards Johnson. For a brief moment Johnson feels threatened. What if the young men were to become violent? Will they beat or stab him? Will they throw him from the moving train? But the youngster is merely cheeky, "give us a kiss" he grins mischievously.

The four young men try one last time to persuade Johnson, but it is futile. He remains stubborn. "Knock it off", says one of the youngsters, "You can't win with his sort. After all, it's his train, isn't it, Mister?" Johnson plays his trump card, "Don't take that tone with me young man; I fought the war for your sort". The youngsters are unimpressed, "I bet you're sorry you won!" quips one of them impertinently. Johnson has had enough, "I shall call the guard" he snaps. The young men have also had enough, "Let's go and get some coffee and leave the kennel to Lassie." Johnson smiles triumphantly believing he has won, but the young men are not finished. As he settles back into his newspaper they screech, "Hey mister can we have our ball back!" They pull grotesque faces, and then, they deploy their secret weapon. Shattering Johnson's composure, they appear, impossibly, outside the train, running and cycling along

* "Appendage" appears in the written screenplay, but not in the film version.

2

the platform. What witchcraft and trickery is this? They have subverted reality and plunged Johnson into a world of bewildering fantasy in which he is confused and unsettled. Now, as if by magic, the young men are back inside the train, mocking Johnson like a pack of unruly schoolboys. Johnson is disoriented by this witchcraft and defeated. He shouts impotently, "Louts! Hooligans! You'll hear more of this!"

Tribalism on a Train

On the surface, this scene, from the 1964 Beatle's film *A Hard Day's Night*, is simply a clash between the lovable "fab four" and one sour old man. But there is far more to it than that. The scene contains a series of mini narratives which express, in essence, the ideology of the Boomer generation. What is taking place is an epic battle between two world views. The screenplay, by Alun Owen, is a generational manifesto in which pre-Boomer values are distorted into a grotesque caricature and portrayed as unreasonable, selfish and bad. At the same time, Boomer values are portrayed as reasonable and good. The scene is a morality play, or mock-heroic saga, in which four noble heroes slay a monster. There are three broad, overlapping themes on display here:

1. Good v Evil.

2. The rights of the tribe v the rights of an individual.

3. Irrealism and unreason.

The most obvious theme, and the most easily misunderstood, is the clash between the Boomer generation and the pre-Boomers. To see it as the age-old clash between youth and old age is to completely miss the point. The Boomers did not see themselves as youthful free spirits who would, in time, mellow into wiser, mature individuals. They saw themselves as a unique generation objectively different from, and better than, any generation that had come before. Boomer Exceptionalism proclaimed that a new age was dawning in which the eternal problems of mankind would be overcome. The scene does not suggest that Fat Man Johnson should be less stuffy and more friendly, instead it is an uncompromising

3

demonization of pre-Boomer values as personified by Johnson. There is no chance of Johnson changing his ways, he is one of yesterday's men, he symbolizes an entire worldview which is past its sell-by date and which must be destroyed. Reduced to its simplest terms, it is a conflict between good and evil.

Described in the original screenplay as "a fat upper class city Englishman", Johnson is not overweight in the film version. He is played by Richard Vernon, who was cast partly because of his resemblance to Harold Macmillan, Britain's aging, aristocratic Prime Minister. The symbolism is pointed. By late 1963 Macmillan was widely viewed as a sick old man, tainted by hypocrisy and corruption. Placing the scene in a railway carriage is also laden with significance. 1963 saw the publication of the Beeching Report which portrayed Britian's railways as a gigantic, inefficient dinosaur, a worn-out relic of the Victorian age. Johnson, who describes himself as traveling on the train "regularly", has evolved to live in a habitat which is rapidly disappearing. He doesn't realize it, but he, and his entire system of values, are doomed. The contrast between Johnson and the youth and vitality of the Beatles, makes it clear that the Beatles could never become Johnson. They are fundamentally different. They belong to different, mutually antagonistic tribes. Tribalism is a key feature of the Boomer Ideology. Boomer Exceptionalism asserts that the Boomers are the in-group — the chosen ones; while the pre-Boomers are the out-group. This inter-generational tribalism is captured by the use of the word "sort", as in, "You can't win with his sort", and "Don't take that tone with me young man; I fought the war for your sort." Tribal identity is also expressed by the different uniforms worn by the Beatles (their distinctive clothes and haircuts), and Johnson (his bowler hat and neatly-rolled umbrella). Communication is impossible across this tribal divide, as evidenced by the Beatles' futile attempts at dialogue. The Boomer Ideology preaches that, ultimately, you either get it, or you don't. You're either one of us, or one of them. Johnson is one of them.

The Boomer Ideology sees rules and regulations as petty, artificial restraints designed to control Boomers and prevent them living life to the full. For example, Johnson uses his knowledge of the "Railway Act's Subsection B & C's blue appendage" as a device to stop the Beatles listening to pop music. While this seems a trivial matter, it reveals the chasm between the assumptions of the Boomer Ideology and Johnson's ideology — Victorian Liberalism. 19th Century thinkers were deeply concerned with how to balance the right of the individual with the need of society as a whole. Theorists identified a specific danger which they labeled the "tyranny of the majority". The solution proposed by Victorian Liberalism lay in creating checks and balances, i.e. rule of law to inhibit the power of the majority to oppress the minority. Hence railway bylaws were created to restrain one individual from annoying another — in this case, all music is banned. However, the screenplay portrays the bylaws very differently, as repressive restrictions, unfair, unnecessary and anti-Boomer. In other words, the law is portrayed as bad because it does not serve the interests of the Boomers.

The Boomer Ideology rejects Victorian Liberalism and interprets the idea of democracy in a different, narrower way. As the script puts it, "there are four of us and we'd like it open" and, "we want to hear it and there's more of us than you." Since the Boomers were the numerically superior cohort, this was a convenient and selfish doctrine. For the Boomers, democracy is rule by the majority, but only if the majority are Boomers. For the Boomers, democracy is a useful tool, a means to an end — a pretext for getting what they want. This may be a crude form of democracy, but it is not *liberal* democracy. Boomer democracy is better described as ochlocracy — the totalitarian rule of the majority tribe. The Boomers' real goal is power — in this case the power to impose their music on Johnson against his will. It is also noteworthy that Paul McCartney invokes socialism as an argument for opening the window and playing loud pop music. As we shall see, the Boomers created an elaborate theoretical framework and mythology to legitimize the gratification of their desires. As part of this process, they re-invented socialism to serve their needs and christened it the "New Left". The most important point, neatly captured by Owen's script, is McCartney's obvious insincerity – Boomer socialism was not supposed to be taken very seriously. McCartney's appeal to socialism "and all that stuff" is, like his trendy suit and haircut, first and foremost a form of signaling that marks him as a Boomer. Paul McCartney was not of course a downtrodden worker, he was a famous, wealthy pop star.[**]

[**]   In December 1966 *Rave Magazine* reported, "there seems little doubt that the four Beatles are now well on the way to becoming multi-millionaires." McCartney was said to have earned £2m that year. He owned several companies, a 183-acre farm in Scotland, an Aston Martin DB6 and a Mini-Cooper S.

Finally, there is the fascinating moment when the Beatles use surrealism as their trump card to defeat Johnson and smash his rational, ordered world. Victorian Liberalism was a well thought-out, rational ideology with solid, empirical foundations. At its base was respect for concrete reality, evidence, reason and logic. The Boomer Ideology could not hope to out-argue Victorian Liberalism so, instead, it brutally assaulted its foundations. The Boomer Ideology embraced all forms of fantasy, irrealism, magic and unreason, and replaced the older generation's love of truth with a subversive fetishizing of truthophobia. However, the Boomer Ideology, which seemed so novel and radical to the Boomers, was in reality an exercise in turning the clock back to pre-Victorian and pre-Renaissance ways of thinking. For example, in October 1967 a group of Boomers attempted (unsuccessfully) to end the Vietnam War by levitating the Pentagon three hundred feet off the ground using ancient Aramaic exorcism rites. Irrealism, cognitive nihilism and truthophobia would become the philosophical weapons of choice for Boomer artists, thought-leaders and public intellectuals during the last third of the 20th Century.

Chapter 2

Immature Dreams and Longings. Inside the Boomer Brain

"I would there were no age between ten and three-and-twenty, or that youth would sleep out the rest; for there is nothing in the between but getting wenches with child, wronging the ancientry, stealing, fighting."

Shakespeare, The Winter's Tale.

A ccording to Generational Cohort Theory, people are shaped by powerful forces during their coming-of-age years, as a result of which, they acquire and share values that remain largely unchanged for the rest of their lives. Cohort Theory was pioneered by the German sociologist Karl Mannheim who argued that membership of a particular generation,

"Endows the individuals sharing in [it] with a common location in the social and historical process, and thereby limit them to a specific range of potential experiences, predisposing them for a certain characteristic mode of thought and experience, and a characteristic type of historically relevant action."[1]

Not all generations exhibit distinctive characteristics, or want to destroy the knowledge handed to them by their parents and start over. But the Boomers did. In 1965 Bob Dylan sang, "You know something's happening, but you don't know what it is, do you Mr Jones?" What was happening was the Boomer generation was changing the dominant ideology of Western society. The constellation of beliefs, social norms, prejudices and attitudes which had guided their parents, grandparents and great grandparents, was being systematically shredded and replaced by a new one. The transformation was so rapid that, by 1981, the sociologist Bernice Martin could state that there had been a total reconstruction of the, "assumptions and habitual practices which form the cultural bedrock of the daily lives of ordinary people." The shift, she wrote,

"Began as a sort of cultural revolution among a small minority of crusading radicals, and finished by altering some of our deepest – and therefore most customary and commonplace – habits and assumptions."[2]

Forty years later, the writer Helen Andrews came to the same conclusion. The transformation had been so complete that, paradoxically, it had become completely invisible,

"The baby boomers have been responsible for the most dramatic sundering of Western civilization since the Protestant Reformation. If that is hard to accept, it is only because the boomer revolution has been so comprehensive that it has become almost impossible to imagine what life was like before it."[3]

8

Like Bob Dylan, everyone agreed that something enormous had happened, but putting it into words was tricky. The journalist, and former hippie, Danny Goldberg, described the elusive "something" as a gigantic "chord" played on some vast ideological guitar. It was, he said, not easily explained because it was the result of,

> "Dozens of separate, sometimes contradictory 'notes' from an assortment of political, spiritual, chemical, demographic, historical, and media influences that collectively created a unique energy."[4]

A major obstacle to understanding the Boomer Ideology is that history is always written by the victors. The vast majority of books and documentaries on Boomer culture therefore offer self-serving, nostalgic and romantic perspectives. The Boomer Version of History is neither innocent nor impartial. On the contrary, it is an exercise in heroificaiton in which Boomers cast themselves as ethical-political heroes. For example, the writers Tariq Ali and Susan Watkins describe their generation's ideology glowingly as a form of pure and intense righteousness,

> "We were justified in the way we acted… we carried within our collective self a vision of a better future. Not for ourselves, but for the oppressed throughout the world: for everyone."[5]

What is noteworthy is how Ali and Watkins hastily add the qualifier "not for ourselves…" In the Boomer mythology, the Boomers are always motivated by virtue and altruism. But were the Boomers really uniquely righteous? or were they merely brilliantly successful at marketing, controlling the narrative and disguising their self-interest behind a mask of impeccable selflessness?

The historian Bruce Cannon Gibney argues that the Boomers were a swarm of generational locust, "United by short-sightedness and self-interest" who consumed everything in their path, leaving their hapless children and grandchildren to face the consequences and pick up the bill. In a book provocatively entitled *A Generation of Sociopaths*, Gibney accuses the Boomers of "the full sociopathic pathology: deceit, selfishness, imprudence, remorselessness, hostility, the works."[6] Although Gibney offers a long-overdue corrective to the self-serving narratives of the Boomers, it is hard to believe that an entire generation was literally sociopathic. A more convincing explanation is not that young people who grew up during the 1960s were sociopaths, but simply that they were young. The mystery of what happened, and why it happened, has been hiding in plain sight. The Boomers were immature, and because they were immature, they thought immature thoughts. Furthermore, a unique combination of circumstances created a powerful feedback loop in which a large cohort of adolescents, all raised with similar expectations and experiences, came to believe that their immature feelings, beliefs and desires, were eternal values, and that those of older people were wrong. In this tribal cyclone, young people learned only from other young people. They shut out and demonized alternative views and embraced only ideas that confirmed their own assumptions. The Boomers created, and were created by, a Vortex of Immaturity.

The Wisdom of the Immature

The study of immaturity has developed dramatically since the beginning of the 21st Century. It is part of a revolution in cognitive science largely driven by technological advances, such as the development of functional magnetic resonance imaging (fMRI) to map activity in the human brain. The ability to peer inside the black box of the human mind has significantly expanded our understanding of mental processes, and provided a range of valuable insights which were unavailable to earlier researchers. For example, there is now compelling evidence that the adolescent brain is immature until approximately the age of twenty-five. The insights of modern cognitive science are able therefore to shine a light on the underlying desires and emotions which drove the Boomers during their formative years, and which helped shape their beliefs and values. Cognitive science offers a powerful new lens through which the Boomer generation appears in a less romantic, more objective light.

The focus of interest for those who research immaturity is the part of the brain known as the prefrontal cortex (PFC). The PFC is associated with executive function; the ability to plan for the future, predict the consequences of our actions, and control impulses, urges and desires. It is associated with the ability to reason critically, but it is also one of the last regions of the brain to reach maturity. Similarly, researchers have discovered that the corpus callosum (the nerve fibers connecting the left and right hemispheres of the brain) are still growing and thickening until the age of twenty-five. It is the maturation of this neural superhighway that helps adults recognize complexity and develop sophisticated responses to uncertainty. As the Dutch researcher Mariam Arain and her colleagues summarize, the human brain is a "work in progress" during adolescence,

> "Significant progress has been made over the last 25 years in understanding the brain's regional morphology and function during adolescence. It is now realized that several major morphological and functional changes occur in the human brain during adolescence... Neurobehavioral, morphological, neurochemical, and pharmacological evidence suggests that the brain remains under construction during adolescence."[7]

The ability of neuroscientists to watch the brain growing, has led to the development of a highly nuanced understanding of adolescence. Immaturity is not a single thing, rather there are many overlapping immaturities. For example, the psychologist Jeffrey Arnett has suggested the category of "emerging adulthood" to describe the period of development stretching from eighteen to twenty-five years of age. According to Arnett, emerging adults think and behave differently from younger adolescents. Researchers also observe that different areas of the brain develop at different rates, i.e. asymmetrically. It is not therefore simply the case that the adolescent brain is "less developed, it is rather that it is "unbalanced" in comparison to a mature brain. This developmental asymmetry leads to a number of distinctive behavioral features in adolescents which include; heightened risk taking and impulsivity, an aversion to rules and restraints, and a reduced ability to recognize the consequences of behavior.

Arnett has produced list of adult and mature traits. Organized under seven broad headings such as 'independence' and 'norm compliance', the list includes: accepting responsibility for the consequences of your actions, having good control over your emotions, avoiding profanity or vulgar language, being financially responsible, becoming less self-orientated, forming your own beliefs and values independently, able to commit to a long-term love relationship, avoiding illegal drugs and petty crime, and being capable of keeping a family physically safe.[8] In other words, it is perfectly normal and healthy for young people to lack maturity. Adolescence is simply the developmental stage appropriate for adolescents, just as childhood is the stage appropriate for children. The concept of immaturity however, implies something inappropriate and unhealthy. It is a morbid condition in which the values of adolescence are inappropriately applied in adulthood. Immaturity is not therefore something to be proud of, it does not refer to the splendor of youth. The salient traits of immaturity - lack of impulse control and irresponsibility — are not well suited to making wise decisions, or to long-term planning. Hence immature people are objectively worse than adults at functioning in the real world. They are always, to some degree, disconnected from reality and trapped within their own immature world view.

Teenagers often interpret adult criticism of their schemes as a subjective difference of opinion. However such analysis is itself immature. It misses the point that what may seem like a good idea to a teenager, may not just seem like a bad idea to an adult, it may actually *be* a bad idea. Relativism, subjectivism and lack of perspective are all symptoms of immaturity. Furthermore, immaturity is not just the inability to think maturely, it is also the inability to recognize that one is unable to think maturely. It is therefore entirely appropriate that the word immature comes from the Latin *immaturitas*, which means not fully developed or unripe.

The behavioral scientist Fernando Almeida argues that people who fail to develop mature traits should be viewed as suffering from Immature Personality Disorder – a disorder that is, curiously, not officially recognized by mental health practitioners. For Almeida, extreme immaturity is exacerbated by environmental factors. For example when children are pampered, or brought up in conditions of comfort and ease which they take for granted,

"Nourished by excessive and unhealthy indulgence, the individuals sometimes develop a feeling of uniqueness, of entitlement to a special status... they acquire behavior that is of unbearable boastfulness, arrogance, haughtiness, intemperate and abusive devaluation of others, which is underlined by a monstrous, given its excess, feeling of self-worth and inability to understand their own limitations, with the individuals revealing the most incredible lack of common sense and manners".[9]

According to Almeida and Arnett, typical markers of immaturity are:

- The urge to instantly gratify one's desires. Hence; impulsiveness and lack of self-regulation. Immature people are uninterested in long-term planning. They prefer to live in the now.

- Hostility to rules that inhibit instant gratification. Contemptuous of traditions and institutions that restrain impulsive behavior.

- Irresponsibility. Excessive risk taking. Unable and unwilling to see complexity and long-term consequences. Hence, attracted to shortcuts and simple solutions. Quick to blame and invent excuses. Refusal to take responsibility. Attracted to irresponsible sexual behavior and substance abuse.

- Righteousness. A feeling of moral superiority and entitlement. Inability to consider opposing points of view. Tunnel vision.

- Fantasy. Immature people are more likely to inhabit an unreal world of Utopian dreams. Consequently, hostile to the limitations imposed on desire by reality.

- Epistemic opportunism. Careless about the truth. Immature people may exhibit a propensity to lie or devalue language. Truth is whatever is currently useful.

- Intuitive. Immature people trust their feelings, emotions and instincts more than they trust evidence and logical thinking.

- Tribal. Unduly susceptible to peer group pressure. Immature people value in-group status and badges of tribal membership. They display strong loyalty to the in-group and hostility to outsiders and traitors.

- Impatience. Frustrated with slow, cautious solutions to complex problems. Immature people may exhibit a capacity for ruthlessness, even a tolerance of cruelty to get the job done quickly.

It would be ridiculous to argue that all these traits were present in every member of the Boomer generation. That is not the claim I am making here. What I am arguing is that these psycho-cognitive forces exerted a profound influence on the Boomer generation as a whole and on the distinctive ideology they constructed. Ideology is always a collective, emergent phenomenon. It is the wisdom of crowds — an expression of the tribal consensus. Like moths drawn to a flame, the Boomer tribe felt the pull of invisible forces and shared intuitions. Their collective dreams and longings would drive the search for new ways of knowing, for a new ideology, and, eventually, a new form of journalism.

Chapter 3

Strange Environments. The Pig in the Python, Affluence, Progress for Ever and Televisionland

"A change not in one point, but in a thousand points; it is a change not of particular details, but of pervading spirit... There has been a change of the sort which, above all, generates other changes – a change of generation."

Walter Bagehot

Psychological immaturity on its own is not enough to account for the dramatic ideological transformation the Boomers unleashed on Western society. It was the combination of psychological and environmental factors that shaped the Boomer's worldview, and the most salient environmental factor was demographic; the Boomers simply outnumbered everyone else. Starting around 1940, the birth rate in the US and the UK began to increase. After the end of the Second World War, it soared. The peak year in the US was 1957 during which 4.3 million babies were born. By 1968, the Boomers were in the majority — 52% of Americans were under the age of 25. In total, a tribe of 76 million Americans were born — 90 million if one includes those born during the early 1940s. But dates do not tell the whole story. The Boomer Ideology was forged in the hearts and minds of the first wave of Boomers who were born between, approximately, 1940-1955. Many of those who came after were post-Boomers; BINOs – Boomers in name only. It was this first wave of Boomers who became role models for the younger, second wave.

The American author Landon Jones uses the metaphor "a pig in a python" to describe the how society struggled unsuccessfully to digest the enormous cohort of Boomer adolescents. The normal mechanism by which society socialises its children and civilizes its young 'barbarians' was overwhelmed by the scale of the task. As Jones explains, there were just not enough grownups to defend the established values from the legions of their immature children,

> "What if a generation of barbarians appeared that, for the first time, abruptly threatened to overwhelm the defenders by force of numbers? This is exactly what happened in the middle of the 1960s. As the baby boom entered the most rebellious years of youth, it gave them a weight and impact they had never had before… Freed from its moorings, the baby boom became a loose cannon on the deck of society, rolling and smashing whatever stood in its path."[1]

To use Jones' striking metaphor, the python was unable to digest the Boomer pig. On the contrary, like the infant alien in Ridley Scott's sci-fi movie, it was the Boomers who violently burst out and devoured the Victorian Liberal society into which they had been born. When the majority are immature, immaturity becomes normal and maturity becomes abnormal. Writing in 1969, the American psychologist Kenneth Keniston referred to this process as "youthful de-socialization". It occurs, he said, when a mass of adolescents, instead of trying to conform to adult society, demand that adult society conforms to their own immature longings and desires. Keniston interviewed dozens of young Boomers and, although

16

he was sympathetic to their youthful idealism, he was also alarmed at their fierce tribalism and intolerance of dissent. The Boomers, he said, saw their own opinions as morally good and the opinions of those who disagreed with them as morally bad. This worried Keniston who accused the Boomers of lacking "awareness of their own ambivalence or potential for corruption — a lack that sometimes allows them to treat their opponents as less-than-human". Keniston concluded that there was something primal and savage about "youthful de-socialization" which was indistinguishable from "a collapse of values into barbarity or nihilism".[2]

The idea that the numerically dominant Boomers might abolish Liberal Democracy altogether was explored in the 1968 Boomer movie *Wild In the Streets*. In the film, the Boomers take control of America, confine people over thirty-five in camps and force-feed them drugs to subdue and control them. The Boomer President, played by actor Chris Jones, explains his plan to an enthusiastic Boomer Congress, "In groovy surroundings we're going to psyche them all out on LSD, babies... they won't draft us; we'll draft them!" In the movie, the Boomers become intoxicated by the knowledge that they are young, strong and numerous, while their parents are old, weak and few. What the Boomers have discovered is the thrill of raw power. Why, asks President Jones, should the majority Boomer tribe not rule over all others,

> "Do you really want a man in his 60s running the country? I mean what do you ask a 60-year-old man? You ask him whether he wants his wheelchair facing the sun, or facing away from the sun. But running our country? Forget it baby!"[3]

The impact of demographics, and the power that comes from being the majority, was reinforced by the fact that the world in which the Boomers grew up, and hence their experience of life, was very different from that of their parents.

The Affluent Society

The Boomers grew up in a world of astonishing material prosperity and economic growth. In the United States, gross national product (GNP) skyrocketed from $200 billion in 1940, to $300 in 1950 and $500 billion in 1960, firmly establishing the US as the most productive, richest and most powerful nation on Earth. By the end of the 1950s, the average American family had 30% more purchasing power than at the start, and were able to buy a dazzling range of consumer goods. Sales of new cars quadrupled between 1945 and 1955. It's estimated that by the end of the 1950s, Americans, who made up 6% of the world's population, consumed 30% of all the world's goods and services. The UK saw a similar trend, though on a less spectacular scale. GDP rose by 40 percent between 1950 and 1966, with real incomes and consumption dramatically increasing. The historian Eric Hobsbawm describes the post war economic boom that swept across Europe, the US and Japan as a Golden Age in which there was full employment, high wages and rising prosperity, "By the 1960s it was plain that there had never been anything like it. World output of manufactures quadrupled between the early 1950s and the early 1970s." At the same time, teenagers found themselves with,

"Far more independent spending power than their predecessors, thanks to the prosperity and full employment of the Golden Age; and thanks to the greater prosperity of their parents, who had less need of their children's contribution to the family budget." [4]

Writing in 1959, the American journalist Vance Packard marveled that he was living in an era of abundance which, "had reached proportions fantastic by any past standards."[5] As the British Prime Minister Harold Macmillan famously observed in 1957, "Let's be frank about it; some of our people have never had it so good". The British journalist Christopher Booker was amazed how quickly everything had changed and pointed out that Macmillan was able to say this just three years after the end of food rationing in the UK, "It was beginning to dawn on the people of Britain that they had embarked on the greatest spending spree in their history... the Golden Age of Macmillan's England had begun." "New money" Booker adds, "Was pouring into tills, pockets and bank accounts at every level of society."[6]

The transformation brought a transformation in mental outlook. In 1953, the American banker Paul Mazur observed that most ordinary Americans already took for granted the right to a "steady improvement of their material well-being." Mazur pointed out that economic prosperity did not simply mean more washing machines, cars and consumer goods;

prosperity also meant access to the higher things of life, "gratifications of a spiritual, intellectual, and artistic nature, as well as the gratifications of love, friendship and public service". These things were now within the reach of everybody, "our economy makes the benefits of culture, as well as material gratifications, possible for all the people instead of limiting the enjoyment and creation of culture to a leisure class."[7] However, Mazur warned that rising standards of living and increased leisure time were only possible because of the delicate, complex balance of economic growth, industrial production and consumption. He noted that prosperity was fragile and that the good times could not last forever. But Mazur's sober realism was already out of fashion. A new, irresistible mood of wild excitement about the seemingly limitless possibilities of the future was breaking out — especially among the young Boomer generation.

In 1958, the economist John Kenneth Galbraith published his influential book *The Affluent Society*. In it he argued that the values of an affluent society, would be fundamentally different from those in which citizens' lives were marked by struggle and hardship. This meant, he said, the values of the War Generation had suddenly become obsolete. We are currently guided, he wrote, by ideas relevant to another world. One could not expect,

> "That the preoccupations of a poverty-ridden world would be relevant in one where the ordinary individual has access to amenities - foods, entertainment, personal transportation, and plumbing - in which not even the rich rejoiced a century ago." [8]

Galbraith's insight was that a different ideology, or "conventional wisdom", would be the inevitable result of transformed economic conditions. Those who possessed the new way of thinking would, he said, constitute a "New Class" and would value individual happiness over material wealth. Members of the New Class would be, and would affect to be, contemptuous of the creation of wealth and view it with a fashionable indifference. They could afford to do this because,

> "The chance to spend one's life in clean and physically comfortable surroundings; and some opportunity for applying one's thoughts to the day's work, are regarded as unimportant only by those who take them completely for granted."[9]

Galbraith predicted that in future, success and status would be gained by the conspicuous display of personal happiness. The more one claimed to be leading a blissful, stress-free life of fulfilment, the more one would be envied and respected. University would, he said, become the New Class's essential finishing school, after which members would move into interesting and meaningful jobs, exempt from danger, toil and boredom. Galbraith predicted that, even if someone hated his job, "he will be expected to assert the contrary in order to affirm his membership in the New Class."[10]

This new elite would work in academia, media, the creative industries, law, technology, and other executive, administrative and managerial roles. Members would have their own "system of morality" in which having leisure time and being seen to be ethical would determine social status. Galbraith also predicted that the New Class would disguise its privilege with sophisticated "social camouflage" to assuage its sense of guilt. To do this, would create narratives of worthiness,

> "It serves the democratic conscience of the more favored groups to identify themselves with those who do hard physical labor. A lurking sense of guilt over a more pleasant, agreeable, and re-munerative life can often be assuaged by the observation, 'I am a worker too'".[11]

Galbraith's insight then, was that increasing wealth would lead to ideological change. Once established, the values of the Age of Affluence would come to resemble religious articles of faith. Expressing them publicly would be an affirmation, as Galbraith put it, "like reading aloud from the Scriptures or going to church."

Progressivism

It was not only affluence that shaped the Boomer's worldview; it was the assumption that affluence was automatic and would continue, effortlessly forever. Progressivism is the belief that progress is natural and assured, and that history flows in one direction, from imperfection towards perfection. Progressivism is also referred to as "historicism" — a doctrine associated with the philosophy of Georg Hegel and Karl

Marx. For example, in classical Marxist theory, society evolves from capitalism into communism, just as an insect metamorphoses from a grub into a butterfly. Progressivism is therefore the doctrine of the unfolding of history. It is a view with a built-in moral dimension. It implies that progress *ought* to happen, and that consequently everyone has a moral duty to remove any obstacles that might be blocking it. Progressivism preaches the importance of being on the "right side of history". Eric Hobsbawm notes that economic progressivism had become widespread by the 1960s — everyone had begun to assume that, "somehow, everything in the economy would go onwards and upwards forever."[12] It was an assumption confirmed by the lived experience of millions of ordinary people in the West. As one British Boomer recalled, during the late 1950s,

> "Jobs were ten-a-penny. You could pick and choose. You could go out as a plumber's mate with no experience, a pipe-fitter's mate with no experience, a scaffolder, a laborer - whatever you wanted to do. There was so much work about, you could pick and choose whatever was the best paying job."[13]

However, progressivism is not the only way of imagining history. The Greek historian Polybius, writing two thousand years ago, took a different view and argued that history is, in fact, cyclical. He said that new generations forget the lessons of the past and are doomed to repeat ancient errors. Polybius wrote that democracy eats itself because the search for something better leads, paradoxically, to something worse,

> "As soon as a new generation has arisen, and the democracy has descended to their children's children, long association weakens their value for equality and freedom, and some seek to become more powerful than the ordinary citizens."[14]

Writing in the 18th Century, the Italian scholar Giambattista Vico also rejected historicism in favor of a cyclical view of history. Civilizations emerge, he said, from barbarism, reject arbitary and capricious law and seek democratic forms of government. This leads to a happy era of flourishing. During this time, philosophy, inspired by democracy, values the search for truth. However, after the long struggle to achieve democracy, people fail to value it, they "delight in pleasures, soon grow dissolute in luxury, and finally go mad squandering their estates."[15] "Learned fools" he said, begin to malign the truth and "false eloquence" arises. Public discourse relapses into "lying, trickery, slander, theft, cowardice and hypocrisy".[16] Unable to govern themselves, the people find themselves governed, or conquered, by other nations. Thus does civilization become corrupt and sink back into barbarism.

However, regressive, gloomy philosophies, such as the cyclical view of history, did not appeal to the Boomer mindset and fell deeply out of fashion. What did appeal were progressive and Utopian theories. So, for example, a popular theme of Boomer progressivism was the widespread desire to abolish "alienation". Alienation was, according to the Boomer political theorist Kenneth Megill, a type of boredom that caused young people to feel, "the life they lead to be unsatisfactory." Megill's 1970 book *The New Democratic Theory* called for "fundamental social change" to "attack alienation in all of its appearances in contemporary society."[17] Life for the Boomers was to be exciting, meaningful and joyful, not boring and dull. Happiness and pleasure for all were within reach; alienation and unhappiness should not be tolerated. As one popular Boomer slogan put it in 1968, "We want nothing of a world in which the certainty of not dying from hunger comes in exchange for the risk of dying from boredom". For the young Boomers, all this felt instinctively right and part of a natural progression. As the American historian Michael Seidman observes, "A hedonistic generation seemed to resist labor and the responsibilities of the adult world. Students actively participated in a fun-loving lifestyle and became its propagandists."[18]

If Boomer progressivism was the belief that a new social order of personal fulfilment and social justice was imminent, then what exactly was holding it back? To the Boomers, the answer seemed to be the rules and restraints of Victorian Liberalism. If only these things could be destroyed, the Boomers believed a better world would, somehow or other, spontaneously appear. The destruction of Victorian Liberal values and restraints became a moral duty. Bernice Martin uses the words "anomic" and "antinomian" to describe the Boomer's war on the values of their parents and grandparents. She says the Boomer project was one long, concerted, "attack on boundaries, limits, certainties, conventions, taboos, roles, system, style, category, predictability, form, structure and ritual".[19] For the Boomers, the only way was up.

Televisionland

The age of affluence was also the age of television. During the 1950s and 1960s, TV ownership soared. By 1962, 90% of American families owned at least one TV set. By 1968, British households had reached the same milestone. In the UK, the BBC's monopoly came to an end in 1956 and American-inspired commercial television went on the air. The impact of TV in the US and the UK was immense. Francis Beckett refers to it as a new religion preaching a new creed. It trained the minds of the young Boomers and made them, "fundamentally different from any earlier generation."[20] The power of TV to colonize the minds of impressionable young viewers was remarkable. In the UK, Christopher Booker observed that the jingles and slogans of TV "had saturated the consciousness of the nation, even coming to replace the age-old nursery rhymes in children's games."[21]

TV meant the Boomer's perception of reality depended far less on first-hand experience of the world than that of any preceding generation. Never before in human history had so many young people been simultaneously exposed to so many homogenous, mass-produced narratives. Landon Jones writes that, for four or five hours a day, TV plunged young Boomers into the alternative reality of Televisionland. Here, "There was death but never emptiness. People didn't work regularly but were rarely hungry or in need. In fact, economic realities were not present at all." In Televisionland there was,

> "Little real despair. Problems can be worked out and almost always are... A child who would believe television would believe that most problems are soluble, usually within the half hour, and that sacrifices and compromises rarely involve human pain... life is fair."[22]

For thousands of years, children's stories, such as Aesop's fables or biblical parables, had been largely designed to teach moral and practical lessons. Traditionally, stories had been "medicine" sweetened with narrative "sugar". Now the age-old formula was reversed. The stories fed to the Boomers were highly refined narrative sugar; entertainment with easily recognizable heroes and villains, and uncomplicated happy endings. In Televisionland, complexity was banished. It was a land of simple tribal binaries; cowboys against Indians, sheriffs against outlaws, space explorers against aliens, good versus evil. One popular show was *The Adventures of Robin Hood* starring the clean-cut Richard Greene. It entranced 32 million Boomers a week in the US and the UK with its tribal formula of taking wealth from the undeserving, evil Normans and giving it to the Saxons. The show's theme song explained that Robin Hood's gang, "handled all the trouble on the English country scene, and still found plenty of time to sing" - adding they were, "Feared by the bad" and "loved by the good". The U.S. equivalent was *The Legend of Jesse James* starring Chris Jones as the handsome, reckless youngster who robbed trains to redistribute the wealth of greedy railroad barons to those who needed it more. Even more influential was *The Lone Ranger* starring Clayton Moore as the masked social justice warrior of the wild west and Jay Silverheels as his companion Tonto. It was one of the most watched TV shows of the 1950s. The spin-off movie described the Lone Ranger as,

"A man who hated thieves and oppression. His face masked, his true name unknown, he thundered across the West upon a silver white stallion. Appearing out of nowhere to strike down injustice or outlawry, and then vanishing as mysteriously as he came"[23]

The Lone Ranger possessed an infallible intuition enabling him to effortlessly distinguish good from evil. In Televisionland there was little moral complexity. As the media historian Stuart Ewen writes, on TV, "nations and people are daily sorted into boxes marked 'good guys', 'villains', 'victims', and 'lucky ones', style becomes the essence, reality becomes the appearance."[24]

Televisionland's simple narratives and happy endings taught the Boomer generation that life ought to be uncomplicated and fair. In doing so, it also vaccinated them against reality. The values of Televisionland even laid the foundations for their radical political beliefs. For example, when the Boomer activist Stew Albert called on soldiers guarding the Pentagon to join the anti-war protest in 1967, he told them he was motivated, not by Karl Marx, but by the Lone Ranger,

"We're really brothers because we grew up listening to the same radio programs and TV programs, and we have the same ideals... I didn't get my ideas from Mao, Lenin or Ho Chi Minh. I got my ideas from the Lone Ranger. You know the Lone Ranger always fought on the side of good and against the forces of evil and injustice."[25]

TV was a communal experience. Millions of young Boomers watched the same shows at the same time and enthusiastically discussed them when they met. The media researcher Aniko Bodroghkozy notes that no Pied Piper ever proved so irresistible as TV which "forged the Boomers into a special community - one that recognized itself as such by the way its members all shared a common television culture."[26] According to the journalist Andrew Anthony, for Boomer children, glued to their sets for hour after hour, the scripted, edited reality of Televisionland seemed more coherent, and therefore more real, than reality itself,

"That's one of the extraordinary aspects of television – its ability to trump reality. If seeing is believing, then there's always a troubling doubt until you've seen it on television. A mass medium delivered to almost every household, it's the communal confirmation of experience."[27]

As Bruce Cannon Gibney summarizes, the Boomers had a "deep and unshakable relationship with TV". They were entranced from their beginnings by a medium which validated a world-view "only loosely tethered to reality."[28]

The Wizards of Televisionland

Televisionland's matrix of sugary entertainment was not, however, the product of random chance. Everything that appeared on screen was carefully designed to groom the Boomer generation to become insatiable consumers — dissatisfied with what they had and eager for something better. The ultimate purpose of commercial TV was to make money by selling advertising. However, the biggest problem identified by advertising executives, and the psychologists who advised them, was the ideology of Victorian Liberalism. The thrifty War Generation, suckled on the values of restraint and self-control, suffered massive guilt feelings when they indulged themselves by buying luxury or unnecessary products. The key target for marketers during the 1950s and 1960s therefore became the young, impressionable Boomers. Vance Packard quotes a 1950s article which explained to advertisers,

> "Eager minds can be molded to want your products! In the grade schools throughout America are nearly 23,000,000 young girls and boys... Here is a vast market for your products. Sell these children on your brand name and they will insist that their parents buy no other."[29]

In another article, advertisers and TV producers were urged to build an army of consumers. Imagine, it said, "a million to ten million who will grow up into adults trained to buy your product as soldiers are trained to advance when they hear the trigger words 'forward march'". Critical thinking inhibits buying decisions, so, in Televisionland, it was discouraged. Emotional thinking, on the other hand, promotes impulse buying and was encouraged. Above all, TV set out to inflame dissatis-faction. The 1950s therefore saw a vast expansion in marketing aimed at training the young Boomer generation to be hedonistic and encouraging them to gratify their desires. By targeting the Boomers, advertisers could slyly bypass the War Generation using a mechanism known as "pester power". As the researcher Vashima Veerkumar explains,

> "Children learn that by asking you may get what you want. Fur-thermore, early peer group influences add to the pressures placed on parents to purchase the latest products for their children so that they will not feel disadvantaged compared to their friends."[30]

Pester power was ruthlessly exploited. For example, in 1955 the General Electric company offered toys including a "magic ray gun, and a space helmet to children who brought their parents into dealers' stores to witness new GE refrigerators being demonstrated."[31]

Many parents were uncomfortable with what they saw as the brain-washing of their children by TV. In Britain, Sir William Haley, a former Director General of the BBC, wrote that TV was responsible for, "a panic flight from all decent values". He accused producers of "televising inan-ities" and promoting a "sick sniggering attitude to life".[32] In the US, campaigner Phyllis Schlafly was appalled at TV's disturbingly violent fantasies. She complained that "the average child by the age of 15 will have witnessed 13,400 televised killings. What is the matter with the parents who permit their children to watch all those murders?" Schlafly noted the changed values of the Boomers and pointed the finger at TV. "The whole generation of Americans who grew to adulthood since World War II" she said, "has been trained to blame its troubles on "society" and to look to the government for the solution to all problems."[33]

In Britain, Schlafly's equivalent, Mary Whitehouse, launched a campaign to "clean up TV" in 1964. Whitehouse believed that TV had become a battlefield for the soul of the Boomer generation which she said was, "pouring into millions of homes the propaganda of disbelief, doubt and dirt". Whitehouse argued that TV was responsible for causing profound ideological change. At stake, she wrote, was nothing less than, "the philosophy on which our civilization has been built".[34]

But these were lonely protests vainly attempting to hold back the incoming tide. The Boomers would "forever be the children of television". It shaped their idealism, their sense of what the world ought to be, contributed to their confusion when they discovered it wasn't, and fueled their desire to change and perfect it. The Boomer Ideology was, at least in part, a denial of the complexity and limitations of reality, and the impulse to make it conform to the simple, sweet narratives and happy endings of TV.

Chapter 4

Boomer Pleasures. Sex, Drugs, Rock 'n' roll, Violence and Debt

"What do we want? Everything! When do we want it? Now!"

"I take my desires for reality because I believe in the reality of my desires."

"Be realistic, demand the impossible".

Boomer slogans.

The Joy of Sex

As it reached adolescence and young adulthood, an immature generation set out to gratify its desires. Sexual liberation was a priority for the Boomers and it appeared as if the planets were aligning to make it happen. In 1960, the US Federal Drug Administration approved the sale of Enovid, the world's first contraceptive pill. By 1967, 13 million women around the world were using it. Meanwhile, between 1967 and 1973, a third of the states decriminalized abortion, a trend culminating in the landmark Supreme Court ruling of Roe v Wade which legalized abortion nationwide.* Divorce law was also liberalized to serve Boomer needs and prevent the 'horror' of Boomers being trapped in unhappy relationships. The introduction of no-fault, quickie divorces in California in 1969 was widely followed by other states during the 1970s. The UK followed in 1971 when the Divorce Reform Act made it far easier to end marriages.

Having separated sex from the consequences of sex, the road was now open for sex to become a pleasurable, recreational activity, rather than a means of making babies. Victorian morality, which valued chastity and denial, and frowned on pre-marital sex, suddenly seemed obsolete. The writer David Allyn observes that, for the Boomer generation, the sexual revolution meant a swinging lifestyle and the "freedom to have sex where and when one wished". The Boomer slogan, "make love not war" he says, brings to mind "naked hippie couples frolicking in a park, or men and women waiting in line to see a hard-core porn film as a first date."[1]

The British fashion photographer David Bailey eulogized the rise of exciting new Boomer values in a 1965 photo-essay *Box of Pinups*. In it, he praised thirty six Boomers for having the courage to pursue hedonistic self-gratification, "Many of the people here have gone all out

---

*   In June 2022 the Supreme Court overturned Roe v Wade and returned decisions about abortion law to individual states.

29

for the immediate rewards of success: quick money, quick fame, quick sex — a brave thing to do." The poet Philip Larkin expressed sadness at missing the sexual revolution because he was too old. In *Annus Mirabilis* he wrote, "Sexual intercourse began in nineteen sixty-three, (which was rather late for me) / Between the end of the "Chatterley" ban, and the Beatles' first LP."

The unrestrained pursuit of sexual gratification was portrayed by the Boomers as liberating and empowering, but it could also be selfish and predatory. Richard Neville was a hero of the Boomer counterculture and a celebrity pornographer. His obituary in *The Guardian* praised him for helping to destroy Victorian morality and its prudish "sexual mores". But the article was silent about his pedophilia. For example, in his 1970 best-selling book *Playpower* Neville boasted,

> "I meet a moderately attractive, intelligent, cherubic fourteen-year-old girl from a nearby London comprehensive school. I ask her home, she rolls a joint… a hurricane fuck, another joint. No feigned love or hollow promises… A farewell kiss, and the girl rushes off to finish her homework."[2]

In this self-serving, sanitized account of child abuse, Neville writes as if he is striking an heroic blow for the sexual revolution. He does not consider the psychological and emotional damage he may be causing, nor of the ethics of using a child for his own sexual gratification. According to Boomer mythology, the sexual revolution was a joyful moment of liberation from the stuffy, repression of 1950s life. But the reality was more complex than the myth. San Francisco's Haight-Ashbury district during the 1960s is today usually portrayed as a beautiful place full of young Boomers living their dreams and helping make the world a better place. For example, a 2016 article tells us,

> "The renowned Psychedelic Shop was opened in January of 1966, providing the community with easy access to drugs by selling marijuana and LSD. Considered a community unifier, the Psychedelic Shop and neighboring coffee shop The Blue Unicorn brought together freaks, heads and hippies alike… A street theatre group known as The Diggers also made history with their ideas of a free society and the good in human nature. They created a

free store and would supply free meals as well as a free medical clinic, the first of its kind."[3]

The reality was different and darker. For example, according to one contemporary account, "a pretty little sixteen-year-old middle-class chick comes to the Haight to see what it's all about and gets picked up by a seventeen year old street dealer who spends all day shooting her full of speed." She is then auctioned for the "biggest Haight Street gangbang since the night before". The author concludes "rape is as common as bullshit on Haight Street."[4]

The cultural critic Gershon Legman, writing in 1967, was another who attacked the sexual revolution saying, "The ostensible goals of the New Freedom are too puerile to discuss." The Boomers, he said, wanted, "Freedom for screwing and turning-on, but this time with perverted chicks, orgies, whippings, sick 'happenings', marijuana, heroin and LSD." Legman asked,

"How will it make over an ailing world that you're so sincerely sorry for, to lay on your side for two days and nights in some dirty girl's even dirtier pad... both of you as high as steamboat whistles on alternate doses of marijuana and LSD? How does that help the ailing world?... How does the sexual piggery of sharing your girl or your wife with three to six other guys, at every end of her pink anatomy, show your rebellion against your parent's bad old world?"[5]

The British-American social critic Duncan Williams attacked Boomer hyposcrisy. They were not creating a better world, as they claimed. Instead, he said, they were creating a "sick society" based on a philosophy of "arrogant primitivism." Writing in 1971, Williams accused the Boomers of destroying the "Old moral sanctions in a search for self-fulfillment."[6] An entire generation was, he said, plunging into a chasm of self-indulgence, "A descent to mere animal gratification, which presents the greatest danger to the immature" because it preaches a morality based on the distorted message, "instant gratification of all appetites with no bill to pay." As Laindon Jones soberly concluded, the carnival, "produced much sexual sophistication but little intimacy... the error of the baby Boomers was believing that sex can satisfy without commitment."[7]

31

Unsurprisingly, many Boomer marriages were fragile; 48% of Americans who married during the 1970s were divorced within 25 years.[8] As a consequence, 43% of American children were raised without fathers — a major contributing factor, according to some analysts, of poverty and crime.[9] There would eventually be a bill, but it was not the Boomers who would have to pay it. Among the consequences of the sexual revolution were soaring divorce rates, single parenthood, and children growing up outside of the stability of family life — something most Boomers had taken for granted.

The Joy of Drugs

The Boomer's fascination with drugs was both a search for sensory pleasure and an escape from reality and responsibility. For the Boomers, the signature drug was LSD which assumed enormous cultural significance between 1965 and 1970. Compared with other drugs which merely intoxified, LSD was a powerful hallucinogenic which altered the user's perception of reality and united them in a community of blown minds. It inspired psychedelia – a craze for surreal, lurid, wobbly music and images. It also promised a shortcut to transcendence. The American psychologist Timothy Leary, who was sacked from Harvard in 1963 for encouraging students to take LSD, played a major role in popularizing and mythologizing the drug. He wrote that LSD freed the mind and enabled it to reach, "that level of understanding variously called liberation, illumination, or enlightenment." Leary described three stages of psychedelic experience, the highest being that of, "complete transcendence — beyond words, beyond space-time, beyond self."[10]

LSD promised the Boomers instant spiritual gratification. The goal that holy men and women had sought for thousands of years — being at one with God and the universe – could now be achieved simply by popping a pill. As George Harrison summarized, "I had such an incredible feeling of well-being, that there was a God and I could see Him in every blade of grass. It was like gaining hundreds of years of experience within twelve hours."[11]

LSD was therefore the Boomer Epistemology in a pill. It demonstrated there was no objective truth, just a slippery, rubbery world of subjective perception and dreams. It taught the Boomers that their knowledge was as valid as the knowledge of their parents. It told the soothing lie that nothing is impossible. In the wonderland of LSD, the complexity and imperfections of the real world were replaced by a technicolor theatre of fantastic illusions. As the Beatles sang in an LSD inspired 1967 song,

"Let me take you down,
'Cause I'm going to Strawberry Fields,
Nothing is real,
And nothing to get hung about."[12]

The Boomer activist Pete the Coyote pointed out the link between acid and ideology, explaining in 1968 that, "LSD is for us what gin was for the Victorians. It lubricates our acceptance of a new age."[13] Timothy Leary agreed, saying that LSD was changing the nature of truth, knowledge and reality. When the Beatles released their trippy, psychedelic *Sgt. Pepper's Lonely Hearts Club Band* in 1967, he said it, "gave voice to the feeling that the old ways were over." However, LSD did not, and could not, change reality. It merely altered the mind's perception of it. Reality remained coldly indifferent to how Boomers perceived it or wanted it to be. For example, Tara Browne was a well-known British socialite who often accompanied rock stars and celebrities on "acid-fueled roller coaster rides". In December 1966, Browne, high on LSD, drove his sports car across London at a hundred miles an hour. Mesmerized by the psychedelic patterns which displaced reality, the "golden child of the sixties"[14] raced through a red traffic light, smashed into a parked van and died instantly. LSD had not revealed reality to Browne, it had concealed it.

The Joy of Rock 'n' Roll

It is hard to overstate the significance of rock music to the Boomers. It was a language - a 'secret alphabet' that the older generation could not understand. As The Who sang rebelliously in 1965, "Why don't you all fade away, don't try to dig what we all say". In the words of a 1969 article in *Rolling Stone* magazine, "rock and roll is more than just music; it is the energy center of the new culture and youth revolution." The Beatles were the most influential and iconic of all Boomer bands. The writer Jonathan Gould says they were a totem for the "broad confluence of pop enthusiasm, student activism, and mass bohemianism that would flood the political, social, and cultural landscape". These avatars of the "great international upheaval" achieved unheard of levels of fame and exerted "the sort of influence that had once been reserved for political, military, and religious leaders."[15]

When John Lennon told an interviewer, "we're more popular than Jesus now; I don't know which will go first – rock 'n' roll or Christianity" he was expressing the growing sense that rock musicians had become the new priesthood and their songs the sermons of a new faith. The British pop star Donovan agreed saying, "Pop is the perfect religious vehicle. It's as if God had come down to earth and seen all the ugliness that was being created and chosen pop to be the great force for love and beauty."[16]

If rock musicians were priests, their acolytes were the new breed of radio disc jockeys. For the Boomers, listening to the radio was an intimate experience made possible by the development of small, battery-operated transistor sets. Transistors meant Boomers could listen to music anywhere. The format of top 40 pop radio developed in the US and fed Boomer audiences a diet of pop music, jingles and simplified snippets of news, served up by hip Boomer deejays. In the UK, the BBC enjoyed a broadcasting monopoly and no independent stations were allowed. However, the situation changed dramatically in March 1964 when the pirate station Radio Caroline began playing pop music from a ship moored off the east coast of England. A law passed in 1967 to outlaw pirate radio only made it more popular. The disc jockey and author Ray Clark listened avidly to pirate radio as a teenager, partly, he says, because it made him feel part of a community from which his parents' generation was excluded,

"In those days people in their late thirties or forties were considered old. They dressed old, they thought old, they wore suits on Sundays! They listened to what Caroline was playing in '67 and '68, with its rebellious attitude, and thought, 'this isn't for me'. So, it became more and more a radio station for the young."[17]

Clark says pirate radio was a shared tribal experience for millions of British teenagers for whom tuning in became an important ritual,

"In '66 and '67 when Caroline and Radio London were huge, they had an audience of 20-30 million between them. We would listen at night and the next morning we would have discussions at school about which was the best station."

Pop radio was the public space that helped forge the Boomer identity. It was a forum where Boomers could discover who was in and who was out, and demonstrate their awareness of the shared tribal knowledge.

The Joy of Violence

Today, the hedonistic, rebellious pleasures of sex, drugs and rock 'n' roll are firmly embedded in Boomer mythology and endlessly romanticized in nostalgic books, films and TV documentaries. However, other Boomer pleasures are less discussed. These include a predilection for the forbidden thrill of violence and law breaking. The statistics however are unambiguous. As the cognitive psychologist Stephen Pinker writes,

"In the 1960s the homicide rate in America went through the roof. After a three-decade free fall that spanned the Great Depression, World War II, and the Cold War, Americans multiplied their homicide rate by more than two and a half, from a low of 4.0 in 1957 to a high of 10.2 in 1980."[18]

Serial killers, for whom killing seems to be an end in itself, were almost unknown in the US during the 1950s. The concept of murder as a macabre sort of sport was a Boomer innovation. Nineteen serial killers became active during the 1960's, 119 in the 1970's, and 200 during the 1980's.[19] It was not just homicide; the number of rapes, assaults, muggings and robberies all soared. American cities became especially dangerous. New York became a symbol of moral decay and lawlessness. Concern about rising crime and violence, and its destabilizing effect on society, was reflected in vigilante fantasies such as the 1971 Clint Eastwood movie *Dirty Harry* or the *Death Wish* movies starring Charles Bronson. In these films, Boomer barbarians are gunned down, usually by the older generation, civilization is protected from chaos and order restored.

In the UK, the Moors Murderers, Ian Brady and Myra Hindley, raped, tortured and killed five children between 1963 and 1965. The judge at their trial said they were "sadistic killers of the utmost depravity". The journalist Christopher Booker noted Brady and Hindley inhabited a "fantasy world of Sadism and Nazism" and the way in which they had gratified their perverted desires, "threw into sharp relief the darker side of the dream into which Britain had been moving".[20]

A distinctively British form of violence erupted in 1964 when rival gangs of Mods and Rockers travelled to sleepy seaside towns to fight each other. Horrified newspapers described the battles, with fists, bottles, bike chains and iron bars, as an invasion of barbarians. The *Daily Express* wrote,

> "There was Dad asleep in a deckchair and Mum making sandcastles with the children, when the 1964 boys took over the beaches at Margate and Brighton yesterday and smeared the traditional postcard scene with blood and violence".[21]

Although the fighting was between rival Boomer sub-tribes, the real target was the settled, civilized world of Victorian Liberalism. Taking over genteel seaside resorts and transforming them into festivals of Boomer violence was the real objective. As 18-year-old John Braden boasted,

> "Yes, I am a Mod and I was at Margate. I joined in a few of the fights. It was a laugh, I haven't enjoyed myself so much for a long time. It was great – the beach was like a battlefield. It was like we were taking over the country. You want to hit back at all the old geezers who try to tell us what to do. We just want to show them we're not going to take it."[22]

In 1972, the Boomer sociologist Stanley Cohen wrote a revisionist analysis of the violence in an influential book *Folk Devils and Moral Panics; The creation of the Mods and Rockers*. In it, he blamed journalists for sensational reporting which had manufactured a problem that did not really exist. Cohen explained, "Much of this study will be devoted to understanding the role of the mass media in creating moral panics and folk devils."[23] Cohen stood the journalistic narrative on its head. According to his radical new view, the behavior of the Boomers was normal; it was the reaction of the War Generation that was deviant. Why, he asked, was it "normal" to want to sit quietly on a beach and build sandcastles? Cohen said,

> "The new tradition is sceptical in the sense that when it sees terms like 'deviant', it asks 'deviant to whom?' or 'deviant from what?'; when told that something is a social problem, it asks 'problematic to whom?'"[24]

Cohen called for new cultural values and for a new type of journalism — one sympathetic to Boomer ways of thinking and hostile to the deviant Victorian values of restraint, denial and self-control. Cohen attacked the "intellectual poverty and total lack of imagination in our society's response to its adolescent trouble-makers during the last twenty years" and suggested radical change was needed to transform the Boomers from folk devils to folk heroes, "our society as presently structured will continue to generate problems for some of its members — like working-class adolescents — and then condemn whatever solution these groups find."[25] For the Boomers, there was nothing wrong with their way of thinking and behaving. Sex, drugs, rock 'n' roll and violence were the new normal. It was the mindset of their parents that was the problem and needed to change.

The Joy of Debt

While only a small minority of Boomers were ever addicted to drugs, vastly more became addicted to debt. Debt made possible the instant gratification of desire. Sexy new forms of debt, such as credit cards, appeared during the 1950s and 1960s. They were based on the idea of 'revolving credit' which allowed borrowers to roll-over debt from one month to the next, effectively allowing debt to be indefinitely postponed and repaid with more debt. It was a formula that became wildly popular. As the bank analyst Warren Marcus put it in 1967, "recently credit cards are becoming as common- place as miniskirts."[26] Or, as the historian Christine Zumello observed, "from cars to vacuum cleaners, consumer credit became essential, and revolving credit grew exponentially as a new debt practice."[27]

The great economist Adam Smith pointed out that money has no intrinsic value. It is simply a convenient means of storing the "toil and trouble" needed to obtain it. Thus, we receive money in exchange for our labor, we use money to buy the labor of others as well as to pay for goods which other peoples' labor produces. As Smith explained, "it is not by gold or silver, but by labor, that all the wealth of the world was originally purchased."[28] According to Smith's classic analysis, debt can be understood therefore as enabling people to enjoy the reward of working without having to work. Debt decouples the gratification of desire from effort. What we want, we can have immediately without effort – thanks to the magic of debt. Debt is also addictive. For the Boomers, debt, not LSD, was the real drug of choice. Debt, like an hallucinogenic drug, alters our perception of reality. It creates a fantasy world in which the iron laws of economics stretch like rubber bands, and apparently no longer apply. All the pleasures of the affluent society can be enjoyed today, with repayments deferred until some distant, later date. Spiraling debt was however viewed with alarm by seasoned economists. Even the usually sanguine Galbraith could not conceal his anxiety over the "tensions associated with debt creation on such a massive scale". He worried about the "gravest results from the way consumer demand is now sustained by the relentless increase in consumer debt."[29] But this was not a fashionable view among Boomers. The Victorian values of thrift, prudence and restraint, along with appeals to 'reality', were ridiculed as obsolete and irrelevant – the stale mutterings of the old.

Chapter 5

The Vortex of Immaturity Seeking an Ideology

The Boomer generation was unique. An enormous cohort of young people was raised at a particular historical moment when a complex and highly unusual matrix of psychological and environmental forces converged to create a self-amplifying, feedback loop. The impact of these forces interacting, feeding, reinforcing and multiplying was that the whole became greater than the sum of the parts. The Boomer Ideology was the product of a Vortex of Immaturity.

Whereas previous generations had learnt from their elders, the Boomers learnt primarily from each other. The psychologist Judith Rich Harris observes that young people are programmed to learn from the dominant social group. For thousands of years, across many different cultures, the dominant group was invariably composed of adults. Historically therefore, the goal of young people had been to learn how to fit into adult society. However, the unique demographics of the post-World War Two era, meant the Boomers' primary goal was to fit into teenage society. The ability to demonstrate immature virtues and reject adult authority, all helped in the competition for social status. The more one signaled radical immaturity, the more one signaled value and usefulness to the tribe. As Harris explains, "The shared environment that leaves permanent marks on children's personalities is the environment they share with their peers." According to what Harris refers to as Group Socialization Theory,

> "In the pre-agricultural societies of our ancestors, group socialization would have begun in mixed-age, mixed-sex play groups. In today's urbanized societies, socialization gets its start in the nursery school or day-care center, gathers momentum in the same-age, same-sex peer groups of school-age children, and approaches asymptote in the mixed-sex crowds of adolescents. It is within these groups, according to GS theory, that the psychological characteristics a child is born with become permanently modified by the environment."[1]

Harris' analysis is supported by recent research in cognitive neuroscience. For example, the neuroscientist Sarah-Jayne Blakemore describes how adolescents are particularly prone to groupthink because the areas of the brain that regulate impulse control develop slowly, whereas the areas associated with the reward system develop earlier faster and earlier. The immature brain is therefore "hyper-responsive" to what the majority feel is a good idea. Consequently, Blakemore says, "decision-making in adolescence may be particularly modulated by emotion and social factors, for example, when adolescents are with peers or in other affective ('hot') contexts."[2] The developmental neuroscientist Elizabeth Shulman makes a similar point, noting that the socioemotional system which makes people seek reward and approval from peers, matures early, whereas, the cognitive control system, which restrains urges and impulses, matures later. Shulman concludes that adolescents are therefore much more likely to behave without regard for long-term consequences when they surrounded by other young people. This is not because they are incapable of logical reasoning, but because the desire to impress other young people becomes their dominant goal. As Shulman explains,

> "When decision making occurs under conditions that excite, or activate, the socioemotional system (e.g., when decisions are made in the presence of friends, under emotionally arousing circumstances, or when there is a potential to obtain an immediate reward) adolescents are more prone than other age groups to pursue exciting, novel, and risky courses of action."[3]

This is a key insight. It means the Boomer generation turned inward and learned from itself. This led to a radical re-wiring of epistemology in which the concepts of truth and knowledge changed profoundly. For example, the 19 year old American Today Malone, who starred in a 1968 documentary, expressed the widely held Boomer view that knowledge was something that emerged from talking to other, like-minded people, not from studying the accumulated wisdom of the past. On the contrary, learning from the past was considered wrong and damaging. Only the Boomer way of knowing, an intuitive, tribal process, was valid. As Today explained,

> "I have learned so much more from going to the drug store cafe and just talking to people than I ever learned in college or high school. Because I think knowledge can be gained much more from contact with people than from books. And the drug store is really a good place to do this. People just go in and order coffee and sit down and rap and talk to each other and learn."[4]

The distinguished anthropologist Margaret Mead, writing in 1972, noted precisely the same epistemic phenomenon; that adolescent Boomers were learning from themselves and were hostile to knowledge from outside. It was the consensus of Boomers that mattered most. Truth was becoming tribal truth, knowledge was becoming tribal knowledge,

> "When the number of such young people is large, they become models for one another and, rejecting the behavior models of adults in the new environment, treat teachers and administrators as opposition forces to be outwitted, not followed."[5]

41

Here then, is the vortex of immaturity. The Boomers were not aspiring to adult status, they were contrasting themselves with adults. The Boomers fetishized and institutionalised immaturity. They did not seek to learn adult values, they sought to unlearn them. In doing so they were often ferociously tribal. The Boomers were constantly asking each other; are you one of us, or one of them? Whose truth do you believe; ours or theirs?

In a flock of birds there is no single, overall leader. Instead each bird keeps a keen eye on what its immediate neighbors are doing and adjusts its position accordingly. This is known as "safer together" behavior, and, as it ripples through the flock, the result is huge, sweeping conformity and group behavior. Thus, a murmuration of tens of thousands of swallows produces magnificent patterns that appear to be carefully choreographed, and in which the entire flock appears to be one living whole. But the appearance of direction and design is an illusion. As the researcher Anne Goodenough and her colleagues observe,

> "Each bird interacts with, and moves according to, six or seven nearest neighbors and it is the proximity of those neighbors, as opposed to all birds within a fixed distance, which dictates individual movement."[6]

The Boomer tribe was a vast herd, or flock, exhibiting an invisible self-adjusting mechanism. The guiding rule was always to pay close attention to what other Boomers were thinking, doing and saying, try to imitate them, keep up with the latest fashions and try to avoid being unfashionable. The vortex of immaturity gave rise to a distinctive culture with distinctive ways of thinking, knowing and doing. Recalling it, the journalist Bernard Levin said,

> "Fashions changed, changed again, changed faster and still faster: fashions in politics, in political style, in causes, in music, in popular culture, in myths, in education, in beauty, in heroes and idols, in attitudes, in responses, in work, in love, in friendship, in food, in newspapers, in entertainment, in fashion. What had once lasted a generation now lasted a year, what had lasted a year lasted a month, a week, a day."[7]

42

The Boomers were driven by an intense tribalism — the combined effect of a huge cohort of immature young people feeding off each other's views. Constant change was the result of the Boomers' ceaseless efforts to be more like each another. Christopher Booker described the Boomers during the mid 1960s as being in the grip of an extraordinary shared fantasy, "feeding on and attracting each other". Being part of the Boomer tribe was all that seemed to matter,

> "There was everywhere unprecedented emphasis on youthful energy, youthful enterprise, youthful idealism... a symptom of the feeling, as yet barely defined, that youth had glamour and power, that England was moving into a new, mysterious age to which the young alone had the key."[8]

The historian Eric Hobsbawm noted the same sense of Boomer Exceptionalism — the belief that immature ways of seeing, thinking and behaving were different to, and better than, anything previously known in human history. Hobsbawm wrote that, during the 1960s, "Youth was seen not as a preparatory stage of adulthood, but, in some sense, as a final stage of full human development". As far as the Boomers were concerned, he said, the fact that they lacked political power and were not in charge of society was, "one more proof of the unsatisfactory way the world was organized."[9]

The film critic Barry Norman remembered, "It seemed as if we had entered upon a new and glorious age in which life, wonderful as it already was, could only get better". Norman added that the Boomers were also intoxicated by the awareness of their numerical superiority and their growing power, "it was the time" he said, "when the authority of parents was challenged and overcome by their children."[10] In Britain, Mary Whitehouse wondered why things seemed to be going wrong. She concluded that her generation, exhausted by the war, had allowed its children too much freedom, given them too little guidance, and abandoned them to learn from each other — and from TV,

> "We abdicated our wider responsibilities in the tired years after the war. Young enough to want the fun we'd missed, part of an affluent society coming to terms with so much, we failed to

grasp at what was slipping unnoticed through our comfortable fingers — our children's and our nation's future."[11]

The Boomer Ideology

Human beings need ideology. Wherever a distinctive community exists with shared cultural assumptions, values, hopes and fears; ideology will begin to form in order to justify it. The psychologist Tom Tyler refers to ideology as group narratives or 'legitimizing myths' that give authority to, and confer normality on, the pre-existing desires and intuitions of the tribe,

> "A legitimating ideology is a set of justifications or 'legitimizing myths' that lead a political or social system, and its authorities and institutions, to be viewed as normatively or morally appropriate by the people within the system."[12]

Ideology is therefore always tribal. It is the social glue that binds members together and helps them cooperate. The social psychologist Herbert Kelman points out that ideology does not just legitimize one set of values, it simultaneously delegitimizes others. According to Kelman, this process of ideological legitimization and delegitimization forms part of a wider power struggle. When one group climbs to power, it plants its ideological flag in the enemy's camp and dictates what should be considered normal and abnormal. This explains, says Kelman, how generational changes sometimes, "turn social norms on their head, such that what was wrong before now becomes right or vice versa."[13] A striking feature of a successful ideology is that it appears normal and unremarkable to those who hold it. It is in other words, completely invisible. It is only other tribes' ideologies that are visible, because they appear abnormal, weird or wrong. As the literary critic and theorist Terry Eagleton neatly puts it, "ideology, like halitosis, is in this sense what the other person has."[14]

The creation of ideology is then, a two stage process. First, there must exist a significant group with shared goals. At first, the group's values are instinctive and intuitive, they are felt rather than stated. Within the group, certain ways of doing things feel right and come to be accepted as normal. At this stage, we can speak of a group having its own culture. The researcher Daniel Feldman points out that this first stage is rarely made explicit, "Although these norms are infrequently written down or openly discussed, they often have a powerful, and consistent, influence on group members' behavior."[15]

In the second stage, the group adopts a formal, legitimizing framework for their pre-existing, intuitions and culture. This involves the construction of fully fledged systems of morality and behavior. This stage occurs only when the group is sufficiently big and involves the writing of texts of various sorts to which group members can refer. Throughout history, this process has often taken the form of a religion with a canon of officially sanctioned scripture. Like trying to draw precise boundaries between the colors of a rainbow, it is hard to point to the exact moment at which an informal tribal culture gives birth to a formal religion or ideology.

Ideology then, serves the social, intellectual, moral and spiritual needs of a community. It confirms and reinforces group members' pre-existing culture — what they already feel and believe. Consequently, when members of a community are presented with a formal ideology, it hits them with a revelatory force. It feels like everything finally makes sense and fits together. Community members respond by saying to themselves, "I knew it"! Psychologists refer to this process of legitimization as 'motivated reasoning'. The cognitive psychologist Jonathan Haidt explains that motivated reasoning is a form of self-deception. Ideological schemes are attempts to justify our pre-existing intuitions, assumptions and prejudices. "When called on to justify these intuitions" says Haidt, theorists generate "post hoc justifications" and "do not realize that they are doing this." [16] Haidt's description perfectly describes the Boomer Ideology. It was a post hoc framework developed by theorists, musicians, artists and public intellectuals, between approximately 1960 and 2000 to legitimize the Boomer's pre-existing intuitions, feelings and desires. The Boomer Ideology was the ethical-political map written to help the Boomer tribe navigate the terrain in which they were living, or believed they were living, during the last third of the 20th Century. It was motivated reasoning on a generational scale.

Chapter 6

Political Philosophy for Boomers. Marcuse and Critical Theory

The Boomer generation was hungry for its legitimizing myths, and for a philosophical framework to support its pre-existing intuitions and desires. What was urgently required was intellectual scaffolding to justify Boomer ways of thinking, knowing and behaving. The existing canon of Enlightenment philosophy was useless because, measured against its standards, the Boomers were simply a mass of immature minds living in a fantasy world — a vast tribe of modern barbarians who rejected the values of Western civilization. One Boomer textbook described the situation as an "intellectual crisis" and argued,

> "The contemporary world projects a perplexing picture of political, social and economic upheaval. In these challenging times the conventional wisdoms of orthodox social thought, whether it be sociology, economics or cultural studies, become inadequate."[1]

The solution was to construct a new canon of texts to make Boomer thinking respectable and explain why the Boomer worldview was superior to what had come before. These new writings would, "transcend the limitations of conventional discourse... in the belief that significant theoretical work is needed to clear the way for a genuine transformation of the existing social order." Or, as Gibney puts it, the Boomers "would create a parallel reality furnished with a more convenient set of books."[2]

One of the first writers to recognize and meet the philosophical needs of the Boomers, was Herbert Marcuse with his uniquely Boomer-friendly 'Critical Theory'. Critical Theory had originally been developed during the 1930s by the German philosopher Max Horkeimer. Horkeimer sought to blend traditional scientific rationalism with Marxist ideas and morality. His aim was to counter Nazi philosophy by introducing an ethical dimension into its cold, relentlessly logical thinking. However, his ideas had little impact and were largely ignored. It was Marcuse, who, during the 1950s and 1960s, breathed new life into Critical Theory and transformed it from a cerebral offshoot of Marxism into a creed legitimizing the gratification of desire and the abandonment of self-control.

According to Marcusian philosophy, emotional and impulsive ways of behaving were ethically and politically good; embracing them would lead to the creation of a better world. This was music to the ears of the Boomers, and Marcuse became a highly influential figure among the Boomer generation of students and academics. To be into Marcuse and Critical Theory became fashionable and cool. In Europe and the US, the slogan "Marx, Mao, Marcuse" was popular during the late 1960s and early 1970s. As the philosopher Arnold Farr notes, "In the 1960s Marcuse ascended to prominence and became one of the best-known philosophers and social theorists in the world. He was often referred to as the Guru of the New Left."[3]

In his 1964 best-selling book *One Dimensional Man*, Marcuse launched a ferocious attack on Western civilization and the concept of individual responsibility. Freedom and democracy were, he said, illusions masking a repressive, totalitarian state. The truth, he argued, was that young people were trapped in a suffocating regime which prevented them from being happy. His opening statement proclaimed, "a comfortable, smooth, reasonable, democratic unfreedom prevails in advanced industrial civilization."[4] Marcuse proceeded to turn reality upside down. He argued that the more society appeared to be free and full of choice, the more repressive it actually was. Freedom, he said, was a tool of enslavement, because it burdened people with responsibility, "under the rule of a repressive whole" he explained, "liberty can be made into a powerful instrument of domination."[5] Every aspect of Western civilization and liberal democracy was, he preached, "intolerably repressive",

> "Domination — in the guise of affluence and liberty – extends to all spheres of private and public existence, integrates all authentic opposition, absorbs all alternatives. Technological rationality reveals its political character as it becomes the great vehicle of better domination, creating a truly totalitarian universe."[6]

One Dimensional Man was a highly truthophobic book. It attacked the concept of truth, dismissing it as a "relic of the past".[7] Critical Theory, he said, required "negative thinking" to "negate" existing forms of thought and reality. He dismissed the old rational way of knowing as, "one dimensional thought" which was an "instrument of domination". He called for new ways of seeing and knowing to "transcend" the old mode of thought which was leading to the "progressive enslavement of man" and ruining, "the lives of those who build and use this apparatus."[8] Marcuse peppered his text with metaphysical speculation derived from German Idealist philosophy in order to question the nature of reality. Words were prized loose from their meanings. There were many different "rationalities" and "realities" — the officially-established "social" or "technological" reality — which must be, "transformed, even subverted in order to become that which it really is"[9] and the new "pre-technological rationality" of Critical Theory which is,

> "The rationality of a two-dimensional universe of discourse which contrasts with the one-dimensional modes of thought and behavior that develop in the execution of the technological project."[10]

In the inverted world of Marcusian philosophy, factual accounts were repressive fictions. It was only in fiction, Marcuse said, that truth could be found, "fiction calls the facts by their name and their reign collapses; fiction subverts everyday experience and shows it to be mutilated and false"[11] To the philosophers of the Enlightenment, the metaphysical and linguistic approach employed by Critical Theory would have seemed an abomination — a ludicrous jumble of sophistry and theology. As David Hume, writing in 1777, had famously insisted,

> "If we take in our hand any volume; of divinity or school metaphysics, for instance; let us ask, Does it contain any abstract reasoning concerning quantity or number? No. Does it contain any experimental reasoning concerning matter of fact and existence? No. Commit it then to the flames: for it can contain nothing but sophistry and illusion."[12]

Marcuse's gnomic writing style, and especially his undermining of the meaning of words, would also have offended writers such as George Orwell who criticized linguistic ambiguity as the "debasement of language" into "sheer cloudy vagueness". Orwell attacked equivocation — slyly attaching new meanings to familiar words such as 'truth' or 'reality'. "Words of this kind" said Orwell,

> "Are often used in a consciously dishonest way. That is, the person who uses them has his own private definition, but allows his hearer to think he means something quite different".

He concluded that the tactic was, "designed to make lies sound truthful and murder respectable, and to give an appearance of solidity to pure wind."[13]

But Boomer readers were delighted by Marcuse's surreal undermining of the foundations of Anglo-American philosophy. If reality was not real, if truth was not truth, and if rationality was irrational, then all the assumptions and logic of their parent's generation collapsed. Marcuse did not provide any evidence for his sweeping assertions, he simply appealed to the Boomers to have faith and accept his opinions as statements of fact. Despite this, or perhaps because of it, *One Dimensional Man* was enormously successful, as the American academic Douglas Kellner notes,

> "Herbert Marcuse's *One Dimensional Man* was one of the most important books of the 1960s. First published in 1964, it was immediately recognized as a significant critical diagnosis of the present age and was soon taken up by the emergent New Left as a damning indictment of contemporary Western societies."[14]

A key feature of Critical Theory was its intolerance. Critical Theory preached that good should not tolerate evil. If the feelings and intuitions arising from the Vortex of Immaturity were good, then it followed that the Boomers should not tolerate the values of their parents. Fighting to destroy the old ways of thinking became an ethical-political duty. Violence, according to Critical Theory, was a legitimate tool in the fight against evil. Compromise was treason. This was, essentially, a reversion to the radical intolerance of the pre-modern era. For example, in the 4th Century, St Augustine preached that those who were passionate, militant and filled with Christian rage were blessed. As the historian Ramsay MacMullen explains,

> "St Augustine addressed his congregation in Carthage with ringing invocations to smash all tangible symbols of paganism they could lay their hands on 'for' he tells them, 'that all super-stition of pagans and heathens should be annihilated is what God wants, God commands, God proclaims!' Words uttered to 'wild applause'.[15]

In his crusade against tolerance, Marcuse was rediscovering the forgotten joys of moral righteousness and theological fanaticism. In 1965, Marcuse launched an attack on liberal tolerance which he labelled "repressive tolerance". "What is proclaimed and practiced as tolerance today" he said is, "serving the cause of oppression." Marcuse suggested a new concept of "discriminating tolerance" – tolerance of what was ethically-politically good, and intolerance of what was bad. It was, he said, a "radical goal" and he called on the Boomer generation to crusade for, "the emergence of a free and sovereign majority... militantly intolerant and disobedient to the rules of behavior which tolerate destruction and suppression."[16] Marcuse had completely inverted the concept of liberal tolerance. Critical Theory instructed the Boomers to only tolerate their own collective impulses, urges and desires.

In 1966, Marcuse took his Boomer-friendly thesis to the next level. He redefined Marxism as a philosophy which advocated the right of the Boomer generation to lead fulfilled lives free from unhappiness and stress. Marxism, he said, should be understood, not as a struggle by the working class to control the means of production as Marx had envisaged it, but as a "protest against unnecessary repression, the struggle for the ultimate form of freedom — to live without anxiety."[17] With his Boomer fan base in mind, he argued that Marxism was, first and foremost, a quest for sexual liberation. Borrowing elements from Freudian psychoanalysis, he claimed that Victorian Liberal ideology was based on the "reality principle". This, he said, was an artificial way of thinking and behaving that stifled the natural urge to gratify one's desires. He explained that "the replacement of the pleasure principle by the reality principle is the great traumatic event in the development of man,"[18] adding that mankind was now involved in a struggle for the "removal of extraneous barriers to his gratification". He proclaimed that the impulses of the Boomer generation were being controlled by "repressive civilization" — the outworn ideology of their parents,

> "Submission to the reality principle is enforced by the parents and other educators.... The primal father, as the archetype of domination, initiates the chain reaction of enslavement, rebellion, and reinforced domination which marks the history of civilization".[19]

Shattering the old rules, for example by having sex before marriage, or by having sex with many different partners was, according to Marcuse, a political duty. "Polymorphous sexuality", he said, was the ultimate subversive, revolutionary act. This was because the ideology of capitalism had artificially diverted energy away from the natural urge to have sex, to economic activity and toil,

> "Since it has not means enough to support life for its members without work on their part, it must see to it that the number of these members is restricted and their energies directed away from sexual activities on to their work."[20]

In the new "non-repressive" and "re-sexualized" society proposed by Marcuse's Critical Theory, sexual pleasure would become the dominant ethical-political goal and going to work would be largely replaced by having sex. The new way of living would, "eroticize the organism to such an extent that it would counteract the desexualization of the organism required by its social utilization as an instrument of labor."[21]

Marcuse had transformed Marxism into a religion of sexual hedonism. Critical Theory unashamedly targeted the Boomer generation. It presented politics as a simple narrative of good v evil, life v death, sexual liberation v chastity, and young rebellious Boomers v their misguided, obsolete parents. He explained,

"On the other side, against the new youth who refuse and rebel, are the representatives of the old order who can no longer protect its life without sacrificing it in the work of destruction and waste and pollution."[22]

Left wing politics had become a fight for the right of the Boomer generation to believe and do whatever it wanted. As Marcuse concluded, "The young are in the forefront of those who live and fight for Eros against Death... Today the fight for life, the fight for Eros, is the political fight."[23]

In a 1967 lecture entitled *Liberation from the Affluent Society*, Marcuse repeated his view that socialism should be redefined to conform to Boomer impulses, dreams and desires. He talked about a future of "joy and pleasure" in which capitalist ugliness "violence and destruction" would be replaced by a new world of "creative imagination and play." "I believe" he told his audience, "the idea of such a universe guided also Marx's concept of socialism." Is personal fulfilment, he asked, "identical with the transition from capitalism to socialism?" Yes, he replied, but first socialism had to be redefined,

"In its most Utopian terms: namely, among others, the abolition of labor, the termination of the struggle for existence – that is to say, life as an end in itself and no longer as a means to an end – and the liberation of human sensibility and sensitivity, not as a private factor, but as a force for transformation of human existence and of its environment. To give sensitivity and sensibility their own right is, I think, one of the basic goals of integral socialism."[24]

Marcuse's genius was his ability to satisfy the ideological needs of the Boomers by giving them a theoretical framework which told them what they wanted to hear. His supreme skill was the ability to blend a delicious cocktail out of ideas which naturally appealed to the immature Boomer tribe. Meanwhile, the founder of Critical Theory, Max Horkheimer, looked with growing horror at the Frankenstein's monster he had helped to create. Marcuse's secular religion of hedonism and ethical-political self-righteousness was, he said, "worse than the disease it is supposed to cure". In 1968, in a thinly veiled attack on Marcuse, he warned that simplistic narratives and Utopian solutions were childish fantasies,

> "In this world, things are complicated and are decided by many factors. We should look at problems from different aspects, not from just one alone. Only those who are subjective, one-sided and superficial in their approach to problems will smugly issue orders or directives the moment they arrive on the scene, without considering the circumstances, without viewing things in their entirety... Such people are bound to trip and fall."[25]

For Horkheimer, Critical Theory had been perverted by Marcuse into a pseudo-religious doctrine of nihilism. It called for a revolution to destroy Victorian Liberalism, the American Dream and the concepts of truth, reality and reason. It criticized self-restraint and every facet of Western civilization. The only thing it was incapable of viewing critically, was itself. In 1972, Horkheimer wrote that Critical Theory had become a dangerous creed that would lead to the establishment of a "totalitarian bureaucracy". He even found himself lining up to defend Enlightenment values and the achievements of Liberal democracy,

> "An open declaration that even a dubious democracy, for all its defects, is always better than the dictatorship which would inevitably result from a revolution today, seems to me necessary for the sake of truth."[26]

However, the Boomers had no appetite for the imperfect compromises of a "dubious democracy". Fueled by the Vortex of Immaturity, they craved a hedonistic Utopia and the radical new ideologies that Marcuse, and others, were happy to supply.

Chapter 7

The Road to Boomertopia. An Exceptional Generation Singing in Perfect Harmony

"Make Love, Not War."
Boomer slogan.

"Nature, Mr. Allnut, is what we are put in this world to rise above."
Katharine Hepburn in The African Queen, 1951.

U topianism — the ability to imagine a perfect future state — is a uniquely human trait. Utopia is paradise, a future world in which we are released from toil, suffering and hardship, and in which all forms of imperfection are abolished. The scholar Ruth Levitas says Utopian thinking is simply the,

> "Expression of the desire for a better way of being… a Utopian impulse, an anthropological given that underpins the human propensity to long for and imagine a life otherwise."[1]

Imagining a better world implies building it. As Levitas notes, once the vision has been established, it follows logically that, "the task before us is to build the Republic of Heaven." A common feature of utopian thinking is that it is vague. In fact, the more concrete and detailed a proposal for Utopia is, the less utopian it will be because there will always be disagreement about what is desirable. One person's idea of heaven is often another's idea of hell. Debate about how to turn a shared dream into reality can quickly sour into disagreement, schism or even violent conflict. Thus, the most successful visions of Utopia are always vague and abstract. Wherever there are people, utopian longing will emerge to inspire and direct them. For example, in his book *Datong Shu*, the 19th Century Chinese philosopher Kang Youwei describes a Utopia in which "complete peace and equality" will exist, and in which selfishness and unhappiness will disappear. The scholar Albert Chen explains that in Kang's Utopia,

> "There will be complete equality between men and women, and society will no longer be divided into classes. The enjoyment of property will be shared in common, and economic activities will not be for private gain but will be directed to the common good… Animals will not be treated cruelly, and in the final stage of the evolution of the Datong world, they will no longer be killed for food."[2]

Kang identified "nine boundaries" which he said were the regressive forces blocking the road to Utopia. Once these were swept away, people would be able to enjoy new levels of fulfillment and happiness under the wise rule of a benevolent world government. Humans would become Gods. As Chen writes, "in the Datong world, the highest attainment in life will be the self-cultivation and practice involved in seeking spiritually enlightenment and becoming Buddhas."

In Western philosophy, the best-known Utopia is the *Republic* written by Plato in 375 BC. In the *Republic,* citizens live communally and private property is not permitted. Children are raised by the state and men and women have equal rights. Society is administered by a caste of powerful para-military guardians. From these are chosen an elite aristocracy of philosopher kings. These incorruptible rulers possess a superior knowledge and wisdom and will rule benevolently for the good of all. Plato's *Republic* is not a democracy. On the contrary, Plato envisages the need for the ruling elite to create a "noble lie" for the sake of social cohesion. The lie will be a simple, easy to understand narrative intended to manipulate the population to be docile and obedient for their own good. Plato's guardians and philosopher kings therefore use propaganda to sustain their power. A number of writers have argued that Plato's proposed Utopia was little more than a totalitarian dictatorship. The philosopher Karl Popper for example, accused Plato of advocating a closed, tribal society motivated by a bitter hatred of Athenian democracy. For Popper, Plato was the philosophical ancestor of Hitler and Stalin,

> "This is the collectivist, the tribal, the totalitarian theory of morality: 'Good is what is in the interest of my group; or my tribe; or my state.' It is easy to see what this morality implied for international relations: that the state itself can never be wrong in any of its actions, as long as it is strong."[3]

Boomertopia

The Boomer generation's vision of Utopia was characteristically vague. It was a shared intuition, not a formal blueprint. For example, the Underground newspaper journalist Tom McGrath looked ahead to a world that was, "just people coming together and grooving. If you don't know what grooving means then you haven't understood what's going on." The future he predicted would operate on, "different conceptions of time and space. The world of the future may have no clocks." He added that it would emerge from those who, "share a common viewpoint — a new way of looking at things." The only non-negotiable feature was sexual liberation. As McGrath explained enthusiastically, "the search for pleasure-orgasm covers every field of human activity from sex, art and inner space, to architecture, the abolition of money, outer space and beyond."[4]

One influence that helped mold the concept of Boomertopia in the minds of young Boomers was the vision of Walt Disney. Disney's TV shows were enormously popular and reached an estimated 75% of homes in the US and the UK. The Disneyfied world was one of sunshine, play, futuristic technology and, of course, happy endings. Its famous motto was, "when you wish upon a star, your dreams come true". In this fantasy world, what ought to be replaces what is. The mechanism of transformation is magic — a force beyond logic and reason. The opening titles of *The Wonderful World of Disney* promised Boomer viewers,

> "Each week, as you enter this timeless land, one of these many worlds will open to you; Frontierland — tall tales and true from the legendary past. Tomorrowland — the promise of things to come. Adventureland — the wonder world of nature's own realm, and Fantasyland — the happiest kingdom of them all..."

But Walt Disney's dream was not confined to TV. During the mid-1960s, he unveiled plans for a real-life city built and run along Disney principles. He named it EPCOT, the Experimental Prototype Community of Tomorrow. EPCOT was to be a functional, self-sufficient Utopian commune. Residents would live either in the central hub, or in the suburbs. Only pollution-free electric cars would be allowed, although most people would ride futuristic monorails on their journeys to work and play. Disney's goal was a community of people with shared values, living contentedly. As he explained in a 1966 promotional film,

> "We must start with the public need. The need is not just for curing the old ills of the old cities. We think the need is for starting from scratch... building a special kind of new community... where people actually live a life they can't find anywhere else in the world. Everything in EPCOT will be dedicated to the happiness of people who live, work and play here."[5]

EPCOT was an anti-urban Utopia. It would be constructed on a pristine site in Florida – far away from the decaying cities of the East and West coast. In EPCOT, poverty would not exist and everyone would be treated equally. Citizens would not own property, but this would bring them happiness,

> "In EPCOT there will be no slum areas, because we won't let them develop; there will be no landowners and therefore no voting control. People will rent houses instead of buying them, and at modest rentals."[6]

What jobs would EPCOT residents have? It wasn't clear. The promotional film promised "employment for all" in "experimental prototype plants, research and development laboratories and computer centers". How would EPCOT be governed? Disney was vague, explaining reassuringly that "we don't presume to know all the answers". He was clear however that citizens would not vote, nor be burdened with the responsibility of having to find out what was true or false, or what was really going on in EPCOT. Instead, Disney's vision suggested a post-democratic future — a community administered by benevolent Disney 'imagineers'. These imagineers would be an elite group possessing the imagination to envision a better future, and the knowledge and will to turn it into reality. However, not everyone was enthusiastic about Disney's plans for Utopia. The American film critic Matt Roth detected a submerged totalitarian instinct along with a disgust for the corrupting influence of the big cities. He observed, "both Hitler's and Disney's anti-urbanism was expressed as back-to-nature primitivism." Roth accused Disney of possessing a, "relentlessly fascist cosmology" and noted that in 1938 Walt Disney had, "regularly attended meetings of the American Nazi Party in Hollywood."[7]

In 1971, John Lennon produced *Imagine* – his famous hymn to Boomertopia. Lennon's lyrics invited the Boomers to,

> "Imagine no possessions, I wonder if you can,
> No need for greed or hunger, a brotherhood of man.
> Imagine all the people, sharing all the world.
> You, you may say I'm a dreamer, but I'm not the only one,
> I hope someday you will join us, and
> the world will live as one."[8]

The song was both a hugely successful pop song and a political prayer. The American journalist Mikal Gilmore called it, "The most radical prayer that ever played widely on radio." Lennon agreed saying the song was intended to be,

"Anti-religious, anti-nationalistic, anti-conventional, anti-capitalistic, but because it is sugarcoated it is accepted. Now I understand what you have to do: Put your political message across with a little honey."[9]

Lennon's message was unashamedly Utopian. It described a world of abundance in which there was no need for anyone to be hungry, or even to own anything. Instead, everyone would simply help themselves to whatever they wanted. In this world of affluence and plenty, scarcity is unknown. Lennon dreams the entire Boomer generation will unite to form a single global community with shared values and ideals. His prayer is therefore both Utopian and tribal. It recognizes that political power comes from the existence of a gigantic tribe of people united by common desires and a common ideology. Two years later, Lennon and Yoko Ono announced plans for a global community called Nutopia. On 1st April 1973, they explained at a press conference, "Nutopia has no land, no boundaries, no passports, only people. Nutopia has no laws other than cosmic." Lennon produced a surreal Nutopian national anthem — three seconds of silence — and included it on his album *Mind Games*.

A few weeks before *Imagine* was released, Coca-Cola produced one of the most famous TV commercials of all time. It featured a group of young Boomers standing on a hilltop singing *I'd Like to Buy the World a Coke*. The song was so popular that a non-commercial version was quickly recorded by the New Seekers and sold more than twelve million copies. Its lyrics proclaimed,

"I'd like to teach the world to sing in perfect harmony, I'd like to hold it in my arms and keep it company. I'd like to see the world for once all standing hand in hand, and hear them echo through the hills, peace throughout the land."[10]

The media analyst Tom Poleman says that the song spoke vividly to the Boomer generation about what the future world ought to be like, "It became a pop culture moment... it spoke to what America was thinking at that time. I was a kid at the time and it was more than a commercial."[11] As with Lennon's Imagine, the *Hill Top Song* was a vision of a deeply tribal future. To Boomers, its message of conformity to shared values was beautiful — refreshingly idealistic and progressive. But to political theorists of Victorian Liberalism, these visions would have appeared immature and sinister. What would happen if someone did not wish to stand "hand in hand" and sing in "perfect harmony"? What if a minority wanted to sing a different song? How would the dispute be resolved? Would people be permitted to dream their own dreams, or compelled to dream Lennon's dream? Seen through the eyes of Victorian Liberalism, *Imagine* and the *Hill Top Song* were advocating the "tyranny of the majority" — the domination of society by a single group.

The prospect of the whole world "living as one" would have horrified Victorian liberal thinkers such as Lord Acton who defined liberty as, "the assurance that every man shall be protected in doing what he believes is his duty against the influence of authority and majorities, custom and opinion." To Victorian theorists, the idea of democracy in a land where everyone thinks the same thoughts would have seemed unrealistic and nonsensical. Liberal democracy was by definition inherently discordant — a cacophony of different songs played on different instruments in different keys. To Victorian liberals, Boomertopia, a place of perfect harmony where the Boomer tribe ruled supreme, would have been a vision of hell. As Acton concluded, "It is bad to be oppressed by a minority, but it is worse to be oppressed by a majority."

Assumptions about Human Nature. Hobbes v Rousseau

Acton and the Boomers lived according to different, incompatible, ideologies. Trying to establish dialogue between the two would have resulted in mutual incomprehension. This is because each ideology rests on fundamentally different philosophical and psychological assumptions, beginning with assumptions about human nature. The foundational beliefs of the Enlightenment, and of Victorian Liberalism, were "Hobbesian" after the English philosopher Thomas Hobbes. Hobbes did not claim, as he is often accused of doing, that human nature was evil. He simply argued that human beings are rational creatures motivated by their own self-interest. In his *Leviathan*, Hobbes wrote that humans must be restrained by rule of law. Without agreed rules and boundaries, there would be only selfishness, violence and, ultimately, the domination of the weak by the strong. In such a lawless state, he famously explained, life was inclined to be, "nasty, brutish and short."[12]

Generations of Enlightenment politicians, basing their philosophy on Hobbesian assumptions, sought ways to create a system of government that would protect minorities from the tyranny of the majority. The American Founding Fathers devoted enormous time and effort to constructing a complex balance of power between the individual, the federal government, the states, the President, the Senate, the House of Representatives and the judiciary. As James Madison put it, "In all cases where a majority are united by a common interest or passion, the rights of the minority are in danger. What motives are to restrain them?"[13] Alexander Hamilton wrote similarly,

"If government is in the hands of the few, they will tyrannize over the many; if in the hands of the many, they will tyrannize over the few. It ought to be in the hands of both."[14]

The most famous of all Victorian Liberal philosophers, John Stuart Mill, said, "Protection, therefore, against the tyranny of the magistrate is not enough: there needs protection also against the tyranny of the prevailing opinion and feeling".[15] In short, Victorian Liberalism saw life as a delicate web of compromises, with different groups of flawed human beings competing for scarce resources in an imperfect world. The job of politics was to find reasonable, temporary solutions to complex problems while preserving everyone's liberty.

The Boomers however, rejected, not just Victorian Liberal thinking, but also the fundamental assumptions about human nature which sustained them. The Boomers believed they were exceptional — superior to any previous generation. Consequently, the old rules no longer applied. The Boomers rejected Hobbesian assumptions and were attracted instead to the theories of the French philosopher Jean-Jacques Rousseau who argued that human beings are not motivated by rational self-interest, but are by nature generous and altruistic. As Rousseau put it, in a thinly-veiled attack on Hobbes,

> "So many writers have hastily concluded that man is naturally cruel, and requires civil institutions to make him more mild; whereas nothing is more gentle than man in his primitive state."[16]

Rousseau asserted that, "There is hardly any inequality in the state of nature, all the inequality which now prevails owes its strength and growth to… the establishment of property and laws." He described primitive human life as one of child-like play and leisure. In fact, his description of it could easily refer to hippie culture during the summer of love of 1967,

> "They accustomed themselves to assemble before their huts round a large tree; singing and dancing, the true offspring of love and leisure, became the amusement, or rather the occupation, of men and women thus assembled together with nothing else to do."

This was far more in keeping with Boomer intuitions and feelings. Rousseau was suggesting there was something evil and depraved about civilization which led to the corruption of man's innate innocence and goodness. As Rousseau explained, the noble savage "breathes only peace and liberty; he desires only to live and be free from labor", whereas civilized man,

> "Is always moving, sweating, toiling and racking his brains to find still more laborious occupations: he goes on in drudgery to his last moment, and even seeks death to put himself in a position to live".

Rousseau's philosophy implied therefore that if Western civilization were destroyed, something better and more beautiful would spontaneously grow up out of the rubble.

A New Consciousness

According to Boomer Exceptionalism, human nature, unchanged for thousands of years, had suddenly evolved to a higher plane. Mankind had become kind, benevolent and selfless and was no longer guided by rational self-interest. If this was true, then all the accumulated wisdom of the past was obsolete and useless. A new beginning could be made based on a new set of assumptions. The stakes were high, and many writers began constructing theories to legitimize and validate this exciting hypothesis.

One of the most successful writers was the American academic Charles Reich whose 1970 book *The Greening of America* became a best-seller. Reich argued that Boomer Exceptionalism was real and that, consequently, human history had crossed into a new epoch called 'Consciousness III'. The Boomer generation, he said, possessed a unique power to understand the concepts of truth and reality. Non-Boomers could not understand this because they lacked Consciousness III, "Consciousness III starts with the self... Consciousness III declares that the individual self is the only true reality".[17] Like Marcuse, Reich explained that the old concept of truth was now obsolete and had been replaced by a new Boomer epistemology,

"For human beings, the only truth must be found in their own humanity, in each other, in their relation to the living world. When the Corporate State forces its 'public interest' truth as a substitute for man's internal truth — for the truth man creates — it cuts him off from the only reality he can live by."[18]

Their unique and exceptional way of knowing, said Reich, would allow the Boomers to create a Utopia based on radically new principles. For example, in Boomertopia, people would be freed from the need to work and would consequenlty be able to stay in bed all day if they wanted to. The future would be characterized by,

"Magic and mystery, romance, play, creativity... imagination, mind-expanding drugs, multi-media experiences (music, light, smell, dance, all together), alterations of time, inner life, responding to own needs (staying in bed when the need is felt), sensuality, new feelings, expanded consciousness, transcendence, myth-making and telling, bare feet, new ways of thinking, non-rational thoughts, new ideas."[19]

The Greening of America was a highly truthophobic book. It argued that truth was 'tribal truth' — the consensus of the inner feelings and intuitions of the Boomer tribe. Truth was whatever the Boomers collectively believed. The opinions of the older generation could be ignored because they lacked Consciousness III. Indeed, their inability to recognize Boomer Exceptionalism and Boomer truth was proof that Boomer Exceptionalism was real. Reich had produced a perfect, circular, self-justifying argument. Because they lacked Consciousness III, non-Boomers could not enter Boomertopia. It was impossible for them, Reich said, "to imagine themselves living according to the new promises". The fact that the Boomers were different and exceptional was, he said, "The truth that the younger generation knows and the older generation cannot know."[20]

In the UK, Richard Neville's 1971 book *Play Power* also made the case for Boomer Exceptionalism. The Boomers were exceptional, he said, because they had rediscovered a primitive and timeless secret. The benevolence and goodness of the human race had been there all along, but was hidden and corrupted by repressive modern civilization. Neville's Rousseauesque book explained,

> "A generation which one day awoke to protest, not only altered the course of politics, but altered their relationship with one another... Within teepees and domes, white tribes are learning to eat weeds, heal themselves with herbs, build solar water-stills, and rediscover secrets of the gypsies and Indians."[21]

To reach Boomertopia, one simply had to unlearn all the toxic knowledge of Western civilization. Destroying the ladder up which people had been forced to climb, would allow them to free fall back into a natural Utopian state liberated from work, anxiety, stress and responsibility, "Like a child taking its first steps, members of the Underground are learning how to live in a future where work is rendered obsolete. They are re-learning how to play."[22] According to Neville, Boomertopia would be a blissful adult kindergarten,

> "Work is done only for fun; as a pastime, obsession, hobby or art-form and thus is not work in the accepted sense. Underground people launch poster, printing, publishing, record and distribution

companies; bookshops, newspapers, information bureau, video and film groups, restaurants; anything that they enjoy doing."[23]

In Boomertopia, there would be abundance for all without the need for economically productive work. People would simply help themselves to whatever they wanted, "who needs money?" he asked.[24] Neville pointed out that "The Deviants, a London rock group, sing 'Let's Loot the Supermarket' and many fans ask 'Why stop there?' The world is over-producing already."[25] The Boomer generation, he said, should prepare for life in Boomertopia by taking things without paying for them. He advised, "picking up food in a supermarket and eating it before you leave the store... is a lot safer than the customary shop-lifting... if you have eaten it, there is no evidence to be used against you."[26] In Boomertopia, wealth would not be produced, only redistributed and consumed. Everybody will have, said Neville, "an absolute right to a guaranteed income"[27] and would spend "all day playing Frisbee". Neville's vision of the future climaxed with a description of the Boomer generation united in "love and laughter", endlessly consuming and gratifying their sexual desires. Boomertopia would be a land of acid trips, mass shoplifting and, "thousands of grown-up children drowning deliciously in a Hog Farm pudding, sucking, fucking and feeding for free. The politics of play."[28]

The prospect of living in Boomertopia was immensely attractive. The American media professional and academic Henry Loeser was an anti-Vietnam War protestor during the late 1960s and early 70s. Typical of many, he dropped out of college in 1972 to live the dream,

> "I hitchhiked down to Florida without a final destination in mind. I got a part time job and would go to the beach four days a week. I got on several beach volleyball teams and became a surfer. You could drink seven beers for a dollar at the Parrot Bar on the beach at Fort Lauderdale and there were lots of beautiful women and sunshine! This was my antidote to the life I wanted to reject."[29]

Many Boomers formed Utopian communities. For example, thousands flocked to a commune set up in Oregon by the charismatic Bhagwan Shree Rajneesh who preached that a state of super consciousness could be obtained through communal living and the gratification of sexual desire. He told his followers,

> "There are two ways. Either repress sex as has been done by all the so-called religious traditions of the world, or transform it. I am for transformation. Hence, I teach my sannyasins to be creative. Create music, create poetry, create pottery, create something. Whatever you do, do it with great creativeness, bring something new into existence, and your sex will be fulfilled on a higher plane."[30]

His personal assistant, Ma Anand Sheela, explained that, by releasing repressed desire and reconnecting with their primitive inner selves, the Boomers could find enlightenment, change human nature and create paradise on Earth. The result would be,

> "A new man that lives in harmony with one another, lives in harmony with nature, where all nationalities, all colors, all religions sit together. This new man has only respect for one another."[31]

Changing human nature however proved more difficult than anticipated. Self-interest, vanity, differences of opinion and the desire for wealth and power were all stubbornly resistant to Utopian desires. In 1984, members of the Bhagwan's tribe carried out a mass poisoning attack on a nearby town. It was the biggest bioterror attack in US history. Amid bitter feuding and personal vendettas, some community members were jailed for crimes including attempted murder. Bhagwan, despite his professed disdain for material possessions, began wearing diamond-encrusted Rolex watches and bought a fleet of 74 Rolls-Royces with money donated by his followers. In 1985 his Utopian community collapsed after he was deported from the US. It was the death of a dream.

Chapter 8

How the
Boomers
Broke Politics

The New Left and the
Colonization of Socialism

The Boomer Ideology required a political vehicle in which to express itself. Socialism offered an attractive, ready-made framework. The rhetoric of socialism preached revolutionary change and the redistribution of wealth and power — all of which strongly appealed to the Boomer mindset. Socialism's division of society into competing groups of workers and capitalists could also be easily adapted to fit the Boomer's own sense of generational tribalism. Unfortunately, the dominant socialist ideology — Marxist-Leninism — was unflinchingly anti-Utopian and was based on a gritty materialism. For the Boomers to successfully colonize socialism, this would have to change; left wing politics would have to be customized and rewritten to meet the needs of the Boomer generation. Another problem was that, pre-Boomer, left-wing politics in the US and Europe had tended to take the form of trade unionism and had prioritized the fight for higher wages and better working conditions for the working class. The revolutionary aspect of socialism had been neglected in favor of the struggle to win a fair day's pay for a fair day's work through negotitation backed by the threat of strikes. The Old Left was therefore more concerned with joining the established social order than overthrowing it. Indeed, during the first half of the 20th Century, socialism gradually became respectable. In 1924, Britain elected its first Labour government, while in the US, the Wagner Act of 1935 recognized the right of all workers to organize into labor unions and strike for better pay.

This spirit of compromise and collective bargaining was anathema to the Boomers. The Vortex of Immaturity did not want to preserve the status quo through gradual, incremental reform. As Margaret Mead observed in 1972,

"The idea of orderly, developmental change is lost for this generation... they are ready to make way for something new by a kind of social bulldozing – like the bulldozing in which every tree and feature of the landscape is destroyed to make way for a new community."[1]

Boomer activists therefore began constructing a 'New Left' to replace the Old Left. In the UK, the influential magazine *New Left Review* appeared in 1960, while, in the US, Boomer activists published their manifesto, the *Port Huron Statement*, in 1962. Describing itself as an "agenda for a generation", it began with a rousing call to put Utopianism back into socialism,

"The decline of Utopia and hope is in fact one of the defining features of social life today. The reasons are various: the dreams of the older left were perverted by Stalinism and never recreated; the congressional stalemate makes men narrow their view of the possible; the specialization of human activity leaves little room for sweeping thought."[2]

The *Port Huron Statement* made it clear that the New Left was a political movement designed to appeal to the Boomer generation. Its author
Tom Hayden explained, "A new left must consist of younger people who
matured in the postwar world, and partially be directed to the recruitment
of younger people." In order to be relevant to Boomers, Hayden said the
New Left must shift the focus of politics from party-political haggling,
to finding solutions to the "private troubles" of individuals. In other
words, politics must be redefined as the process of changing the world
to make it a place where the dreams and desires of the Boomers could
be gratified. Hayden concluded that the New Left must,

> "Transform modern complexity into issues that can be understood
> and felt close-up by every human being. It must give form to the
> feelings of helplessness and indifference, so that people may see
> the political, social and economic sources of their private troubles
> and organize to change society."

Historically, personal happiness had been the business of religion,
not politics. Finding inner peace, making sense of the human condition,
coming to terms with suffering and death, and searching for answers
about how to live, had been problems for priests and holy men. Politics,
on the other hand, had been a purely material business — in the words
of the theorist Harold Lasswell, a debate about "who gets what, when,
and how". This separation of politics from religion was an important
element of Liberal Democracy. Fusing them was viewed as sliding down
a slippery path towards the sort of intolerant theocratic society that had
characterized Europe during the Middle Ages and which had led to the
wars of religion of the 16th and 17th Centuries. A significant feature of
the New Left was then, that it pulled down the firewall separating church
and state. By injecting Utopianism into politics, the Boomers politicized
morality and in effect created a new type of secular religion. In future it
would be increasingly difficult for people with divergent political views
to negotiate, or agree to disagree. Dissent from the agenda of the New
Left could no longer be seen as a purely political choice, it would mark
the dissenter as a bad person. The Boomer feminist writer Carol Hanisch
also saw politics in Utopian terms as the abolition of unhappiness. In
a famous 1969 essay entitled *The Personal is Political*, she described her
life as "grim" and expressed the desire to rid herself of guilt and "self-
blame". Hanisch wrote that politics should be thought of as "political

therapy" and said, "personal problems are political problems. There are no personal solutions at this time. There is only collective action for a collective solution."[3]

The American psychologist Kenneth Keniston spent several months with a group of Boomer political activists in 1967 and concluded that the New Left was not one thing, but a "scattered and uncoordinated group of young Americans who share certain basic criticisms of contemporary life."[4] Keniston said that, while they were all sincere and passionate about "radically transforming American society and the world,"[5] there was a conspicuous lack of any concrete political vision, just a vague feeling that Utopia would automatically emerge if existing society was destroyed. Keniston described, "the characteristic vagueness of these New Leftists as to the specifics of their vision of a just, free, peaceful, participatory society."[6]

The Boomers, said Keniston, understood politics almost entirely in terms of their own personal feelings of alienation and unhappiness, and their search for satisfaction and gratification. It proved impossible, "to talk only about 'political' matters, for the interviewees often spontaneously brought up the role of family, early conflicts, and non-political events in their political lives."[7] One Boomer told Keniston that joining the New Left felt like a religious experience "translated into secular terms."[8] "One of the central characteristics of today's youth in general and young radicals in particular" Keniston said, was they "insist on taking seriously a great variety of political, personal, and social principles that 'no one in his right mind' ever before thought of attempting."[9] Although he was a sympathetic observer, Keniston could not escape the conclusion that the Boomers were sharing an immature fantasy of "protracted adolescence". In the final analysis he wrote soberly, what the Boomers were trying to deny were the harsh realities of human existence and adult life,

"The determination and optimism of these young radicals about their continuing commitment to the New Left, however sincere and deeply felt, may not be a realistic judgement of the difficulties that lie ahead of them."[10]

Marxism Without Marx

Demand for ideological doctrine to legitimize the Vortex of Immaturity gave rise to a "theory boom" during the 1960s and 1970s, as academics hunted for the magic formula to blend Marxism seamlessly with the Boomer Ideology. The quest produced a prodigious literature of books and papers exploring new Boomer-friendly interpretations of Marxism. These included: Neo-Marxism, Post-Marxism, Post-Modern Marxism, Analytical Marxism, Structural Marxism and surreal Freudo-Marxism. The writings of forgotten activists, such as the Italian communist leader Antonio Gramsci, were rediscovered and scrutinized for ideological inspiration. New Left writers, such as Louis Althusser and Michel Foucault, blended elements of Marxism with psychology and semiotic linguistics to produce exotic theoretical brews which became highly fashionable with Boomer intellectuals. As the British cultural theorist Stuart Hall put it, there was an urgent need for, "a sustained work of theoretical clarification" in order to "reconstitute existing knowledge under the sign of new questions."[11]

The Boomers were obliged to "reconstitute" Marxism because, in its original form, it was deeply hostile to Utopian thinking. Karl Marx and Friedrich Engels had set out to provide socialism with a robust, scientific base, and would have been horrified to see how their ideas had been co-opted by the affluent, hedonsitic Boomer generation. Engels for example, had referred to Utopian socialism as a form of "insanity". Utopian schemes, he said, were always vague and unrealistic, and attempts to put them into practice inevitably resulted in them "drifting off into pure phantasies".[12] Engels said Utopian socialism, such as that developed by the French theorist Saint-Simon, was really religion dressed up as politics. It offered, he said, "a new religious bond, destined to restore that unity of religious ideas which had been lost since the time of the Reformation – a necessarily mystic and rigidly hierarchic 'new Christianity'". Because it was a theological doctrine, Engels pointed out that Utopian socialism always found it necessary to redefine the concepts of truth and reality. To Utopian socialists, "Socialism is the expression of absolute truth, reason and justice, and has only to be discovered to conquer all the world by virtue of its own power." Marx strongly agreed and dismissed the "ideological nonsense" of the Utopian French socialists labelling it "vulgar socialism". He scathingly said, "what a crime it is to attempt, on the one hand, to force on our Party again, as dogmas, ideas which in a certain period had some meaning but have now become obsolete verbal rubbish."[13]

Marx and Engels would no doubt also have howled with laughter at the concept of Boomer Exceptionalism. The idea that human nature had suddenly evolved into a new consciousness, with a new way of seeing and knowing, would have seemed to them the height of arrogance and folly. As Engels put it, such "stupendously grand thoughts and germs of thought that everywhere break out through their phantastic covering" were the hubristic delusions of those convinced of the "superiority of their own bald reasoning." They were delusions, he said, "which today only make us smile".

The literary theorist Leonard Jackson summarizes that, during the late 20th Century, Boomer academics were engaged in a, "process of creative transformation" in which Marxism was turned into its opposite. In their quest for doctrine to justify the Vortex of Immaturity, Boomer academics re-interpreted the "sacred texts" and subverted their original meanings. Leonard writes that the ghost of Karl Marx haunts Boomer academic theory saying, "'That is not what I meant at all!' When a modern theorist calls himself a materialist, the ghost of Marx says indignantly: 'I was talking about the economy.'"[14] The socialist commentator Peter Sedgwick, writing in 1964, observed that the New Left had abandoned Marx and transformed socialism into a "socio-cultural" movement dedicated to the values of immaturity. It had, "captured youth in a purely mental fashion, by recording the detail of the teenage masquerade". Socialism, he continued, had been turned into an expression of immature nonconformity, "as 'millennial', 'utopian', 'heroic' and 'romantic' as its proponents have supposed revolutionary Marxism to be."[15]

Socialist Standard magazine was also angered by the hijacking of socialism by the Boomers. In February 1968 it said, "one of the most widespread of their illusions is the feeling that the fundamental division in society is between the young and old, rather than between the working class and the propertied class." The following year, in an article entitled *Hippies: an Abortion of Socialist Understanding*, the paper suggested the Boomer Ideology and the New Left were simply products of advanced consumer society which had groomed a generation to expect something for nothing. Boomer thinking was not socialist, it was, "a product of the youth cult, the commercialization of young people and the 'generation gap'".[16]

Radical Chic

The need to justify our behavior and feel good about ourselves is one of the highest form of self-gratification. Utopian idealism therefore allowed the Boomers to enjoy the pleasure being ethical and to bask in the warm glow of virtue. The hedonism of the Boomers was not satisfied by the creature comforts that excited their parents. The Boomers wanted more than new washing machines, vacuum cleaners, fitted carpets, central heating and bigger, better cars and lawn mowers. They wanted the exquisite pleasure that comes from being righteous, and from being seen to be righteous by their peers. The sociologist Colin Campbell refers to this sort of indulgent, idealistic thinking as a form of "luxury consumption",

"Modern hedonism tends to be covert and self-illusory; that is to say, individuals employ their imaginative and creative powers to construct mental images which they consume for the intrinsic pleasure they provide, a practice best described as day-dreaming or fantasizing."[17]

Campbell describes the pleasure gained from ethical fantasies as "illusory or imaginative hedonism" and concludes that, "A certain dissatisfaction with reality is thus bound to mark the outlook of the dedicated hedonist, something which may, under appropriate circumstances, prompt a turning to fantasy."

The self-indulgent nature of Boomer politics often appeared as blatant insincerity which deserved to be mocked. Richard Neville describes how a group of New Left activists met in 1968 to discuss how to start the revolution, change the world and create Boomertopia. "In the discussion which followed" writes Neville, "three hours were spent arguing over the definition of 'neo-capitalism'. Ken Tynan was the first to leave, in despair."[18] Calling for the destruction of the American Dream and Victorian Liberalism became a fashionable form of social signaling — a way to increase one's prestige with other Boomers. In New York, the journalist Tom Wolfe called it "radical chic". Wolfe described a society party at which the revolutionary Black Panthers were celebrity guests. "Amid the sconces, silver bowls full of white and lavender anemones, and uniformed servants serving drinks and Roquefort cheese morsels rolled in crushed nuts" Wolfe observed, the wealthy audience gushingly agreed when the Panthers lectured them, "This country is the most oppressive country in the world, maybe in the history of the world."[19] However, while the affluent, white partygoers were professing their deep commitment to social and racial justice, what they were secretly admiring, Wolfe noted, were the Black Panthers' "Tight pants, the tight black turtlenecks, the leather coats, Cuban shades, Afros. But real Afros... funky, natural, scraggly." Radical politics had become a Boomer fashion accessory. In making the personal political, they had also made the political personal. Egotistical motives, such as wanting to be seen to have the correct political views, had become hopelessly tangled with a sincere desire to make the world a better place.

A penetrating observer of Boomer hypocrisy and hubris during the 1960s and 1970s was the activist Emmett Grogan, leader of the radical Diggers movement in the US. Grogan was scathing about college-educated radicals lecturing poor, working class families that they should reject the values of Liberal Democracy and the American Dream. It was, he said, "A mockery, a derisive imitation of their existence."[20] For Grogan, Boomer radicals too often used working class people as pawns in a game of self-indulgent virtue signaling,

"Their dreams of someday makin' it out of what they regard as a sewer are very important to them, 'n when hippies come along riffin' about how unhip it is to make it into middle class society... these low money people get confused and upset because here are these creepy longhaired punks who grew up with meat at every meal and backyards to play in and the kind of education which is prayed to God for, and they threw it all away for what? To become junkies like at least one member of every family on the Lower East Side? To live with garbage and violence, and rats and violence, and no heat or hot water and violence, and disease and violence?" [21]

Grogan's verdict was, "You're still the children of the ruling class-es... you're just having an adventure in poverty which, if you aren't careful, may prove more real than you're ready to deal with."[21]

The British radical Jeff Nuttall also complained of the blatant insin-cerity and immaturity of Boomer politics. He said the Boomer Ideology was not a genuine desire to make the world a better place, it was a herd mentality, the result of a,

"Large number of teenagers... incapable of thinking more than half an hour ahead. Things like promises and responsible un-dertakings, honor, indeed, any principles at all, are, of course impossible in minds so conditioned."

It was a blueprint, he said, for a nihilistic way of life, "devoted to the sensation of the moment."[23]

By the late 1960s, some of the older cohort of Boomers were finding the pretentiousness of the New Left irritating, if not alarmingly fanat-ical. Boomer politics branched into two camps; those who believed Boomertopia could be created by revolutionary political action, and those for whom Boomertopia simply meant living the dream — turning on, tuning in and dropping out. The schism is captured by an argument which erupted in 1968 over the Beatles' song *Revolution* the lyrics of which which explained,

"You say you want a revolution,
Well, you know, We all want to change the world...
But when you talk about destruction, don't you know that you can count me out.
Don't you know it's gonna be all right..."[23]

John Lennon's lyrics also complained about the vagueness of the New Left's proposals for a new political order, "You say you got a real solution, well, you know, we'd all love to see the plan..." The song also expressed concern about the Boomer's normalization of violence. Lennon could detect a disturbing streak of cruelty and savagery lurking just beneath the surface of their radical, Utopian politics. His lyrics continued "If you want money for people with minds that hate, All I can tell you is brother you have to wait." The song infuriated the New Left and prompted an angry letter from John Hoyland, a student activist, to the Underground newspaper *Black Dwarf*. Hoyland said that to build a better society, it was first necessary to smash the existing one, "In order to change the world we've got to understand what's wrong with the world and then destroy it. Ruthlessly." Hoyland added that this was the only way to force the "system" to "hand over their power."[25] Stung by accusations that he was disloyal to the Boomer tribe, Lennon wrote back asking for detail about the New Left's plan for a better society, "What kind of system do you propose" he asked, "and who would run it?" Noting Hoyland's eagerness to behave "ruthlessly", Lennon said that what was wrong with the world was human nature,

"You're obviously on a destruction kick. I'll tell you what's wrong with it – People – so do you want to destroy them? Ruthlessly? Until you/we change your/our heads – there's no chance. Tell me of one successful revolution."[26]

Hoyland responded in a second letter in which he walked back some of this more extreme proposals, "We wouldn't want to shoot all the capitalists", he conceded before retreating to the safer ground of vague Utopian slogans. He called for the abolition of the "system" which encouraged people to compete against one another, he said he was opposed to putting "profit before principle", and placing "power and privilege in the hands of the few at the expense of the many." Hoyland closed by repeating his faith in Boomer Exceptionalism and progressivism, "I know it's possible for us to create a world which could one day become a loving paradise for every human-being" he said. We know this will happen, "because we see history moving inexorably towards this kind of society."[27]

Benevolent Humanity and Responsibility for Knowing

The belief that the Boomers were naturally altruistic and benevolent, is a foundational assumption that underpins the entire Boomer Ideology. According to the Boomer worldview, competition and conflict is artificial and unnecessary. It is the product of advanced industrial societies which corrupt the essential goodness of human nature. Therefore, the solution to the problems of the world lies in unwinding civilization. Doing so, will remove selfishness and return mankind to the golden age that existed in pre-industrial society. According to Boomer primitivism, the Anglo-American Enlightenment and Victorian Liberalism are toxic aberrations responsible for untold misery and strife. For example, although Boomer opposition to the Vietnam War was complex and multi-layered, it was explained, at least in part, by this Rousseauesque conviction. To Boomers, the US was not protecting South Vietnam from North Vietnamese aggression, it was causing unnecessary hatred and bitterness. As the American Underground paper *Fire* wrote in 1969, "THE VIETNAM WAR ISN'T THE ISSUE ANY MORE". Vietnam, it said, merely symbolized the wider crusade against Liberal Democracy and its mistaken, Hobbesian assumptions,

"For lots of us our whole life is a defiance of Amerika. Everything we do and have — our street actions, our friendships, our ideas — all show our contempt for the pig death culture of this country".[28]

The article concluded,

"It's not so much that we're against the war... The thing to get a handle on is what's necessary to build a revolution in the world... Revolt! Tear it down! Rip it up! Chicago, Washington, and Your Town USA. The time is right for fighting in the streets! The time is right for violent revolution!"

In other words, the Boomers assumed Victorian Liberalism was not a solution to the world's problems, but the cause of them. Therefore, destroying American values would release man's inner goodness and bring about an age of peace, love and happiness. All this makes perfect sense if human nature is indeed perfectly benevolent.

Belief in the essential goodness of mankind is also intimately related to the question of whether individuals should take responsibility for their own knowledge and belief, or whether they should entrust them to others. In a Rousseauesque world, it is safe to abandon personal responsibility and place power in the hands of an elite group of tribal leaders. This is because their benevolence and wisdom can be relied upon to produce the best outcomes for all. In this world, ordinary people can, and should, leave government to the experts and concentrate on leading fulfilling personal lives and gratifying their desires. In this world, there is no need to waste time and effort researching things for oneself. Unlimited trust becomes both an epistemic virtue and an ethical-political duty. Questioning the wisdom of those in positions of power and authority, on the other hand, is a tribal sin which can only stir up doubt, division and discord. In a Rousseauesque world, skepticism and lack of faith are ethical-political crimes.

This is no mere arcane, philosophical point. A great deal rests on it. If human nature is not perfectly benevolent — if Boomer assumptions are wrong — then none of the above applies. If people are motivated by their own rational self-interest, then even the most public-spirited leaders will be flawed and corruptible human beings. In a Hobbesian world, putting unlimited trust in other people is foolish and dangerous. There will always be the suspicion they are secretly pursuing their own interests, not yours. In the Victorian Liberal worldview, individuals have a duty to be skeptical and find things out for themselves. Failure to do so is an epistemic and ethical-political crime.

For example, during the Nuremberg trials of Nazi war criminals in 1946, great emphasis was placed on the importance of personal responsibility for knowing. The Nazis attempted to hide behind the excuse they were not responsible because they did not know what was going on. The American Prosecutor Robert H. Jackson refused to accept this, insisting it was the duty of all citizens to be inquisitive and not to allow themselves to fall into ignorance. As Jackson sardonically observed, "These men saw no evil, spoke none, and none was uttered in their presence." He ridiculed the idea the Third Reich was therefore composed of,

"A Number Two man who knew nothing of the excesses of the Gestapo which he created, and never suspected the Jewish extermination program although he was the signer of over a score of decrees which instituted the persecutions of that race; A Number Three man who was merely an innocent middleman transmitting Hitler's orders without even reading them, like a postman or delivery boy... A security chief who was of the impression that the policing functions of his Gestapo and SD were somewhat on the order of directing traffic."[29]

Jackson accused the Nazis of opting for, "an abdication of personal intelligence and moral responsibility" as a result of which they had, "bathed the world in blood and set civilization back a century." The Nazis also famously sought to evade their responsibility by claiming they were only following orders from higher authority. Field Marshall Wilhelm Keitel for example had,

> "Put his name to invasion plans, policy documents on stripping food and looting in occupied areas, orders for sending prisoners-of-war to industry, transporting foreign workers to Germany, seizing and executing hostages, but could not see that he bore any moral responsibility for them. Not for Keitel the old cliché 'I was only obeying orders': for him it was 'I was only writing orders.'"[30]

The Nuremberg trials therefore represented the high water mark of Victorian Liberalism and its doctrine of personal responsibility. As Jackson told the court, what was at stake were values and principles so important, "civilization cannot tolerate their being ignored". Above all else, was the principle that individuals must take personal responsibility for knowing and for making choices. As Jackson put it,

> "One who has committed criminal acts may not take refuge in superior orders nor in the doctrine that his crimes were acts of states... Modern civilization puts unlimited weapons of destruction in the hands of men. It cannot tolerate so vast an area of legal irresponsibility."[31]

Jackson argued it is when individuals abandon personal responsibility, stop questioning the official narrative, and allow themselves to become passive bystanders that acts of great evil take place. Personal accountability is the only thing capable of restraining the anonymous, unlimited cruelty of the tribe. Each of the accused, he said,

> "Was entrusted with broad discretion and exercised great power. Their responsibility is correspondingly great and may not

be shifted to that fictional being, "the state", which cannot be produced for trial, cannot plead, cannot testify and cannot be sentenced."[32]

As Jackson summarized, "Nowhere do we find a single instance where any one of the defendants stood up against the rest and said: "this thing is wrong, and I will not go along with it."[33]

The Dutch psychologist Joost Meerloo lived through Nazi occupation and studied the totalitarianism mindset. He became convinced that self-government by free people cannot survive when individuals abandon responsibility for knowing. He accepted that epistemic responsibility requires time and effort, and that consequently, it is very tempting to leave the task to others. Meerloo wrote of the "womb state" — a nirvana-like political Utopia in which "everything will be regulated, just as it was for the fetus in the womb, the land of bliss and equanimity." For Meerloo, this "infantile irresponsibility" led to the belief that, "Freedom is a danger, while dependence is a pleasurable safety" hence, "Totalitarianism is man's escape from the fearful realities of life into the virtual womb".[34] Meerloo believed that soothing Utopian fantasies are always immature and will always lead to tyranny and oppression. The choice, he said, was between hard, effortful freedom; or easy, effortless slavery,

> "Stepping out of a relatively safe childish dependence into freedom and responsibility is both hazardous and dangerous... Living takes us away from the dream of being protected and demands that we expose our weaknesses and strengths daily to our fellow men, with all their hostilities as well as their affections."[35]

In the analysis of Meerloo and Jackson, Nazism was not uniquely evil. Totalitarianism is simply the default condition of humanity which is held back only with much effort. It was the achievement of the Anglo-American Enlightenment and Victorian Liberalism to devise an ideology and epistemology capable of restraining it. The Nazi project set out to undo these restraints and release mankind's primitive, tribal hopes and fears. However, to the Boomers, the views of Meerloo and Jackson were obsolete because they were based on obsolete assumptions about human nature. According to Boomer Exceptionalism, human nature had changed. Removing the restraints would lead therefore, not to the gates of Hell, but to the gates of Boomertopia.

How the Boomers Broke Politics

The Boomer colonization of socialism redfined 'left-wing' and transformed the meaning of the old political labels. Henceforth, being 'left-wing' would mean being sympathetic to the ideals of the New Left. This meant being a believer in the Boomer Ideology, in Boomer Exceptionalism, having Rousseauesque beliefs about human nature, and being opposed to the ideology of Victorian Liberalism. 'Left-wing' therefore meant; normal, idealistic, humane, kind, compassionate and ethically-politically good. 'Right-wing' meant the opposite of these things. 'Right-wing' meant being deviant, inhumane, unidealistic, selfish and ethically-politically bad. To the Boomers, the phrases had become badges of tribal membership and synonyms for good and evil. Claiming to have left-wing beliefs, like having long hair or wearing flared trousers, signalled you were 'one of us'. Not having them, signalled you were 'one of them'.

The Boomers believed they had injected a refreshing new, ethical dimension into the stale parliamentary politics of Victorian Liberalism. However, to many observers, what they had really done was steer public discourse back towards the emotional, pre-Enlightenment standards of the 16th and 17th Centuries. The Boomer transformation of politics would lead some 21st Century thinkers, such as the historian Hyrum Lewis, to conclude that, "Left and right are entirely tribal designations and have no unifying philosophy or principle behind them." According to Lewis, by the 2020s, the labels 'left-wing' and 'right-wing' had become,

> "Tools of self-delusion – they let us indulge the fantasy that our partisanship is principled rather than tribal, i.e., that there is some noble ideal connecting all the distinct and unrelated issues that our party happens to support."[36]

Socialism, a political movement originally built to serve the interests of the working class, had become an opportunistic bricolage of political and cultural assumptions designed to serve the needs of the college-educated Boomer generation. As the American author Helen Andrews put it,

"For all their claims to be the most progressive generation ever, the main result of the boomers' involvement in politics has been the destruction of the Left... if a left-wing party is no longer the party of the working class, what good is it? What left is it?"[37]

The Victorians had worked hard to dial down the temperature of politics. Committed, passionate politics went out of fashion during the 19th Century both in Britain, and after the reconstruction era, in the US. It was replaced by a calmer style which emphasized debate and compromise. Victorian Liberal Journalism was designed to support this style of consensual, participative democracy. The older generation therefore viewed the rise of Boomer politics at first with dismay and then with horror. In 1969, Vice President Spiro Agnew warned the Boomers they were blindly galloping down a slope towards totalitarianism and tyranny,

"It is time to stop dignifying the immature actions of arrogant, reckless, inexperienced elements within our society. The reason is compelling. It is simply that their tantrums are insidiously destroying the fabric of American democracy... We have reached the crossroads. Because at this moment totalitarianism's threat does not necessarily have a foreign accent. Because we have a home-grown menace, made and manufactured in the U.S.A. Because if we are lazy or foolish, this nation could forfeit its integrity, never to be free again."[38]

Writing in 1971, Duncan Williams said Boomer politics was characterized by selfish "emotionalism" and an "arrogant primitivism". The Boomers, he said, were abandoning civilized politics and were, "all moving in one direction, shouting hysterically and manifesting a tendency towards violence, destruction and anarchy."[39] He quoted T. S. Eliot's harrowing prophecy that the future would be a place of, "Internecine fighting... people killing one another in the streets". The Vortex of Immaturity, he said was leading mankind, "Back to the primitive jungle from whence he came... the trousered ape returns to its pristine state, the only ultimate victor."[40] Agnew and Williams were warning that, if pre-Enlightenment, tribal politics was what the Boomers really wanted; then pre-Enlightenment, tribal politics is what they would get.

PART TWO

A GOLDEN AGE?
JOURNALISM
BEFORE THE
BOOMERS

Chapter 9

Prologue.
Epistemology for
a Cruel World

"Data! data! data!" he cried impatiently. "I can't make bricks without clay."

Sherlock Holmes, The Adventure of the Copper Beeches. Arthur Conan Doyle

The German submarine struck at night, silently and unseen. One by one, the cargo ships were torpedoed, burned and sank - their terrified crews dying in the cold, dark waters of the Atlantic. For the British escort ships trying to protect them, finding the U-boats seemed an almost impossible task. ASDIC, their rudimentary sonar equipment, was unreliable and confusing. Shoals of fish, wrecks, or even layers of different temperature water all produced false positives.

It was just after dawn when HMS Compass Rose made contact with a U-boat. Below deck, the ASDIC operator, Sub Lieutenant Lockhart, bent over his tiny screen focusing on the unusually crisp and well-defined image. "Echo bearing two-two-five," he shouted excitedly. "Submarine sir — can't be anything else." Up on the bridge, Captain Ericson ordered the ship to begin its attack run. The ship changed course and increased its speed. It was then Ericson, peering through his binoculars, noticed a group of around forty men in the water straight ahead — survivors from a recently torpedoed cargo ship. The place where he had to drop his depth charges was alive with swimmers. If he attacked the submarine, he would kill them all. Ericson drew breath sharply. He desperately needed more information.

Nicholas Monsarrat's 1951 novel *The Cruel Sea* was one of the most authentic, and highly acclaimed, books written about the Battle of the Atlantic during World War Two. Based on Monsarrat's experience in the navy, it resonated with the war generation, became a best-seller, and, as a movie, a box office success both in Britain and the US. It dealt with two interrelated themes; epistemology — the limitations of human knowledge; and individual responsibility — having to face the conse-quences of decisions made from imperfect knowledge. If *A Hard Day's Night* contains clues to the Boomer Ideology, then *The Cruel Sea* is equally revealing about the ideology of the War Generation,

"What's it look like now?" Ericson called out. "The same sir — solid echo — exactly the right size – must be a U-boat."

Ericson's mind is racing — calculating, weighing. As the seconds speed by, and the range closes, he fights against the softening instincts of doubt and mercy. Six hundred yards. More information, he must have more information.

"What's it look like now, Number One?" "Just the same – seems to be stationary – it's the strongest con-tact we've ever had."

"There are some chaps in the water."

"Well, there's a U-boat just underneath them."

Ericson hesitates. Four hundred yards. He imagines the devastating effect his depth charges will have on the men in the water. But he also trusts Lockhart's expertise to interpret the ASDIC data. Three hundred yards. No more time to think. He rasps out the order, "Attacking — stand by!" The depth charges, barrels full of high explosive, plop into the water amid the appalled and disbelieving swimmers. Then, with a hammer crack they explode. Monsarrat describes the gruesome aftermath,

"Men floated high on the surface like dead goldfish in a film of blood. Most of them were disintegrated, or pulped out of human shape... [others were] split open from chin to crutch, they had been as neatly gutted as any herring. Some seagulls were already busy on the scene, screaming with excitement and delight."[1]

Ericson meanwhile is,

"Deep in self-torture, and appalled by what he had done, he had already decided that there had been no U-boat there in the first place: the contact was probably the torpedoed ship, sliding slowly to the bottom, or the disturbed water of her sinking."[2]

Was it a submarine, or had it been a false echo? It could have been either. It was impossible to know, impossible to be certain. Later, Ericson, haunted by what he has done, talks to three ships' captains and explains, "I really thought there was a submarine there, otherwise I wouldn't have done it. I had to make up my mind." "There is no blame" says one of the captains, "but there will be thoughts. For that there is gin." When Lockhart approaches Ericson, he is surprised to find him weeping, "I identified it as a submarine. If anyone killed those men, I killed them," Lockhart says consolingly. To which Ericson replies, "No one killed them, it's the war, the whole bloody war, we've just got to do these things, and say our prayers at the end."[3]

Human Knowledge is Imperfect Knowledge

In Monsarrat's novel, the sea is cruel because it is indifferent to human hope and fear. It lacks compassion. It is inhumane and unforgiving. It feels nothing. It is brutally, cruelly impartial. Above all, the sea has no sympathy for human hubris, for those who fool themselves with fantasies and illusions, and who allow themselves to be destroyed with false hope. Monsarrat describes the sea as a wild, inhuman force — unfathomable and unpredictable. No human can ever know, "its moods, its violence, its gentle balm, its treachery: what men can do with it, and what it can do with men."[4]

The sea is nature in the raw, without any of the trappings and niceties of civilization. When people stand face to face with it, they discover it is volatile, uncertain, complex and ambiguous. In this cosmology, knowledge becomes a mysterious paradox. Possessing it is of supreme importance for survival, yet truth will always be uncertain and elusive — always tantalizingly just out of reach. The hunt for the submarine becomes a metaphor for the epistemology of the War Generation. Sealed in a windowless box in the bowels of the ship, Lockhart must use all his skill and experience to decode the unreliable clues supplied by the ASDIC.

Captain Ericson has to quickly weigh this uncertain testimony against a host of competing factors, epistemic, emotional and ethical, and make a momentous decision under enormous pressure. He will never know if he is right or wrong. Yet, the heavy burden of responsibility is his alone and he must find the emotional strength to bear it. He must not succumb to weakness and indecision. The safety of his ship, his life and the lives of his crew depend on his strength. In the middle of the Atlantic Ocean there is escape; no one else to blame, nowhere to hide.

This is how the concept of truth was understood by the Anglo-American Enlightenment, by Victorian Liberalism and by the War Generation. Reality was a concrete, objectively existing thing independent of human belief. In other words, millions of people might believe something which was, in reality, false. The challenge for each individual was to narrow the gap between their belief and reality, and build an accurate picture of what is, not what ought to be. The Victorians devoted much time and trouble to developing methodologies to help them do this. They developed the scientific method and introduced scientific thinking to professions such as medicine and law. Popular fictional heroes, such as Sherlock Holmes preached the virtues of meticulously observing reality and thinking logically. Holmes made pronouncements such as, "emotional qualities are antagonistic to clear reasoning" and, "when you have eliminated the impossible, whatever remains, however improbable, must be the truth". The Victorian Liberal concept of truth also made possible the creation of Victorian Liberal Journalism with its professional, quasi-scientific methodology of accuracy, impartiality and its strict divide between fact and opinion. All these innovations were designed to restrain the natural human urge to lapse back into lazy, primitive ways of knowing based on emotion, intuition, prejudice and groupthink.

The belief that all human knowledge is uncertain and fallible, led Victorian Liberal thinkers towards an uncomfortable epistemic and moral dilemma. If certitude is an illusion — if what we believe to be true today may turn out to be untrue tomorrow — how can we avoid paralysis and indecision? Why should we believe anything at all? As the famous Victorian Liberal philosopher James Fitzjames Stephen put it,

> "Mankind appear to me to be in the following difficulty, from which I see no means of extrication. Either they must confine their conclusions to matters which can be verified by actual experience, in which case the questions which principally interest them must be dismissed from consideration as insoluble riddles; or they must be satisfied with probable solutions to them, in which case their solutions will always contain a certain degree or error and will require reconstruction from age to age as circumstances change. Moreover, more solutions than one will always be possible and there will be no means of deciding conclusively which is right."[5]

Another philosopher, Leonard Hobhouse, put it more succinctly, "We are never to suppose that we are in the possession of complete and final truth... there are endless opportunities of error."[6]

The Victorian journalist John Morley described this epistemic approach as a "doctrine of intellectual responsibility" requiring the courage to admit that knowledge was fragile,

"There is a certain grave acquiescence in ignorance, a recognition of our impotence to solve momentous and urgent questions, which has a satisfaction of its own."[7]

The only certain knowledge, said Morley, was that there was no such thing as certain knowledge. This "negative truth" was, he said, the foundation of rational thinking, "The negative truth that nothing can be known is in fact a truth that guides us. It leads us away from sterile and irreclaimable tracts of thought and emotion."[8] Morley acknowledged that embracing ignorance makes us uncomfortable because we are hard-wired to crave certainty. Thus, most of the time, we prefer soothing, comforting narratives to independent, critical thinking,

"There is a corresponding fashion of placing truth second and emotional comfort first... This choice of emotional gratification before truth and upright dealing with one's own understanding... is an everyday plea for self-deception, and a current justification for illusion."[9]

The solution which the Victorians proposed to life's uncertainty and complexity was epistemic vigilance and toil. It was every individual's responsibility to gather facts, formulate opinions and constantly test them against alternative views. Truth was an endless journey without a destination. To the Victorians, everybody was expected to copy Sherlock Holmes' example. But, even so, truth would always remain provisional — an educated guess supported by imperfect evidence. To the Victorians, there were degrees of truth. Some assertions were better supported by evidence and hence more probable than others. The philosopher Bertrand Russell, writing during World War Two, summarized that truth "is neither completely attainable nor completely unobtainable; it is attainable to a certain degree, and that only with difficulty."[10] Susan Stebbing, another philosopher writing during wartime, said this epistemology applied equally to journalism because journalists were human and therefore fallible. She advised the public to compare contradictory accounts from different sources by reading, "newspapers of different political complexions if we wish to be well informed of what is taking place."[11]

The need for apparently limitless epistemic effort brought Victorian Liberal theorists to another dilemma – the impossibility, in the real world, of expending infinite effort to research, find out and know. Ultimately, wrote James Fitzjames Stephen, each individual must do his best and take responsibility for his own choices and behavior, in the full knowledge he might be wrong. He must also allow others the same freedom. Stephen produced a vivid metaphor for the limitations of human knowledge, the fallibility of belief, and the necessity of taking individual moral and epistemic responsibility,

> "We stand on a mountain pass in the midst of whirling snow and blinding mist, through which we get glimpses now and then of paths which may be deceptive. If we stand still, we shall be frozen to death. If we take the wrong road, we shall be dashed to pieces. We do not certainly know whether there is any right one. What must we do? 'Be strong and of a good courage.' Act for the best, hope for the best, and take what comes. Above all, let us dream no dreams, and tell no lies, but go our way, wherever it may lead, with our eyes open and our heads erect. If death ends all, we cannot meet it better. If not, let us enter whatever may be the next scene like honest men, with no sophistry in our mouths and no masks on our faces."[12]

The Truth Gap

To the Boomers, all of this was obsolete. There were no convoys, no U-Boats and no world war. Modern life required new, better ways of seeing and knowing. This chasm in understanding was neatly captured by the novelist Gerald Kersh. In his best-selling 1941 novel *They Die With Their Boots Clean*, Kersh imagines a post-war scene in which a teenager, raised in comfort and affluence, sneers at a group of war veterans and their strange, outmoded values. Communication is impossible between the two sides. There is only mutual incomprehension. To the teenager, the old soldiers are dinosaurs. To the soldiers, the teenager appears to lack any common sense or maturity. As they angrily tell him,

> "We were keeping you and your mum safe in your beds when you were too little to walk, and keeping this country all clear for you to grow up and do nothing in... We've known what it

feels like to come face to face with a day or a night that must be the last, only somehow we came through, and saw the dark, or the daylight, and laughed it off whatever we felt… Where has it got us? Son — didn't anybody ever tell you? Manhood! That is what it's got us."[13]

Kersh developed this theme in a 1946 book in which he predicted that the intensity of the war experience would make it impossible for his children and grandchildren to understand him. He prophesized they would be,

"Untidy, raucous young men with rumpled hair; or smelly, neglected young women… they will laugh at me for a God-forsaken old fool, and when, with senile persistence, I try to tell them of the glory that was Britain's, they will say: 'Listen Comrade Grandfather, why don't you lie down and die, you doddering old anachronism.'"[14]

In the future imagined by the Boomer generation, citizens would be liberated from epistemic toil and effort. Individuals would not be expected to work things out for themselves. Instead, benevolent Boomer experts would think out solutions and make policy decisions on behalf of the tribe. Freed from the tedious duty to be epistemically responsible, individuals would be free to spend their time in Boomertopia gratifying their desires and pursuing personal pleasure and fulfilment. The generation gap was therefore about far more than different tastes in music, fashion and hairstyles. It was an epistemic gap between two entirely different understandings of what makes knowledge legitimate. The generation gap was fundamentally, a truth gap.

Chapter 10

Aletheia - The Four Pillars of Journalistic Truth

"The greatest challenge facing mankind is the challenge of distinguishing reality from fantasy, truth from propaganda. We must daily decide whether the threats we face are real, whether the solutions we are offered will do any good".

Michael Crighton

Since absolute truth was unobtainable for mortals, Victorian Liberal Journalism set its sight on a lesser, more practical goal — Journalistic Truth. Victorian Liberal Journalism can be understood as a quasi-scientific, or quasi-judicial, methodolgy that scrutinizes information and subjects it to a series of quality control checks. In other words, the professional procedures introduced by Victorian Liberal Journalism were intended to deter journalists from relying on prejudice, guesswork, superstition and the host of cognitive biases that constantly afflict human decision making. It was an epistemology designed to limit the number of mistakes, filter out improbabilities and steer journalists away from error. The goal was not perfection, but the management of imperfection. This, then, was Victorian Liberal Journalism; half art, half science — a set of professional routines which, taken together, created a provisional, uncertain verdict, one that was always temporary and fragile, always awaiting further evidence. Audiences were not expected to have blind, uncritical faith in the testimony of journalism. Ultimately, it was for each individual to decide what to believe, after having heard all the available evidence, and listened to both sides of the story.

The temple of Victorian Liberal Journalism rested on four mighty pillars:

1. The separation of fact from opinion.

2. Journalism's arrow must always point from fact towards opinion, never the other way.

3. Accuracy — providing a factual account which was as close as possible to reality.

4. Impartiality — the complete picture must be given, not a partial, one-sided account.

First, facts and opinions had to be separated. As the British newspaper editor C.P. Scott famously explained in 1921, the primary function of journalism was the reporting of factual news. Facts should never be confused, or contaminated, with opinion, comment, analysis, prediction or speculation. As Scott put it, at the peril of its soul journalism, "must see that the supply is not tainted... Comment is free, but facts are sacred".[1]

The first pillar of Victorian Liberal Journalism was therefore intended to separate evidence from the conclusions drawn from evidence. This was to minimize the danger of confusing speculative hypotheses with genuine facts. As James Fitzjames Stephen said, it was essential to,

"Abstain as far as possible from the process of piling inference upon inference, each inference becoming more improbable in a geometric ratio as it becomes more remote from actual observation... A probability upon a probability closely resembles an improbability."[2]

The second pillar was related to the first. Explanation, opinion, forecasting and speculation must always be firmly supported by fact. Journalism's arrow must point from fact to opinion and must never be reversed. This was designed to control the natural human tendency to see the world as a series of simplified narratives. The Victorians viewed Narrative-Led Journalism as highly dangerous; the product of a theological, tribal way of knowing based on faith. Once a narrative became established in the collective mind, it created the illusion of certainty and encouraged intolerance and fanaticism. Facts would be chosen to support the narrative and inconvenient facts would be suppressed and ignored. Isaac Newton had championed this mode of self-disciplined, rational thinking, famously saying, "*hypotheses non fingo*" — "I frame no hypotheses" — meaning his mission was to observe reality and describe its laws, not attempt to explain them. It was a revolutionary and counter-intuitive way of knowing compared to the epistemology of the Middle Ages which was based on shared faith and deference to authority. Hence, Newton's methodology, which inspired the Anglo-American Enlightenment, and laid the foundations for Victorian Liberal Journalism, freed the mind from the slavery of narrative, speculation and theory. As Newton put it,

"The best and safest method of philosophizing seems to be, first to inquire diligently into the properties of things, and establishing those properties by experiments and then to proceed more slowly to hypotheses for the explanation of them. For hypotheses should be subservient only in explaining the properties of things, but not assumed in determining them; unless so far as they may furnish experiments. For if the possibility of hypotheses is to be the test of truth and reality of things, I see not how certainty can be obtained in any science; since numerous hypotheses may be devised, which shall seem to overcome new difficulties."[3]

The Victorian Liberal theorist Henry Buckle used the label "inductive" to refer to this modern, scientific way of knowing which pointed from fact to explanation; and "deductive" to refer to the theological, or magical, way of knowing which led from explanation to fact. Buckle said the great achievement of the scientific method was that it defeated superstition by refusing to,

> "Accept principles which could not be substantiated by facts; while the opposite and theological plan is, to force the facts to yield to the principles... In theology, certain principles are taken for granted; and, it being deemed impious to question them, all that remains for us is to reason from them downwards. On the other hand, the inductive method will concede nothing, but insists upon reasoning upwards, and demands that we shall have the liberty of ascertaining the principles for ourselves."[4]

In an 1891 short story, Sherlock Holmes put it more succinctly, "It is a capital mistake to theorize before one has data. Insensibly one begins to twist facts to suit theories, instead of theories to suit facts."[5]

Victorian Liberal Journalism was not hostile to theories, opinion and analysis. Many newspaper editors thundered their political and moral views from their leader pages with passion. However, the *modus operandi* of Victorian Liberal Journalism was to maintain a fire-gap between fact and opinion and try to restrain the urge to allow pre-existing prejudice to dictate which facts were reported. Keeping the arrow of journalism pointing in the correct direction was essential to prevent journalists falling into the chasm of Narrative-Led Journalism.

The third pillar demanded that facts were reported as accurately as possible. Journalists were to confine themselves to asking a set of questions designed to elicit only factual answers. Thus, the classic five questions of Victorian Liberal Journalism were: 'who?', 'what?', 'when?', 'where?' and 'how?' Journalists recognized, as had Isaac Newton, that the question 'why?' was a completely different type of question designed to elicit an opinion. For example, a journalist might report that Jack the Ripper had murdered Kate Eddowes, who was a prostitute, in Mitre Square in the East End of London at around 01.40 am on the morning of 30th September 1888. The killer had slit her throat with a knife. All of these were statements of fact. Asking why Jack the Ripper had murdered her, or why Eddowes had become a prostitute, or why sex work was rife in

Victorian London, or what measures ought to be taken to reduce it, were questions that could only be answered by opinion, analysis, theorizing and speculation. These, in turn, would provoke moral judgments and further opinions about ethical-political remedies. Hence, asking 'why?" was the job of leader writers, priests and politicians, not journalists. The high-minded Victorians had plenty to say about social and moral issues, but their newspapers made it a rule to confine comment to the opinion columns and keep it out of the news pages. However, maintaining this separation and reporting facts accurately was no easy task. The Victorians recognized that facts are often disputed and uncertain, and based on the unreliable testimony of witnesses who might be mistaken or deceitful. The source of a factual claim was therefore attributed to the person making it. This would, it was hoped, help readers judge the reliability of the claim for themselves.

Impartiality, the fourth pillar, was intimately related to all the others, and was understood as giving a full and complete account. An impartial report was therefore the opposite of a partial report, in the same way one might say an airport is partially open, or a new building is partially finished.* Impartial journalism was characterized by reporting both sides of the story and attempting, as honestly as possible, not to leave out any strategic, or relevant information. In practice, this generally meant seeking an opposing point of view. Journalistic impartiality was therefore equivalent to presenting the jury in a trial with both the case for the prosecution, and the case for the defense. Partial journalism, on the other hand, was journalism that favored one side by omitting information, or presenting it in a slanted, incomplete and misleading way.

Journalistic Truth then, like judicial truth, is a technical, practical thing which should not be confused with the abstract concept of objective, or absolute, truth. For example, in a criminal trial, there are frequently strong differences of opinion between jurors about what really happened, even though each juror has heard exactly the same evidence. Debate in the jury room can last for days as jurors argue about what the evidence

---

* Originally, the word 'partial' meant 'partly'. Hence a partial account of events was an incomplete one i.e., only part of the story. An impartial account, on the other hand, was a complete one. The distinction is between telling the truth and telling the whole truth. Confusingly, in modern English usage, the opposite of 'impartial' is 'biased' - the original meaning of 'partial' having been lost. Semantic shift has therefore made the concept of impartiality highly confusing for students of journalism.

means, how it should be interpreted and how much weight should be given to each element. The verdict in a trial is not therefore the same thing as what *really* happened — which is unknowable. Thus, somebody may be found guilty of a crime he did not commit, or acquitted of one which he did. This apparent contradiction is neatly captured in lines from Terence Rattigan's play *The Winslow Boy*,

> "Catherine: Many people believed him innocent, you know.
> Sir Robert: So I understand. (A faint pause.) As it happens, however, he was guilty."[6]

Here, each character is using the words 'innocent' and 'guilty'. In different ways. Catherine uses 'innocent' to mean objectively, absolutely innocent; whereas Sir Robert uses 'guilty' to mean merely that the accused received a fair trial and was found guilty by the jurors. He was, in other words, *legally* guilty. Similarly, information produced according to the methodology of Victorian Liberal Journalism, could be considered journalistically true. It might turn out to be wrong, but that is beside the point. Victorian Liberal Journalism was not supposed to be accepted as an unchallengeable gospel. It was simply testimony that had been inspected, checked and approved by journalists using a recognized methodology. Journalistic Truth was a badge of approval; a hallmark denoting that reasonable care had been taken by fair-minded professionals to avoid narrative, restrain groupthink, and provide an impartial, honest account. After that, it was for readers to discuss among themselves and make up their own minds. Ultimately, responsibility for believing rested with the individual.

Chapter 11

A Very Short Epistemic History of Journalism – Part One

The End of the End of History

It is very difficult, from the perspective of the early 21st Century, to appreciate the epistemic achievement of Victorian Liberal Journalism. This is largely due to the dominance of Boomer truthophobia. As we have already noted, from the late 1960s onwards, Boomer revisionist historians manufactured a new version of history from which epistemology was expunged. At the same time, the Boomer generation of scholars in the humanities and social sciences re-drew the acceptable boundaries of academic discourse and made the concept of Journalistic Truth largely unavailable to writers — except as a subject for ridicule. Failure to adopt the Boomer paradigm was to defy intellectual fashion and commit an embarrassing faux pas; like saying one preferred 1930s dance bands to the Rolling Stones. Writing about truth, except to undermine it, was to exclude oneself from the intellectual community and identify onself as the tribal other.

A mischievous consequence of Boomer truthophobia is therefore that, in the early 21st Century, the intellectual tools needed to understand Victorian Liberal Journalism's commitment to truth, no longer exist. To recapture what has been lost, it is necessary to look, with fresh eyes at what pre-Boomer journalists were trying to do and how they attempted to do it. It is only by reconnecting with the minds of pre-Boomer journalists that one can gather the clues necessary to reconstruct their concept of Journalistic Truth and break free from the mental and linguistic cage of Boomer truthophobia.

This chapter is a time machine in which we will travel back to the pre-Boomer era. It is a very brief epistemic history of Anglo-American journalism containing the sort of information Boomer historians omitted and suppressed. Because it is an epistemic history, it recognizes the concept of Journalistic Truth and is neither embarrassed nor frightened by it. Pre-Boomer journalists were, first and foremost, seekers of Journalistic Truth, therefore bringing back their lost thoughts helps us see the ideology and epistemology of the Boomers in perspective; not as an eternal, objectively correct set of values, but as an opportunistic collection of views that were useful to a unique generation living at a particular moment of history.

The Boomers found it hard to tolerate a way of thinking different to their own. The Boomer historian Francis Fukuyama even famously claimed the human race had arrived at the "end of history" — a perfect, final state that would never change.[1] But what the Boomers had constructed was in reality only the Boomer Version of History — a comforting and flattering reflection of their own values and assumptions. Only a uniquely hubristic generation could claim it represented the final stage of human evolution and that history had ended — with itself. Re-engaging with pre-Boomer views allows us to see something very different, the end of the end of history. It enables us to escape the cultural and intellectual stagnation of the Boomers and makes possible new beginnings.

Journalism Before the Victorians

Victorian Liberal Journalism, with its goal of truth-seeking, was innovative and revolutionary. It was also a reaction to the chaotic, untrustworthy journalism of the 18th Century. 18th Century journalism in England and America had a rowdy, Hogarthian flavor. Journalists and publishers were largely indifferent to what was objectively true or false and wrote what would sell, or what they were paid to write. Journalistic Truth had a tribal quality and was understood as the official narrative — the consensus of opinions of the great and good of our side. Fake news and misinformation were the narratives of the other side. The journalistic business model was based on patronage and subsidy. For example, the British Prime Minister Robert Walpole was notorious for paying editors and journalists to write partisan narratives and suppress inconvenient facts. As the historian Thomas Horne wrote, in a paper aptly entitled *Politics in a Corrupt Society*, one of England's best-known journalists, William Arnall, was secretly paid £11,000 from public funds to write government-friendly narratives for the *Free Briton* and other pamphlets between 1732 and 1735,

> "A subsequent investigation by a committee of the House of Commons uncovered payments from the Walpole administration to various writers and publishers for the sum of £50,077 during the period 1732-41."[2]

The home of English, partisan, narrative-led journalism was London's Grub Street. According to one description it "abounded with mean and old houses" and was home to a tribe of,

> "Miserable, poverty-stricken scribblers, whose main chance of existence depended upon their power of virulence at a libel, and who last residence in this world was almost invariably the gaol."[3]

Nor was this mere hyperbole. One well-known newspaper editor, William Dodd, was hanged for forgery in London 1777. Hence, during the 18th Century, telling the truth was relegated to a position of secondary importance behind the *consequences* of telling the truth. As Dr Johnson complained,

"The first demand made by the reader of a journal is, that he should find an accurate account of foreign transactions and domestic incidents. This is always expected, but this is very rarely performed. Of those writers who have taken upon themselves the task of intelligence, some have given and others have sold their abilities, whether small or great, to one or other of the parties that divide us".[4]

As one modern historian concludes, being a journalist during the 18th Century was to be a writer of partisan propaganda and fake news. It was not considered a respectable occupation,

"The assumption that a newspaper writer was little more than a paid agent of politicians ensured that 'journalist' would be a term of opprobrium... It was thought mildly degrading to fight a duel against a newspaper man. To have taken paid employment for a newspaper also ensured a man would be barred from the legal profession in England, according to a regulation of 1807."[5]

Perhaps the most damning portrait of 18th Century journalism was a satire by Richard Savage which portrayed the profession as a sewer of lies and partisan narratives written purely for financial gain. Savage's imaginary journalist boasts his methodology is to embellish rumor, hearsay and gossip and transform it into news, "My bribe is a pot of ale, and my intelligence the scraps of conversation that fall at the table of great ministers." Savage's verdict was that journalists were scoundrels who deserved to be, "Pump'd, duck'd, pillory'd, pissed and shat on."[6]

Truthophobic 18th Century journalism was a product of the ideology of its time and of the prevailing system of government. Although early 18th Century England was the most democratic nation on Earth, its understanding of 'democracy' was quite different to how it would later be understood. It was by modern standards a proto-democracy, limited to the one percent of the population entitled to vote and in whom wealth and political power resided. This small oligarchy sat at the apex of a hierarchical society in which people were encouraged to remain in their place. Social mobility, except in modest degree, was discouraged. Happiness and the common good depended on ordinary people trusting the wisdom and benevolence of their rulers. As the historian Jean Hecht puts it,

"The cultural tone of eighteenth-century England was set by an elite composed of the highest nobility, the wealthiest gentry and their satellites… this small group constituted the fount of norms and values. No level of the social structure escaped the impact of its scheme of life, its modes of behaviour."[7]

Questioning the right of the oligarchy to rule was to question a natural and divinely ordained hierarchy. In this world, it was often more useful to know what one should believe, than what was objectively true. Widening the franchise and enlarging democracy was thought of as dangerous populism and a recipe for barbarism. In Doctor Johnson's words, it would lead to chaos, anarchy and rule by the "riot and filth of the meanest and most profligate of the rabble."[8] Even John Bowdler, an English writer who favored a more representative system of government, was horrified at the idea of *full* democracy which he said would inevitably lead to mob rule and political corruption. In 1797 he asked,

"If every man in the Kingdom had a vote for a Member of Parliament, what would be the consequence? Why, each Member would be chosen by a mob. And whom would a mob choose? Why, the man that made the loudest speech and the largest promises. And who would this be? Why he, that, having neither property nor character to lose, was ready to say anything to get into the House in hopes of being paid for breaking every promise he made."[9]

Growing pressure for a wider democracy, especially in the wake of the French Revolution of 1789, alarmed the British government which became less tolerant of dissent and free speech. Censorship, in the form of prosecutions for seditious libel, became common. By the end of the 18th Century, it was the newly independent United States of America that had become the freest nation on Earth. In 1791 the Federal Constitution was amended to include the following, famous declaration,

"Congress shall make no law respecting an establishment of religion, or prohibiting the free exercise thereof; or abridging the freedom of speech, or of the press; or the right of the people peaceably to assemble, and to petition the Government for a redress of grievances."

American journalists were free, but free to do what? The answer was, to continue the partisan tradition of the 18th century. Freedom did not translate into an attempt to be more truthful. On the contrary, American freedom of the press was simply the freedom to write stories to please one's patrons. It was the same journalism described by Dr Johnson as a corrupt occupation that produced "many narratives" by concealing, manipulating and misrepresenting facts, as well as by outright lying "without a wish for truth or thought of decency". American newspapers blended fact with opinion and reported only stories that supported their tribal cause. Political and financial motives came first, telling the truth was optional. In other words, *arete* and *nomisma* dominated, *aletheia* was a poor third. Publications were either pro-Federalist, or pro-Democratic-Republican, and vicious personal attacks, intended to damage the reputation of public figures, were frequently made by both sides. "There is a liberty of the press," observed the *Columbian Centinel* dejectedly in 1797, "which is very little short of the liberty of burning our houses." As President, Thomas Jefferson was tormented by partisan, fake news and concluded that a citizen who never opened a newspaper would be "better informed than he who reads them". Writing to the young, aspiring journalist John Norvell, he said,

"Nothing can now be believed which is seen in a newspaper. Truth itself becomes suspicious by being put into that polluted vehicle. The real extent of this state of misinformation is known only to those who are in situations to confront facts within their knowledge with the lies of the day."[10]

As the historian Frank Mott gloomily summarized,

"The whole period of 1801-1833 was in many respects disgraceful — a kind of "Dark Ages" of American journalism. Few papers were ably edited; they reflected the crassness of the American society of the times. Scurrility, assaults, corruption, blatancy were commonplace."[11]

The Birth of Victorian Liberal Journalism

The early 19th century saw the slow, painful birth of participative democracy in Britain. The Great Reform Bill of 1832 signaled a new way of thinking. The zeitgeist of the age was one of scientific enquiry and progress; toleration and truth seeking. A new philosophy, Victorian Liberalism, captured the public imagination. It stressed the liberty of the individual and sought a meritocratic democracy — a society composed of responsible, informed citizens each contributing to the public good, in which the most talented, virtuous and industrious would prosper. It was a world of piety and austerity which turned its back on the licentiousness of the 18th Century. Luxury and self-indulgence were viewed as destructive sins. Self-denial, self-management and self-improvement were virtues.

The Victorians launched an assault on the inefficiency, patronage and corruption of the preceding century. For example, during the 18th and early 19th Centuries, appointment, promotion and advancement had depended largely on group membership. As one historian observes, "Membership of a well-known family gave a young man an assured position in politics, the army, the Church, or the Law, often regardless of personal ability."[12]   To remedy this, the Victorians introduced merito-cratic competition. For example, in 1870 Gladstone's Liberal government opened entry to most branches of the Civil Service to competitive exam-ination.   Many other institutions followed suit and introduced written examinations as a condition of entry. The underlying philosophy was to allow the appointment of the most talented individuals regardless of their tribal or group identity.

How Journalistic Truth was understood also became more demo-cratic. It was no longer seen as the property of a tribal group or ruling elite. Instead of truth being the consensus of the powerful, the rich, the great and the good, it came to be understood as a destination that could be approached by any rational, reasonable individual. The road towards it was paved with open-minded, evidence-based enquiry, discussion and freedom of thought. It was the epistemology of the Anglo-American En-lightenment and Isaac Newton, but, now in the hands of the Victorians, it was being treated with a high-minded seriousness.

To serve the new mood, a new journalism emerged. It scorned the corrupt, Narrative-Led Journalism of the 18th Century and set itself the task of reporting reality as honestly as possible. It created a new journalistic methodology and a new professionalism. Techniques were developed to restrain the natural tendency towards bias and narrative. By the 1830s, the word "journalist" was beginning to take on its modern meaning. Henceforth, it would refer to someone whose goal was to report the news truthfully, not a hired Grub Street hack, manufacturing stories to reinforce the pre-determined narrative. In response to its increasing importance to Victorian Liberal Democracy, the social status of journalists rose.

The Times of London, under the editorships of Thomas Barnes (1817-1841) and John Thaddeus Delane (1841-1877), became the symbol of this novel, responsible journalism. Its self-appointed mission was to supply trustworthy information to inform Britain's newly enfranchised voters. *The Times* thundered its political views, but it scrupulously distinguished between fact and opinion, confining the latter to its leader columns. It revelled in its impartiality and independence which meant it might praise a politician one day and criticize him the next. As a *Times* editorial of 1817 put it,

> "We estimate measures by their merits... those who praise actions on account, universally, of their authors, have only [one] enquiry to make – 'who performs them?' Their course is easy, but it is a humble one. Ours is more arduous and more honourable."[13]

To those used to committed, partisan reporting, Victorian Liberal Journalism seemed maddeningly inconsistent and unpredictable. Journalistic impartiality was an acquired taste. As Barnes' biographer explains,

> "The mass of readers did not know that a struggle for their instruction rather than their deception was proceeding between one man and host of political and professional corrupters."[14]

Even threats from government ministers were unable to shake *The Times* from its commitment to *aletheia*. During the early 1850s, extreme political pressure was brought to bear on the paper to make it reign-in its criticism of the French President Louis Napoléon who had become,

"Irritated and annoyed beyond measure" by what *The Times* was writing. *The Times* responded in a series of famous editorials defending its right to publish information, even when politicians said it was contrary to the public interest. In January 1852 the paper explained,

> "The responsibility of journalists is in proportion to the liberty they enjoy. No moral obligation can be graver. But their duties are not the same, I think, as those of statesmen. To find out the true state of facts, to report them with fidelity, to apply to them strict and fixed principles of justice, humanity, and law, to inform as far as possible, the very conscience of nations and to call down the judgement of the world on what is false, or base, or tyrannical, appear to me to be the first duties of those who write."[15]

This celebrated mid-century clash between *The Times* and the British government was, first and foremost, a clash between *aletheia* — the desire to tell the truth regardless of consequences, and *arete* — the desire to do or say whatever is ethically-politically expedient. A follow-up editorial of 6 February, explained the two motives belonged to different worlds. Well-intentioned deception might be acceptable in politics, but never in journalism,

> "The statesman collects his information secretly and by secret means; he keeps back even the current intelligence of the day with ludicrous precautions... The press lives by disclosures; whatever passes into its keeping becomes a part of the knowledge and the history of our times."

By the 1850s, the enigma of *The Times'* brand of journalism had become both well understood and highly respected. When the German writer Max Schlesinger visited the paper's London offices, he noted that although, "The politics of *The Times* are an inscrutable mystery to most men", the explanation lay in its impartiality and independence. Thus, he explained, "On certain questions it supported the ministers of the day, on others it opposed them; but it never made opposition for the sake of opposition."[16]

Thus did journalism progress to the status of the Fourth Estate, arm in arm with the development of Britain's fledgling democracy. The rapidly expanding number of literate voters demanded high quality, relevant information and Victorian Liberal Journalism set out to supply it. The relationship between Victorian Liberal Democracy and Victorian Liberal Journalism was therefore organic and intimate. The expectation that individuals should think independently and critically, fuelled demand for truthful journalism. As one historian explains, it produced newspapers, "governed by a sense of obligation to their readers to give them the truth." The result was, "The working man, given the vote by Disraeli's 1867 Reform Act, could buy a penny newspaper which presented news in a dignified and unsensational manner."[17]

Since advertising is always attracted to audiences, and because audiences wanted truthful Victorian Liberal Journalism, truth-telling was also profitable. The mass production of news by steam powered presses quickly became a wonder of the world. By 1866, *The Times* was selling an impressive 71,000 copies a day. In 1869 it installed a Walter rotary press capable of printing 12,000 pages per hour. Other British newspapers imitated *The Times'* formula and adopted the methodology of Victorian Liberal Journalism. By 1862, sales of *The Daily Telegraph* were exceeding 140,000 copies per day, *The Standard* was selling 185,000 copies by 1874, while *Lloyd's Weekly News* reported sales of almost a million per week by 1890.[18] Advertising revenue bolstered independence from political influence and patronage. Victorian Liberal Journalism and its business model was a happy marriage of *aletheia* and *nomisma*. *Arete,* in the form of political and moral opinion, was tamed, controlled and confined to clearly labelled leader articles and op-eds.

Victorian Liberal Journalism in the US

Throughout the first half of the 19th century, American journalism proved stubbornly resistant to the new, responsible journalism coming into the fashion in Britain. In an 1850 census, only five percent of newspapers claimed to be impartial or independent. "Neutrality in this country and this age," noted the *Richmond Times and Compiler* in August 1844 "is an anomaly". Audiences preferred the rough honesty of partisan journalism and regarded it as superior to morally timid, impartial reporting. One American newspaper editor recalled this era of committed journalism as a time when,

"Every editor wore his conscience on his arm, and carried his dueling weapon in his hand, walked always in the light where the whole world could see him, and was prepared to defend his published opinions with his life if need be."[19]

However, not everyone was so enthusiastic. The novelist James Fennimore Cooper, writing in 1838, expressed exasperation at the sly, misleading mixture of truth, half-truth and lies that defined American journalism,

"The admixture of truth and falsehood in the intelligence circulated by the press, is one of the chief causes of its evils. A journal that gave utterance to nothing but untruths, would lose its influence with its character, but there are none so ignorant as not to see the necessity of occasionally issuing truths."[20]

It was not until after the trauma and bitterness of the civil war and reconstruction eras had begun to fade, that a new cultural landscape began to emerge in the US, and with it new journalisms. As early as 1872, the journalist Whitelaw Reid was able to detect the new trend,

"Independent journalism! that is the watchword of the future in the profession. An end of concealments because it would hurt the party; an end of one-sided expositions... of hesitation to print the news because it may hurt the party."[21]

Melville Stone, who launched the *Chicago Daily News* in 1876, was one of the first American editors to embrace the epistemology and methodology of Victorian Liberal Journalism and make it profitable. Stone described the new approach as being like a, "Witness in court, bound to 'tell the truth, the whole truth, and nothing but the truth'."[22]

However, Victorian Liberal Journalism was not the only game in town. Towards the end of the 19th Century, it faced stiff competition from an entirely different genre. "Yellow Journalism", or "Muckraking Journalism", employed a proto-tabloid style and reveled in sensationalism and political campaigning. Famous for faked interviews, melodrama, lurid accounts of crime, poverty and human suffering, Yellow Journalism was partial, emotional, indifferent to truth and frequently attacked for peddling fake, or distorted, news. The prototype for Yellow Journalism was the *New York Herald* which specialized in dramatic "stories of illicit sex relations" and scandalous allegations which, according to Mott, were often "more or less fictitious"[23] For example, in 1874 *The Herald* invented a story about wild animals escaping from New York's Central Park Zoo. In huge headlines, the paper's 9 November edition proclaimed,

"Awful Calamity. Wild Animals Broken Loose from Central Park. Terrible Scenes of Mutilation. Savage Brutes at Large. Awful Combats between the Beasts and Citizens".

The story reported that a lion had seized four small children and "mangled the delicate little things past all signs of recognition". Another lion was described as "tugging and crunching at the arms of a corpse, now letting go with his teeth to plant his paws upon the bleeding remains". A panther, the paper said, "sprang upon the shoulders of an aged lady, burying its fangs in her neck". Only at the end of the report, did the paper mention, "the entire story given above is a pure fabrication. Not one word of it is true. Not a single act or incident described has taken place." The hoax created wild panic in New York and was condemned as an, "Insane jest... intensely stupid and unfeeling" by *The New York Times*.[23]

Yellow Journalism was blatantly truthophobic. Its goal was not to tell the truth, but to make as much money as possible for its owners by whatever means. Yellow newspapers, like their British tabloid imitators, was a lurch towards undiluted *nomisma*. As one historian summarizes,

"Their aim was to interest, excite and amuse their readers... Sensational headlines, 'bright' writing and photographs all attracted the reader's attention and caused him the minimum of effort."[24]

To satisfy public demand for its Yellow Journalism, the *New York Herald* installed the latest Hoe sextuple rotary press in 1891. It was a machine capable of printing and folding an astonishing 90,000 four-page newspapers per hour. Yellow Journalism was popular and profitable, and helped make fortunes for publishers such as Joseph Pulitzer and William Randolph Hearst, however it also attracted widespread criticism. William Jay Gaynor, a Supreme Court Justice and later Mayor of New York, was one of many who attacked Yellow Journalists calling them "scoundrels",

"The journalism of New York City has been dragged to the lowest depths of degradation. The grossest railleries and libels, instead of honest statements and fair discussion, have gone on unchecked."[25]

Yellow Journalism retained much of the excitement, wildness and disregard for truth of American journalism of the antebellum era. But the spirit of the age was changing. The swashbuckling, frontier spirit was giving way to the desire for something more respectable. Partisan, tribal journalism was starting to become unfashionable. By 1890 a third of American newspapers were describing themselves as "independent," "neutral," or "local". The newspaper that symbolized this new mood most of all was *The New York Times*, under the ownership of Adolph Ochs. Ochs rejected the values of Yellow Journalism and promised in August 1896 to,

"Give the news impartially, without fear or favor, regardless of any party, sect or interest involved; to make of the columns of The New York Times a forum for the consideration of all questions of public importance, and to that end to invite intelligent discussion from all shades of opinion."[26]

Appropriately, the *New York Times* struck a deal to share resources and news stories with its London namesake. It also adhered to the same epistemic methodology; scrupulously distinguishing between fact and opinion. Fact was reported on the news pages, opinion explained what the facts might mean, but only appeared on the leader pages. This separation was crucial to the business of truth-seeking journalism. As the historian of the *New York Times*, Elmer Holmes Davis explained, "the general reader may disagree with the editorial interpretation. That is his privilege, for it is presented only as an interpretation." As Davis put it,

"The news department of a paper should not be, and that of *The Times* is not, influenced by editorial policies… it has been found advisable to print all the news and leave to the editorial page the assessment of its relative worth."[27]

The eminent journalist H.L. Mencken was grateful for the demise of Yellow Journalism and the rise of truthful, responsible reporting. He was skeptical about Yellow Journalism's claims that it was fighting nobly to make the world a better place. In reality, he said, it simply whipped audiences into an emotional frenzy to sell papers and make money,

"This crusading business is one of the worst curses of journalism, and perhaps the main enemy of that fairness and accuracy and intelligent purpose which should mark the self-respecting newspaper... is not war; it is lynching — and lynching is surely no sport for men presumably of honor."[28]

Charles Moreau Harger, Editor of the *Abilene Reflector*, also welcomed the new age of impartial, truthful journalism,

"That there is a new journalism, with principles and methods in harmony with new political and social conditions and new developments in news-transmission and the printing art, is evident."

Painstaking research, the search for truth, professionalism and "fairness" he said, were replacing the old amateur, "say what you like" style, "The new journalism demands men of high character and good habits",

"The old story of the special writer who, when asked what he needed to turn out a good story for the next day's paper, replied, 'a desk, some paper, and a quart of whiskey,' does not apply."[29]

This era of transition to responsible Victorian Liberal Journalism in the US was brilliantly captured by Orson Welles in his fictional history of American journalism *Citizen Kane*. Kane, a character loosely based on Hearst, abandons the lurid, fake news of Yellow Journalism, for sober, professional New Journalism and prints an Ochs-style declaration of principles on the front page of his *Enquirer*,

"I'll provide the people of this city with a daily paper that will tell all the news honestly... They're going to get the truth from the Enquirer, quickly and simply and entertainingly and no special interests are going to be allowed to interfere with that truth."[30]

In the movie Kane ultimately fails to keep his pledge. But his failure, indeed the impossibility of producing genuinely objective, impartial news, is irrelevant. What was distinctive about Victorian Liberal Journalism was not that it supplied an unblemished stream of pure Journalistic Truth, but that it set itself the *goal* of doing so. It was the *motive* of truth-telling that was significant. As Och's biographer explains,

"It was his intent, not always his accomplishment, for who attains his ideal in this frustrated world? But it is a lordly intent, one of the highest goals of human endeavor; for to be impartial, truly and thoroughly impartial, a man must divest himself of all the passions, whether as low as lust and greed, or as high as the crusader's zeal, that subtly color his vision and draw veils between his eyes and naked Truth. It is, flatly, a goal no mere mortal has ever attained; but this man strove for it."[31]

Journalism Between the Wars

Aletheia hibernated during the First World War, sheltering from the cold winds of partisan propaganda which howled through Anglo-American journalism. However, it emerged into the post-war spring with a renewed sense of optimism and maturity. During the 1920s, journalists devoted much time and energy to reasserting the values of Victorian Liberal Journalism and refocusing their profession on the goal of Journalistic Truth. The four pillars of Journalistic Truth, scarred by epistemic shrapnel from the war, were given a coat of bright new paint. For example, in April 1923 the newly formed American Society of Newspapers Editors (ASNE) published its *Code of Ethics*. Its seven rules explained the first duty of journalism was to the reporting of fact, "the primary function of newspapers is to communicate to the human race what its members do, feel and think." The ASNE code stressed that journalists must be able to recognize the distinction between fact and opinion, "Sound practice makes clear distinction between news reports and expressions of opinion. News reports should be free from opinion or bias of any kind." Consequently the codes demanded that, "responsible" journalism should strive to be "impartial" and aspire to "fair play" and "decency". Incomplete, partial, Narrative-Led News, which omitted half the story, was condemned,

"Partisanship, in editorial comment which knowingly departs from the truth, does violence to the best spirit of American journalism; in the news columns it is subversive of a fundamental principle of the profession."[32]

The ASNE code was a classic restatement of the four pillars of Victorian Liberal Journalism. It provided practical guidelines to help keep reporters on the epistemic highwire and concluded that journalists must constantly restrain themselves from "pandering to vicious instincts" and follow their professional methodology in order to stay maintain their balance.

During the 1920s and 1930s, newspaper editors and proprietors frequently spoke about the need to make *aletheia* a reality. Even the former champion of Yellow Journalism, William Randolph Hearst, the owner of the USA's largest newspaper chain, offered his own seven rules for Journalistic Truth. These included, "Be fair and impartial. Don't make a paper for Democrats or Republicans... make a paper for all the people and give unbiased news of all creeds and parties." Hearst, a reformed character, spelled out the need for responsible journalism to support democracy, saying it was the sacred duty of all journalists to tell,

"The truth, all the truth, and nothing but the truth as news. And it is its equal duty to print honest opinion as belief, and propaganda as dishonest opinion and distorted fact. Truth is the firm basis of democracy. Accurate information and complete information are a prime necessity for the citizens of a republic... Free discussion to establish the truth is the very life-sustaining blood stream of democracy."[33]

The journalist Willard Grosvenor Bleyer, writing in 1918, also stressed the need for impartial reporting driven by *aletheia*. Liberal democracy, he said, could only exist if citizens were able to hear both sides of the debate,

"In order to furnish the average citizen with material from which to form opinions on all current issues, so that he may vote intelligently on men and measures, newspapers must supply significant news in as complete and as accurate a form as possible. The only important limitations to completeness are those imposed by the commonly accepted ideas of decency embodied in the phrase, 'All the news that's fit to print,' and by the rights of privacy."[34]

Some were uneasy at the rapaciousness of press barons such as Hearst. Oswald Garrison Villard, Editor of the *New York Evening Post*, warned that newspaper moguls were buying up, and merging, hundreds of small, independent papers across the US. "We drift toward consolidation" he said, "on a resistless economic current, which foams past numberless rocks, and leads no man knows whither". The danger, he argued, was that diversity of opinion would be lost and monolithic news narratives would dominate. It was a peril, he said because, "democracy depends largely upon the presenting of both sides of every issue."[35]

Joseph Pulitzer, publisher of the *St. Louis Post-Dispatch* and the *New York World,* and a passionate supporter of Democrat politics, demanded his journalists should be "scrupulously accurate." "It is not enough to refrain from publishing fake news", he said, the entire staff of his newspapers must embrace the search for Journalistic Truth,

> "There is not a crime, there is not a dodge, there is not a trick, there is not a swindle, there is not a vice which does not live by secrecy. Get these things out in the open, describe them, attack them, ridicule them in the press, and sooner or later public opinion will sweep them away."[36]

John Cowles, editor of the *Minneapolis Star* and *Minneapolis Tribune*, pointed out the provisional nature of Journalistic Truth, admitting with epistemic humility, "we make lots of mistakes, and at times we perform our functions badly". Nonetheless, *aletheia* must always be pursued using the tried and tested methodology of Victorian Liberal Journalism,

> "The primary obligation of a newspaper is to give its readers the news, all the news, without bias or slant or distortion or suppression, in the news columns. We believe that only on our editorial pages should our own opinions be expressed... On our editorial pages we express our opinions and viewpoints as vigorously and persuasively as we know how, but there is a complete separation between our editorial pages and our news columns."[37]

Colonel Robert McCormick, publisher of the *Chicago Tribune*, agreed, stressing the importance of the classic distinction between fact and opinion,

"The emergence of news from opinion, from what an editor wishes somebody else to believe, to what is - this is the principal development of American journalism during the last half century. It is the duty and responsibility of a newspaper that the news shall be treated as news, and that news shall be printed according to its news value and not distorted."[38]

Arthur Hays Sulzberger, publisher of the *New York Times*, warned of the perils of Narrative-Led Journalism. Facts, he said, must come first, "whichever way the cat may jump", he wrote, "we should record it." Sulzberger agreed with his many peers that the strict separation of news and opinion was vital,

"We do not crusade in our news columns. We are anxious to see wrongs corrected, and we attempt to make our position very clear in such matters on our editorial page. But we believe that no matter how we view the world, our chief responsibility lies in reporting accurately that which happens."[39]

The journalist Roy W. Howard warned of grave danger if journalists tried to take epistemic responsibility away from audiences. "Intellectual dictatorship" he said, must be avoided. The proper function of journalism is to help readers, "think intelligently for themselves, instead of having their thinking done for them."

"Its function is to illuminate, not dictate. The public would be just as averse to seeing the country governed by its newspapers as it is to seeing it misgoverned by partisan political bosses... we draw the line against those people only, who, whether stupid or sinister, parroting the cliches of phony 'liberalism' seek to edge our nation towards statism and totalitarianism."[40]

Arthur Krock, a Pulitzer Prize winning journalist, described journalism as a contract which called for a single-mined devotion to Journalistic Truth, "This responsibility" he explained, "is best expressed when no outside or inside pressure is able to induce the suppression or omission of a line of legitimate news or opinion." Journalists, he said, must be guided only by the desire to tell the whole truth and be immune to the influence of any, "political, religious, or economic doctrine and personal prejudice". Hence a journalist was someone, "intent only on writing the news as objectively and factually as it is within the limitations of fallible humanity to do."[41]

Writing in 1920, the best-known observer of American journalism Walter Lippmann, expressed concern about the combination of misleading news and the "boundless credulity" and "downright lack of common sense" of readers who believed everything they read. These people were abandoning individual responsibility and delegating it to journalists. He criticized journalism that confirmed readers' prejudices and reported, "not what was, but what men wished to see."[42] Society, argued Lippmann, needed critical, skeptical readers and a "steady supply of trustworthy and relevant news". Without these he said, liberal democracy could not survive, "incompetence and aimlessness, corruption and disloyalty, panic and ultimate disaster, must come to any people which is denied an assured access to the facts."[43] As an experienced reporter, Lippmann acknowledged that balancing on the epistemic highwire was a tough act, "I have few illusions as to the difficulty of truthful reporting", he wrote. Nevertheless, "there can be no higher law in journalism than to tell the truth and shame the devil."[44]

Lippmann's warning was timely. Journalism, especially in Britain, was slipping from the high ideals of impartial, Victorian Liberal Journalism. Doing what those in positions of power and authority believed to be ethically and politically right, was trumping the public's right to know. A low point was the news blackout of Edward VIII's relationship with the twice-divorced American Wallace Simpson. Although the affair led to a constitutional crisis and to the King's abdication in 1936, the British public was kept ignorant of events which were being prominently reported in the US and Europe. It was a bizarre situation. As the historian George Young summarized,

"The voluntary discretion of the English papers concealed from the public a situation which the people of the United States were watching with excitement, France with amusement, and Canada with some anger and alarm."[45]

116

But worse was to follow. Over the next three years, the British media failed to impartially report the growing threat posed by Nazi Germany. Instead, most news outlets meekly adopted the UK government's policy of appeasement. The shared ethical-political goal was to avoid offending or provoking Germany. Stories that showed the Nazis in a negative light were downplayed or omitted altogether. Winston Churchill, a stern critic of Hitler, found himself effectively banned by the BBC because his opinions didn't fit the official narrative and because they might enflame public opinion. Although he made broadcasts on American radio, his warnings about Nazi aggression were not heard in the UK. As he later bitterly remarked, "For eleven years they kept me off the air. They prevented me from expressing views that proved to be right. Their behaviour has been tyrannical."[46]

The well-intentioned desire to do the right thing and avert war had promoted the interests of the Third Reich, hidden the truth from the public, and silenced those who argued the case for standing up to the Nazis. Inevitably, there was a bill to pay — confidence in journalism slumped. As the historian of journalism Tim Luckhurst observes, after their failure to tell the truth about the abdication crisis and Nazi Germany, "Britain's national newspapers entered the Second World War widely read but little trusted."[47]

Chapter 12

A Very Short Epistemic History of Journalism – Part Two

The Impact of World War Two on Journalism

The Second World War led Victorian Liberal Journalism into a second period of hibernation. The dominant goal in Britain and the US was winning the war, not telling the truth regardless of consequences. However, not everyone was comfortable that truth-telling had become subservient to propaganda. In 1941, Gerald Kersh, a best-selling British author asked, "What kind of silly men are they", who offend the intelligence and integrity of brave men and women, "with evasion and empty falsehood in the struggling grapevine of information about this war." Kersh argued that telling the truth, even in wartime, should remain a priority. Misleading the population with well-intentioned propaganda was counterproductive. Writing for the *Daily Herald* newspaper, one of his semi-fictional soldiers says gruffly, "I'll fight, but I'll not be lied to".[1]

George Orwell was also disturbed by the abrupt suspension of Journalistic Truth and its replacement by ethical-political expediency. In an essay written in 1943, he said propaganda was a form lying for the benefit of our side - good lying. But it was still lying, and therefore it was morally dangerous. The war, said Orwell, had released people from the moral duty to search for truth, and replaced it with the moral duty to believe official lies. It awakened a primitive epistemic tribalism,

> "Atrocities are believed in or disbelieved in solely on grounds of political predilection. Everyone believes in the atrocities of the enemy and disbelieves in those of his own side, without ever bothering to examine the evidence... The truth, it is felt, becomes untruth when your enemy utters it... This kind of thing is frightening to me, because it often gives me the feeling that the very concept of objective truth is fading out of the world."[2]

To Kersh and Orwell, the ability of human beings to recognize and value the concept of objective truth was a distinguishing feature of civilization. When the love of objectivity and impartiality are destroyed, Orwell said, all that remains is a brutal, Darwinian struggle between rival Tribal Truths,

> "It is just this common basis of agreement, with its implication that human beings are all one species of animal, that totalitarianism destroys... Nazi theory indeed specifically denies that such a thing as 'the truth' exists. There is, for instance, no such thing as 'science'. There is only 'German science', 'Jewish science' etc. The implied objective of this line of thought is a nightmare world."[3]

Hence, World War Two, was, amongst many other things, a fight to defend the right of individuals to search for objective truth. In epistemic terms, the war was a conflict between the Victorian Liberal way of knowing; and tribal, totalitarian truth. The War Generation witnessed how the Nazi way of knowing had helped transform millions of ordinary people into fanatics capable of the utmost inhumanity and cruelty. These epistemic issues fascinated Orwell who developed them further after the war in his famous anti-Utopian novel *1984.*

In 1945, the victorious allies charged many senior Nazis with crimes against humanity and put them on trial at Nuremberg. One of the most chilling remarks made during the trials was the Nazi leader Hermann Goering's assertion that any population could be persuaded to carry out, or turn a blind eye to, atrocities. All that was required, he said, was for the media to manipulate the information the public received in order to generate fear. After nudging them in the required direction, a primitive tribalism and the herd instinct would take over,

> "It is always a simple matter to drag the people along, whether it is a democracy, or a fascist dictatorship, or a parliament, or a communist dictatorship... All you have to do is tell them they are being attacked and denounce the peacemakers for lack of patriotism and exposing the country to danger. It works the same in any country."[4]

To those living in the liberal democracies, Goering's testimony was deeply unsettling. Was civilization really so fragile? Could it be swept away simply by rekindling mankind's primitive emotions, anxieties and hatreds? Was responsible, truth-telling journalism all that stood between Liberal Democracy and totalitarian government?

World War Two was quickly followed by the outbreak of the cold war. Anglo-American Liberal Democracy had vanquished the fascist dictatorships of Germany, Italy and Japan, it now stood face-to-face with another ideological foe, the communism of Stalin's USSR. For journalists of the War Generation, the epistemic highwire had never seemed so high, the consequences of falling, never so great. The post-war period saw renewed efforts to strengthen the four pillars of Journalistic Truth and encourage a return to *aletheia*. Orwell, writing in 1946, complained that the pursuit of Journalistic Truth was being hampered by the rise of "political speech". Ambiguous language permitted people to mislead without actually lying. The result was a hollow shell of words produced without the motive to be truthful,

"The great enemy of clear language is insincerity. When there is a gap between one's real and one's declared aims, one turns, as it were instinctively, to long words and exhausted idioms, like a cuttlefish squirting out ink. In our age there is no such thing as "keeping out of politics." All issues are political issues, and politics itself is a mass of lies, evasions, folly, hatred and schizophrenia."[5]

Britain's 1949 Royal Commission on the Press was also troubled that *aletheia* was a wounded animal. The report noted that responsible journalism was "vital to the future of democracy"[6] but warned journalists often abandoned their duty to pursue Journalistic Truth, "newspapers, with few exceptions, fail to supply the electorate with adequate materials for sound political judgements."[7] The report acknowledged that reporting facts accurately was difficult. Journalism was an imperfect art which had to contend with innumerable epistemic challenges,

"Facts which are not beyond dispute are often news… much of its information is obtained by one fallible human being from another… Not all news reports come from one person or from people in a position to know the truth."[8]

The report stressed the importance of impartiality and the dangers of Narrative-Led Journalism which could be factually accurate and yet misleading. The report said that by, "consistently selecting items of news which supported its own policy and omitting others" a news organization could produce in the minds of its audience, "an impression totally divorced from the truth. And it could do this while preserving the most meticulous accuracy in its statement of the facts reported."[9]

The Commission concluded that journalism's arrow was too often reversed and that partisan journalism was becoming commonplace. Instead of evidence-based narrative, there was a tendency towards narrative-based evidence in which the conclusion "derives from pre-determined party policy rather than from a balanced presentation of all available evidence." Facts were then included "to justify a position already arrived at."[10] Wartime propaganda had become a difficult habit to lose.

In the US, The 1947 Hutchins Commission, chaired by the philosopher Robert Hutchins, was also anxious about the standard of journalism and explored some of the underlying political issues. The report opened dramatically, "The Commission set out to answer the question: Is the freedom of the press in danger? Its answer to that question is: Yes."[11] Hutchins noted that responsible journalism had "always been in danger."[12] However it currently faced two threats: First there was the ever-present possibility that journalism would fall from the epistemic highwire and stop providing the Journalistic Truth on which democracy depended. Second, that citizens, greedy for something better, might fail to value democratic society altogether. Hutchins argued that the two threats were intimately related. New technologies, such as TV, were increasing journalist's power which was,

> "Increasing every day as new instruments become available to them. These instruments can spread lies faster and farther than our forefathers dreamed when they enshrined the freedom of the press in the First Amendment to our Constitution."[13]

Hutchins reminded journalists of their obligation to *aletheia* and the four pillars of Journalistic Truth. "The first requirement" he wrote, "is that the media should be accurate. They should not lie".[14] Impartiality, he said, was also essential. Presenting some facts, and suppressing others in the service of a pre-existing narrative must be resisted,

> "The account of an isolated fact, however accurate in itself, may be misleading and, in effect, untrue... It is no longer enough to report the fact truthfully. It is now necessary to report the truth about the fact."[15]

The Commission restated the need for the classic separation of fact and opinion, "Of equal importance with reportorial accuracy are the identification of fact as fact and opinion as opinion, and their separation, so far as possible."[16] Finally, it restated the Victorian Liberal assumption that human beings are fallible, and frequently deceitful. Human knowledge is therefore always unreliable. The path to Journalistic Truth was to encourage the competition of ideas and resist the temptation to censor dissenting voices, no matter how unpalatable they might be,

"Many a lying, venal, and scoundrelly public expression must continue to find shelter under a 'freedom of the press' built for widely different purposes, for to impair the legal right even when the moral right is gone may easily be a cure worse than the disease." [17]

Hutchins closed by reflecting on the second, more profound threat; that Journalistic Truth could only exist in a society that valued and wanted it. *Aletheia* was a necessary consequence of Liberal Democratic ideology. But being a responsible citizen and an independent, critical thinker was hard work. If citizens should ever grow weary of their responsibility, democratic ideology would wither and be replaced with something less effortful. If this happened, a different type of journalism would evolve to support it. Impartial, truthful journalism would no longer be useful. In other words, society gets the form of government, and the form of journalism, it deserves. As Hutchins put it,

"The freedom we have been examining has assumed a type of public mentality which may seem to us standard and universal, but which is, in many respects, a product of our special history... These mental conditions may be lost. They may also be created. The press itself is always one of the chief agents in destroying or in building the bases of its own significance."[18]

This profound insight, that journalism always evolves to support the dominant ideology of the age, and that this might change, was developed by the American media scholar Fred Siebert. In 1956 he wrote an influential book based on the assumption that,

"The press always takes on the form and coloration of the social and political structures within which it operates. Especially, it reflects the system of social control whereby the relations of individuals and institutions are adjusted."[19]

Siebert was pointing out that there is no eternal, unchanging thing called 'journalism'. There are a number of 'journalisms'. To understand them, one first has to understand the societies and ideologies they exist to serve. This involves understanding the philosophical, moral and political assumptions of the people who live in those societies. As Siebert put it,

"One has to look at certain basic beliefs and assumptions which the society holds: the nature of man, the nature of society and the state, the relation of man to the state, and the nature of knowledge and truth."[20]

Siebert identified four different journalisms which had evolved to meet the needs of different political ideologies. For example, he contrasted Victorian Liberal Journalism, which he labelled "socially responsible" journalism, with the "authoritarian" journalism of totalitarian regimes such as the USSR. Authoritarian regimes, he wrote, are those that assume responsibility for man's happiness. A feature of these states is the existence of a powerful oligarchy of, "'wise men' capable of analyzing and synthesizing". This elite group, reminiscent of Plato's philosopher kings, creates the official knowledge which,

"Becomes the standard for all members of society and acquires an absolutist aura which makes challenge undesirable and stability or continuity a virtue in itself. In addition, the authoritarian's theory demanded a unity of intellectual activity since only through unity could the state operate successfully for the good of all."[21]

In such states, the role of journalism is to maintain the official narratives and myths, and suppress undesirable, dangerous ones. For example, in the Soviet model, Siebert pointed out there was no such thing as journalism independent of the state. On the contrary, journalism was the state's public relations department, tasked with promoting Official Truth. This model, Siebert noted, was the very opposite of the Victorian Liberal ideal which existed to stir debate and enlighten the public, "so as to make it capable of self-government." Whereas, in the Soviet model,

"The media should be used as instruments to convey the 'word' as interpreted by the Kremlin. The media should be used as instruments of social change and social control... In other words, the Soviet media have grown so as to reflect the Soviet official ideology."[22]

In the Soviet model, the role of journalism was to communicate the official narrative and inform citizens what they ought to believe so they could be good citizens. Journalistic Truth was Official Truth.

124

Protecting Journalistic Truth;
Smith-Mundt and the Fairness Doctrine

The late 1940s and 1950s witnessed the dramatic growth in TV owner-ship in Western nations and the arrival of the "mass media" age. Journalism's power was becoming more concentrated. Instead of reading different accounts produced by independently owned national and local newspapers, Americans were increasingly likely to receive the same information from the same source at the same time. As the media historian Frank Mott put it, by the 1950s, "a large part of the population — as many as 60 or even 75 million on occasion — was exposed to a single item of communication at the same moment of time."[23] An awareness of the growing power of the media to influence and persuade, triggered moves to safeguard the public from the threat of misleading, or dishonest, journalism. In the US, Congress introduced legislation which it hoped would help journalists keep their precarious balance on the epistemic highwire.

One safeguard, introduced in 1948, was the Smith-Mundt Act. It was, in essence, a law to protect US citizens from state propaganda. While politicians realized the cold war required an energetic propaganda effort to combat that of the USSR, they were equally determined the federal government should not be allowed to pollute public discourse at home. The spirit of Smith-Mundt was therefore very much in the tradition of Victorian Liberal Democracy. It assumed citizens must be able to make rational decisions for themselves based on accurate information, and after listening to unrestricted, free debate. Citizens whose decisions were influenced by government propaganda could not truly be said to be free, nor could the society in which they lived be a Liberal Democracy. As the writer Terence Qualter explained in 1962, "In a dictatorship all propaganda is government propaganda; in a democracy there is great reluctance to allow the government to enter into the propaganda field at all."[24] The goal of protecting *aletheia* from *arete* was at the heart of the Smith-Mundt philosophy. Journalism should be as free as possible from the influence of government. As the political historian Matthew Armstrong notes, resolution HR 3342, which became the Smith-Mundt Act, stated its purpose was to "tell the truth",

"General Eisenhower, testifying twice in front of Congress, was emphatic on both the importance of HR 3342 and the importance of telling the truth. Truth was a central facet of the Act. Reports and testimony before and after the passage of HR 3342 stressed the importance of truth and noted the Act would provide the "urgent, forthright, and dynamic measures to disseminate truth.""[25]

Congress later strengthened Smith-Mundt to make the ban on domestic propaganda even more explicit. Senator Edward Zorinsky introduced an amendment to the act stating, "No funds authorized to be appropriated to the United States Information Agency shall be used to influence public opinion in the United States." Zorinsky told Congress his intention was to protect the public from a single, state-approved set of facts and opinions. "This distinguishes us" he said,

"From the Soviet Union where domestic propaganda is a principal government activity... The American taxpayer certainly does not need or want his tax dollars used to support U.S. Government propaganda directed at him or her. My amendment ensures that this will not occur."[26]

In 1949 another important piece of regulation was introduced to safeguard Victorian Liberal Journalism in the US. In a report entitled *Editorializing by Broadcast Licensees*, the Federal Communications Commission (FCC) considered the "proper resolution of the difficult and complex problems involved in the presentation of radio news and comment in a democracy."[27] The report restated the core principles of Victorian Liberal Journalism,

"It is axiomatic that one of the most vital questions of mass communication in a democracy is the development of an informed public opinion through the public dissemination of news and ideas."

The FCC went on to contrast the *positive* liberty of a broadcaster to broadcast one-sided news by excluding dissenting voices, with the *negative* liberty of the excluded voices to be heard. It was a sophisticated argument which the great Victorian liberal theorists would have recognized and applauded. The FCC was seeking to restrain the powerful and ensure that different shades of opinion were heard. The underlying goal was the creation of an informed citizenry able to think for themselves and participate in the effortful business of Liberal Democracy. Hence, the FCC wrote broadcasting,

> "Should not be used for the private interest, whims, or caprices of the particular persons who have been granted licenses, but in a manner which will serve the community generally and the various groups which make up the community."

The FCC required all TV and radio broadcasters in the US to devote a reasonable portion of airtime to the, "discussion and consideration of controversial issues of public importance" and to do so in a fair and balanced way by broadcasting, "varying and conflicting views held by responsible elements of the community." This demand, that US broadcasters should produce impartial journalism, became known as the Fairness Doctrine.

The 1950s - Twilight of Victorian Liberal Journalism

In 1954 the British government created its own version of the FCC, the Independent Television Authority (ITA), to regulate commercial TV. Partly inspired by the Fairness Doctrine, the 1954 Television Act directed the ITA to ensure that news on commercial TV was presented with "due accuracy and impartiality" and maintained "due impartiality as regards matters of political or industrial controversy". The ITA was also to ensure that commercial TV included, "no matter designed to serve the interests of any political party, except [for]... properly balanced discussions." This was the first time British journalists had been placed under a regulatory obligation to produce responsible, impartial journalism.*

In 1954 the BBC broadcast its first TV news bulletin. In the tradition of Victorian Liberal Journalism, it confined itself to strictly factual reporting and took elaborate precautions to eliminate anything that might be considered to be an opinion. For example, newsreaders did not appear

---

* The BBC remained self-regulating. It was not until 1996 that it became obliged, by Royal Charter, to treat, "controversial subjects with due accuracy and impartiality".

in-vision in case a particular look, or raised eyebrow, might suggest a personal opinion or feeling. As the BBC's first TV newsreader Richard Baker recalled, "In those early days, newsreaders were never seen because it was feared our facial expressions might not always look impartial".[28] At the same time however, powerful new forces were beginning to shake the epistemic highwire. An unforeseen consequence of the rapid spread of TV news was to push newspaper journalism away from the reporting of bare, unvarnished facts. If audiences could watch the news on TV, why would they buy a newspaper the following day to read an account of what they had already seen? Fearing obsolescence, print journalism began to seek alternative approaches. One tempting possibility was to explore the fuzzy boundary between fact and opinion. If broadcasters were obliged to be impartial, then partiality offered uninhabited territory into which the print media could expand.

Supplying more interpretation and explanation also proved popular with younger Boomer readers for whom simple narratives seemed vastly more appealing than the confusing complexity and cautiousness of Victorian Liberal Journalism. However, for journalists of the War Generation, mixing explanation with fact seemed dangerously like reversing journalism's arrow. It assumed that complex events could be explained and that journalists were qualified to provide the explanations. Kent Cooper, executive director of the Associated Press, wrote uneasily during the 1950s that journalists were beginning to feel torn by the need to report purely factual information and simultaneously satisfy the growing demand for explanation. Nothing, he said, should obstruct the public's "right to know" which included the right to know *why* things happen. Therefore, he said, news reports,

"Must tell how and why an event came about and what it means, in spite of the fact that this may lead away from safe ground - of purely factual reporting, of setting down the visible or quotable facts, of straight, police-blotter reporting – and into the potentially treacherous ground of interpretation. Yet the task must be undertaken. For there is a tremendous increase in the interpretive story."

However, he concluded journalists should not lean too far in the direction of explanation. Ultimately, he said, journalism's job was to help the audience reach its own conclusions, "with good morals in mind, it must leave deductions to the reader."[29]

Denis Weaver, writing a journalism textbook in 1961, also noticed journalism's explanatory turn which he attributed to the rise of TV journalism. Modern readers, he said, like their news presented "with something more than bare facts." Merely informing readers, he said, "leaves many readers unsatisfied, and it is precisely the explanatory detail they cannot always get on screen that they look for in print." Weaver observed that a new form of journalism was beginning to emerge which, "tells the reader not only what has occurred, but why. A new word, 'news feature', has been coined to describe this type of writing."[30] Weaver warned however, that excessive explanation was the enemy of, "the balance of truth which it is the proud tradition of journalism to preserve". He suggested readers should therefore buy several different papers, with different narratives, in the hope that Journalistic Truth would emerge from the process of comparing them, "one remedy the public has found for itself is to buy more than one paper."[31]

Oveta Culp Hobby, Editor of the *Houston Post* during the 1950s, expressed concern that the golden threads connecting Victorian Liberal Democracy to Victorian Liberal Journalism were starting to fray. Echoing Hutchins and Siebert, who feared that citizens might become bored with Liberal Democracy, she detected "warning signs of weakened fabric". The first symptom, she said, was, "we take freedom too much for granted. The fight for freedom is never won permanently." Hobby also detected a growing taste for Narrative-Led News,

"There was a time when every citizen was adjudged innocent of crime until legally proved guilty in court. This was a precedent we inherited from English common law. Today that precedent seems to be forgotten. When sensational charges are made by anyone against anyone - not by a grand jury, not by a district attorney, but sometimes by vacant-minded, hysterical or irresponsible people - the public instinct is often to accept charges as proof."[32]

Journalists, she said, were losing sight of the goal of truth-telling and beginning to climb down from the epistemic highwire. The nature of Journalistic Truth seemed to be changing. *Aletheia* was dangerously ill.

She called for journalists to take a professional oath, similar to the Hippocratic oath taken by doctors. They must all, she suggested, promise to,

> "Strive to write the truth with complete accuracy, with no expression of my own personal bias or opinion... I serve all men, rather than myself; that man's right to know, rather than the private furtherance of my own career, is, and must always be, the first goal of my endeavor."[33]

Summarizing the "explanatory turn" of the late 1950s and early 1960s, Mott noted that "debate on the question of 'interpretive' or 'objective' reporting had become common among newspapermen"[34] Adding that, in the view of older reporters, "interpreting might suggest too much freedom of comment, editorializing, 'slanting' of the news." But the views of older reporters were becoming less important. The winds of change had started to blow. In the following decades they would reach hurricane force.

Chapter 13

Pre-Boomer Journalism at the BBC

The BBC had a good war. It redeemed itself after its pre-war failures. Its broadcasts from London provided occupied Europe with an alternative to official, pro-Nazi narratives. For millions of people, the BBC was the voice of freedom, hope and resistance. It was also seen as a supplier of truthful journalism. In spite of the pressure of wartime conditions, and the need to propagandize, the BBC still managed to keep a grip on the values and methodology of Victorian Liberal Journalism. It separated fact from opinion and attempted, as best it could, to report news stories accurately and impartially. For the most part, the BBC succeeded in the difficult task of juggling the twin goals of supporting the war effort and supplying information which was journalistically true. As the French historian Aurélie Luneau puts it,

"During the occupation, the French turned to the BBC for their news. France was under the German boot but people knew the BBC would tell the truth even if the news was bad, and this countered German propaganda. With the BBC, people knew they were hearing the truth."[1]

The BBC emerged from the war with a shining reputation for truth-telling. Whereas American broadcasters were commercial entities that needed to pursue the goal of profit-making, the BBC could boast it pursued *aletheia* with an unrivalled devotion. As the historian of journalism Tim Luckhurst notes, "by the end of the war, colossal audiences often consisting of half the adult population listened to the main 9.00 pm radio news bulletin".[2] By 1945, the BBC had become, arguably, the most principled and truthful news organization in the world. Those who led it and gave it direction, its Director Generals, became highly respected for their views about Journalistic Truth, and how to pursue it. Between 1944 and 1977, there were four Director Generals. William Haley, Hugh Carleton Green and Charles Curran were the most significant. Their writings provide an important snapshot of Victorian Liberal Journalism in the hands of the War Generation, and its collision with the radically different epistemology of the Boomer generation.*

William Haley – the High-Water Mark of Victorian Liberal Journalism

William Haley was a professional journalist who left the BBC in 1952 to become editor of *The Times*. He set out his philosophy of journalism in three thoughtful essays published in 1954. Inspired by classic Victorian Liberal thinkers such as John Sturat Mill, James Fitzjames Stephen, John Morley and Frederic Harrison, Haley sought to apply the four pillars of Victorian Liberal journalism to the TV age. Haley was clear about the historical origins of truthful journalism, "like so many other good things in our modern life it is the product of the Victorian Age."[3] Everything,

---

*   Ian Jacob was Director General between 1952-1959. A former army General, he was a strong believer in Victorian Liberal Journalism and the need to prioritize truth-telling. When asked by the government to censor opinions critical of the Suez invasion of 1956, he replied, "If the BBC is found for the first time to be suppressing significant items of news its reputation would rapidly vanish, and the harm to the national interest done in that event would enormously outweigh any damage caused by displaying to the world the workings of a free democracy." However, Jacob did not write in detail about Journalistic Truth and so is omitted from this chapter.

he said, must begin with the honest desire to seek and communicate Journalistic Truth. The guiding principle of the BBC must be *aletheia*, "the need endlessly to search for truth". Hence the prime duty of the BBC "should come in essence to one thing. Broadcasting should play its part in bringing about the reign of Truth." All other considerations, said Haley, such as entertaining audiences, instructing them, or improving their morals, must remain secondary. The hunt for truth, he wrote, should be "the living Law". Journalists should

> "Hold fast to it, work under it, test all their conduct by it, and know no other master. For if only we will give undivided allegiance to the True and the Beautiful, the third partner, the Good, will eventually come into its own."[4]

Haley explained that journalists must think of their audience as rational individuals, not as a herd to be led. These individuals were responsible members of a participative democracy and should be exposed to a multitude of competing opinions. It was not for journalists to oversimplify or explain, doing so would be manipulative. As Haley explained in his 1948 lecture, *The Responsibilities of Broadcasting*, "The essence of Democracy is that issues shall be decided by the people after they have heard all sides."[5] It followed that journalists must resist the temptation to censor; the role of news was not to tell people what to think, but to serve thought, "so that people shall think for themselves."[6] Consequently, the BBC should,

> "Pour through the world hour by hour, day by day, and year by year an unending, undeviating, irrigating flow of truthful news given as objectively and as impartially as British professional men and women could make it."[7]

Since the world was volatile, uncertain, complex and ambiguous; one of the greatest perils to *aletheia* was the journalist who arrogantly believed he possessed certain knowledge. This dangerous delusion would encourage him to be intolerant of information which contradicted his own beliefs. Hubris would cause him to lose his balance and fall from the epistemic highwire into an abyss of self-righteous certitude and self-censorship. Haley warned his journalists, "suppression of information or opinion is a cancerous growth." In order to stay on the highwire,

"Freedom in Broadcasting must be maintained to the uttermost limits within the climate of public opinion. Broadcasters should be vigilant and vigorous in resisting any attempts at encroachment upon that freedom from without. They must be equally vigilant and vigorous at resisting encroachments from within."[8]

In summary, Journalistic Truth was not something possessed by journalists which could be neatly packaged and delivered to an ignorant and grateful public. Journalism's deeper purpose was to teach the truth about truth; that it was always just out of reach and could only be approached with considerable, ceaseless effort. Journalism's higher task was therefore to, "show that the search for truth is endless, and an end in itself." Haley's eloquently-stated views were, in short, an impeccable restatement of the epistemology of Victorian Liberal Journalism.

Hugh Carleton Greene – Tolerating Intolerance

Hugh Carleton Greene, who was Director General between 1960 and 1969, was also a professional journalist. Greene reported from Berlin during the 1930s and spent much of the war in charge of British propaganda broadcasts to Germany. After the war he supervised British, anti-communist propaganda during the conflict in Malaya. His view of journalism was therefore uniquely flavored by his training in psychological warfare. For example, he distinguished between 'black' propaganda — information deliberately designed to mislead in the short-term, and 'white' propaganda — designed to persuade and influence over the long-term. Black propaganda he described as little more than lying, cheating and forging. Producing it could be exhilarating. The joy of lying, he wrote, "appeals to the small boy's heart… what fun."[9] In the long-term however, audiences would realize they were being lied to, and 'black' propaganda would be revealed as dishonest, fraudulent fake news. The key to successful 'white' propaganda was, paradoxically, telling the truth. Greene said that British propaganda during the Second World War aimed to,

"Tell the truth and tell it consistently and frankly. This involved a determination never to play down a disaster. It would for instance, be tempting from time to time within the limits of one news bulletin to give more prominence to a minor success than to a major defeat. This was a temptation to be avoided."[10]

Greene wrote that it was important to recruit skilful, talented propagandists to do the job well, and he discovered "journalists and university dons turned out to be the best". It was under Greene's reign that young Boomer journalists and producers first began to arrive at the BBC. The new recruits brought with them an intolerance of the ideology of Victorian Liberalism and began to attack it. For example, in 1962 the BBC introduced the satirical current affairs show *That Was The Week That Was*, or *TW3* for short. *TW3* was rebellious and irreverent. Produced and presented largely by Boomers, it caught the mood of the time and was extremely popular. But it was incompatible with the old virtues of *aletheia* and journalistic impartiality. It did not seek Journalistic Truth, nor did it aspire to give both sides a fair hearing. On the contrary, it heaped mockery and ridicule on those with pre-Boomer values. The cultural critic Christopher Booker described *TW3* as a mass of, "personal abuse and bitter attacks on every kind of authority", adding that much of it was immature, "amateurish", "juvenile and stereotyped in attitude."[11] When, in 1963, Prime Minister Harold Macmillan was succeeded by Sir Alec Douglas-Home, Booker says *TW3* marked the event "with an attack of such savage contempt that for the first time the Director General himself actually ordered cuts before the programme went on the air."[12] According to Booker, *TW3* marked the BBC's "final breach" with Victorian Liberal ideology.

Responding to the winds of change, Greene cautiously started to allow the mixing of fact and opinion. He did this by encouraging a closer working relationship between the News Department – which dealt strictly with matters of fact; and the Current Affairs Department – whose currency was analysis. "In those days" Greene recalled, referring to the early 1960s,

"News was news and current affairs were current affairs and never the twain should meet. They had been living in water-tight compartments for many years in an atmosphere of mutual distrust and even contempt. My job as I saw it was to weld together the news and current affairs elements in radio and television

135

so that they could carry out their respective functions against a background of shared policy and journalistic assumptions."[13]

Greene's reforms were disturbing to those schooled in the tradition of Victorian Liberal Journalism. Greene said he was reacting to demand for more explanation and opinion which he described as, "The new facts of life in the Sixties". However, to traditionalists, he was beginning to saw through the four pillars of Journalistic Truth. Greene replied that, according to the traditionalists, the BBC would have to be, "completely impartial and not risk saying or reporting anything that might affect the way in which any member of the public exercised his vote."[14] However, he felt there was room for compromise, and that "responsible and impartial" journalism could be achieved without slavish, uncritical adherence to the Victorian methodology. But this was not a view shared by many long-serving journalists. Greene notes, "By the early 1960s many of the old hands in the BBC who thought we were going too fast and too far were leaving. A new younger generation was in control."[15] However, Greene was exaggerating. The Boomer generation was exerting a powerful influence, but it was not in control of journalism at the BBC. It would not be until the 1980s that Boomer journalists would rise to positions of power and authority.

Greene's relationship with the Boomers was like that of an indulgent, but wise father. He encouraged novelty and new ideas and defended the Boomers when they offended traditionalists. However, Greene did not tolerate the Boomer Ideology because he agreed with it; he tolerated it because he believed it was his duty to be tolerant. As an advocate of Victorian Liberalism, Greene saw the Boomer Ideology as a legitimate point of view which should not censored. However, he ensured it was kept under control and properly managed. Under Greene, Boomer ideas were subject to discipline and only allowed to go so far. Senior editorial figures, such as Grace Wyndham Goldie, who was Head of BBC News and Current Affairs, were tasked with "stimulating creative innovation by her producers", while at the same time, "maintaining an iron control over the editorial concepts which were deployed."[16]

Greene believed that Victorian Liberalism implied a commitment to wide debate and that uncomfortable views should not be suppressed. Therefore, he rejected the arguments of conservatives who viewed the Boomer Ideology as nihilistic and dangerously anti-democratic. In a 1965 speech to the International Catholic Association for Radio and Television, he explained his philosophy of tolerance. The objective, he said, was not the "conversion" of the audience to a particular point of view, nor the "scoring of victories", but rather the "breaking down of barriers" so that each side might emerge "with a deeper knowledge of the other."[17] Central to this objective was freedom of speech. Hence it was essential to open up TV and radio to, "the widest possible range of subjects and to the best exponents available of the differing views on any given subject, to let the debate decide, or not decide, as the case may be".[18] It was not, he argued, for journalists to preach the truth, because the truth was unknowable. Instead it was the duty of journalists to examine all points of view impartially with a "healthy scepticism." Above all he wanted journalism to resist censorship in all its forms. This included any social, political or moral pressure which encouraged journalists to limit their enquiries or self-censor,

> "I believe that broadcasters have a duty not to be diverted by arguments in favour of what is, in fact, disguised censorship. I believe we have a duty to take account of the changes in society, to be ahead of public opinion rather than always to wait upon it."[19]

In a 1968 lecture, Greene said his experience as a journalist in Nazi Germany caused him to, "hate intolerance and the degradation of character to which the deprivation of freedom leads." It was blind conformity which offended Greene – slavish tribal loyalty which would attack "whatever does not underwrite a set of prior assumptions, assumptions which are anti-intellectual and unimaginative".[20] This is what he had witnessed in Germany where journalism had become corrupted and turned into an "instrument of totalitarian dictatorship."[21] I have, he said, "always remained, incorrigibly, a journalist." To the end his values remained those of Victorian Liberal Journalism, "the highest standards of truth, accuracy and impartiality."[22]

Charles Curran – Holding Back the Tide

Charles Curran inherited a very different BBC when he took over in 1970. His urgent task was not to gently indulge the Boomers and their new ideas, but to try to steady the journalistic ship and prevent it from sinking under the weight of the Boomer Ideology. Curran, who had served as an infantry officer during the war, launched a counter-offensive and attempted to reintroduce some of the restraints of Victorian Liberal Journalism. As *The Guardian* later summarized, Curran was a "steadying force, after the whirlwind of Greene".[23] Curran explained his push-back against the Boomer Ideology in his 1979 book *A Seamless Robe*. In it he restated the foundational purpose of Victorian Liberal Journalism. It was, he said, designed to make possible Liberal Democracy. Therefore, the BBC had one supreme bias. It was,

> "Biased in favour of parliamentary democracy. That form of democracy depends on there being a plurality of opinions, on the freedom of their expression, on their public dissemination, and on the resolution, in circumstances of tolerance, of the differences of view which will then arise."[24]

From this premise, everything else followed. For example, the classic distinction between fact and opinion was essential to aid clear, critical thinking and prevent the return of pre-democratic Narrative-Led News. Journalism's arrow must not be reversed. "The news programmes" Curran said, "are intended to provide the participants in the British democracy with the material which forms the ground of the variety of their opinions." Once people were aware of the facts, then it would be possible for them to debate their significance. The programmes of opinion, he continued, "are intended to provide an opportunity for democracy to express itself in public argument." Curran accepted that in practice, fact and opinion were often entangled. Nonetheless, journalists must always work hard to try to separate them,

> "Information is not some kind of pure gold which can readily be identified and separated from the dross of opinion. Beyond a very simple level, every piece of information incorporates an attitude of mind. But I believe it is possible to present information and opinion in a way which will generally be recognized as fair."[25]

In other words, the job of the BBC was to run an informational supermarket and fill its shelves with a wide choice of fact and opinion. It should not only offer customers a single brand. Journalists must not fall into the epistemic trap of believing they knew the truth and believing it was their job is to enlighten those who did not. That would be to confuse the function of a journalist with that of a priest. Curran explained the role of the journalist was not to,

> "Preach a particular form of conduct. They do not see it as their job to adopt a particular morality as their own and then to use the broadcasting medium in order to persuade everybody else to follow that morality."[26]

Curran restated the Victorian Liberal view that citizens must take responsibility for their own beliefs and not delegate responsibility for knowing to elite experts. Journalism's role was to help individuals think for themselves and avoid groupthink,

> "It is emphatically not the broadcasters' job to persuade their audiences about the truth of particular propositions which may be put forward by one interest or another - including by one party or another. But it is their duty, for the sake of the successful government of society, to persuade their audiences to feel themselves involved in the issues which have to debated."[27]

Above all, journalists must not confuse reporting what *is* with what *ought* to be, "The BBC's position is one of quasi-judicial impartiality... the BBC's programme philosophy seeks to display what the world is like, and to present what might be."[28]

Curran was deeply alarmed by the rising tide of Boomer intolerance. The fashion for activism and the zeal of the Boomers to make the world a better place, were, he thought, reminiscent of the burning of heretics of the pre-Enlightenment era. He responded by stressing it was the duty of broadcasters to place as many different points of view as possible before the public. This implied a high degree of tolerance, even for uncomfortable views that some people might find offensive. One person's right to avoid being offended, Curran said, should not outweigh another's right to be heard. Curran also attacked those who cynically claimed to be offended in order to silence their opponents. This, he said, was intolerance masquerading as sensitivity,

"Those who may switch on a programme in order to experience the sensation of not enjoying it, or of being offended by it. That seems to be a misuse of the rational faculty of choice."[29]

He added pointedly, "The darkness of intolerance begins to close in when the torch-carriers begin to want to burn the sinners, instead of to forgive them."[30] Curran concluded his book on an ambiguous note. He was convinced, he said, that the tree of Victorian Liberal Democracy was so strongly rooted, it was unlikely to ever fall. Victorian Liberal Journalism was, he believed, here to stay,

> "The long argument about the proper role of news and current affairs broadcasting will never be decisively concluded. But it seems to me, in 1978, that the broad principles - editorial freedom, impartiality in its exercise, and balance in the presentation of views - are now solid assumptions which will not again be challenged, so long as Britain continues to be a living parliamentary democracy."[31]

However, Curran's optimism contained a vital qualification. *Aletheia* – the goal of hunting for Journalistic Truth – is only desirable if the overriding objective is the creation of independent thinkers to participate in the business of Liberal Democracy. But what would happen if people wanted something 'better', or easier, than Liberal Democracy? For example, what would happen if a new generation preferred an illiberal democracy to a liberal one? In that case, the whole justification for Victorian Liberal Journalism would collapse. Impartial journalism would serve no useful purpose and become obsolete. If that should happen, a new type of journalism would be needed to serve the needs of the new system.

Chapter 14

The Tipping Point. Boomers with Votes, "Worse than Barbarism"

In 1968 a wave of violence exploded across the Western world as the Boomer generation took to the streets to overthrow Victorian Liberal Democracy and create a new world-order. In Washington, London, Paris and many other cities, the Boomers rioted and turned their full fury on the social structures they felt restrained them and barred their path to Boomertopia and political power. As Tariq Ali and Susan Watkins explain, 1968 was the year the Boomers attempted to, "change the human condition for ever. It was a year of hope... 1968 was an attempt to create a new world, a new starting point for politics, for culture, for personal relations."[1]

History has been kind to the orgy of violence unleashed by the Boomers in 1968. Innumerable books and TV documentaries, all of them written and produced by Boomers, have mythologized events and created a narrative according to which the heroic Boomer tribe rose up to destroy the forces of darkness and oppression to create a better world. However, as the lens of history slowly rotates, and as the Boomers begin to fade from the landscape, a less romantic and more realistic picture starts to come into focus. Psychologists describe a tantrum as an immature outburst of unrestrained screaming, defiance, and resistance to all reasonable attempts at pacification. A tantrum is therefore a cluster of aggressive behaviors including the display of anger, the use of violence and the destruction of property to get what one wants.[2] The violence of 1968 was a generational tantrum. The Boomer tribe, suddenly aware of its collective strength and power, violently lashed out at the restraints of Victorian Liberalism. The feeling of generational self-righteousness and tribal power were intoxicating and exhilarating. One rioter, Barbara Brick, recalled, "There was a readiness for violence which came from an enormous anger, a rage… Yes, emotionally, we were out for war now, civil war."[3] Mike Wallace, who took part in the occupation of Columbia University in April 1968, described it as an intensely tribal experience,

"I was in the midst of an enormous tide of people. There was so much constant collective reaffirmation of it. The ecstasy was stepping out of time… The usual rules of the game in capitalist society had been set aside. It was phenomenally liberating."[4]

Another rioter, Elsa Gili, says that the aim was to sweep away the world of their parents and create a new society based on Boomer desires and values,

"We had the idea that the social revolution had to start from daily life. Start from even the smallest unbearable aspects of daily life, like the wearing a tie or make-up… start to take things back into our hands, reappropriate what had been expropriated from us. The revolution must be a festival."[5]

As the historian Ronald Fraser summarizes, the violence of 1968 can be traced to the collective feeling that the ideology of Victorian Liberalism was out of sync with,

"The rising expectations seemingly afforded by rapid economic growth; and to the increasing awareness on the part of a new generation, conscious for the first time of its weight in society, that these structures were blocking its development."[6]

1968 was the year of the smashing of the old restraints, duties and responsibilities. It was a volcanic expression of the Vortex of Immaturity and the belief in Boomer Exceptionalism. It was the collective conviction that, if the existing order was destroyed, something better would spontaneously appear. It was an attempt to force open the gates of Boomertopia — a place where the Boomers would be free to pursue the instant gratification of their desires and find fulfilment and satisfaction. In 1968 it was impossible to disentangle political motives from personal, hedonistic ones. Popular Boomer slogans included; "Take your desires for reality", "Never work" and "The more I make revolution, the more I want to make love". Rioting in France was sparked by the demand by male students to spend the night in female dormitories at the Nanterre campus of the University of Paris. The French journalist Christian Charrière, wrote that at Nanterre there was "no life without love". He described the campus as a pressure cooker of adolescent hormones and desire, "fifteen thousand jutting breasts, ready for wicked love-making."[7]

In the US, it was also impossible to separate the motive of sexual gratification from the desire to destroy the existing world order and create a new one. The Weathermen, a group made up of Boomer extremists, explained their philosophy as, "people who fuck together fight together."[8] The Weathermen planted bombs, carried out armed robberies and held orgies to stop the war in Vietnam and undermine Liberal Democracy. The orgies were intended as revolutionary acts and referred to as the 'Smash Monogamy program'. One member recalled,

"I took the hand of this girl and exchanged a few pleasantries to give it a slightly personal quality, and then we fucked. And there were people fucking and thrashing around all over. They'd sort of roll over on you, and sometimes you found yourself spread over more than one person. The room was like some modern sculpture. There'd be all these humps in a row. You'd see a knee and then buttocks and then three knees and four buttocks. They were all moving up and down, rolling around... one woman piped up, 'I'm sure they have to do it this way in Vietnam.'"[9]

In 1968, unrestrained violence and rage seemed to offer a path to Utopia. It would be a blissful life free from toil and responsibility in which unfairness and unhappiness were banished forever. As the historian Michael Seidman notes,

"Even apolitical young people from various social classes could agree that the new consumption was considerably more amusing than working. A hedonistic generation seemed to resist labor and the responsibilities of the adult world."[10]

Boomer violence sputtered on for several years. In August 1970, four radical Boomers detonated two thousand pounds of explosives at Wisconsin University. A postdoctoral researcher was killed and three others injured. The bombers said they were protesting the Vietnam War and the draft. Henry Loeser was a freshman at Wisconsin and recalls the mood was dominated by the opposition of young men to the draft, "We wanted to end the Vietnam war, and one of the reasons was, I didn't want to go over there and die. I had a personal as well as a political interest." Loeser took part in numerous anti-war demonstrations and recalls an overwhelming feeling of loyalty, passion and commitment to the Boomer tribe. Being impartial, or being prepared to listen to the other side of the argument, was not acceptable,

"I got clubbed by police, tear-gassed and jailed. Remember, I was a 17-year-old freshman at college. People got hurt. Our whole aim was to push people off the fence. Either you're for the war or you're against the war. You can't be sitting on the fence anymore. That was the philosophy."[11]

Although never violent himself, Loeser says there was a lot of sympathy for those who were, because their motives were ethically-politically good, "We wanted to tear it down," says Loeser, "We wanted to critically change things for the better. It's like renovating a house. You've got to have demolition first. You've got to get the rot out".

In May 1970, violent protest turned to tragedy at Kent State University in Ohio when the National Guard was called-out to stop protestors throwing rocks and setting fire to buildings. In the ensuing clashes, four students were shot dead and nine wounded. Nor was Boomer violence confined to the US. In Germany, the Baader-Meinhof gang carried out bombings, shootings and kidnappings in an attempt to destroy Liberal Democracy and bring about a new world order. In the UK, the Angry Brigade carried out 25 bombings between 1970 and 1971. Described by the press as, "dissolute middle-class revolutionaries plotting to undermine civilized values", they said violence was justified to bring about radical social change. As one member explained, "What we were doing was a new form of politics."[12]

The journalist Bryan Burrough chronicled the bombings, robberies and murders carried out by Boomer radicals across the US to help make the world a better place. During the early 1970s, he says it reached epidemic proportions,

> "'People have completely forgotten that in 1972 we had over nineteen hundred domestic bombings in the United States,' notes a retired FBI agent, Max Noel. 'People don't want to listen to that. They can't believe it... It was every day. Buildings getting bombed, policemen getting killed. It was commonplace.'"[13]

Boomers who hoped to witness the creation of Utopia after the violent tantrum of 1968, were disappointed. As Seidman writes, 1968 was "ineffective politically" — it produced no immediate, dramatic, transformation of society. However, despite this, there was a widespread feeling that 1968 represented the "beginning of a new value system". Indeed, after 1968, things would never be the same again. Shaken by the specter of an entire generation in revolt, the War Generation shifted towards a policy of appeasing their wild and violent children. The real message of 1968 was therefore that the price of defending Victorian Liberalism from the Boomer Ideology was no longer one the War Generation was prepared to pay. Even the hardline French President Charles De Gaulle was forced to admit that, after 1968, he had become "more open to reforms."[14]

The most important change that followed the Boomer violence of 1968 was the decision by the War Generation to lower the voting age from twenty-one to eighteen. In 1969 in Britain, and in 1971 in the US, young Boomers were given the vote. France followed suit in 1974. It is hard to overstate the importance of the enfranchisement of adolescent Boomers. Its significance was not due to the fact that adolescents suddenly began to vote in large numbers, indeed the majority of Boomers seemed bored by the prospect of voting and didn't bother to do so. The significance lies in the fact that politicians were now aware that Boomers *could* vote if they wanted to. Henceforth, the Boomer Ideology had to be reckoned with and taken into account by policy makers. In all areas of public life; political, economic, educational, intellectual and cultural, Boomer sensitivities, aspirations and desires would have to be appeased. Problems would have to be solved with solutions that would appeal to the Boomer Generation. The Boomer Ideology, like a boulder being pushed up a hill, reached the top in 1968. Now it began to roll down the other side with a momentum of its own. After 1968, the power of the Boomer Ideology would prove irresistible, relentless and unstoppable.

Worse than Barbarism

The fact that society now had to reckon with millions of immature voters with a strong tribal identity, had a profound impact on the nature of democracy itself. Democracy, like journalism, is not one unchanging, eternal thing. There are different types of democracy. Victorian Liberal Democracy assumed voters would be mature, independent thinkers. Voting was considered a privilege which carried with it responsibilities, not just rights. In Britain, as successive reforms gradually widened the franchise during the 19th Century, there was considerable unease that democracy would be devoured by large numbers of irresponsible voters. The historian Robert Saunders describes this as the "Liberal Dilemma". It was the fear that a mass of ignorant, uneducated people would use the democratic process to vote for their own, short-term, selfish interests. This would sweep away the delicate structure of Victorian Liberalism leaving in its place the tyranny of the majority; mob rule in the form of an intolerant, totalitarian ochlocracy.* It would be democracy, but not

---

* The political scientist Jasmin Hasanović describes ochlocracy as

146

Liberal Democracy. Conscious of this danger, Sir Thomas Hare, the Victorian political scientist, described voting as a "great social duty" for which each individual was personally responsible,

> "The opening to every elector of the power of performing his electoral duty is the first and prime necessity, in order to re-establish the sense of personal responsibility, or the empire of conscience, in electoral action."[15]

Hare added that, before the franchise was widened, it was essential to create a culture in which voters appreciated they were being asked to perform a solemn duty. Any extension of voting, he said,

> "Should be preceded by such an electoral system as will make every man feel that the suffrage is a solemn duty to be prepared for in the quiet of his chamber, and not with drinking and clamor of a tavern, or amidst the shoutings of a mob."[16]

Victorian Liberals agonized over how the mass of people could be encouraged to engage with complex political and economic issues, take part in civilized debate, and reach wise conclusions, if they had neither the time nor ability to research or understand them. Full democracy therefore seemed a hopelessly unrealistic, self-destructive ideal. Lack of education seemed to be at the heart of the problem. As Saunders summarizes, "few denied the existence of a huge stratum of coarse, reckless and ignorant individuals, whose knowledge of politics was painfully inadequate."[17]

If lack of education was the problem, then more education had to be the solution. Thomas Jefferson explained this philosophy neatly in a letter written in 1820,

> "I know no safe depository of the ultimate powers of the society, but the people themselves: and if we think them not enlightened enough to exercise their control with a wholesome discretion, the

fake democracy, "the rule of the general populace is democracy as the rule of the people spoiled by demagoguery, tyranny of the majority, and the rule of passion over reason. Ochlocracy is therefore a type of tyranny, held by crypto-practices, corruption, mediocrities etc" Hasanović, Jasmin. (2015). Ochlocracy in the practices of civil society: a threat for democracy? *Studia Juridica et Politica Jaurinensis.* 2. 56-66.

remedy is, not to take it from them, but to inform their discretion by education."[18]

John Stuart Mill, writing forty years later, defined a responsible voter as an educated adult. He wanted to see, "People universally educated, and every grown-up human being possessed of a vote."[19] However, Mill made it clear that democracy was not for the immature,

> "It is, perhaps, hardly necessary to say... that this doctrine is meant to apply only to human beings in the maturity of their faculties. We are not speaking of children, or of young persons below the age which the law may fix as that of manhood or womanhood."[20]

This guiding principal was thought of as simple common sense and barely worth discussing. James Fitzjames Stephen, who did discuss it, said, with characteristic bluntness, that treating adolescents as the equals of adults, for example by allowing them to vote, would lead to, "something infinitely worse than barbarism", something "So utterly monstrous and irrational that I suppose it never entered into the head of the wildest zealot for equality to propose it."[21]

American statesmen, with a longer experience of popular democracy, had grappled with the same problem eighty years earlier. Jefferson frequently argued that democracy would be impossible without an informed electorate. It was essential he said,

> "To illuminate, as far as practicable, the minds of the people at large, and more especially to give them knowledge of those facts which history exhibits, that possessed thereby of the experience of other ages and countries, they may be enabled to know ambition under all its shapes, and prompt to exert their natural powers to defeat its purposes."[22]

Victorian Liberal Democracy therefore required individual epistemic responsibility — the desire of voters to educate themselves and spend time and effort seeking the truth. Epistemic laziness and democracy were incompatible. As Jefferson famously put it, "if a nation expects to be ignorant and free in a state of civilization, it expects what never was and never will be."[23] The alternatives to Victorian Liberal Democracy were the different shades of oligarchy, feudalism and autocratic rule that had preceded it. It was, ultimately a choice therefore between freedom and enslavement. As Benjamin Franklin summarized in 1773, "if you make yourself a Sheep, the Wolves will eat you."[24]

Because it was seen as essential to Liberal Democracy, public education advanced in tandem with the widening franchise. For example, in the UK, Forster's Education Act of 1870 encouraged elementary education for all children aged between 5 and 12, while the subsequent Mundella Act of 1880 made it compulsory. In the US, Massachusetts became the first state to introduce compulsory schooling in 1852, while Mississippi was the last in 1918. If public education was one of the supporting legs of democracy, journalism was the other. The British historian Thomas Carlyle famously said that Victorian Liberal Journalism had become so indispensable to Victorian Liberal Democracy, it was its 'Fourth Estate' — a means by which voters could discuss the issues of the day and share information and opinion,

> "Does not, though the name Parliament subsists, the parliamen-
> tary debate go on now, everywhere and at all times, in a far more
> comprehensive way, out of Parliament altogether? Burke said
> there were Three Estates in Parliament; but, in the Reporters'
> Gallery yonder, there sat a Fourth Estate more important by far
> than they all. It is not a figure of speech, or a witty saying; it is a
> literal fact, — very momentous to us in these times."[25]

Journalism he continued, "is equivalent to Democracy: invent Writing, Democracy is inevitable... whoever can speak, speaking now to the whole nation, becomes a power". Moreover, said Carlyle, it was rapidly becoming the single most important element of democracy, "How the Press is to such a degree superseding the Pulpit, the Senate, the Senatus Academicus and much else, has been admitted for a good while; and recognized often enough."[26]

Carlyle's 'Fourth Estate' became the classic way of describing the relationship between Victorian Liberal Democracy and Victorian Liberal Journalism. Together they would create and maintain a self-governing community of free individuals with the minimum of state control. In

Abraham Lincoln's famous phrase, it would be "government of the people, by the people, for the people."

The Dawning of the Age of the Boomers

The proposal to lower the voting age to eighteen to appease the Boomers was greeted with horror by traditionalists. It appeared to make a mockery of the concept of Victorian Liberal Democracy. In Britain John Collins, a Labour politician, believed the world had gone mad,

> "An odd type of national madness seems to have swept over the country with regard to this question of youth. One hears from every quarter the cry, 'Youth, youth! We must have more young people, young ideas. The young people are the people to do it', and so forth. I am not denying that youth has many excellent qualities, but it does not have them all… it does lack very much other qualities, such as experience, wisdom from having lived in the world for some time and seen how it works, and various other qualities of that sort."[27]

Speaking against the proposal in the House of Lords, Collins argued that it was a grave mistake to enfranchise immature minds. What was at stake, he said, was Liberal Democracy itself,

> "Voting is a very serious matter. It is not just a game… If democratic election, which we all pride ourselves on as one of our great traditions, is to mean anything at all, we must first make certain that the electors know something of what they are voting about, and this knowledge can be gained only by living in the world for a certain number of years and seeing what the problems are; seeing both sides, both pro and con."[28]

In the US, House Judiciary chairman Emanuel Cellar, a New York Democrat, made the same point, saying teenagers were "easily enflamed" and usually saw things "in patterns of black and white without shadings." Because of the tempestuousness inherent in young people, Cellar asserted, "there are sound psychological reasons why the age of twenty-one has been considered the beginning of maturity."[29] Cellar had argued since the 1940s that eighteen-year-olds were unable to evaluate intricate questions of economics and government and should not be allowed to vote. In 1954, he had attacked such proposals as dangerously naïve, pointing out it was, "significant that Hitler and Mussolini lowered the voting age to help create their dictatorships."[30] When confronted with the argument that those who were old enough to serve in the military must be old enough to vote, he replied,

> "Voting is as different from fighting as chalk is from cheese… Young men under twenty-one are more pliable and more amenable to indoctrination. Instant and unquestioning obedience may be most desirable from soldiers in the battlefield, but in a voter such obedience would be most undesirable. Self-interested groups and corrupt politicians would find such obedience a fertile playground."[31]

But Collins and Cellar were voices shouting against the wind, drowned out by the noise and fury of 1968. What resonated now were the Boomer-friendly thoughts of writers like Charles Reich. According to Reich, transferring political, economic and cultural power to the Boomers would create a new world order based on the, "liberation of each individual in which he is enabled to grow towards the highest possibilities of the human spirit."[32] This "satisfying and beautiful" vision of the future, was he said invisible to non-Boomers. According to Reich, it could be "comprehended only by seeing contemporary America through the eyes of a new generation." The more non-Boomers objected, the more they demonstrated their inability to understand.

The first visible sign that a new ideology was guiding public policy came just five months after Congress gave the Boomers the vote. In August 1971, President Nixon told the American people, "The time has come for a new economic policy." He went on to announce the abandonment of the gold standard and the end of the Bretton Woods Agreement – an event known to history as the 'Nixon Shock'. The gold standard had been a creation of the Victorian Liberal world order. It was widely adopted by nations during the second half of the 19th Century. First and foremost, the gold standard was a symbol of restraint. It signified, in the words of the American economist, Hugh Rockoff,

"Evidence of financial probity — like the 'good housekeeping' seal of approval — it would signal that a country followed prudent fiscal and monetary policies and would only temporarily run large fiscal deficits in well understood emergencies."[33]

At a fundamental level therefore, the gold standard represented an ideological commitment, or a pledge, by citizens to be responsible, to work hard, to repay debt and to live within their means. Those who played by the rules of the gold standard were proclaiming they could be trusted to consume only in proportion to what they produced. At a philosophical level, the gold standard acknowledged the iron law that wealth was the result of economically productive work. It could not be summoned into existence *ex nihilo* out of thin air. The existence of the gold standard shielded populations from the temptation to cheat by printing money, or engage in other economic trickery. As Rockoff put it, "transparency and simplicity avoided the problems of moral hazard".

The Nixon Shock was therefore a highly symbolic act which signaled the abandonment of the old assumptions and the embrace of radical new ones. The underlying message was that economic problems need not entail sacrifice, hardship and self-denial, but could be solved creatively. Wealth, or at least the illusion of wealth, would henceforth be created by the artful manipulation of fiscal and monetary policy, through debt, redistribution and by printing paper money. It was a paradigm shift from an economic regime developed to serve the interests of the Victorians, to one designed to serve the interests of Boomers. Some economists believe they can trace a series of trends from 1971, the year American Boomers got the vote. For example, the blogger Ben Prentice detects the start of a dramatic expansion of debt, the widening of income inequality, the growth of unproductive bureaucracy and of economic inflation. He says 1971 marks a "fundamental change in our society." By studying a range of economic metrics, he concludes that 1971 represents an "interesting inflection in the data that you can point to and say, "look what happened here, everything went crazy!"[34] The age of the Boomers had arrived.

PART THREE

HOW THE BOOMERS BROKE JOURNALISM

Chapter 15

Prologue.
Mick Jagger and the
Sins of Victorian
Liberal Journalism

ick Jagger, high on LSD, was sitting on a couch trying to make
sense of what was happening. His girlfriend Marianne Faithfull
sat next to him, naked except for a fur skin rug. From time
to time the rug slipped from her shoulders revealing her body to the
police officers searching their house. One officer examined the pockets
of Jagger's green velvet jacket and discovered four amphetamine pills. It
was the evening of 12 February 1967. The world's most famous rock star
had been busted for possessing drugs. But what was more remarkable
than Jagger's arrest was the role of journalism in organizing it. It was a
sordid tale of Victorian Liberal Journalism at its worst.

A few weeks earlier, the British tabloid *The News of the World*, published an article headlined, "Pop Stars and Drugs — Facts That Will Shock

You" in which it claimed Mick Jagger had taken LSD. Unfortunately for the paper, its undercover journalists had confused Mick Jagger with his fellow Rolling Stone Brian Jones. Jagger, who was planning to take LSD, but who had not actually done so, sued for libel. Embarrassed by its own incompetence, and fearful of having to pay huge damages, *The News of The World* hatched a sly plan. The paper bribed a member of Jagger's entourage to tell them when the rock star really was taking drugs. When they received the tip-off, the newspaper called the police who raided Jagger's home and arrested him.

Jagger, even more than the Beatles, symbolized the rebelliousness of the Boomer generation. His music, his attitude and his public utterances preached rebellion against the shackles of Victorian Liberalism. "Anarchy" he told an interviewer in September 1967 "is the only slight glimmer of hope… politics, like the legal system, is dominated by old men."[1] Jagger was a spokesman for the Boomer generation. His music was a sermon preaching the Boomer's shared desire for satisfaction, fulfilment and a new way of thinking,

> "I see a great deal of danger in the air. Teenagers are not screaming over pop music any more, they're screaming for much deeper reasons. We're only serving as a means of giving them an outlet… Teenagers the world over are weary of being pushed around by half-witted politicians who attempt to dominate their way of thinking and set a code for their living. This is a protest against the system. I see a lot of trouble coming in the dawn."[2]

When Jagger was sentenced to three months in prison there was uproar. In court, one of his fans screamed, "You're only jailing him because he has long hair." The symbolism was unmistakable. To the Boomers, it seemed the older generation had declared war on them. The jailing of Jagger appeared to be a blatant attempt to squash their dreams, discredit their values and destroy their heroes. As the historian Simon Wells explains, the case was the,

> "*Cause célèbre* of its era, raising issues of far greater significance than the simple possession of a bit of pot and a few pep pills. For several months it seemed that the entire establishment of Great Britain had taken up arms against the young."[3]

155

But what was most significant was the role of *The News of the World*. Its journalists had not reported the facts honestly, impartially and objectively. On the contrary, they had plotted to manufacture a story which would not otherwise have existed. To many Boomers, the Jagger case was the moment that professional journalism exposed itself as a corrupt force opposed to the Boomer Ideology. Instead of being fair and honest, professional journalists had shown themselves to be part of a cozy establishment cartel of press, police and judiciary — reactionary forces fighting to protect the status quo. The underground magazine *Oz* ranted that the gloves were now off, ideological war had been declared,

> "Just as the Stones symbolise the new permissiveness – hence the vicious exemplary punishments... [*The News of The World*] epitomises the money-grabbing, witch-hunting, God-playing fascism of a decaying hypocrisy."[4]

Even neutral observers could see *The News of The World* had conspicuously failed to follow the ethical code of Victorian Liberal Journalism. Lord Lambton, a Conservative MP, described the paper's behavior as "indefensible" pointing out that, "It is the business of a newspaper to present the news... it is surely not the function of a newspaper to become an agent of the police." The London *Times*, in a famous editorial entitled "Who Breaks a Butterfly on a Wheel?" said the case symbolized a clash of ideologies which did not show Victorian Liberalism in a flattering light. Its Editor William Rees-Mogg wrote,

> "If we are going to make any case a symbol of the conflict between the sound traditional values of Britain and the new hedonism, then we must be sure that the sound traditional values include those of tolerance and equity... There must remain a suspicion in this case that Mr. Jagger received a more severe sentence than would have been thought proper for any purely anonymous young man."[5]

For many Boomers, the takeaway from the Jagger affair was that Victorian Liberal Journalism was irredeemably corrupt and broken. Its high-sounding talk about searching for truth was a smokescreen for anti-Boomer conspiracies and propaganda. It was time for the old journalism to be swept away and replaced by something better. What was needed was something more idealistic, something more in tune with the values, hopes and desires of the Boomer generation — something more committed to changing the world and making it a better place.

Chapter 16

The Assault on Victorian Liberal Journalism

"Need woman of any age for senior help on established underground paper. Must have interest in social change and journalism."

Advert. *Other Scenes*, April 1969.

Boomer Journalism and the Underground Press

Boomer Journalism first appeared as the underground journalism of the counterculture. It's estimated more than 2,600 different underground titles were produced in the US between 1965 and 1975. Well-known papers included the *Berkeley Barb*, the *San Francisco Oracle*, *The Los Angeles Free Press*, *RAT* and *The Rag*. In the UK the best known were the *International Times (IT)*, *Oz* and *Black Dwarf*. As Danny Goldberg recalls, for millions of Boomers, underground journalism was, not just a way of communicating information, but a tool for creating a better world. As Goldberg puts it, "The media was an indispensable tool for social change. It was certainly what got to me as a teenager."[1] Boomer Journalism rejected the rules and restraints of Victorian Liberal Journalism and took sides. As Goldberg explains, whereas the old journalism felt obliged to be objective, "People in the underground media regarded themselves as advocates of the counterculture, not merely as reporters. Their unabashed enthusiasm was part of what made us trust them."[2] For example, when the *Berkeley Barb* covered the story of a student protest, it set out to construct a narrative in which an attractive, female Boomer student is brutally attacked by a giant, thuggish policeman,

> "A bulky pasty-faced cop went up to her and told her to go home. Twenty-year old Suzanne Workman looked up defiantly with a sneer that seemed to say - 'Go fuck yourself cop!' This reporter heard no sound. For a moment the 6'4", 250 pound Berkeley bull stood hovering over the slim blond-haired chick. Then he went to grab her, she squirmed away. 'Get away from me, pig!'... With rage written on his face, the cop grabbed Suzanne, threw her to the ground, and straddled her dog-style."[3]

Boomer Journalism scorned complexity. Stories were tribal narratives of our side v theirs, right v wrong and good v evil. In the UK, the Boomer journalist Richard Neville explained that a willingness to take sides and fight for Boomer values made the new journalism "instantly identifiable" adding, "If you don't read Underground papers you don't know what's going on in the world."[4] Boomer Journalism scorned the impartial methodology of the old journalism, as Neville put it, "Pseudo 'objectivity' is a liberal shibboleth discarded by new-style journalists. The tone of Underground papers is pugnaciously partisan."[5]

Boomer Journalism set out to explain the news, not report it, by weaving together fact and opinion to create a seamless fabric — an explanatory narrative that confirmed the Boomers' pre-existing intuitions and beliefs. After reading the narratives of Boomer Journalism, everything seemed to make sense. As Neville put it,

> "Good Underground papers analyse key issues and, unlike everyday papers, attempt to relate and interweave them into a coherent critique of society. The violence in Vietnam is not seen

in isolation — it is related to the violence inherent in corporate bureaucracy: the violence of poverty, the violence of Chicago and the ghettoes, the unconscious violence of the conveyor belt."[6]

The news narratives of Boomer Journalism played an important role in uniting the Boomer tribe. To Boomer journalists, factual reporting was soulless and produced an unsatisfying, "scattered needle-spray of unrelated, often ephemeral, facts and events which confuse the readers more than they inform them."[7] Narrative was seen as a powerful epistemic explosive capable of bringing down Victorian Liberal Journalism by demolishing the wall separating fact from opinion. The American Boomer journalists Thorne Dreyer and Victoria Smith, writing in 1969, described Boomer Journalism as intentionally seeking the destruction of Victorian Liberal Journalism. In a famous manifesto, they wrote it was, "an often tacit, and sometimes explicit, 'Fuck You' to establishment papers everywhere". Having dispensed with the old rules of accuracy and impartiality, Boomer journalists were free to report the world as it ought to be, rather than as it was. As Dreyer and Smith explained, "Involvement and experience are prerequisites for good journalism, for a liberated journalism. Once freed from the illusory constraints of objectivity, you can explore new levels of creativity and communication."[8]

Boomer Journalism painted a picture of how a generation imagined itself. It cast the Boomers as actors in a drama set in a world operating according to Boomer rules and Boomer laws. Dreyer and Smith said it was a type of journalism designed make the world a better place by leading audiences towards ethically-politically desirable conclusions. Hence, narrative-led, underground journalism,

> "Puts isolated events and data into a context. Not only does the commercial media fail to tie together the facts it presents, but it actually destroys a sense of continuity and history in the minds of the American people. In the name of journalistic objectivity, it reports events; the readers are supposedly free to make their own judgments, but the people read their daily papers and make no judgment at all."[9]

In other words, whereas Victorian Liberal Journalism aspired to teach readers *how* to think, Boomer Journalism aspired to teach people *what* to think. According to Dreyer and Smith, ordinary people did not want to, nor were capable of, thinking for themselves,

> "Why can't people connect these events for themselves, why can't they put phenomena into a context? The answer would entail a discussion of the manipulation or the American mind by all forms of power."[10]

The task of underground journalism was therefore to make the task of understanding complex events easy and less effortful by constructing simplified narratives. The reluctance of Victorian Liberal Journalism to do this, was seen, not as an epistemic strength, but as a fatal weakness,

> "The press assumes that one thing, like the Vietnam War, can be discussed in complete isolation from another thing, like the U.S. economy. The radical press responds with cries of 'fallacy' and 'bullshit': phenomena necessarily relate, and it is more accurate to draw those connections."[11]

Boomer Journalism was then, proudly partisan and tribal. Its role was to be persuasive; to shape belief and behavior. As Dreyer and Smith concluded, its functions were twofold,

> "First, internal education and communication among people already in the movement, and the other, reaching out to new, presently un-hip people who must become part of a revolutionary class."

Underground journalism was the expression of a shared generational dream — a "new conception of news". It was also however, a return to pre-Victorian models. As the *Los Angeles Free Press* shrewdly noted in 1968, "We have returned to the concept of 18th and 19th century American journalism when newspapermen were passionately partisan."[12] Or, as the same paper commented in 1969, "there is a new spirit in journalism... a vital amateurishness in the spirit of the pamphleteering journalism of the American Revolution of 1776."[13] By abandoning Victorian Liberal Journalism, the Boomers had rediscovered the wildness of 18th Century journalism — its swashbuckling disregard for Journalistic Truth, its appetite for vitriol and invective, and its willingness to distort truth in pursuit of ethical-political goals. Ironically therefore, Boomer journalists who attacked Victorian Liberal Journalism as, "just more of that same old descriptive, non-committal, liberal crap" were in fact replacing it, not with something radically new, but with something radically old.[14]

Many college-educated Boomer journalists found inspiration in the writing of the media theorist Marshall McLuhan. McLuhan published a series of books during the 1960s arguing that journalism was not an impartial and objective guide to truth. Journalism, he said, was obsolete because it was a "hot" medium which belonged to a bygone age. He said the current era was the "electric age" in which media should be "cool". Consequently, nothing written by Victorian Liberal journalists should be believed. Journalism ought to be understood simply as a tool used by journalists to construct reality. Victorian Liberal journalists used it to construct one reality, now Boomer Journalists should use it to construct another. As one Underground journalist explained in 1966, everything had been transformed thanks to these insights,

> "One year ago, in the first issue of *The Paper*, I discussed the loyalty I felt I had to the traditional ideals of journalism... In the year since we began publishing, a very significant evolution has taken place in and around the American press".[15]

The writer attributed, "a great deal of importance to McLuhan" who had empowered him to abandon the old journalism. "We really didn't have the slightest ideas what we were getting into last year, when we thought we cared mainly about journalistic ideals". Now, having abandoned objectivity and impartiality, the writer says he has learnt to embrace "the tendency to enlightened and interpretative subjectivity". By being less accurate and more subjective, the writer concludes his journalism is now, "portraying a more accurate, objective picture of the action of our time than can be given through the use of linear-objective, formula journalism."

The need to abandon impartial Victorian Liberal Journalism was a favorite theme of Boomer journalists. A 1965 article, featuring an interview with the Ghanaian politician Kwame Nkrumah, called for a new, committed journalism explaining,

"We cannot be neutral between the oppressor and the oppressed, the corrupter and the victim of corruption, between the exploiter and the exploited, the betrayer and the betrayed. We do not believe that there are necessarily two sides to every question; we see right and wrong, just and unjust, progressive and reactionary, positive and negative, friend and foe. We are partisan."[16]

The Boomer journalist Joseph Barbato, in an article headlined *The Obsolete Press*, complained, "We are caught up in a revolutionary time; yet, for most of us, news of this daily change is filtered through a tradition-bound, conservative Colossus — The Press." The codes of the old Journalism, said Barbato, encouraged restraint and compromise. It was time, he argued, for something better,

"In addition to its antiquated reporting and editing methods, the press, more often than not, is itself one of the social institutions that make up the status quo. Can it report the real grievances of a radical movement and long remain loyal to the existing community structure?"[17]

Barbato reasoned that the Boomer's project to build a new world required a new journalism, "The press can start performing a new social function only after it transcends the bonds of current journalistic standards." These 'standards' comprised the entire epistemology and worldview of Victorian Liberalism. Objective, accurate reporting had to go — it was part of the problem. As Marc Furstenberg, explained to readers of *The Seed* in 1969,

"The original role of a reporter was to be an objective observer of events and an impartial recorder of them. The 'New Journalism' of the underground press allowed the reporter to be a partisan. Some, myself included, have tried to extend this idea and become a participant and even an instigator... I go to demonstrations, outside agitate, and write... We've thrown a lot of rocks and carried a lot of signs... We're doing everything but what needs to be done — take power."[18]

Boomer Journalism rejected the idea that journalists should be impartial bystanders. Furstenberg's rock-throwing reporter was the epitome of the new journalist — half warrior, half troubadour. British underground journalism followed the same principle. Black Dwarf's coverage of the Paris violence of 1968 was unapologetically partisan. Its front page reported how student demonstrators, "have been fighting with such skill and courage against a savage police force."[19] It described the police's response to Boomer violence as the, "extreme ferocity of fascism." The paper reported the feelings of a protestor who told the paper, "I had the impression of being free for the first time in my life. We marched, we laughed, we sang, we cried". This was Boomer Journalism in its purest form; committed, emotional and passionate.

Boomer Journalism, in other words, recognized its responsibility to help create Boomertopia — a place where unfairness, suffering and unhappiness would be abolished. In Boomertopia, freed from toil, competition and alienation; everyone would be able to gratify their desires, find fulfilment and live in peace and harmony. As the *Los Angeles Free Press* explained, "Our fundamental and overall concern is with the creation of those conditions where each one of us can really live a deeply personal life as we see fit and with due regard for our fellow human beings."[20] John Wilcock, writing for *RAT* in 1968, reported widespread agreement among Boomer journalists that their first loyalty was to change the world and promote the agenda of their generation, not search for Journalistic Truth,

> "Virtually all of the editors at last week's underground media conference in Ann Arbor were agreed that the press should be an organizing tool for 'the revolution' rather than merely a vehicle for information (which, in the case of the straight press, is distorted information serving the ruling class). But some dichotomy arose over such questions as 'Are we going to be journalists or revolutionaries?' Surely the answer is: both."[21]

The less balanced and less impartial a news report was, the more the Boomers liked it – provided it undermined the values of their parents and furthered the Boomer project. For example, in 1968 the Boomer journalist Jefferson Fuck Poland* reported a speech by Bobby Kennedy. His methodology was to get stoned, shout abuse at the senator, and then

---

* Poland founded the Psychedelic Venus Church in 1970, a cult which practiced orgies as a form of religious ritual. He was jailed in 1988 for child sex abuse.

get thrown out of the event. "I have an excuse, folks" he explained to readers of the *Berkeley Barb*,

> "I was high on SWP, a fearsome psychic energizer which I'd scored earlier in the day from notorious pusher Pete Camejo... So, there I was, standing two feet from Bobby, screaming "Fascist Pig!' into his calm, unshakeable, icy blue eyes."[22]

The response of Kennedy, who would be assassinated four weeks later, were not included in Poland's report. But Poland's truthophobic reporting style was all part of the fun, "Oh well," he concluded, "the speech was probably dull anyway, so I was just obeying Canon 36 of the Protocols of Underground Journalism: If there's no good story, make one up."

Boomer Journalism reported different facts and different opinions. It recognized a different reality and produced a different truth. As a college student during the late 1960s, Henry Loeser remembers being at home reading the underground *Madison Kaleidoscope*, while his dad sat on the opposite side of the room reading the *Milwaukee Sentinel*. Between them was an invisible, epistemic curtain which made dialogue and debate impossible,

> "The Underground press was telling what we felt was the real story. We were big consumers of that because we rejected mainstream media. We were reading the alternative press to get a critical view of things. There was truth here. There was real truth in the alternative press that we could see, but it was not what our parents were reading. I had a completely different idea about things because I was reading the alternative press, so I was seeing the real truth, not the truth he was reading in his paper. We couldn't really have a conversation."[23]

Boomer Journalism was incompatible with Victorian Liberal Journalism, because the Boomer Ideology was incompatible with Victorian Liberalism. The two journalisms, and the two ideologies they existed to serve, were mutually hostile. Boomer Journalism saw its role as helping to tear down the fabric of Victorian Liberalism and replace it with something better. Victorian Liberal Journalism saw its role as making debate possible between different, opposing groups. However, in Boomertopia there would be no messy squabbling or debating. The views of the other side would not have to be listened to politely because they wouldn't exist. No-one would have to tolerate what was obviously wrong because everyone would intuitively know what was right. For example, *Black Dwarf* dismissed the idea of debate about Vietnam as, "parliamentary cretinism". It dismissed rational, fact-based argument as a "brand of social democracy" which existed solely to "preserve the existing social structure". Evidence and logic belonged to the old way of knowing and were irrelevant. The article continued,

> "We do not want any more teach-ins on Vietnam - our minds are made up. We support the National Liberation Front of South Vietnam and want it to defeat United States Imperialism. We do not want any more petitions to Parliament. The House of Commons is as irrelevant as those who sit inside it."[24]

The US underground paper *Fire* also saw no need for debate or independent, critical thinking. Making the world a better place, it said, could only be achieved through direct action and street violence,

> "We moved through the streets in groups, marching, dancing, running, chanting, singing, downing jugs of wine. Running together with the people we knew well and trusted a lot. We carried VC flags and used the flagpoles as weapons. Trashing windows and pig cars. Setting fires at street corners."[25]

Boomer journalists used a variety of abusive labels to demonize the journalism of the War Generation. It was referred to as: "bullshit journalism", "doctrinaire liberal journalism", "prostitute journalism", "American flag journalism", "paranoid journalism", "flagrant yellow journalism", "violent, authoritarian and often times repulsive journalism", "official journalism", "establishment journalism" and, "stereotyped, unimaginative, knee-deep in the ochre mud, big city journalism." The Boomer activist Jerry Rubin paid a visit to the newspaper where he had once worked as sportswriter and youth page editor. Whereas Rubin had discovered the Boomer Ideology and become part of the movement, his erstwhile colleagues had not. Rubin therefore described them as soulless robots, barely human,

"The reporters were sitting at their desks just like I left them 13 years ago. They arrived at work at the same time. They got a Coke from the same Coke machine at the same time. They took a shit at the same time. They took the same bus to the same house".[26]

Rubin predicted that Victorian Liberal Journalism and its outmoded ideology would soon be destroyed in a blaze of Boomer activism, "High school students will seize radio, TV and newspaper offices across the land. Police stations will blow up. Revolutionaries will break into jails and free all the prisoners." From the rubble, the Boomers believed, a new, beautiful world would spontaneously blossom.

New Journalisms

Growing from the same ideological roots as underground journalism was the 'New Journalism' of Tom Wolfe and Truman Capote. The New Journalism attempted to fuse fact and fiction. Objectivity, accuracy and impartiality were rejected in favor of an artistic attempt to empathize with the characters and recreate their thoughts and feelings. The goal was not Journalistic Truth, but something better — something "more real than reality" and "more true than truth". Capote's 1966 *In Cold Blood* dramatized the true story of the murder of four members of the same family in a small Kansas town. As part of his research, Capote interviewed the murderers on death row. He called the result a "nonfiction novel". Wolfe described his New Journalism as able to give the reader, "the feeling of being inside the character's mind and experiencing the emotional reality of the scene as he experiences it."[27] Bridging the gap between New Journalism and underground journalism was the "Gonzo Journalism" of Hunter S. Thompson. As with other Boomer Journalisms, the Gonzo genre abandoned the classic values of objectivity and impartiality, as well as the distinction between fact and opinion. Gonzo journalism had attitude, it was part of the solution — it was committed and passionate. It combined journalism with activism. Facts were embellished or even invented to make the narrative more compelling. As Thompson explained,

"I don't get any satisfaction out of the old traditional journalist's view... Objective journalism is one of the main reasons American politics has been allowed to be so corrupt for so long. You can't be objective about Nixon. How can you be objective about Clinton?... I don't quite understand this worship of objectivity in journalism."[28]

For Thompson, the goal of journalism was to help change the world. Therefore, being subjective and partisan were not journalistic sins, but virtues. Dispassionate objectivity should be replaced by emotion and rage,

> "You're talking about your objective journalism?... speak no evil of the dead. Well, why not? What the fuck? Nixon goes out as a champion of the American dream and a hero. It enraged me. So it was the rage that tapped the vein."

In his 1970 essay *The Kentucky Derby is Decadent and Depraved*, Thompson mocked the legendary sporting event which he portrayed as a squalid assembly of old people with stagnant, obsolete values, "the result of too much inbreeding in a closed and ignorant culture." At the Kentucky Derby, which has taken place since 1875, Thompson discovers,

> "Thousands of raving, stumbling drunks, getting angrier and angrier as they lose more and more money. By midafternoon they'll be guzzling mint juleps with both hands and vomiting on each other between races."[29]

Thompson fantasizes about gassing the elderly, establishment figures, along with members of the mainstream media, with mace. He tells his colleague, the artist Ralph Steadman,

> "'Just pretend you're visiting a huge outdoor loony bin,' I said. 'If the inmates get out of control we'll soak them down with Mace.' I showed him the can of 'Chemical Billy,' resisting the urge to fire it across the room at a rat-faced man typing diligently in the Associated Press section."

Thompson gleefully describes the reaction of a mainstream journalist whom he and Steadman 'accidentally' mace,

"Bug off, you worthless faggot! You twisted pigfucker! (Crazed laughter.) If I weren't sick I'd kick your ass all the way to Bowling Green — you scumsucking foreign geek. Mace is too good for you — we can do without your kind in Kentucky."

It was entertaining and deliciously irreverent, but for non-Boomers, it simply wasn't journalism. The American writer Dwight Macdonald attacked the New Journalism as a "bastard form" — fiction in journalism's clothes,

"A new kind of journalism is being born, or spawned. It might be called 'parajournalism'... in which rational forms are used to express delusions. Parajournalism seems to be journalism - 'the collection and dissemination of current news' — but the appearance is deceptive. It is a bastard form, having it both ways, exploiting the factual authority of journalism and the atmospheric license of fiction."[30]

But Boomers were immune to this sort of criticism. Indeed, it only served to prove their point. They rejected the entire worldview represented by Macdonald along with all his assumptions and values. For the Boomers, what they were producing was indeed 'journalism' because they had redefined both the concept and the epistemology that legitimized it. To the Boomers, it was Victorian Liberal Journalism that wasn't really 'journalism' because the old concept of Journalistic Truth wasn't really 'truth'. By the mid-1970s, there existed two competing journalisms. There was Victorian Liberal Journalism — dispassionately searching for Journalistic Truth to preserve Victorian Liberal Democracy; and there was Boomer Journalism — producing simplified, tribal narratives to help destroy Victorian Liberal Democracy and create Boomertopia.

Chapter 17

Arete. Narrative & Pro-social Lying to Make the World a Better Place

"And hence she lied, her heart persuaded thoroughly,
'Twas worth her soul to be a moment kind."

Thomas Hardy, Her Dilemma.

If the goal of Victorian Liberal Journalism was *aletheia* — the desire to communicate Journalistic Truth regardless of consequences, the goal of Boomer Journalism was *arete* — the desire to change the world and make it a better place. Although the two motives are different, they are not always incompatible. Often, they can live together peacefully together. However, on other occasions, there will be friction between them.

When different goals conflict, people are forced to choose and concentrate on what's most relevant and important. In the language of cognitive psychology, people will inhibit the competing alternative to the "focal goal". With practice, this behavior becomes second nature and quite natural, a process referred to as "over-learning". In the context of journalism it means that journalists who are committed to the dominant goal of *arete* (making the world a better place), will sacrifice the "interfering temptation" to scrupulously tell the truth (*aletheia*) if the two conflict. Telling the truth becomes the low-priority goal, compared with, for example, promoting social, racial or environmental justice. Self-censorship then becomes automatic — part of the skill set of professional journalism. As the psychologist Arie Kruglanski explains, "Habitual behavior is purposive or goal-driven... The more often one performs a given behavior, the more likely they are to do so in the future."[1]

What this means is that contemporary journalists will be perfectly happy to search for, and report, Journalistic Truth, provided it does not conflict with the dominant, focal goal of making the world a better place. However, if the two goals conflict, *arete* will prevail over *aletheia*. Trying to produce outcomes that are ethically, socially or politically desirable will triumph over the indiscriminate and irresponsible reporting of facts. If, for example, the member of a marginalized group commits a serious crime, journalists will have to make a complex calculation about the ethical-political consequences of reporting it. This will affect the detail of what information is included and what is excluded, as well as how prominently, or discreetly, the story is reported. In other words, if reporting might cause the marginalized group to be feared or hated, then journalists will be expected to apply a discriminating incuriosity. When telling the whole truth would harm the cause of social, racial or environmental justice, or threaten social harmony, journalists working in the Boomer tradition are expected to consider the consequences of their journalism and self-censor. Psychologists refer to this type of behavior as 'pro-social lying'.

Pro-social lies are 'white lies' — statements that are technically untrue or misleading, but which are altruistic, well-intentioned and socially beneficial. As the behavioral scientist Emma Levine puts it, "when benevolence and integrity conflict, benevolence will often be more important than integrity." Levine points to research showing that gang members who lie in order to protect the gang are valued far more than those who always tell the truth. Truth and lies, honesty and dishonesty are not moral absolutes, they are contextual. What matters is the *intention* to produce outcomes that benefit the community. As Levine explains, when it comes to how we feel about deception, it is not the deception that matters, but the consequences of the deception,

"Individuals trust in-group members, but distrust out-group members. Individuals within the group are trusted because they care for and protect in-group members, even if they have demonstrated low integrity with respect to their interactions with out-group members"[2]

Brian Gunia, an academic who studies ethical decision-making, notes that in some professions deception is not merely tolerated, it is expected. Gunia categorizes jobs as either 'High In Sales Orientation' (HISO) or 'Low In Sales Orientation' (LISO). HISO jobs, he says, include advertising, marketing, sales, investment banking, consulting and politics. These are all roles that require the ability to persuade and manipulate other people. Gunia notes the ability to deceive is highly valued among HISO occupations and seen as a signal of competence, whereas, in LISO jobs, it is frowned upon. In HISO occupations, pro-social deception and manipulation are given a range of positive labels such as 'making a difference' or 'closing a sale'. As Gunia summarizes, "perceivers do not entirely disapprove of deceivers. Instead, they interpret deception as a signal that the deceiver will be competent in occupations stereotyped as HISO."[3]

Using Gunia's model, the impartiality inherent in Victorian Liberal Journalism can be understood as the lack of desire to persuade. In Victorian Liberal Journalism, fact and opinion are separated. This epistemic quarantining signals the journalist is presenting factual evidence without any desire to lead the audience to a particular conclusion about what the facts mean. However, this is not the case with Boomer Journalism. The fusion of fact and opinion into persuasive news narratives signals audiences *ought* to believe both the individual facts and the wider explanatory framework. According to Gunia's model, Boomer Journalism would qualify as a HISO occupation, whereas Victorian Liberal Journalism would not. When the goal of journalism is *arete*, journalists who are able to produce engaging narratives that persuade the audience and 'make a difference', will be more highly valued by their peers and employers than those who simply report facts.

The conflict between *aletheia* and *arete* is an ancient one. For example, in *The Republic*, written around 350 B.C., Plato describes the perfect society as one in which an enlightened and benevolent aristocracy of Guardians rules with totalitarian power for the benefit of all. In this Utopia, ordinary people, lacking the ability to make intelligent political decisions, will be freed from the need to do so. Instead, they will be guided, like children, by those who know better. Plato calls for the pro-social deception of the masses through a "magnificent myth", or "noble lie"

> "'I wonder if we could contrive one of those convenient stories we were talking about a few minutes ago, I asked, some magnificent myth that would in itself carry conviction to our whole community, including, if possible, the Guardians themselves?'
> 'What sort of story?'
> 'Nothing new — a fairy story like those the poets tell and have persuaded people to believe...'"[4]

Plato describes an "audacious" myth, a pro-social lie of epic proportions which involves rewriting history and fabricating science. For Plato, it is not merely excusable to deceive people in a good cause, it is irresponsible not to.

However, *arete* need not be understood as telling lies – noble or otherwise. This is because there are many forms of manipulative and persuasive communication short of lying. The behavioral psychologist Joseph Gaspar explains that deception exists along a cline or spectrum. He rejects as misguided the "belief that all forms of deception are immoral". Once again, it is the *intent* of the deceiver and the *consequences* of the deception, that matter. As Gaspar explains, deception is a "multi-dimensional construct with outcomes that range along a continuum from harmful to helpful".[5] Similarly, the journalism academic Caroline Fisher has constructed a typology of ten ways of avoiding telling the whole truth. In a world of complexity, Fisher argues truth is never simple — accounts of it will always be fragmentary and incomplete. This presents many enticing opportunities for journalists to offer their preferred narratives,

"A news story is not just a list of facts – it is a narrative, which also includes interpretation, inferences to causal explanation and linkages to broader context. Through a process of selection a journalist identifies what story will or won't be told. He or she then selects who to interview, what quotes and information to use and places them in a certain order to tell a story that explains an event to the public."[6]

According to Fisher, journalists rarely tell clear-cut lies because they don't need to. What they more commonly supply is "selective truth".

The behavioral psychologist Todd Rogers and his colleagues use the word "paltering" to describe the art of using factually accurate information to mislead. Paltering is dissembling — the "active use of truthful statements to create a false impression." Rogers uses the example of a car salesman who stresses the good points of a used car, but who slyly neglects to mention its faults. Paltering is therefore a form of lying by omission. According to Rogers, because every word uttered is true, it absolves the communicator from some of the ethical problems associated with lying,

"By using truthful, but misleading statements, those who palter may be able to effectively mislead others while justifying their behavior and maintaining a positive self-image. As a result, many deceivers may prefer to palter than lie by commission."[7]

The construction of news narratives by Boomer journalists, who pro-socially include some facts and omit others, matches Roger's definition of "artful paltering".

When the dominant goal of journalism is the creation of ethically-politically desirable outcomes, journalists become epistemic opportunists. When telling the whole truth would achieve the desired outcome, then the correct thing to do will be to produce truthful journalism. However, if the outcome requires the creation of a persuasive narrative, then paltering, dissembling, or some other form of prosocial deception, will be justified. The American philosopher Harry Frankfurt uses the earthy noun "bullshit" to describe this type of epistemic pragmatism. A bullshitter, writes Frankfurt, is someone who is not primarily concerned with "the truth-values of his statements". His intention, says Frankfurt, is, "neither to report the truth nor conceal it." Frankfurt's label happens to also be a close, albeit highly unflattering, fit for journalism driven by *arete*. Hence, an activist journalist whose focal goal is making the world a better place, is,

> "Neither on the side of the true nor on the side of the false. His eye is not on the facts at all, as the eyes of the honest man and of the liar are, except insofar as they may be pertinent to his interest in getting away with what he says. He does not care whether the things he says describe reality correctly. He just picks them out, or makes them up, to suit his purpose."[8]

In other words, although telling the truth is important in Boomer Journalism, it is not as important as making the world a better place. When reporting Journalistic Truth ceases to be useful, then it must step aside and accept its secondary position in the hierarchy of goals.

What is Social Justice?

Journalism based on *arete* privileges ethical and political criteria above epistemic ones. However, escaping epistemology is not as easy as it might appear. A range of difficult epistemic questions confront the journalism of *arete*. For example: What does 'making the world a better place' actually mean? How can we be certain who is oppressor and who is oppressed? Which news narrative will be most effective at helping to make the world a better place? and, perhaps most importantly, Who gets to decide these things? At first glance it might seem that our feelings and emotions offer an easy path to ethical-political knowledge compared with the effortful task of searching for truth using evidence-based enquiry and logical thinking. However, appearances can be deceptive. Our feelings about what is right and wrong quickly change when the facts change. Our sympathy for a victim can turn to anger if we learn we have been lied to and deceived. Our righteous anger with a ruthless killer evaporates when we learn he was framed for a crime he did not commit. Changing the goal of journalism from truth-seeking to seeking ethical-political justice merely shifts the problem of knowing from one place to another. As the philosopher Jonathan Wolff observes,

> "Morality is a puzzle. It's not like science, where we make observations and conduct experiments to gain and improve knowledge... There seem to be moral rules, or at least moral standards. What are they? What do they require of us? Where do they come from? How do we know what they are? Are moral rules ... like rules of fashion, coming and going, varying in time and place, at the whim of a few leaders in the field - in the case of fashion, by designers and journalists; in the case of morality, by priests, prophets, and perhaps philosophers?"[9]

In Boomer Journalism, 'making the world a better place' is usually understood in terms of 'social justice'. Therefore, *arete* can be rephrased as 'journalism whose focal goal is promoting social justice.' However, the epistemic questions refuse to go away. For example, what exactly is social justice and how should it be achieved? There are many different definitions of social justice. The prominent US theorist Maxine Greene explains,

> "To teach for social justice is to teach for enhanced perception and imaginative explorations, for the recognition of social wrongs, of sufferings, of pestilences wherever and whenever they arise. It is to find models in literature and in history of the indignant ones who have taken the side of the victims of pestilences, whatever their names or places of origin. It is to teach so that the young may be awakened to the joy of working for transformation in the smallest places, so that they may become healers and change their worlds."[10]

Greene's poetic description suggests that social justice is something vague and intangible — something that feels right intuitively and emotionally. As the political philosopher Fazal Rizvi reluctantly admits, the concept of social justice is plagued by ambiguity,

"The immediate difficulty one confronts when examining the idea of social justice is the fact that it does not have a single essential meaning - it is embedded within discourses that are historically constituted and that are sites of conflicting and divergent political endeavors."[11]

In practice, the concept of social justice usually involves the redistribution of wealth and power from those who have too much, to those who have too little. For example, an American university website explains,

"Today, the concept of social justice often refers to human rights, centered around improving the lives of groups historically marginalized based on race, ethnicity, nationality, gender, sexual orientation, age, religion and disability… those who strive for social justice seek the redistribution of power to enhance the well-being of individuals through equal access to healthcare, justice and economic opportunity."[12]

This theme is echoed in the writing of the political theorist David Miller who says redistribution lies at the heart of the concept of social justice,

"Very crudely, I think, we are discussing how the good and bad things in life should be distributed among the members of a human society. When, more concretely, we attack some policy or some state of affairs as socially unjust, we are claiming that a person, or more usually a category of persons, enjoys fewer advantages than the person or group of persons ought to enjoy."[13]

If the redistribution of wealth and power does indeed lie at the heart of the concept of social justice, then this begs a multitude of epistemic questions such as; How can we be certain who has too much and who has too little? How much wealth and power should be redistributed to achieve social justice? How can we define 'fairness'? When people and groups of people clamor for fair shares, it is to be expected that these questions will be hotly contested. Inevitably, there will be many bitter disputes cloaked in deception and fraud as different coalitions jockey for power and wealth at the expense of others and try to disguise their real status. It is unsurprising that, in practice, the details of social justice become highly politicized. The writer Ben O'Neill argues that social justice is a zero-sum game, thus giving power and wealth to one group, means taking it from another, a process which fuels the division of society into endlessly competing groups. He sees the modern quest for social justice as self-interest masquerading as virtue,

"As the critics of social justice are compelled to point out ad nauseam, to assert a right to some tangible good or service like clean water, healthcare, education, prenatal care, or ice cream, requires that someone else must supply that good. It asserts the moral prerogative to have others supply you with your desires, at the expense of their effort. When coupled with an appeal to government provision (as is always the intention), it asserts the moral prerogative to use force to attain one's desires — to force others to give you their ice cream, their clean water, their medical skills, and so on. It is the principle of the thief, the rapist, the criminal, who sees his whims and desires as reason to impose himself forcibly on others."[14]

The underlying epistemic point here is that real world disputes about what is fair and unfair hinge on questions of fact. Doing what is right is parasitic on *knowing* what is right, which in turn depends on knowing what is true. Thus, *arete* is unavoidably parasitic upon *aletheia*. In other words, there is a direction to moral judgements which leads from knowledge of reality, to judgement — not the other way round. The trial must come before the verdict. This dilemma was also discussed by Plato. In the *Meno* Socrates says the desire to do good (*arete*) is potentially dangerous, unless it is subject to thoughtful and detailed enquiry (*aletheia*). For Plato, the streets of hell are paved with good intentions,

"Isn't it clear then that this class [of people], who don't recognize evils for what they are, don't desire evil, but what they think is good, though in fact it is evil; those who through ignorance mistake bad things for good obviously desire the good... In short, everything that the human spirit undertakes or suffers will lead to happiness when it is guided by wisdom, but to the opposite when guided by folly".[15]

The psychologist Paul Bloom makes a similar point — that the desire to do good without reliable factual knowledge about what actually *is* good, leads to evil,

"In the real world, evildoers see themselves as good people doing good things, or good people forced to do difficult things because of special circumstances, or, at worst, good people who are forced, tricked, or goaded into doing bad things, against the grain of their fine characters".[16]

Another difficulty is that our sense of good and evil is deeply tribal. Our moral intuition has evolved over tens of thousands of years to help us cooperate with other members of our group and be good members of society. This means the more ethical we try to be, the more tribal we become. Being ethical implies being loyal to our group and intolerant of those who reject our group's morality. Hence, when people question our values and our understanding of social justice, they mark themselves as the tribal other — potentially dangerous outsiders. As the evolutionary psychologist Joshua Greene explains,

"In the modern tragedy, the very same thinking that enables cooperation *within* groups, undermines cooperation *between* groups... morality did not evolve to promote universal cooperation. On the contrary, it evolved as a device for successful intergroup competition."[17]

According to Greene, our sense of what is fair is unconsciously distorted, not just by our *individual* self-interest, but by our *tribal* self-interest. Thus, the more enthusiastically we fight for social justice, the more intolerant we grow of those who disagree with us. The more we believe we are good, the more we believe those with different views are evil. This "biased fairness" changes the way we process information. In a dispute about what is ethical and fair, we tend to favor the option that benefits our own group, because we feel certain we are the good guys. As Greene summarizes, "Our social impulses take us out of the frying pan of personal conflict and into the fire of tribal conflict."[18]

The fundamental problem then, when journalism is guided by *arete*, remains epistemic. How can we know how to achieve social justice? How can we be certain our actions are fair? How can we be sure our noble motives are not merely self-serving tribal impulses and unconscious biases? In practice, journalism based on *arete* usually ignores these difficult questions and becomes a form of pro-social, manipulative-persuasive communication. Its creators simply assume infallible knowledge about what is fair and unfair, who is good and bad and which causes are just and unjust. Once these questions crystalize into unchallengable assumptions, action becomes all important.

One contemporary version of pro-social, manipulative-persuasive communication is Nudge Theory. Nudge theory was developed as a practical form of manipulation in which 'architects' create content to 'nudge' the audience in a certain direction. The nudges are designed to be so subtle people won't realize they are being nudged. Nudge Theory architects will, for example, offer choices in sly, artful ways knowing that how the choice is framed will make people more likely to choose the architect's preferred outcome. The Australian academic Cynthia Cai explains,

"We can deliberately design how information/choices are presented to individuals, and hence influence their behavior. That is, people can be nudged to achieve desired results."[19]

In Nudge Theory, people have the illusion that they are making up their own minds freely and rationally, but the game is rigged. In reality, "the probability of an individual choosing any one option becomes the choice of the architect, and not of the individual." Contemporary Nudge Theory has a long ancestry. For example, in 1947 the American 'father of PR' Edward Bernays argued that people could be led like a herd of animals, without the awareness they were being led. He called this technique the 'engineering of consent'. Bernays said the process would require specialists in communication and experts in the use of mass media to mold public opinion. These elite manipulators he referred to as "consent engineers",

"Communication is the key to engineering consent for social action... The public's attitudes, assumptions, ideas, or prejudices result from definite influences. One must try to find out what they are in any situation in which one is working."[20]

Bernays identified narrative and journalism as two of the most potent manipulative tools, "the engineer of consent" he said, must employ "what in fiction is called the 'story line'" and they must also, "create news. News is not an inanimate thing. It is the overt act that makes news, and news in turn shapes the attitudes and actions of people." The reporting of news, Bernays continued, should be, "planned deliberately to accomplish a purpose, to influence our ideas and actions". Bernays believed these techniques were morally neutral or amoral — they could be used to make the world better, or they could be subverted and make the world worse, "demagogues can utilize the techniques for antidemocratic purposes with as much success as can those who employ them for socially desirable ends."

In summary, the difference between Victorian Liberal Journalism and Boomer Journalism is that, according to the former, journalists should always tell the truth, regardless of consequences. According to the latter, journalists should only tell the truth if it helps make the world a better place. In Boomer Journalism, journalists must consider the *consequences* of telling the truth and be prepared to self-censor, or engage in other forms of benign, pro-social deception, if they believe the causes of social, racial or environmental justice are threatened. Although this type of journalism is plagued with innumerable, complex philosophical and psychological questions, none of them unduly bothered the Boomers. Their goal was to replace Victorian Liberal Democracy, its epistemology and its journalism with something better and more useful to their generation. In this cultural war, the Boomers, from the early 1970s onwards, began to deploy their elite shock troops — intellectuals and academics whose role was to construct new theoretical frameworks, redefine 'truth' and 'knowledge' and legitimize and glorify the Boomer way of knowing.

Chapter 18

Three Eminent Scholars. From Truthophobia to Official Truth

The Evolution of Truth

The Boomer generation of academics produced a prodigious body of intellectual theory in the fields of media, journalism, cultural and communication studies. Within this canon, it is possible to identify three distinct historical phases. During these phases, the Boomer generation first destroyed, then rebuilt, the concept of Journalistic Truth. Like the new owners of an old house, they demolished the existing structure, before replacing it with a sleek new modern design and then redecorating it to suit their changing needs. In reality the three phases are fuzzy and overlapping, not neatly delineated. However, for convenience, we can label them as follows:

- 1965-1980. The phase of Truthophobia. Demolition of the old structure.

- 1980-1995. The phase of Tribal Truth. The new building takes shape.

- 1995-2025.* The phase of Official Truth. Completion and consolidation.

These phases reflect the growing power and dominance of the Boomer generation. For example, during the Truthophobic Phase, the Boomers were on the outside looking in. Their pressing need was to destroy the authority of Victorian Liberalism and its epistemology. Academics therefore set out to undermine the foundations of existing knowledge. In the Tribal Truth phase, the Boomers were moving into positions of power in journalism and academia. The need was to legitimize their own values and ways of thinking. Instead of arguing that knowledge was impossible and relative, the Boomers now argued that legitimate knowledge came from the shared intuition of the Boomers — the tribal consensus. The Phase of Official Truth marks a period of consolidation. The Boomers have now reached the apex of power and are passing their values to their children — the Millennial generation. The Boomer way of knowing becomes the new orthodoxy and hardens into a settled doctrine taught in schools and colleges. Boomer narratives become Official Truths that resist challenge and which must be defended from dissent. In the space of approximately fifty years therefore, Boomer academics progressed from arguing that there was no truth for journalists to report, to arguing that truth could be intuitively known by Boomers, and finally to the increasingly authoritarian position that it was ethically-politically wrong to question the Boomer's Official Truth.

* During the early 2020s, the last of the Boomer generation were retiring and leaving the workplace. Subsequent phases should therefore really be considered as part of the Millennial Epistemology — the way of knowing of the children of the Boomers.

Colleges and universities played a major role in the codification of the Boomer Ideology. They were crucibles of Boomer thinking — finishing schools where large numbers of Boomers came together to vocalize their shared feelings and intuitions. More Boomers went to university than any previous generation. As one US government report noted,

"College enrolment rose by 49 percent in the 1950s... during the 1960s, enrolment rose by 120 percent. By 1969, college enrolment was as large as 35 percent of the 18 to 24-year-old population."[1]

However, higher education did not simply get bigger — it changed. The Boomers wanted education to confirm their pre-existing values and assumptions, not contradict them. As the historian Helen Horowitz puts it, the Boomers, "began to request courses designed to meet their own agenda."[2] While campus sit-ins and violent protests grabbed the headlines during the late 1960s, a much more significant revolution was quietly taking place. It was an intellectual revolution in which theories, not bricks and bottles, were the weapons. As Horowitz explains, the site of ideological struggle shifted, "All the energies that had once gone into campus high jinks, or political demonstrations focused on the curriculum."[3] The sociologist and political theorist Paul Hirst, writing in 1973, noticed how Boomer students were actively, "seeking an intellectual basis for their political rejection of modern society." Hirst observed that Boomer intellectual theories were deliberately designed to attract, "radical critics oriented towards the questioning of the modern social system as a totality."

The Australian cultural studies academic Graeme Turner, writing in 1990, looked back with approval on the profound "shift" in his discipline since 1960. It had succeeded in shattering, "elitist assumptions in order to examine the everyday and the ordinary."[4] The old Enlightenment focus on evidence, reason and the search for truth had been replaced, he said, with new assumptions drawn from, "language, semiotics, Marxism and ideology, individualism, subjectivity and discourse." What had taken place was a profound epistemic shift. New criteria had been introduced to redefine what counted as legitimate knowledge and truth. Turner said this radical change, "has enabled the crossing of disciplinary borders and the re-framing of our ways of knowing."[5] Concepts such as accuracy, impartiality and the distinction between fact and opinion, were jettisoned and ridiculed. New subjects, new attitudes, new ways of seeing and knowing replaced the old. The underlying goal was to help create Boomertopia. As Turner proudly wrote,

> "Cultural Studies' commitment to understanding the construction of everyday life has the admirable objective of doing so in order to change our lives for the better. Not all academic pursuits have such a practical political objective."[6]

This epistemic shift was not an innocent enterprise. As well as providing Boomer students with intellectual justification for their pre-existing impulses and beliefs, Boomer Education also served to give status and employment to the Boomer generation of academics. Once established, this became a self-supporting, self-referential framework. Many insightful and self-critical Boomer scholars were troubled however that what they were creating was in reality a semi-theological doctrine based, not on evidence, but on faith. Hirst, for example, described the "Theory Boom" of the 1970s as a production line for Utopian "ideologies of self-deception". He concluded uneasily, "like most truths of this kind the part that is hidden is the most serious and unpalatable aspect of the whole of the matter."[7]

Despite its lack of empirical rigor, or perhaps because of it, Boomer academic doctrine was wildly popular with Boomers. As the sociologist Bernice Martin observed in 1980, "starting in the universities and spreading outwards and downwards through the system... the reverberations of the movement spread wide."[8] Nowhere was the impact of radical Boomer theory more evident than in the disciplines of Media, Journalism, Cultural and Communication Studies. Particularly appealing to Boomers was the idea that journalism was a weapon for cultural change, and an instrument they could use for getting what they wanted.

This is the generational context that helps us understand the vogue for radical intellectual theories during the last third of the 20th Century. As one writer summarizes, they were a set of "strategic and rhetorical practices" sharing a common motive to destabilize and subvert concepts such as reason, the meaning of words and "epistemic certainty".[9] In other words, to take control of journalism and bend it to their purpose, the Boomers first had to demolish Victorian Liberal Journalism and its supporting epistemic scaffolding. The old concept of impartial, Journalistic Truth was their first and most important target.

The Truthophobia of Tuchmanism

One of the best known intellectuals of the Phase of Truthophobia was the sociologist Gaye Tuchman who published an influential paper *Objectivity as Strategic Ritual* in 1972. It was so successful, she expanded it into a full-length book *Making News; A Study in the Construction of Reality* which was published in 1980. In the 1972 version, Tuchman argued the methodology of Victorian Liberal Journalism served no real epistemic purpose. Its function was to act as a fig leaf to conceal journalism's nakedness. According to Tuchman, objectivity should be understood as a form of superstition,

> "To journalists, like social scientists, the term 'objectivity' stands as a bulwark between themselves and critics. Attacked for a controversial presentation of 'facts,' newspapermen invoke their objectivity almost the way a Mediterranean peasant might wear a clove of garlic around his neck to ward off evil spirits".[10]

In other words, journalists who checked their facts and tried to produce balanced reports were, in reality, deluding themselves and taking part in a meaningless pantomime. Tuchman adopted an ethnographic style, portraying herself as an explorer from sophisticated Boomer society visiting a primitive pre-Boomer tribe. This rhetorical trick endowed her with a privileged vantage point from which to look down on the mistaken views of the "newsmen" whom she describes as acting out "performance strategies" and using "objectivity as strategic ritual" to "defend themselves from critical onslaught." Tuchman says the tribe of "newsmen" makes ritualized, yet essentially meaningless and random, editorial decisions. For example, she said, "The top editor might simply 'blue pencil' or alter a 'bad story,' grumbling because subordinates had done a poor job." Tuchman says this behavior should be understood as social scolding. As she puts it, "scoldings and 'blue penciling' are part of a system of social control potentially affecting promotions, keeping one's job, and drawing good assignments."[11]

Tuchman ridiculed Victorian Liberal Journalism describing it as an absurd series of rituals in which the tribe of 'newsmen' run around the newsroom trying to verify unimportant details, "such as telephoning a marriage license bureau to determine whether Robert Jones had married Fay Smith."[12] In the 1980 version, Tuchman continued her truthophobic blitz with a series of philosophical claims intended to deny that journalism could possibly have any relationship with truth. According to Tuchman, all narratives have the same epistemic status. For example she argued, "Ultimately, both the fairy tale and the news account are stories... Jack Kennedy and Jack of beanstalk fame are both cultural myths."[13]

To support this view, she employed a form of extreme philosophical skepticism to argue that even arithmetical calculations were socially constructed, "Taken by itself, a fact has no meaning. Indeed, even 'two and two equals four' is factual only within certain mathematical systems or theories."[14] All of this led her to the truthophobic conclusion that news is not a "mirror of events", and that it was time to "cast aside the identification of news as a crusade for truth."[15] Instead of facts, Tuchman asserted there was only a "web of facticity" which produced the illusion of facts. News reports,

> "When taken together, present themselves as both individually and collectively self-validating. Together they constitute a web of facticity by establishing themselves as cross-referents to one another."[16]

Tuchman was a lavish user of a technique known as naïve relativism which argues that facts do not exist. It is however, a self-defeating tactic because it requires readers to accept that the statement 'there are no facts' is itself a fact. This is equivalent to asking readers to believe that the statement 'there is no such thing as truth' is true, or asserting 'there is no such thing as a thing', or that 'reality is not real'. It is impossible to accept these claims because they are literally nonsensical and irrational. Like other types of philosophical paradox, they are self-referential and lie in the twilight zone at the edge of meaning and human understanding. Hence, because there is no evidence to support Tuchmanism, and because its conclusions cannot be either proven or disproven, Tuchmanism is best described as a quasi-theological doctrine. Belief in it requires an act of faith. Another difficulty for Tuchmanism is that the arguments it uses against journalism must logically also apply to itself. If journalists weave "webs of facticity" and create the illusion of knowledge, then so too must academics. If the methodology of journalism is merely an empty "ritual", then so too is Tuchman's ethnographic methodology and the academic "ritual" of peer review. What's sauce for the goose is sauce for the gander.

Tuchman was one of many Boomer intellectuals who found inspiration in the work of the Austrian-American theological writers Peter Berger and Thomas Luckmann. Berger and Luckmann's 1966 book *The Social Construction of Reality; A Treatise in the Sociology of Knowledge* became a best-seller and the title of Tuchman's own 1980 book, *Making News; A Study in the Construction of Reality* echoes Berger and Luckmann's. Indeed, Tuchman's book is largely Berger and Luckmann's constructivist thesis applied to journalism. However, it is important to recognize that Berger and Luckmann were not trying to argue that human knowledge, or facts, are literally "constructed". On the contrary, they make it clear that epistemic questions are outside the realm of their enquiry,

> "The sociologist is in no position to supply answers to these questions. What he can do, however, is to ask how it is that the notion of 'freedom' has come to be taken for granted in one society and not in another."[17]

In other words, the sociology of knowledge is the study of intellectual fashion. It asks; why do certain ideas gain traction with certain groups of people at certain times? Why do ideas fall out of fashion? Why are they replaced by other ideas? It does not attempt to judge whether any particular belief is actually true or false. Berger and Luckmann later complained bitterly that their ideas had been hijacked by theorists of the Boomer generation and used inappropriately to justify a wide variety of radical and irrational stances,

> "It was, of course, the orgy of ideology and utopianism that erupted all over the academic scene in the late 1960's, almost immediately after the publication of our book. Neither Luckmann nor I had any sympathy with this Zeitgeist, but even if we had been more sympathetic, our sort of sociology was not what all these putative revolutionaries were clamoring for. It is not possible to play chamber music at a rock festival."[18]

In a pivotal moment in her 1972 paper, in an attempt to escape the sticky web of irrational, naïve relativism in which she is stuck, Tuchman attempts to argue that while Victorian Liberal Journalists believe facts exist, this cannot be true because sociologists know they do not. Tuchman plays her trump card by appealing to the authority of the respected Japanese-American sociologist Tamotsu Shibutani,

> "The newsmen's assertion that 'the facts speak for themselves' is instructive... Of course, it is sociological commonplace that 'facts' do not speak for themselves. For instance, Shibutani (1966) demonstrates that the assessment and acceptance of 'facts' is highly dependent upon social processes"[19]

But Tuchman's decision to rely on Shibutani is disastrous because what he says is, in fact, the exact opposite of what Tuchman claims he says. In his 1966 book *Improvised News; A Sociological Study of Rumor*, Shibutani makes it clear that professional journalism is trustworthy precisely because of the checks performed by journalists,

> "In modern mass societies complex procedures have been established for the gathering, processing and dissemination of news... blatant error is easily exposed. In times of crisis people turn first to these channels, and they serve as the standard against which all other reports are checked".[20]

Shibutani applauds the rigorous professional processes Victorian Liberal Journalists, especially in the US and the UK, have developed. These, he points out, are guardians of epistemic good practice that help journalists report factually and accurately,

> "Possibilities for deception are considerable, but the professional ideology of newsmen helps to maintain standards of reliability. The announced ideal in journalism is the clear, impartial, and, accurate description of significant events... Journalists in the United States and England take great pride in their standards of fairness and accuracy... News agencies throughout the world have standardized procedures that tend to maximize reliability".[21]

Shibutani approves of Victorian Liberal Journalism and the tradition of Enlightenment rationalism. For Shibutani, all epistemic questions must face the ultimate tribunal of human observation and reason,

"All communication channels, both formal and informal, are subject to repeated pragmatic tests, and their reputation for reliability depends on adequate performance... The frequent presentation of false information, however, discredits the channel... Human beings are not gullible. Once a source is defined as unreliable for certain kinds of news, it is not trusted."[22]

But no-one seemed to notice, or care, that the authorities on which Tuchman relied contradicted her thesis, nor that its naïve relativism was philosophically self-defeating. Tuchmanism was eagerly embraced during the truthophobic phase of the Boomer's intellectual project because its motive was to delegitimize Victorian Liberal Journalism and the concept of Journalistic Truth. As Tuchman proclaimed in 1978, her intention was to demonize and undermine professional journalism,

"The aim of this research has not been to strengthen journalism as a profession. Indeed, I read the work on news-professionalism as a challenge to and debunking of that very concept. Rather, the aim has been to explore news as an agent of legitimation and social control."[23]

During the 1970s and 1980s, Boomer academics and intellectuals frequently quoted Tuchman as proof that journalism could not be a search for truth, because truth did not exist. Truthophobia had become so widespread in academia, the theorist Catherine Belsey could state confidently in 1980 that, "The notion of a text which tells a, or the, truth... is not only untenable but literally unthinkable, because the framework which supported it... no longer stands".[24]

However, by 1980 the truthophobic phase was coming to an end and Tuchmanism was becoming obsolescent. The Boomers were moving into positions of power. A more subtle intellectual framework was required — one that would delegitimize the old journalism, while at the same time legitimize their own. In other words, by the 1980s there was demand for a theory that would claim that facts did exist, and that certain knowledge was possible — but only for Boomers. The solution to this delicate intellectual problem, was provided by the eminent theorist Stuart Hall.

Stuart Hall - Consensus Truth

Although best known today for his writing on cultural identity and race, Hall was also a highly influential media theorist who continues to influence academics, students and journalists in the 21st Century. Hall stood the concept of journalism on its head. Whereas Victorian Liberal Journalists had developed ways to restrain political bias, Hall embraced it. Instead of news reports being true or false, Hall measured them according to whether they were ethical or unethical, politically helpful or politically unhelpful. In his influential 1978 book *Policing the Crisis; Mugging, the State, and Law and Order*, Hall argued that journalists who describe a problem, create the problem. For example, Hall claimed that journalists reporting the fact that young black men were disproportionately involved in mugging in the UK, were responsible for creating a problem that would not otherwise have existed, "Part of what is standing in the way — producing crime, so to speak, as a simple and transparent fact — is the label 'mugging' itself".[25] Since journalists had constructed the problem, Hall said the solution had to lie in journalistic self-censorship,

> "If we could abolish the word, that would have been our principal — perhaps our only — 'practical proposal'. It has done incalculable harm — raising the wrong things into sensational focus, hiding and mystifying the deeper causes. A moratorium should now be declared on its highly suspect use, especially by politicians, judges, the police, criminal statisticians, the mass media and our moral guardians".

Here, Hall is outlining a fundamental principle of the journalism of *arete*; a news story should only be reported if its consequences are ethically and politically good. It should not be reported if its consequences harm the causes of social, racial or environmental justice. Hall was troubled however by the obvious epistemic questions which this approach raised. For example, how can a journalist foresee all the future ethical-political consequences of reporting, or suppressing, a story? More generally, if news stories are ethically-politically good rather than true, how can audiences know what to believe when faced with different, contradictory, accounts? Hall had run into the ancient, eternal questions of epistemology and moral philosophy.

Hall attempted to answer these vexed questions in a famous paper entitled *Encoding/Decoding*. When it was first published in 1973 it aroused little interest. However, when he revised it and republished it in 1980, it quickly became a canonical text which has been quoted in media studies textbooks ever since. As the Danish media theorist Henrik Bødker notes, the Encoding-Decoding model is often treated as a sacred gospel by media teachers and academics. It has, he says, become the "dominant theoretical approach" and now sits atop the syllabi of communication studies everywhere. The "canonization" of this text means it is often "ritually invoked" rather than, "something to be thought with or about, engaged with and argued over, contended and challenged".[26]

In *Encoding/Decoding*, Hall explains that when audiences hear a news story they 'decode' it with either the "dominant code" — which means they believe it, or with a "negotiated code" — which means they neither wholly believe nor disbelieve it, or with an "oppositional code" — which means they reject it and refuse to believe any of it. So how do people know which code to use? Why should the audience believe one thing and not another? It is only at the very end of his paper that Hall provides an example to illustrate his solution. He describes a viewer watching a TV debate about the need to limit wages to control inflation. Hall says this viewer chooses to "decode" what he hears with the "oppositional code",

> "It is possible for a viewer perfectly to understand both the literal and the connotative inflection given by a discourse but to decode the message in a globally contrary way... This is the case of the viewer who listens to a debate on the need to limit wages but 'reads' every mention of the 'national interes' as 'class interest'".[27]

Hall ends his paper on a triumphant note, saying this revelatory moment, when the message supplied by Victorian Liberal Journalism is rejected, and the oppositional code chosen, is a profound moment of ideological conversion. It is, says Hall,

> "One of the most significant political moments... the point when events which are normally signified and decoded in a negotiated way begin to be given an oppositional reading. Here the 'politics of signification' — the struggle in discourse — is joined".

It finally becomes clear that the correct code is chosen simply through intuition. Hall's viewer does not research the complex economic issues involved. He is not persuaded by the weight of evidence, nor by superior logic. Hall's viewer breaks free from journalism's "complex structure in dominance" by *feeling* what to believe. The feminist theorist Patrick Love has described this sort of emotion-led epistemology as a "woman's way of knowing". According to Love, women often rely on,

"Intuition and the direct perception of truth — independent of any conscious reasoning process. Many distrusted books and the written word, preferring to learn through direct sensory experience and personal involvement. Other people's opinions did not often change the mind of the subjective knower because she was locked inside her own subjectivity; however, like-minded people might be sought out to affirm her opinions."[28]

Another word used to express the Hallist concept of felt truth is "truthiness" — a term coined by the American comedian Stephen Colbert. Colbert defined truthiness as, "the belief in what you feel to be true rather than what the facts will support". On his TV show he told his audience "the truthiness is, anyone can read the news to you. I promise to *feel* the news at you".[29] Colbert's satire was aimed at the growing trend towards emotion, intuition and narrative in journalism. On another occasion he explained, "That's where the truth lies; right down here in the gut... Every night on my show, the Colbert Report, I speak straight from the gut. I give people the truth unfiltered by rational argument".[30]

The cognitive nihilism of Tuchmanism argued there was no such thing as Journalistic Truth. This was useful to the Boomers during the 1960s and early 1970s. However, Hallism provided something much more useful for the late 1970s and 1980s — epistemic justification for the intuition and feelings of the Boomer generation. According to *Encoding/ Decoding*, truth could be sensed, but only by the numerically dominant Boomers. But Hall's model only provided the illusion of an explanation. The big questions remained unanswered; how exactly does his TV viewer intuitively feel which code to choose? What guided his intuition? Hall never explained this. His paper ends as soon as the viewer makes his choice. Hall gets off the intellectual bus at a stop that suits him.

The psychologist Cory Clark, writing in 2020, provides the vital cognitive and epistemic analysis missing from Hall's model. Clark says that humans are tribal animals who have evolved over hundreds of thousands of years in the context of competing coalitions. The default epistemic position for all humans is therefore a protribe bias — the tendency for homogenous groups to see the world through the lens of their own values and sacred narratives. As Clark writes,

> "Most reasoning is strategic, and is designed to persuade, defend, and signal commitment to others, not to adjudicate calmly between different propositions. Belief is guided like iron filings around a magnetic field by the forces of tribalism."[31]

Hall's TV viewer chooses the "oppositional code" because he is a member of the Boomer generation. He chooses to oppose the ideology of Victorian Liberalism and restraint because he intuitively feels this is what the majority of his peers would do. Hall's viewer is not interested in what is objectively true on the balance of probabilities, he is loyal to his group and adjusts his beliefs accordingly. As Clark writes, people generally,

> "Do not argue to discover the truth; they argue to advance their tribe's interests in order to advance their own. Similarly, they are selectively skeptical of information that is incongruent with their tribe's preferences because they were designed to combat evidence that undermines their tribe's ideology."

The question Hall's viewer asks himself, after watching the complex political-economic debate on TV, is what *should* he believe as a loyal, valuable group member? The calculation he makes is essentially tribal; what would other Boomers be likely to think? What is the consensus view? What would my friends and peers expect me to think? In *Encoding/Decoding*, Hall promotes the view that legitimate knowledge is the consensus belief of our group. As Clark explains,

> "The social consequences of beliefs are often more important than having true beliefs, especially when the truth is difficult to know, which is often the case for many political issues and puzzles of human nature."[32]

Social psychologists who study collective belief and crowd dynamics point out that this way of knowing is normal and natural for most species. The spontaneous adjustment of belief and behavior to our perception of the group norm is a phenomenon known as "herding". As the psychologist Inbar Marton explains,

> "Herding requires each group member to recognize and anticipate not only the actions of one other member, but rather the entire group's continuously changing trajectory. Thus, herding requires simultaneously paying attention to numerous social cues from different origins while accounting for their distinct saliency and dependency."[33]

Being misaligned with the human herd produces feelings of anxiety. It exposes us to stigma and social pressure to conform. There are penalties for social deviance and for being different. In extreme cases we might even find ourselves ostracized or banished from the community. To avoid this, we are constantly wondering; What should I believe? How should I behave? What would people who are popular and respected do? According to social psychologists, we have evolved a sophisticated "consensus-finding mechanism" to help us make these calculations. It operates both consciously and unconsciously and processes the constant flow of social cues and signals we receive from other people. Because of it, we feel pulled by an invisible force to believe what others in our tribe believe. However, paradoxically, the confidence of herding animals in their leaders, and even in the group consensus, is not absolute. On the contrary it is surprisingly fragile. When leaders are perceived to be leading the herd towards danger, the consensus rapidly collapses. When this happens, trust disappears and new leaders emerge to take the herd in new directions. The zoologist Isobel Watts points out that flock leaders who attempt to give birds incorrect information about their direction of travel can find themselves overruled and ignored,

> "In animal groups where certain individuals have disproportionate influence over collective decisions, the whole group's performance may suffer if these individuals possess inaccurate information... when leaders hold inaccurate information they lose their influence over the flock."[34]

The French social psychologist Gustave le Bon described the same mechanism of Tribal Truth as the "religious sentiments of crowds". Le Bon observed that, "crowds do not reason", instead they "accept or reject ideas as a whole" and "tolerate neither discussion nor contradiction."[35]

Stuart Hall's Encoding/Decoding model brilliantly encapsulated this new understanding of what makes knowledge legitimate. It rejected the empiricism of Victorian Liberalism and bypassed the Anglo-American Enlightenment's obsession with independent, evidence-based thinking. Instead, it provided a much-needed theoretical validation of the Boomer way of knowing — one based on the shared feelings of Boomers. Tribal Truth, the ethical-political consensus of the Boomers, was an attractive epistemic formula — one perfectly suited to the needs of a generation that had begun to place its hands on the levers of power.

Hall's Regret; God Save Us From Our Friends

Instead of asking; What is true? or Is this belief justified by evidence? Hallism asks; Are the consequences of believing this ethically-politically good or bad? Is it safe for me to believe this? and, Are my beliefs in tune with the current group consensus? Lawrence Grossberg, an American media theorist and friend of Stuart Hall, notes that when this epistemology is applied to the production of news, it produces a form of journalism intimately tied to the political interest of the group which produces it. Consequently, faith in the narrative signals tribal loyalty while disbelief signals disloyalty,

> "The various forms and statements of knowledge, are really political struggles. And the choice comes down not to some judgment about the relative merits of epistemological claims but to a statement of political commitments."[36]

Towards the end of the 1980s, Hall started to become uncomfortable with the formula of Tribal Truth he had popularized. In 1987, in an attempt to apply the intellectual brakes, he noted that generational consensus was evolving into a fierce intolerance of dissent,

"Our mode of political calculation is that of the taking of absolutist positions, the attribution of bad faith to those genuinely convinced otherwise — and thereby, the steady advance of the death-watch beetle of sectarian self-righteousness and fragmentation."[37]

In 1994 he intensified his warning, saying the Boomers had become so certain their intuitions and feelings were right, they risked establishing an epistemic tyranny more totalitarian than anything they had inherited from their parents,

"What is being legislated is another single, homogeneous truth — our truth to replace theirs... The last thing we need is the model of one authority substituting one set of identities or truths with another set of 'more correct' ones".[38]

Sensing a creeping fanaticism, he complained, "There are those who believe that politics consists of getting 'our side' where 'their side' used to be and then exercising power in exactly the same way they did", adding dryly, "Our enemies are bad enough; God save us from our friends".[39] Hall also attempted to distance himself from his Encoding/Decoding model. With endearing candor he criticized it for its lack of intellectual rigor,

"The encoding/decoding model wasn't a grand model... I didn't think of it as generating a model which would last for the next twenty-five years for research. I don't think it has the theoretical rigor, the internal logic and conceptual consistency for that".[40]

By the 1990s, Hallism had run its course. The needs of the Boomer generation were evolving. The War Generation was retiring and taking its commitment to Victorian Liberal Journalism with it. The Boomers were now in positions of power and responsibility in the newsrooms of the US and the UK. What was required was a new theoretical approach, one capable of cementing the authority of the Boomers and their way of seeing and knowing. Hallism argued that legitimate knowledge was the consensus of the group, and that individuals could use their intuition to sense it. This framework would now need to be adjusted to legitimize intolerance of non-Boomer views. The theorist who best expressed this new authoritarian mood was the French intellectual Pierre Bourdieu.

Bourdieuism, and the New Journocracy

Pierre Bourdieu was a sociologist and public intellectual in the French Marxisant tradition. He was opposed to Victorian Liberalism and its impartial style of journalism, thus his project was not a purely scholarly one. As the American sociologist David Gartman puts it, "Bourdieu's theory also has a critical intent — it aims not merely to understand society but also to criticize and change it."[41]

Bourdieu set out his vision for journalism in *On Television*, an influential book which was translated into English in 1998. Bourdieu began by criticizing Victorian Liberal Journalism for pandering to the worst, lowest instincts of audiences. In emotive language, Bourdieu argues that popular, tabloid journalism stirs the "most primitive drives and emotions" of the mob and can therefore be considered as a form of journalistic "lynching",

> "This same search for sensational news, and hence market success, can also lead to the selection of stories that... can stir up great excitement by catering to the most primitive drives and emotions (with stories of kidnapped children and scandals likely to arouse public indignation)... aggressive enough almost to qualify as symbolic lynching".[42]

Having equated Victorian Liberal Journalism with sensational, tabloid journalism, Bourdieu then argues the problem is caused by competition between journalists which is a product of Victorian Liberalism itself,

> "Economic competition between networks or newspapers for viewers, readers, or for market share, takes place concretely in the form of a contest between journalists. This contest has its own, specific stakes — the scoop, the 'exclusive,' professional reputations, and so on." [43]

At first it appears Bourdieu is arguing for more accurate and more truthful journalism, but that is not where his argument is heading. Bourdieu says his quarrel with human interest stories is they lack a guiding ethical-political framework. For Bourdieu, news stories should always fit into a wider explanatory narrative. Journalism that fails to do this is objectionable,

> "Human interest stories create a political vacuum. They de-politicize and reduce what goes on in the world to the level of anecdote or scandal... In short, the focus is on those things which are apt to arouse curiosity but require no analysis, especially in the political sphere".[44]

It is now clear that Bourdieu is arguing, not for less tabloidization, but for politicized, Narrative-Led News. He follows this logic relentlessly and reaches the conclusion that there is no place for purely truth-seeking journalism. Whereas Hall called for Boomer Journalists to self-censor, Bourdieu calls for the outright suppression of views that prevent the creation of a better world. Bourdieu realizes this is a delicate matter, so he writes euphemistically that only "heteronomous" voices should be banned. Heteronomous voices, he says, are those which are deviant, peripheral to the consensus and therefore undesirable. As he explains, "It seems to me indispensable to combat these heteronomous intellec-tuals."[45] Bourdieu calls for an ideological "entry fee" — a bar of ethical and political merit which must be met before anyone is allowed on the air. This, he says, will suppress undesirable, hetronomous voices — even if they represent the views of large sections of society,

> "What I find difficult to justify is the fact that the extension of the audience is used to legitimate the lowering of the standards for entry into the field... we must work to maintain, even to raise the requirements for the right of entry — the entry fee — into the fields of production".[46]

Bourdieu gives an example of the voices he believes should be sup-pressed. They are voices that are "liable to unleash strong, often negative feelings, such as racism, chauvinism, the fear-hatred of the foreigner or xenophobia. I am referring, of course" he says, "to the National Front".** He prophesizes that, when Victorian Liberal Journalism is finally de-

---

** *Le Front National*, a French populist party highly critical of mass immigration. In 2018 it changed its name to The National Rally (*Rassemblement National*).

stroyed, a new type of journalism will emerge in which journalists will be empowered to silence these unwanted, heteronomous voices,

> "Journalists might agree to forget about audience ratings for once and refuse to open their talk shows to political leaders known for and by their xenophobia. Further, they could agree not to broadcast what these characters say".[47]

Bourdieu says this new type of Boomer Journalism will be conscious of its ethical-political responsibilities and will permit only the voices of the "guardians of collective values" to be heard.[51]

Bourdieu began by arguing that the tabloidization of news panders to the tastes of an ignorant and vulgar mob. By a series of leaps and jumps of logic he ends with the neo-Platonic conclusion that there should be an intellectual aristocracy of "guardians" with the power to dictate which opinions are heard and which are silenced. Bourdieu's vision of journalistic Utopia — "All of this is utopian, and I know it"[49] — legitimizes the establishment of a journocracy in which elite journocrats will construct and manage the official, tribal narrative and control access to the channels of communication. Only voices that reinforce "collective values" will be heard. Stuart Hall understood truth as an expression of the collective consciousness of the Boomer generation. Bourdieu goes further and transforms Tribal Truth into Official Truth — the expression of the tribal consensus after it has been interpreted, codified and curated by tribal leaders. It was an appealing formula that promised the Boomers a monopoly on truth and legitimate knowledge.

Bourdieu's Journocracy and Soviet Journalism

Bourdieu's model of journalism is largely indistinguishable from the journalistic doctrine of the Communist Party of the Soviet Union during the cold war. Both adopted a high ethical-political tone and were contemptuous of their audiences. The Soviet era journalist Stanislav Kondrashov for example boasted of the moral superiority of communist journalism over that of the West, "Our reportage is not based on commercial interests which, especially at the lower end of the market, exploit people's baser instincts, and arouse the darker side of their character. This we don't have".[50]

Bourdieu also follows orthodox Soviet media theory by rejecting the impartiality and depoliticization characteristic of Victorian Liberal Journalism. The Soviet approach to news was known as *narodnost* — the privileging of important political education over trivial entertainment. It was an approach described in detail by Lenin,

> "While ruthlessly suppressing the thoroughly mendacious and insolently slanderous bourgeois press, we must set to work systematically to create a press that will not entertain and fool the people with political sensation and trivialities, but which will submit the questions of everyday economic life to the people's judgement and assist in the serious study of these questions".[51]

In other words, journalism in the USSR was partial. The impartiality that was so important to Victorian Liberal Journalism was despised. The essential function of Soviet journalism was to persuade audiences to believe in the ethical-political merits of Marxist-Leninist communism and exclude dissenting voices. However, willful lying and falsification were just as contemptible to Soviet journalists as to their liberal Western counterparts. For example, according to the introduction of the 1958 edition of Lenin's writings on the press,

> "Lenin taught that the revolutionary Marxist press... must stand on a firm foundation of facts, reflecting the events and phenomena of social life in their dialectical development, and in relation to concrete historical conditions".[52]

However, to a Soviet journalist, impartiality was equally as abhorrent as inaccuracy. The tactic routinely used was therefore to include some facts, but omit others so as to construct a narrative. Soviet journalists were trained to tell the truth, but not the whole truth. Soviet journalists were advocates. Journalistic Truth was understood as being accuracy without impartiality. In fact partiality (*partiinost*) was as precious to Soviet journalists as impartiality was to their Western counterparts. As the media scholar Brian McNair explains,

"The most important principle of Soviet journalism was, for Lenin, partiality, expressed in Russian by the terms *partiinost* and *ideonost*... Partiality assumes that social consciousness and the means by which it is expressed, such as communication, have a class nature. There can be no neutrality in cultural production".[53]

Thus, Soviet journalists distinguished between *pravdivost* (accuracy) and *obyektivnost* (impartiality). Journalism of the Soviet era was intended to portray facts accurately (*pravdivost*), but at the same time be unapologetically one-sided and partial. However, where there is partiality, it is essential that journalists know which facts they should include and which they should omit. All the facts must support the approved narrative and contrary evidence must be excluded. Therefore, to ensure that only the narrative of the "guardians of collective values" is heard, the Soviet regime established a formidable apparatus of state control. As Lipovchenko's textbook for Soviet journalists put it,

"Mass media are not independent, 'autonomous' elements in the political system. Journalism is subordinate to the aims laid down for it by the political forces governing it".[54]

Bourdieu does not argue for formal state control of journalism, instead he suggests this will be the job of journocrats whom he flatteringly describes as a special caste of "journalist-intellectuals"[55] and "professional cultural producers"[56] chosen because they possess a superior "enlightened scientific judgment".[57] Bourdieu calls on journalists to abandon their outmoded objectivity and impartiality, step down from their "ivory tower" and become ethically-politically committed agents. Like Hall, Bourdieu believes the job of journalists is not to search for truth. Instead he says, they need to recognize they are, "part of the political field."[58]

Like Soviet journalism, Bourdieuism is not concerned with whether a news story is objectively 'true' or 'untrue'. It is concerned only with whether it is ethically-politically useful — whether it will help bring power to those trying to make the world a better place. It is the ethical-political *consequence* of news story that matters. However, because *arete* replaces *aletheia*, this epistemic approach also implies a denial of reality. This uncomfortable fact was brought home to McNair who was in Moscow in 1986 when the nuclear reactor at Chernobyl exploded showering radioactive debris over a large part of Europe. The disaster posed an epistemic challenge to Soviet journalism because the goal of making the world a better place by promoting the successes and achievements of the socialist state, clashed with the goal of telling the truth and warning citizens they were in danger. The result was a journalism of wishful thinking that described the world as it ideally ought to exist, not the world that actually did. It was, says McNair,

"A period of ten anxious days... during which the Soviet government, through the media, kept its own citizens, foreign guests, and the international community as a whole in virtual ignorance about a nuclear catastrophe of unprecedented seriousness... While western tabloids spoke of thousands dead... one had little choice but to stock up with plentiful supplies of champagne, get therapeutically drunk, and hope for the best".[59]

In summary, during the last third of the 20th Century, Boomer academics created a dense, self-supporting web of texts designed to delegitimize the truthful journalism of Victorian liberalism and legitimize the Vortex of Immaturity, the Boomer Ideology and the aspirations of the Boomer generation. It was an epistemic revolution that saw the old concept of Journalistic Truth erased and replaced by the concept of consensus, or Tribal Truth and then a more authoritarian version of it — Official Truth. The intellectual theories produced during the last third of the 20th century were therefore the product of the unique discontents of the Boomers. The activist and journalist Jack Newfield, writing in 1966, described them as, "powerlessness, moral disaffection, the purposelessness of middle-class life — all of which are the special products of an abundant, technocratic urban culture."[60] The job of intellectuals was to legitimize the evolving feelings, hopes and fears of the Boomers, provide theoretical scaffolding to support their generational quest for power and redefine fundamental epistemic questions such as, What is sane and what is insane? and Who decides? As Newfield concluded, it was above all else, a fight to control the definition of truth, "One generation's revolt against the last one's definition of reality." This epistemic revolution was not confined to college media departments and high school text books. By the late 1980s, professional journalism in the US and the UK was also rapidly changing. Victorian Liberal Journalism was being replaced by a radically different journalism — one based on the new, truthophobic assumptions of the Boomers.

Chapter 19

A Mission to Explain. From Journalism to Journocracy at the BBC

During the late 1980s, the BBC's highly-respected Victorian Liberal Journalism was replaced by Boomer Journalism. The transformation of the world's biggest, and most influential news broadcaster, was masterminded by John Birt who joined the BBC as a senior executive in 1987 and who was in overall charge of the organization between 1992 and 2000. Born in 1944 in Liverpool, Birt was a self-confessed child of the sixties and champion of Boomer values. As a boy, he enjoyed solving problems by looking for the grand, unifying framework that created sense and order. At St Mary's Catholic boys' school he was fascinated by a teacher who seemed to have the magical ability to simplify complexity and reduce it to easily digestible nuggets. As Birt recalled in his autobiography, the math teacher, "explained the most difficult and abstruse concepts brilliantly" which encouraged Birt to enjoy the process of "dissecting complex problems, [and] making the imaginative leap to a solution."[1]

As a TV journalist, his big break came in 1967 after Mick Jagger was freed from jail. Birt persuaded the rock star to be interviewed by a panel of establishment figures in a "dialogue between generations". In a 2005 speech, recalling his Jagger scoop, Birt described the erotic thrill of being pressed against Jagger's girlfriend Marianne Faithfull in a small helicopter on their way to the filming location,

> "We swooped exhilaratingly over a verdant countryside on a glorious, cloudless, summer's day. Faithfull – relieved her man was not in jail – snogged him ferociously, unselfconsciously grinding her bum against me as she did."[2]

As a young TV producer, Birt recalls the shared tribal intuition of the Boomers and their desire to change the world and make it a better place, "We knew what we liked and didn't like... We bridled against stuffy, out of touch, unaccountable institutions." Birt adds, "We didn't yet understand how to achieve these goals, but in the event the liberal values and notions of our generation would indeed change the world, generally for the better."[3]

Between February 1975 and September 1976, Birt, and his colleague Peter Jay, wrote five historically important articles for the London *Times*. The articles formed a manifesto for a new type of journalism. Their thesis was a declaration of war on Victorian Liberal Journalism and a plan for its destruction. In the first article, Birt attacked the traditional journalistic questions; 'Who', 'What', 'Where', 'When' and 'How' claiming they represented a "bias against understanding". He argued the most important question, and the one which should be answered first, was 'Why'. This reversed the old journalistic methodology which prioritized factual reporting, and confined explanation and opinion to the editorial columns. Birt's justification was not epistemic, it was ethical and political. Like the Boomer journalists of the Underground press, he wanted a journalism based on *arete* — one that would make the world a better place. The bias against understanding, he said, "aggravates the difficulties which our society suffers in solving its problems and reconciling its differences."[4] Reporting bald facts, Birt said, was "unsatisfying",

> "With no time to put the story in context, [it] gives the viewer no sense of how any of these problems relate to each other. It is more likely to leave him confused and uneasy."

For example, a report about unemployment, said Birt, should aim to explain, "the real causes of unemployment." What was urgently required, he said, was journalism that solved problems,

> "The constant emphasis placed on societies' sores by television feature journalists, with little or no attempt to seek out the root causes or discuss the ways by which the sore might be removed, may even be dangerous."

In his second article, Birt attacked the classic Victorian Liberal distinction between fact and "news analysis". It was, he said, "the basic misconception, the reigning error. It is a distinction without any proper difference." He also attacked the old journalism for reporting events, "as separate stories, each a collection of discrete 'facts'".[5] This, he said, was wrong because life was not a complex collection of random events, it had patterns that could be analyzed and understood,

> "The reality is a seamless garment of interacting and developing processes while journalism is organized to collect innumerable nuggets of self-contained fact, to report an atomized world of a million tiny tales."

Birt argued it was the primary job of the journalist to seek out and identify the wider narratives. Journalists should not allow themselves to be distracted by the fine detail. In order to construct these explanatory narratives, a different type of journalist would be required. Birt had undisguised contempt for the old sort of fact-finding hacks who cut their teeth working on provincial newspapers. These working-class reporters lacked the ability, he said, to make the necessary leap from factual reporting to Narrative-Led Journalism. Instead, he explained, a new generation of elite, university-educated journocrats was urgently required. The problem, he said, was due to a,

> "Cultural lag in the qualifications and background of the broad mass of reporters, news editors and the like. If the archetype is the cub reporter who, having left school at 16, wins his spurs covering crime in Gateshead, it is not to be expected that the profession will be well adapted to explaining a world of continuing economic malaise and increasing social stress."[*]

Birt called for the creation of crack squads of Boomer journocrats whose role would be to construct news narratives to help people understand the world's problems. Anything less, he claimed, would be "amateur". What was required were many,

> "Knowledgeable and educated journalists, sometimes working in teams and continuously blending inquiry and analysis, so that the needs of understanding direct the inquiry and the fruits of inquiry inform the analysis."

In another article, Birt gave more detail about the "radical changes" required to create the "new style of journalism."[6] He explained that once the elite journocrats had constructed their narratives, the next challenge would be to efficiently communicate them down through the hierarchy of the news organization and to audiences. Birt called for a revolution in the methodology and organization of news,

> "We urgently need profound change in television journalism - even in journalism as such… It means building a new structure of programmes, a new concept of programme making and a new organization of properly qualified producers and journalists, custom-designed for the purpose. In this way the pervasive bias against understanding, which is now the chief disfigurement of contemporary journalism in all media, can be corrected."

---

[*]Gateshead is a town in the north east of England. Birt uses it derisively. The US equivalent would be Palookaville or Hickville — an unremarkable place in the back of beyond characterized by mediocrity and blandness.

In his final article, Birt repeated his view that Victorian Liberal Journalism was out of date and no longer relevant, "In sum, most journalists, including television journalists, work to obsolete and muddled concepts which need to be replaced by the values of a new journalism-value."[7] Birt could only identify one possible drawback to his grand scheme. He admitted it was conceivable that centralized, top-down, Narrative-Led Journalism might become, "monolithic and that this would lead to a set of constricting values determining 'the line' which journalists are to take when covering a particular story." Having raised this possibility however, he quickly dismissed it. The risk of creating an Official Truth with a set of inflexible, official narratives was, he said, worth taking, "much is at stake", he urged, "if we do not move towards, this new journalism."

Birt finished his manifesto with a dramatic flourish and a nod to fashionable Boomer media theory. Referring to Marshall McLuhan's categories of 'hot' and 'cool' media, he claimed Victorian Liberal Journalism was 'hot' and therefore ethically-politically bad. The old journalism was, he said, "anti-social",

> "If television does not provide a cool exposition of the complicated and deep-rooted problems which face our society and our world... if instead, it simply provides a hot diet of the manifestations of those problems, then it may reasonably be said that television journalism has become an obstacle, rather than an aid, to understanding and so has become anti-social."

Birt's plan to create an aristocracy of university-educated Boomer journocrats to explain the news, was a repudiation of the entire Enlightenment way of knowing — a reversal of Newton's dictum "*hypotheses non fingo*" — "I frame no hypotheses". Birt's methodology was to create the hypothesis first and then seek evidence to confirm it. "*Narrantes fingo*" might have been Birt's Latin motto — "I construct explanatory narratives". This approach was, in turn, the logical outcome of the radically different metaphysical and ontological assumptions of the Boomer Ideology compared to those of the Anglo-American Enlightenment. For example, the Newtonian Universe was cruelly indifferent to human wishes. It was an imperfect place where nature bestowed her gifts unequally and capriciously. It was unpredictable, inscrutable, unknowable — a place where human knowledge was uncertain and fragile. In this Universe, the role of man was to understand nature and work within the limitations she imposed.

The moral Universe of the Boomers was a very different place. It was responsive to the hopes and dreams of the Boomers. It was progressive; inexorably moving towards a final destination — a place where unfairness, unhappiness, suffering and injustice would be abolished. In Boomertopia, the Boomers would have it all, provided they dared to dream. These two worldviews are incompatible and gave birth to different epistemologies and journalisms. The epistemology of Victorian Liberalism assumed the world was volatile, complex and ambiguous. Simple solutions to life's problems were likely to be illusions — the product of wishful thinking. To the Victorians, those peddling simple narratives should be viewed with suspicion, as dangerous fanatics or unscrupulous hucksters. The philosopher Isaiah Berlin described narrative-led thinking as superstitious thinking, "a craving for the certainties of childhood or the absolute values of our primitive past". It led, he warned, to a longing for "quasi-religious myths" and was symptomatic of a dangerous "moral and political immaturity."[8] Unsurprisingly therefore, Birt's blueprint for elite Boomer journalism was greeted with hostility by journalists schooled in the Victorian Liberal tradition. Everything Birt was saying, and all his underlying assumptions, seemed hopelessly wrong, immature and alarming. The TV journalist Llew Gardner attacked Birt and Jay's epistemic arrogance and their,

> "Awful elitism, their smug conviction that they know best and have somehow hit on a truth about television journalism which could only have been discovered by people as wise as themselves."[9]

Another outspoken critic was Charles Curran, BBC Director General when Birt's manifesto was published. Curran told the Royal Television Society that journalism must not be allowed to become a sermon.[**] Explaining the news, he said, was not in the best interest of audiences. He

[**] Interestingly, Birt says in his autobiography he was not merely a "child of the sixties... seeking to build a new Britain", but also "culturally a Catholic, committed to, branded with, the essential values inculcated in me when I was growing up" (op cit, 244). Interestingly, Birt's vision for a centrally controlled, benevolent journocracy resembles the organization of the Catholic Church. Both rest on the assumption that those at the top possess superior, infallible knowledge of truth from which they derive the authority to instruct those below and lead them to salvation.

damningly referred to Birt as "the man who wants to wash their brains".[10] One of the strongest responses to the Birt-Jay Thesis came from Louis Heren, Foreign Correspondent of *The Times*. Heren lectured Birt on the value of epistemic humility. The job of a journalist, he said, was to try to find out what was going on and report it as honestly as possible. It was not for journalists to decide what caused the world's problems, nor preach about how they should be solved. The reason for this, he said, was journalists had no means of knowing these things,

> "I did my best as a young reporter to tell the readers what really happened. I was not very successful. At first, I blamed my inexperience, but as I got older I realized that very few observers, and indeed some of the participants in the events reported, knew what had really happened. The best one could hope for was to write an honest report, which did not mislead, and leave the rest to further investigation or history."[11]

Heren added that, recognizing one's own ignorance was the essential first step to producing honest, mature journalism,

> "It was the true beginning of the learning of my curious craft, of humility if not wisdom. It remains the indispensable discipline, along with deadlines, space, and the laws of libel and contempt, of journalism. That it was ignored by John Birt and Peter Jay in their articles on television news makes suspect their case for what they chose to call the New Journalism."

Heren also attacked the naïve philosophical relativism of the Boomer generation of academics. He referred to their truthophobic claim that facts did not exist as an,

> "Obscure philosophical argument of no relevance to journalism... There are facts and events which can be factually reported: indeed, which must be factually reported without comment. Instant analysis and comment by pundits who cannot possibly know what really happened can diminish the impact of the event and be dangerously misleading."

Heren said it was not for elite journalists to tell the audience what they should believe. Instead, he said, "readers and viewers should be allowed to draw their own conclusions." Heren ended with a stern warning. Birt's elite journocrats would not be infallible and would therefore inevitably fall prey to normal human biases and prejudices. The result would be a return to pre-Victorian Narrative-Led News,

> "Commentators and analysts are prone to the weaknesses and failings of reporters, and a few more. The reporter is at least disciplined by the requirements of his craft. Above all, he realizes that he rarely knows what really happened immediately after an event. He has to keep an open mind. That is not always easy, and it could be impossible if facts and comment were allowed to become inseparable."

But Birt was immune to this sort of criticism. He did not want to preserve Victorian Liberal Journalism and its epistemology. He wanted to destroy it.

A Mission to Destroy.
Flooding the BBC with Journocrats

After joining the BBC, Birt lost no time in declaring war on Victorian Liberal Journalism and all those who practiced it. He labelled his project the "Mission to Explain". In his autobiography he describes it as an epic David v Goliath battle and casts himself in the role of David. Birt contrasts exciting, committed, ethical-political Boomer Journalism with dreary, boring, impartial Victorian Liberal Journalism and complains that when he arrived at the BBC, "From the beginning, I was struck by how little overt idealism was in evidence."[12] Birt says his strategic objective was the destruction of the separation of fact and opinion. Birt is disgusted that, "the BBC's journalistic tradition overall was descriptive rather than analytical."[13] He says the BBC was clinging to outdated, pre-Boomer values, "Many of the BBC's journalists and programme makers seemed trapped in their West London prisons. Unaware of the swirl of ideas around them." It was, he says, fundamentally a generational clash,

"There was a huge cohort – chiefly in their forties or fifties – for whom news and current affairs were a process. They covered and responded to events. They were competent and experienced, but they had long since ceased to think enquiringly. They were in a groove serving time."[14]

Birt describes the hostile reaction of pre-Boomers to his arrival. They responded, he says, with,

"Sullen resentment... The centre of the BBC seemed stuck in the 1950s, and, as someone whose values and attitudes had been formed in the 1960s, I stood out... My modern clothes were obviously a cause of great fascination too."[15]

Birt notes there were some Boomers at the BBC, "among these listless legions were many glorious individual exceptions, generally in their twenties and thirties — a younger generation, in both radio and television, of a different hue."[16] But the problem was the "glorious" Boomers "were not in positions of power." Birt's solution was simple; he began to replace the non-Boomers with elite, university-educated Boomer journocrats, "I set out to reform and to modernize one part of this enormous, uncontrolled leviathan, BBC News" and bring about a spectacular transformation from, "the old world to a new journalistic era at the BBC."[17]

Birt flooded BBC News with Boomer journocrats many of whom were parachuted directly into senior positions of power and influence. Birt says he filled,

"Key slots on the team from both inside and outside the BBC, and — in defiance of BBC tradition — by direct appointment, without formal interview boards. I was certain we had to skip a generation or two to fill the lead management positions."[18]

The new journocrats all shared the Boomer's ethical-political values. They even looked reassuringly like members of the Boomer tribe. For example, Birt says one new arrival, Ian Hargreaves, looked like "a young, radical university lecturer."[19] Of the eighty new recruits, Birt says proudly his, "biggest catch was the brilliant, edgy Polly Toynbee, a real authority, who joined from *The Guardian* as social affairs editor."[20] Toynbee was no impartial reporter of fact. An Oxford-educated political activist, described as the, "*grande dame* of the Left" by one newspaper, she made no secret of her desire to use journalism to promote radical social change and social justice.[21] Birt says his "young lions" were recruited to "edit a new generation of news programmes", and notes with satisfaction the horrified reaction of the old guard. Birt gleefully writes that one pre-Boomer described his revolution as a "most violent act", and that it, "prompted a flock of early retirements."[22] Eradicating Victorian Liberal Journalism at the BBC and replacing it with Boomer Journalism would not be painless. However, the momentum was now with the Boomers. As Birt gleefully put it, "a new generation was now in charge."

Lime Grove – Demolishing the Dragon's Lair

At the BBC, the job of the News Department was to report fact, while the job of the Current Affairs Department was to add analysis and opinion. Birt set out to break down the firewall between them by merging the two departments into one. He immediately ran into fierce resistance from the Current Affairs team based at Lime Grove in West London. To Birt, everything about Lime Grove reeked of Victorian Liberal Journalism and its traditions. Even its architecture seemed to suggest that life was a complex, insoluble mystery, rather than a set of patterns to be simplified and explained. Lime Grove had been constructed in 1915 as one of the first purpose-built film studios in Britain. John Tusa, a senior old-school BBC journalist, described it affectionately as a, "scruffy maze of cubbyholes, rat runs and Escher-like stairs carved out of narrow corridors".[23] To Birt, it was a shrine to Victorian Liberal Journalism — the dragon's lair. He described it with contempt as a, "labyrinthine building of bewildering complexity, run-down and ramshackle, unsuitable for modern programme-making, a festering rabbit-warren sheltering hidden cliques."[24]

In July 1987, Birt visited Lime Grove and told a meeting of current affairs journalists, their world was about to change. David Wickham, a senior producer, remembers that Birt and his "troops" marched in and made it, "very clear that this was a new beginning, that nothing we had done before was good enough and that we were going to start again."[25] Birt's zeal for his mission was intense, almost religious. Tusa said it was totalitarian,

"I noted that one of the tactics of the new regime was to portray itself as founder of 'Year Zero'. Everything new and worthy, on this view, began with them; naturally, everything that existed before 'Year Zero' was worthless."[26]

Another senior BBC journalist recalls gloomily,

"We were told in a big meeting that we didn't know what we were doing, that the award-winning journalism the BBC had done was crap. I'd just spent months in Lebanon being shot at, I'd been mustard gassed in the Iran-Iraq war, and I'm being told I don't know what journalism is and it's all going to change."[27]

Birt reorganized journalism. He introduced a new methodology and imposed it on his reluctant journalists. Scripts would be written by elite journocrats in the newsroom, and then reporters would be sent out to film interviews and collect footage to fit the pre-existing scripts. In this way, reality would be forced to conform to the narrative. At another meeting, Birt told producers he wanted to see far more "scripting and planning in advance". When asked which BBC current affairs shows he liked, "to be honest", he replied, "there's nothing I like." The truth of a news story, he implied, "could be arrived at intellectually." The media historian Georgina Born explains that Birt's methodology privileged narrative over factual reporting, "In the name of rigor and efficiency, scripts were to be prepared and the logic of argument fully worked out before filming, which would follow the dictates of the argument."[28]

By the 1990s, BBC reporters out in the field were increasingly being told what was 'really' happening and how they should report it, regardless of the evidence of their own eyes. One journalist recalls,

"They'd say, 'Now by the way, the way we see this story is...', and tell you what your story ought to say when you were out there actually at the story. That sounds like a joke, but that is the way it became. And it became that way out of a sort of slightly centralizing, control freaky thing that was going on around the new bureaucracy."[29]

Birt had pioneered this type of journalism before he joined the BBC. In 1979, at London Weekend Television, he over-ruled journalists in Iran who were reporting the fall of the Shah. Birt refused to believe them because the narrative he had worked out in advance predicted the Shah would remain in power. As one frustrated reporter explained, "Back at LWT they said, 'stick with the script.' People in the field were saying, 'it's not happening,' but the decision was, that is the slant, that is what we're going to do."[30]

Narrative management became the most important journalistic skill. Born notes the result was a more homogenous news agenda dictated from above. In Birt's BBC, "vertical controls were introduced… scripts were vetted and an inhibited intellectual tone took hold. In this climate investigative journalism was not welcomed."[31]

Journalists complained of the growing tyranny of narrative, and of "Stalinist pressures to take the 'BBC line' editorially".[32] As the news agenda was increasingly worked-out in the office by teams of senior journocrats, many reporters began to feel uncomfortable. One admitted often having no idea if the stories he reported were true or not,

"It's bizarre; you become a kind of virtual journalist, stuck in a bureau reprocessing material and not actually going out and witnessing events, not experiencing what you're reporting."[33]

John Tusa was damning about the new Journalism. He said it was a formula powered by wishful thinking which produced fantasy not truth,

"I think his theory of news is almost total rubbish. It bears no relationship to the nature of events. It bears no relation to what gathering news on the ground is like... I have no time for his journalism and I think it was bad, misdirected and usually completely unviewable."[34]

However, the discomfort and despair of the BBC's Victorian Liberal journalists was music to Birt's ear. He felt his mission was to do to journalism, what the Beatles and Mick Jagger had done to music — change it, revolutionize it and make it serve the needs of the Boomer generation. He saw himself as a journalistic rock star trashing his hotel room

— a radical, destructive force breaking the old rules and smashing ancient taboos. Describing his impact on the older generation of BBC journalists, Birt wrote with satisfaction, "I was the person who had blasted their world apart."[35] All that remained was one final symbolic gesture. Lime Grove, the stronghold of pre-Boomer values, was sold and the building razed to the ground. "It was a happy day for me" Birt recalled, "when Lime Grove was bulldozed to the ground, and a centre for the homeless built in its place."[36] The triumph of Boomer Journalism was complete.

Boomer Journalism for Boomer Democracy

If Lime Grove was hell, then the BBC's new building at Milbank was John Birt's vision of heaven. It was symbolically located in Westminster just across the road from the Houses of Parliament. It spoke of a new type of collusive journalism in which journocrats and policy makers would work together to design and build a better world, based on shared Boomer values and assumptions. This collusive approach to journalism was very different to the Victorian Liberal ideal in which journalism was the "Fourth Estate" — a watchdog keeping an ever-vigilant eye on the activities of those in power. Boomer Journalism saw its role as working alongside politicians to help shape the consensus and pursue the goals of social justice. However, the new alliance between Boomer technocrats and Boomer journocrats drew sharp criticism from commentators such as Peter Oborne for whom the new arrangement was both undemocratic and sinister,

> "The Media Class and Political share identical assumptions about life and politics. They are affluent, progressive, middle and upper-middle class. This triumphant metropolitan elite has completely lost its links with a wider civil society... politicians and the media have far more in common with each other than they do with voters, readers and the public."[37]

Oborne argued that Boomer Journalism was politicized journalism and its methodology involved pro-social lying. Thus, he said, collusive Boomer Journalism was largely indistinguishable from propaganda,

"To put the matter at its simplest, journalists became instruments of government. Reporters and governments joined a conspiracy against the public to create a semi-fictitious political world whose most striking features were media events and fabricated stories."[38]

According to Oborne, narrative-led Boomer Journalism was creating a "complex new world, where fact and fiction merge" and in which "manipulation and deceit" have come to,

"Dominate almost all of British mainstream culture... lying, deception, manipulation and fabrication of the truth have become routine and to a large extent systemic."[39]

In other words, the Boomer consensus was becoming an elite consensus serving the interests of a narrow section of Boomers — those in positions of power. Official Truth had become elite truth. As one troubled BBC producer put it, "They've come from the same universities, the same social background, there is no standing back, no objective role there. It's a cozy working relationship... it's completely undemocratic."[40]

The new Boomer Journalism was intended to help create Boomertopia and meet the needs of those living there. In Boomertopia, citizens would be liberated from the tedious task of searching for truth. Instead, they would be free to spend their time seeking personal fulfilment, gratifying their desires, pursuing their dreams and making the world a better place. In Boomertopia, citizens would delegate responsibility for governing to benevolent Boomer technocrats. They would delegate responsibility for knowing to benevolent Boomer journocrats. The American media scholar Michael Schudson, writing in 1998, proposed a new name for citizens of this new type of Boomer democracy. Instead of "informed citizens", he proposed "monitorial citizens". "A headline service", Schudson said, "is what, in the first instance, citizens require." In Boomertopia, simple, explanatory news narratives would replace the confusing uncertainty produced by the old journalism. Schudson painted a beguiling picture of citizens lazing in the sun beside a swimming pool,

"The monitorial citizen engages in environmental surveillance more than information-gathering. Picture parents watching small children at the community pool. They are not gathering information; they are keeping an eye on the scene."[41]

In Schudson's version of Boomertopia, journocrats would be informational 'lifeguards'. Boomer citizens could switch off their epistemic vigilance and doze contentedly in the sun. The British sociologist Colin Crouch labelled the new low-effort, Booomer democracy 'Post Democracy'. It was a form of government in which individuals could abdicate personal responsibility and put their trust in the wise rule of tribal leaders and expert policy makers,

> "A post-democratic society therefore is one that continues to have and to use all the institutions of democracy, but in which they increasingly become a formal shell. The energy and innovative drive pass away from the democratic arena and into small circles of a politico-economic elite."[42]

It was the War Generation, said Crouch, who had brought Victorian Liberal Democracy to its peak of democratic perfection, "In most of western Europe and North America we had our democratic moment around the mid-point of the 20th century."

Looking back on his achievements, Birt recalled he had entered broadcasting as a Boomer with "hair heading for my shoulders" at a time of ideological change. He described himself as one of the new generation of "media radicals" whose mission was to "prise open this industry and to connect it more effectively to the shifts taking place in wider society." His greatest pride came from unchaining ethical-political tribalism, the very thing the Victorians had worked so hard to restrain. He called on journalists to continue to collaborate with policy makers and encourage them to,

> "Do the right thing, to diagnose the deeper causes of our problems, many of which have been decades in the making, and to devise and to pursue robust long-term solutions to them. As I put it in an article in *The Times* exactly thirty years ago '...there is a danger that the pressure brought to bear on politicians...will lead them to deal with the symptoms of crisis rather than to take a longer time to search out fundamental causes and to deal with them'."[43]

The verdict of the historian Georgina Born was less generous. Birt succeeded, she says, in introducing into journalism "unprecedented forces for editorial control",

> "The pincer movement applied by Birt to news – centralization and commodification – had the effect of diminishing editorial bravery and originality, reinforcing institutional caution and homogenizing news content ready to be repackaged for new outlets."[44]

Birt redirected journalism. The commitment to search for truth, became a commitment to make the world a better place. The question, Is this story true? took second place to, Is this story well-intentioned? or Are its consequences ethically-politically good? Editorial decision-making became aware of its ethical-political responsibilities. The role of elite journocrats was to help shape the tribal consensus by constructing official news narratives. The role of rank-and-file journalists was to curate these narratives and communicate them to citizens. A willingness to self-censor replaced the ability to enquire impartially as one of the most valuable journalistic skills. Born concludes that Birt's legacy was the replacement of "editorial autonomy" with obedient "anxious hierarchies."[45]

Chapter 20

Truthophobia US Style. Sullivan v *The New York Times* and the Death of Fairness

In the US, Boomer Journalism took a different path, but arrived at the same place. Unlike the UK, where the leviathan of the publicly funded BBC casts its long shadow, the US media ecosystem is fragmented. Historically it was composed of numerous independent, small and medium sized enterprises gathered together in a patchwork quilt of networks and affiliates. In the US, it was demand from Boomer audiences that brought about legislative change and drove the transition from

Victorian Liberal to Boomer Journalism. Along the road from truth to truthophobia, two legal milestones stand out; the 1964 Supreme Court ruling in the case of *The New York Times* v Sullivan, and the 1987 repeal of the Fairness Doctrine. The first undermined the obligation for journalists to report facts accurately, the second undermined the obligation for them to be impartial. Together they kicked away two of the epistemic pillars supporting Victorian Liberal Journalism in the US.

The New York Times v Sullivan

Every society places limits on free speech. The right to free expression is not absolute. Where it collides with the right to protect one's reputation from defamation, or to live without fear of violence, the limits of freedom are reached. Where precisely these boundaries should be placed is always controversial. In the US, free speech and the right of journalists to say what they like, is protected by the First Amendment which states, "Congress shall make no law... abridging the freedom of speech, or of the press." Nonetheless, despite this constitutional protection, a number of restrictions still apply. For example, "fighting words" which might incite violence are prohibited.* Another restraint on the freedom of the press is libel. Historically, in the US and the UK, truth was generally accepted as a complete defense in all defamation cases. In other words, no news organization could be successfully prosecuted for publishing a statement that was factually accurate. On the other hand, getting the facts wrong could easily result in an expensive payout for libel. Therefore, the legal requirement to tell the truth acted as an important incentive to keep journalism honest. In 1964, all of that changed. A highly truthophobic decision by the Supreme Court in the case of *The New York Times* v Sullivan, made it legal for journalists to lie, provided their motives were ethically-politically pure.

---

* The US Supreme Court (SCOTUS) defined "fighting words" in Chaplinsky v New Hampshire, 315 U.S. 568 (1942) as words which "by their very utterance, inflict injury or tend to incite an immediate breach of the peace. It has been well observed that such utterances are no essential part of any exposition of ideas, and are of such slight social value as a step to truth that any benefit that may be derived from them is clearly outweighed by the social interest in order and morality." Note the importance placed on the goal of truth-seeking (*aletheia*) by the justices in 1942.

The Sullivan decision was the culmination of a four-year legal battle which took place at the height of the civil rights campaign. On 29 March 1960, *The New York Times* published a full-page advertisement under the headline, "Heed Their Rising Voices",

> "In Montgomery, Alabama, after students sang 'My Country, 'Tis of Thee' on the State Capitol steps, their leaders were expelled from school, and truckloads of police armed with shotguns and tear-gas ringed the Alabama State College Campus. When the entire student body protested to state authorities by refusing to re-register, their dining hall was padlocked in an attempt to starve them into submission."[1]

The advert was emotional and affective. However, it also contained a number of inaccuracies. The campus dining hall had not been padlocked, students were not expelled for singing, nor did police "ring" the campus. L. B. Sullivan, the Montgomery Public Safety Commissioner, argued that, although he was not named, the word "police" obviously referred to him. Sullivan sued *The Times* for libel and a jury in Alabama awarded him damages of $500,000 — a huge amount at the time. *The New York Times* assembled a formidable legal team and appealed to the Supreme Court. After a three-month hearing, SCOTUS overturned centuries of common law tradition and ruled that publishing a false statement about a public official was acceptable, provided it was not motivated by hatred. In a momentous decision, the Court decided that, in any future libel case, public officials would have to prove "actual malice" in order to win a case for libel. Since this is an extremely difficult thing to do, the case represented a huge blow to journalistic truth, and an equally huge victory for the forces of truthophobia. The decision, in effect, legalized pro-social lying.

The Role of the Media in the Civil Rights Campaign

Sullivan was not an ordinary court case. It took place in a highly charged atmosphere. Looking back from the early 21st Century, it is difficult to fully appreciate the context in which it was heard. The summer of 1963 had been marked by angry clashes in and around Birmingham Alabama in which white police officers used high pressure fire hoses and dogs to break up peaceful protests by black civil rights campaigners. In August, a quarter of a million people marched on Washington DC and assembled in front of the Lincoln Memorial to hear Martin Luther King Jr's stirring "I Have a Dream" speech. The summer climaxed with a horrific bombing which killed four black girls at a church.

Media coverage of these events proved decisive. Images of police brutality in Birmingham were seen around the world and caused profound soul-searching across the US. As President Kennedy summarized on live TV,

> "The events in Birmingham and elsewhere have so increased the cries for equality that no city or state or legislative body can prudently choose to ignore them."

Kennedy vowed to urgently introduce legislation and the Senate passed the Civil Rights Act into law the following year — though not without furious opposition from the South. Then, in November 1963, just two months before SCOTUS heard the Sullivan case, came the shattering news of Kennedy's assassination. Finally, and highly symbolically, in February 1964, in the middle of the Sullivan case, the Beatles made their first appearance in the US playing live on the Ed Sullivan Show to an audience of 75 million people — most of them Boomers. It was an event that signaled the arrival of powerful new generational forces. To many, it seemed as if the old world was violently splitting apart and a new one was being born, like a butterfly emerging from its chrysalis. Sullivan was not therefore a purely legal case decided impartially on its merits. The Supreme Court was being asked to take a stand. It could either choose to put its weight behind racial bigotry and segregation and encourage those resisting change; or it could send a signal that it stood aligned with the forces of progress, anti-racism and civil rights. The court unhesitatingly chose the latter. The Supreme Court justices were not Boomers, however they shared with the Boomers a willingness to elevate ethical-political goals over the need to protect the abstract concept of truth. In 1964, it seemed an easy choice to make.

During the civil rights campaign, the media played an important role in shaping public opinion, especially in the North and among the Washington elites. Jack Nelson, a journalist who covered the civil rights movement during the 1960s recalls, "It was only after the news media began to cover Martin Luther King's protests extensively, and the broader public began to respond, that real reform began to take place." He adds that King knew,

> "Coverage on the evening television news was essential to moving public opinion. Riveting images of Birmingham Police Commissioner Bull Connor's officers using dogs and fire hoses to attack defenseless blacks, including women and children, sparked such national outrage that Congress passed the 1964 Public Accommodations Act."[2]

Andrew Young, one of King's most trusted advisors, also understood that sympathetic media coverage was essential in the fight to win the hearts and minds of elite decision makers and the wider public. According to Young, journalism was,

> "Essential to the conduct of non-violent demonstrations... It was no accident that our demonstrations were always in the morning; that we completed them by two o'clock in the afternoon so that we could make the evening news; and so that reporters could file their deadlines for the coming day."[3]

The media strategy of the civil rights campaigners involved creating simple, but powerful narratives and repeating them day after day in the press and on TV. These narratives were especially successful at galvanizing the young, idealistic, and numerically huge, Boomer generation. As the American academics Aldon Morris and Dan Clawson summarize,

> "Social disruption framed as struggles between good and evil, and between democracy and oppression attracted the media. Real human drama is hard to ignore, and leaders and grassroots people who are willing to confront oppressors in dramatic fashion generate it."[4]

Because the civil rights movement depended on sympathetic news coverage to spread its message, Sullivan's decision to sue for libel was, first and foremost, an attempt to deal *The New York Times* a harsh financial blow to deter it, and other news organizations, from supporting the movement. Therefore, if the Court found against *The Times*, the consequences would have been catastrophic for civil rights in the US. As the legal scholar David Anderson explains,

"The Southern press, for the most part, either ignored the movement or was hostile to it... The Northern press was important to the movement because its funding and volunteers came largely from the Northern audiences."[5]

The Supreme Court was clear where its duty lay. It had already played an important role in the struggle against segregation in the South when, in 1954, it ruled public school segregation based on race was unconstitutional. In 1958 it refused to allow schools in Little Rock Arkansas to delay desegregation, and it made sympathetic judgments in the sit-in cases that began in 1961. Indeed, several Supreme Court justices were well-known supporters of social and racial justice. For example, William Brennan was an outspoken champion of civil rights and later became, according to his biographers, a "symbol of judicial activism" and a, "hero to two generations of progressive lawyers, including Presidents Bill Clinton and Barack Obama". Brennan was known for his willingness to employ, "an assertive vision for the courts in which judges aggressively tackled the nation's most complicated and divisive social problems."[6] Another Justice, Arthur Goldberg, was also a staunch advocate of civil rights reform and hence, when Martin Luther King Jr. attended court on January 6th he was treated as,

"Something of an honored guest: Justice Arthur Goldberg quietly sent down a copy of King's account of the Montgomery bus boycott, *Stride Toward Freedom*, asking for an autograph."[7]

On 9 March 1964, the Supreme Court reversed the libel damages judgment against *The Times*. It was a righteous decision which arguably saved the civil rights movement. However, from a strictly legal point of view, the decision was harder to justify. The legal scholar Mary-Rose Papandrea says the good guys "plainly won this case", though she also

226

describes it as an "over-reaction" made in a "charged political atmosphere". Writing shortly after the ruling, the jurist Harry Kalven Jr said it was clearly an ethical-political decision, not a purely legal one. Kalven said the court had been "compelled by the political realities of the case to decide it in favor of *The Times*" adding , the justices were, "Prepared to pay the high price of destroying a considerable part of the common law of defamation" in order to obtain the desired ethical-political results.[8]

Outside the South, the decision was widely applauded. The eminent jurist Alexander Meiklejohn said it was wonderful news, "an occasion for dancing in the streets."[9]

The Consequences of Sullivan

In the Sullivan case, the Court was being asked whether modest pro-social lying in journalism was lawful. The underlying conflict was not between Sullivan and *The New York Times*, but between truth and truthophobia. The central question was, 'could a news organization report inaccurately and misleadingly in order to help the cause of social and racial justice?' In 1964, the choice seemed obvious. However, the judgment had unintended and unforeseen consequences. The Supreme Court, in doing what was right, had released a genie from its bottle. The landmark judgment created, in effect, a new category of 'morally good libel' and gave it legal protection. Sullivan rudely disturbed journalism's delicate dance with truth. In the hands of the new generation of Boomer journalists, its impact was to release the hand brake holding back their natural impulse to use pro-social lying to change the world and make it a better place. A door which the Victorians had bolted shut was now unlocked.

By the late 1980s, when Boomer journalists were in positions of power, the consequence of the Sullivan decision were rippling far and wide across the pond of US journalism. Referring to Alexander Meiklejohn's joyous reaction, the legal scholar Richard Epstein dolefully noted, "A generation has now passed, and the dancing has stopped." Epstein said the tree of Sullivan was bearing a bitter fruit, "The question on everyone's lips is: What went wrong? Why a winter of discontent after a springtime of unrestrained joy?" "The greatest cost of the present system is", he penetratingly observed, that, "it makes no provision for determining truth."[10] Journalists in the US were now free to lie about public figures, provided they claimed to be motivated by ethical-political goals. Pro-social lying would have no legal consequences. Epstein complained, "The centrality of truth is of critical importance" and concluded that, by permitting "morally good libel", Sullivan had created a dangerous, toxic legacy. He called for a return to the old, common law test of whether a statement was actually true or false,

> "Now that the exigencies of the immediate case, and of the segregation crisis that brought it to the fore have passed, the sensible constitutional conclusion is to abandon the actual malice rule in *New York Times*. In its institutional sense, *New York Times* v. Sullivan was wrongly decided."

During the mid-1980s' even the Supreme Court itself started to express unease with the Sullivan decision. As its implications became clearer, Justice Byron White wrote glumly, "New York Times Co. v. Sullivan was the first major step in what proved to be a seemingly irreversible process." Commenting on the truthophobic consequences of the ruling, he argued, "There is no constitutional value in false statements of fact. Neither the intentional lie nor the careless error materially advances society's interest in 'uninhibited, robust, and wide-open' debate on public issues."

> "*The New York Times* rule thus countenances two evils: first, the stream of information about public officials and public affairs is polluted and often remains polluted by false information; and second, the reputation and professional life of the defeated plaintiff may be destroyed by falsehoods that might have been avoided with a reasonable effort to investigate the facts."[11]

In 2020, the juror David Logan linked the Sullivan judgment to the contemporary epidemic of fake news. He observed, "We are subject to waves of falsehoods that swamp the ability of citizens to effectively self-govern" and he pointed to Sullivan as the cause,

> "With more than half a century of perspective, it is now clear that the Court's constraints on defamation law have facilitated

a miasma of misinformation that harms democracy by making it more difficult for citizens to become informed voters. The time has come to ask a once heretical question: "What if *New York Times* got it wrong?""[12]

The Sullivan decision was, he said, made recklessly without regard for long-term consequences, "In this one remarkable opinion, the Court struck down centuries of libel law" and "remade defamation law in a dizzying array of ways." It had, he said, resulted in, "what amounts to an absolute immunity from damages actions for false statements" which had led in turn to a, "torrent of false information entering our public square." Logan noted that new generations of journalists had "weaponized" Sullivan and used it to create a type of journalism, "rife with fake news and alternative facts".

The Sullivan case raised a series of exceptionally challenging moral and epistemic questions: Can short term ethical-political expediency justify inaccurate or dishonest journalism? And, How can journalists, or judges, avoid the unforeseen long-term consequences of well-intentioned acts? In *New York Times* v Sullivan, we see the eternal, vexed conflict between *aletheia* and *arete* — between the desire to tell the truth and the desire to do what is right.

The Abolition of the Fairness Doctrine

If the Sullivan decision chopped away one of the legs of Victorian Liberal Journalism, then the abolition of the Fairness Doctrine in 1987 chopped away the other. What Sullivan did for journalistic accuracy, abolition did for objectivity and impartiality. Although US newspapers have never been obliged to be impartial, the Fairness Doctrine did require TV and radio stations to devote time to controversial political issues and present them fairly by reporting both sides of the argument. The guiding principle was that impartial journalism was necessary to create an informed public and a functioning Liberal Democracy. However, the Boomer generation was militantly opposed to Victorian Liberal Democracy and wanted something better. To the Boomers therefore, the Fairness Doctrine was the relic of a bygone age — an arbitrary rule forcing them to listen to boring, complicated current affairs programing and to views with which they strongly disagreed.

As the Boomer generation bristled against this relic of Victorian Liberal Journalism and sought to dismantle it, one solution seemed to offer a magical quick fix — deregulation. The sweeping away of outmoded rules and restraints, was the perfect Boomer-friendly policy, and it became wildly fashionable on both sides of the political divide during the 1980s. Deregulation to the Boomers was subversive and radical. It was as if the Beatles on the train had suddenly gained the power to cancel all the old railway by-laws created by Fat Man Johnson's generation. The natural outcome of deregulation was the 'free market'. To the Boomers during the 1980s, the free market seemed to be a highly attractive proposition. Whatever the Boomers demanded, the free market would, at least in theory, supply. If the Boomer majority wanted an ethical consumer society, then the mechanism of the market would deliver it. If Boomer audiences wanted Boomer Journalism, then the market would deliver that too.

Looking back on the 1980s, Joseph Stiglitz, Chief Economist at the World Bank and a Nobel Prize winning economist, describes the enthusiasm for deregulation as a manifestation of wishful thinking and "irrational optimism" which was shared by most people at the time regardless of political affiliation. Hence the Democrats "joined in the fray — sometimes pushing things even further than under the Reagan administration." It quickly became, he said, the "mindless pursuit of deregulation."[13]

Stiglitz says the Boomer's "seemingly limitless faith" in the beneficial effects of deregulation and the market, underestimated the "drive for domination" that would inevitably follow. He observed that "advocates of deregulation had forgotten, or deliberately ignored, the market failures which had originally given rise to the regulations."[14] In other words, deregulation is never innocent and must always be considered in context. What is important is who is deregulating what, and who benefits from the deregulation. During the 1980s, it was the Boomers who were dismantling the regulations imposed on them by their parents' generation. It was against this background that Mark Fowler, the newly appointed Chair of the Federal Communications Commission, began his attack on the Fairness Doctrine in 1982.

The Fairness Doctrine was a well-entrenched piece of regulation. Previous attempts to weaken it had failed. For example, in 1969 the Supreme Court ruled that the purpose of broadcasting in the US was not primarily to entertain, but to help create, "an informed public capable of conducting its own affairs." The Court said that guaranteeing impartial news was in the spirit of the First Amendment, "Freedom of the press from governmental interference under the First Amendment does not sanction repression of that freedom by private interests."[15] Arguments based on the importance of free competition and market forces had also failed in the past. For example, in 1972 *WEFM*, a classical music radio station in Chicago, was sold to new owners who wanted to turn it into a rock music station for Boomers. The plan was strongly opposed by classical music fans of the War Generation. When the FCC refused to intervene, the classical fans went to court claiming the change was not in the public interest. This obscure inter-generational battle between classical music and rock 'n' roll ended with a victory for the War Generation who successfully used the Communications Act of 1934 to keep Bach on the air, and the Beatles off it. What was significant was the court's rejection of arguments based on market forces. "A policy of free competition" it said, would not bring "the maximum benefits of radio to all the people of the United States." Specifically, the court reasoned, a free market approach would favor the Boomers who had become numerically and economically dominant,

"The end result would be radio programs in line with the tastes of young adults with larger discretionary incomes, to the detriment of the preferences of older audiences with less discretionary income."[16]

However, although the older generation had won the battle, they were about to lose the war. In March 1981 the Supreme Court abandoned the "*WEFM* Doctrine" and ruled the FCC was free to decide what was, and was not, in the public interest. Justice Byron White accepted the FCC's case that,

"The public interest is best served by promoting diversity in a radio station's entertainment formats through market forces and competition among broadcasters."[17]

The decision was described as "disastrous" by Kristin Glen, a lawyer representing a group of classical music fans, who recognized the decision signaled, "an end to the trusteeship concept of broadcast licensing."[18] With the legal obstructions cleared away, Mark Fowler was now free to introduce sweeping changes to US broadcasting. "We're not going to regulate, we're not going to deregulate, we're going to *unregulate*!" he cheerfully announced.[19]

Fowler launched his offensive early in 1982 with a paper published in the *Texas Law Review*. In it he criticized the old ideology which had sought to protect informed debate by forcing TV and radio stations to broadcast both sides of a political argument. Fowler sneered at this philosophy and labelled it with the old-fashioned, pompous-sounding word "fiduciary". He said, under his leadership, the FCC's "fiduciary approach to broadcast regulation may be ending at last".** Fowler ridiculed the idea that Boomer broadcasters and journalists needed to be restrained by regulations imposed on them by the War Generation. Instead, he argued, the new values of deregulation and the free market would help fulfill "public desires,"

> "The perception of broadcasters as community trustees should be replaced by a view of broadcasters as marketplace participants. Communications policy should be directed toward maximizing the services the public desires."[20]

Fowler framed the issue as a simple, tribal conflict between "fiduciaries" — parental figures who wanted to preserve the status-quo; and "the market" — a vibrant force for radical change. Broadcasters and journalists, he said, should be viewed, "not as fiduciaries of the public, as their regulators have historically perceived them, but as marketplace competitors". He called for the abolition of the Fairness Doctrine and the political speech rules adding, "This new approach concludes that broadcasters best serve the public by responding to market forces rather than governmental directives."

In 1985, Fowler's FCC produced *The Fairness Report*, a one hundred and ten page document setting out in even greater detail the case against the Fairness Doctrine. Fowler argued that forcing journalists to cover both

** Fiduciary refers to the right of a parent to do things on behalf of a child who is incapable of doing them for himself. It survives as a legal term.

sides of an argument, deterred them from covering it at all. His report claimed a "chilling effect" arose because journalists feared getting into trouble for being insufficiently impartial,

> "The record reflects that broadcasters from television network anchors to small radio station journalists perceive the fairness doctrine to operate as a demonstrable deterrent in the coverage of controversial issues. Indeed, the record is replete with descriptions from broadcasters who have candidly recounted specific instances in which they decided not to air controversial matters of public importance."[21]

The report accused the Fairness Doctrine of creating, "a climate of timidity and fear, unexperienced by print journalists, that is antithetical to journalistic freedom." This, it said, "significantly impairs the journalistic freedom of broadcasters" because, "Once a newsperson has to stop and consider what a Government agency will think of something he or she wants to put on the air, an invaluable element of freedom has been lost." The report concluded, "There exists within the framework of fairness doctrine administration and enforcement the potential for undue governmental interference in the processes of broadcast journalism."

Fowler added a personal note to the document in which he framed the issue as the, "freedom of a broadcast press to cover a controversial issue of public importance in the manner they saw fit." It was, he said, a choice between, "the right of the press to criticize freely and the authority of the government to channel that criticism". He added the right thing to do would be to, "head ballistically toward liberty of the press for radio and television." What Fowler was doing was subtly changing the direction of the argument to assert the rights of *journalists*, not the rights of *audiences*. This represented a reversal of the argument used by the framers of the Fairness Doctrine in 1949 who prioritized the liberty of the audience to be informed, not the liberty of journalists to be partisan. For example, in 1949, the FCC had insisted,

> "It is this right of the public to be informed, rather than any right on the part of the Government, any broadcast licensee or any individual member of the public to broadcast his own particular

views on any matter, which is the foundation stone of the American system of broadcasting."[22]

Here then, was the seismic generational shift in ideology that separated the Boomers from the War Generation. The Boomers wanted the positive liberty to hear only their own narratives. The War Generation wanted the negative liberty to be free from partisan, Narrative-Led Journalism. Victorian Liberalism sought to protect the rights of the minority from the tyranny of the majority through regulation and rule of law. The attraction of the free market to Boomers during the 1980s, was it gave them power because they were the majority. The final act of the drama came in August 1987 when the FCC refused to enforce the Fairness Doctrine against the New York TV station *WTVH*. Citing their own Fairness Report, as well as previous court decisions, the FCC ruled,

"The fairness doctrine, on its face, violates the First Amendment and contravenes the public interest... the fairness doctrine can no longer be used against *WTVH* in any subsequent renewal proceedings or in any other context."[23]

The Fairness Doctrine was dead. Mark Fowler and the Boomer generation had killed it.

The Consequences of the Death of the Fairness Doctrine

US broadcasting began to change dramatically within weeks of the demise of the Fairness Doctrine. In July 1988 *WABC* Radio in New York launched The Rush Limbaugh Show which was soon syndicated across the country. Limbaugh pioneered a new style of talk radio in which he commented on news and current affairs in highly opinionated monologues. Limbaugh made no attempt to be impartial. Indeed, the more partial he was, the more his audience liked him. He was wildly popular with those who shared his views, and wildly unpopular with those who did not. He was, as the journalist Brian Anderson put it, "boisterously opinionated, unafraid to name names, informative, and, if you disagree with the host's politics, infuriating."[24]

Limbaugh's brand of opinionated quasi-journalism would have been unthinkable during the era of the Fairness Doctrine. Each of his opinionated comments would have had to be balanced by an alternative, competing view. Now, released from the shackles of the old regulations, new formats were possible. News organizations were free to supply politicized news narratives to meet demand from Boomer audiences. Boomers, like the broadcaster Adrian Cronauer, welcomed the new committed journalism which was being produced. Those who didn't like it, he said, were free to shop around and find views they preferred,

> "No responsible viewpoint is in danger of being stifled simply because it is denied access to a particular station – so long as there are other available stations. If a demand for a product exists, someone will eventually undertake to cater to that demand. If all television stations in a given area shut out a specific viewpoint, there is always radio."[25]

The Boomers did not need, nor want, impartial journalism because they were working from an entirely different set of epistemic assumptions. Truth was now Tribal Truth — the ethical-political consensus of their generation. It was something that could be felt intuitively and without considering the other side of the argument. As Cronauer put it, the American people,

> "Have an almost intuitive feeling for what is fair and what is not. They neither need, nor deserve, governmental censorship masquerading in the guise of fairness."[26]

Ironically however, the dominance of Boomer Journalism had arrived at precisely the same time the Boomer consensus was beginning to unravel. The schism within the Boomer tribe was symbolized by the falling-out between two former icons of the underground counterculture, Jerry Rubin and Abbie Hoffman. Close comrades during the 1960s, by 1985 they were politically estranged. They both still wanted to build Boomertopia, but disagreed about what it should look like. Rubin reinvented himself as a businessman and Wall Street stockbroker, and ran a company that organized business networking events. Rubin the Yippie, the leader of the radical Youth International Party, had become Rubin the Yuppie, the young upwardly-mobile professional. Rubin said he was still passionate about social justice, but argued the best way to achieve it was through small government and maximum freedom of the individual. Hoffman was skeptical and accused Rubin of selfishness and selling-out. The two clashed during a series of public debates with Rubin explaining,

> "You can be wealthy and still care about changing the world. As a matter of fact, it's OK to be successful. We were against success in the '60s. We're for success in the '80s. The only difference is, now we're going to combine success with a social conscience."[27]

Hoffman disagreed and argued that only a big, powerful state run by benevolent Boomer experts could bring about the necessary, radical social change. Hoffman said Rubin had abandoned Utopian political activism and was ignoring the needs of the oppressed, "I'm not against entrepreneurship" he insisted,

> "But you can't say to a black woman living in Harlem with ten kids and no education, 'go out an invent an Apple computer'... I'm not afraid of big government, I'm not afraid of the size of government... the Yuppie attitude lacks basic compassion for those who can't get in on the big deal."

Rubin insisted he wanted to change the world and make it better just as much as Hoffman. Hoffman, he said, was stuck in the 1960s and failed to realize that the Boomers were no longer rebellious teenagers. They had grown up and were now on the cusp of real political power,

> "Once we have the White House, which is going to happen. Once the Baby Boom generation has economic security which it doesn't yet have – it's today in middle management... When that is done... then you're going to see government policies using the taxation system, low cost loans to minority business people and a massive campaign, a crusade in North America to wipe out poverty, a crusade to clean up the environment."

By a twist of fate therefore, by the time the Boomers had gained the power to change the world and make it a better place, they no longer agreed about how to do it. The Boomer consensus had fractured into two different consensuses. The result was the rapid development of politically partisan journalism as the deregulated market responded to demand. Boomer Journalism, with its simplified, ethical-political narratives, was produced in two flavors so audiences could consume the narratives they liked and avoid the ones they disliked. It was a 'pop music' model of journalism. Audiences were free to spin the radio dial and tune into the channel that played what they wanted to hear. Journalism was commodified as never before.

Freedom From Choice

The legal scholar Cass Sunstein observes that when people only listen to a single set of comforting opinions, the result is 'group polarization'. When this happens, bubbles of prejudice form and those inside them become more certain they're right, and more certain those outside them are wrong. Group polarization is therefore a self-reinforcing, tribal feedback loop that encourages fanaticism. As Sunstein puts it, "When people find themselves in groups of like-minded types, they are especially likely to move to extremes".[28] The antidote to group polarization, he says, is the "public forum", in which different viewpoints are forced to confront each other. It is a process that can feel uncomfortable at first, however it tends to lead, over time, to mutual understanding, respect and compromise. Sunstein believes the public forum,

> "Promotes cognitive diversity. It makes it difficult for like-minded people to insulate themselves from those who think differently... it helps to check the effects of echo chambers and ensure that those with blinders, or those who prefer information cocoons, occasionally see elsewhere. What they see may change their minds."[29]

Sunstein is, perhaps without realizing it, describing the methodology of Victorian Liberal Journalism — the solution to tribalism that his generation discarded in its search for something better and more committed.

Interestingly, although deregulation was equally fashionable in the UK during the 1980s, arguments in favor of the market led politicians and regulators there to very different conclusions about broadcasting. For example, the economist Alan Peacock, author of the 1986 *Peacock Report* into the future of the BBC, argued that a marketplace of ideas could only exist if buyers were able to sample and compare alternative opinions simultaneously.

> "If freedom of expression is to have a positive value to a community in which it is assumed that persons have the right to accept or to reject the goods and services on offer, its members must have the opportunity for testing the product. The usual way to do this is to 'sample' the product."[30]

According to Peacock, for choice to exist consumers must be presented with alternatives. If an alternative is hidden, hard to find or not readily accessible, then choice exists in name only. In the context of journalism, a news report should therefore contain a balance of different opinions for audiences to 'sample'. One-sided, Narrative-Led Journalism does not allow this to happen. Therefore, in Peacock's view, no free market can truly be said to exist. As he put it, "Freedom of expression must be presented in a form where acceptance or rejection is feasible."[31] Seen from this perspective, the Fairness Doctrine compelled US broadcasters to serve audiences with a choice of opinions which they could sample at the same time. Hence, during the era of the Fairness Doctrine, US broadcasters were like restaurants that offered a rich and diverse menu. After deregulation, the menu changed and offered far fewer flavors. Diners with an appetite for different things now had to make a conscious effort to shop around and visit other restaurants. Those not willing, or able, to do so, had to be content with narrowed choice and an increasingly homogenous diet of news and opinion. What Mark Fowler argued was freedom of choice, was to Alan Peacock freedom *from* choice. What Fowler claimed was a free market, was to Peacock merely a series of monopolies — isolated trading posts of opinion spaced far apart. The veteran journalist Walter Lippmann made a similar point about the need for a one-stop epistemic shop. He wrote that Journalistic Truth required the confrontation of opinions where "the same audience hears all the sides of the disputation" at the same time. Lippmann was uncomfortable about the rise of modern, broadcast journalism that only had time for short soundbites which made it hard for audiences to,

"Have the benefit of the process by which truth is sifted from error — the dialectic of debate in which there is immediate challenge, reply, cross-examination, and rebuttal."[32]

The Fairness Doctrine was a product of Liberal Democracy. It compelled journalists to expose audiences to a range of diverse views at the same time. It offered them samples of different opinion from which to choose and prevented ideological and political insulation. An unregulated market however, operates in the other direction. It allows people to choose comfortable narratives and avoid uncomfortable ones. Unpopular opinion becomes unprofitable opinion — which means it is heard only faintly or not at all. Market forces amplify the tyranny of the majority. They may be democratic, but they are not Liberal. As the political historian Julian Zelizer summarizes, the impact of the death of the Fairness Doctrine was profound,

"The decision was huge. Radio and television broadcasters understood that the regulatory obstacles toward politicized news had been dramatically lowered... Later the left would mimic what the right had done... without federal restraints and with unlimited access to broadcasting, the nation moved deeper and deeper into an age of polarized news without anything to hold these forces back."[33]

The Fairness Doctrine was not the only piece of regulation removed by Mark Fowler's FCC. Numerous anti-monopoly restrictions were also relaxed. With the abolition of multiple-ownership and cross-ownership restrictions, the US saw a frenzy of corporate take-overs, acquisitions and mergers. The result was the consolidation of media ownership and a media oligopoly. As CBS Senior Vice President David Fuchs commented in 1987, deregulation had a, "colossal effect. It's the reason for Capital Cities merging with ABC, it's the reason for Ted Turner trying to buy CBS, it's the reason for NBC being acquired."[34] A feature of oligopolies is they tend to produce products that are close substitutes for one another. Although each has its own distinguishing characteristics, they all monitor each other's behavior and act like a herd. In journalism, this phenomenon means less diversity and more homogeneous news. As the President of the National Cable TV Association James P. Mooney put it, "Mark Fowler leaves very deep footprints."[35]

During the 1980s, the Boomer generation of journalists and media executives, both in the UK and the US, wrought radical change. Although working in different media ecosystems, the results were indistinguishable. By the end of the decade, the underlying epistemology of Victorian Liberal Journalism had been undermined and was being rapidly abandoned. The boundary between fact and opinion was dissolving. Simple, easy to understand, ethical-political narratives were the norm. Boomer audiences heard what they wanted to hear on TV and radio courtesy of a deregulated market place. Boomer Journalism reigned supreme. *Arete* was vanquishing *aletheia*. Truthophobia was vanquishing truth.

Chapter 21

Martin Bell and the Punditocracy. The Zenith of Boomer Journalism

"Philip Ernst omitted a pine
from his painting because it
'spoiled the composition'
until remorseful at
misrepresenting the scene
he attacked the tree with an axe."

Chris Greenhalgh, *The Cool End of Red.*

Martin Bell; Boomer Journalism Marches on

The last decade of the 20th Century saw the pendulum continuing to swing with an unstoppable momentum towards Boomer Journalism. No one exemplified the trend more than the British celebrity reporter Martin Bell. Bell, well-known for appearing on screen in his trademark white suit, was the BBC's Foreign Affairs Correspondent and one of John Birt's senior journocrats. In 1997, Bell published a manifesto calling for a new type of journalism which he called the 'Journalism of Attachment'. Journalists, he suggested, should no longer pretend to be impartial, but should take sides and openly fight to make the world a better place. Victorian Liberal Journalism, he scathingly said, was "bystanders' journalism",

> "I started out as a war reporter in the mid-sixties, I worked in the shadow of my distinguished predecessors and of a long and honourable BBC tradition of distance and detachment. I thought of it then as objective and necessary. I would now call it bystanders' journalism."[1]

Objectivity, explained Bell, was an "illusion". Journalism should be understood as a "moral enterprise" informed by knowledge of "right and wrong". Journalists should not be neutral, but should ask themselves, "What do we believe in?" The job of a journalist, he urged, was not to report events impartially, but to take sides,

> "In place of the dispassionate practices of the past I now believe in what I call the journalism of attachment. By this I mean a journalism that cares as well as knows; that is aware of its responsibilities; and will not stand neutrally between good and evil, right and wrong, the victim and the oppressor... we in the press, and especially in television, which is its most powerful division, do not stand apart from the world. We are a part of it. We exercise a certain influence and we have to know that."

Bell was following John Birt's Mission to Explain to its logical end point. Birt saw the primary job of journalism as constructing narratives to explain complex events to audiences. However, when narratives, and their casts of good and bad actors are established, then moral and political judgements inevitably follow. Bell was suggesting a form of activist, or advocacy, journalism in which pro-social lying is not merely tolerated, it is encouraged, to help change the world and make it a better place. Bell's manifesto received widespread international publicity because it struck a chord with the idealism and Utopianism on which the Boomers had been suckled. It also signaled the overt politicization of journalism. Bell resigned from the BBC and, in 1997, entered the world of politics as an MP.

Bell's call for a Journalism of Attachment was warmly received by many, though not by all. The Canadian journalist Stephen J. Ward pointed out that objectivity and impartiality had been developed to protect journalists from their own human frailties and biases. Ward accused Bell of recklessly putting tribal passions ahead of the objective search for truth,

"Objectivity controls our penchant to speculate and promote... A journalism of attachment that stresses feelings, value judgements, and interpretation is reckless without objectivity."[2]

Ward argued that determining the truth about events, or the rightness of a cause, was either extremely difficult or completely impossible. The whole point of journalism, he said, was to help audiences judge these complex matters for themselves. He warned that the Journalism of Attachment, like other forms of Boomer Journalism, stripped away the old, much-needed restraints, "I fear that an unfettered journalism of attachment... would devolve into unsubstantiated journalism where biases parade as moral principles... that road leads to disaster."

The British journalist Brendan O'Neill agreed and pointed out,

"In emphasizing attachment over neutrality, and emotionalism over objectivity, the new breed of attached reporter became more like an activist, an international campaigner, rather than a dispassionate recorder of fact and truth."[3]

Bell later attempted to back-pedal and suggested he had been misunderstood. In a radio debate with O'Neill in 2012, Bell said his aim was not to encourage partisan journalism, nor to release journalists from the duty to tell the truth,

"I'm absolutely against partisan journalism... I did advance in the Bosnian war the theory which I called the Journalism of Attachment — a journalism that cares as well as knows. It was set around with all kinds of qualifications, like meticulous attention to the details, seeking out supposed bad guys, explaining what's happening, why they're doing what they're doing."[4]

But O'Neill replied that the damage had been done and could not be undone. Bell had become the poster boy for Boomer Journalism — he had played a prominent role in demoting the importance of impartial reporting, and promoting committed, ethical-political journalism driven by the desire to change the world and make it a better place. As O'Neill explained,

> "Historically... the role of journalists in wars was to report what they saw and to report the facts. Now we have journalists who, even before they go to a conflict zone, have decided which side is good, which side is bad, which side they will take.... There's a real danger that if you see things in terms of black and white, good and evil, you will only take the side of the suffering of the people that you like. And you will ignore the very human suffering of the people you dislike."

The journalist Mick Hume added his voice to criticism of Bell's philosophy. Writing in 1997, he said the Journalism of Attachment transformed complex reality into a set of fairy stories,

> "Rather than exposing the political and social roots of wars, the Journalism of Attachment depicts them as exclusively moral struggles in which Right fights Wrong. It reduces complex conflicts to simple fairy tale confrontations between the innocent and the forces of darkness. To achieve that, journalists have to appoint themselves as judges of who is Good or Evil in the world. And that means a journalist's responsibility to report all of the facts can come a poor second to broadcasting what is considered the morally correct line."[5]

Hume had correctly identified the key difference between Victorian Liberal Journalism and Boomer Journalism. The dominant goal of the former was *aletheia* — the impartial search for truth. The dominant goal of the latter was *arete* — ethical-political virtue. Hume criticized elite journocrats who he labelled "celebrity journalists". They suffered, he said, from hubris and were deluding themselves that they were uniquely wise, saintly figures blessed with infallible knowledge, "on a self-appointed mission to save the world."

Another critic was the academic Richard Landes who pointed to media coverage of the Arab-Israeli conflict as an example of what happens when journalists report news stories based on pre-existing prejudices about who is morally good and bad. The result was, he said, "lethal journalism" in which Israeli Jews were automatically cast as baddies — stereotyped, devilish oppressors; while Palestinian Moslems were automatically cast as goodies — noble, innocent victims struggling against injustice. Lethal journalism, Landes said, was indistinguishable from "demented anti-Israel invective". Its methodology was to reverse the chronology of violence so that when Israel responded to aggression, it was falsely portrayed as the aggressor. In order to generate "lethal narratives about evil Israel", some Palestinian leaders, said Landes, had even adopted a cynical policy of self-harm. This pattern of 21st Century press behavior,

> "Has given birth to one of the most grotesque (and profoundly inhumane) war strategies in the history of asymmetrical war: Provoke the enemy to attack, so as to maximize your own civilian casualties, exploiting the compassion of outsiders to get outsiders to hate your enemy as much as you do. This cannibalistic strategy of inflicting damage on your own people to win a propaganda war against your enemy can only work if the outside media tell the story as you want it told: highlight your suffering; use your statistics; blame the enemy for disproportionate response; accuse it of war crimes and ethnic cleansing."[6]

The journalist and Middle East analyst Douglas Davis, also saw the existence of ingrained institutional anti-Israel narratives as indistinguishable from something much darker. Davis singled out the BBC for fanning the flames of an ancient racial hatred,

> "In my judgement, the volume and intensity of this unchallenged diatribe has now transcended mere criticism of Israel. Hatred is in the air. Wittingly or not, the BBC has become the principal agent for re-infecting British society with the virus of anti-Semitism".[7]

Hanoch Marmari, former Editor of the Israeli newspaper Ha'aretz, was also troubled by the dominance of crude tribal narratives and the uncritical eagerness of journalists to believe and perpetuate them,

> "One day, historians examining this period of crisis will have to consider the circular process by which the media were transformed from observers to participants. From covering the story to playing a major part in it, to stimulating and sometimes agitating the environment for their own media purposes".[8]

Bell's significance to the history of journalism lies, not in the originality or novelty of his ideas, but in the fact they were expressed by such a high-profile, celebrity journalist working for the much-trusted BBC. His manifesto symbolized the very public triumph of Boomer Journalism and Boomer ways of knowing. There was something almost religious about the white-suited Bell's high-profile conversion to the values of the Journalism of Attachment, and his decision to leave the BBC for politics. In abjuring the Victorian Liberal tradition, Bell was widely seen as giving the BBC's blessing to Boomer Journalism. Bell's turn marked the arrival of a new age in which mainstream journalism would tolerate, and embrace, far higher levels of activism and pro-social lying.

In the US, the well-known journalist Roy Gutman played a similar role to Bell. Gutman was European Bureau Chief for *Newsday* during the 1980s and early 1990s. Like Bell, he reported on the Bosnian War and argued for more ethically-politically committed journalism. In 1993, in a much-publicized interview, he said journalists ought to be motivated by the desire to make the world a better place, not the desire to search for truth. Gutman said journalists needed to recalibrate their priorities and "get their compasses straight". For Gutman, as for Bell, Boomer Journalism was far superior to the old, impartial variety. "We can't watch passively" he said Gutman, "while people are being killed in front of us",

> "There are higher requirements. As a reporter, you can't simply sit there and report passively. You've got to do everything in

your power to stop these things... Some issues simply are not equally balanced, and we can't give the impression that for every argument on one side, there is an equal one on the other side. I don't believe the fairness doctrine applies equally to victims and perpetrators."[9]

Like the small fraction of an iceberg visible above the water, Bell and Gutman were the high-profile symbols of a more widespread change in Anglo-American journalism. To many observers, it was obvious that the shift was generational. Writing in 1993, the American journalist Kim Mills observed that values had changed, "particularly in the last decade, from the traditional view that a journalist is supposed to be a detached observer of society and not a participant." Linda Grist Cunningham, a member of the American Society of News Editors ethics committee, agreed. Boomer journalists, she said, had brought their ideology and values into the workplace,

"The people who are in journalism today, and certainly those in management positions and experienced reporters, are all prod-ucts of the 1960s, where involvement and helping to make the world a better place was a big part of who we were and who we are... I don't think we ever forgot those ideals, and just because we're journalists doesn't mean we gave up the desire to make the world better."[10]

Stephen Isaacs, Ethics Professor at Columbia University's Graduate School of Journalism, was of the same opinion. According to Isaacs,

"A lot of the reporters are coming in, more than half are either minorities or women, and many of them come with a cause, which is the righting of decades, centuries, whatever, of wrong... It is hard for them to suppress their advocacy, so they insist on being able to march in civil rights marches or anti-abortion marches or whatever. And that may have changed the face of journalism."[11]

In the UK, Mick Hume also disapproved of the new way of reporting the news. The reality, he said, was that the ethical-political narratives constructed by elite journocrats were a "twisted sort of therapy" which functioned, "not so much to find out the truth as to find themselves".

Narrative-Led Journalism allowed journalists to indulge their innate prejudices and "force the facts into their preconceived framework". Once a news narrative had been established, it dictated the news agenda and determined which facts would be reported and which left out. Major news organizations, he said, now routinely, "ignored and distorted any evidence that did not correspond with the battle cry of their moral crusade,"

> "Those facts which fit into their Good v Evil scenario might indeed be treated as sacred. The status of those facts that do not quite fit into the framework, however, can be much more negotiable."[12]

Any journalists still clinging to the old values of Victorian Liberal impartiality, Hume said, were discovering they were fishes out of water, "Those journalists who transgress against the new moral correctness, and stray outside the Good v Evil framework in their reports, are the ones who can expect to be treated as heretics."

Other commentators referred to the shift to Boomer Journalism as journalism's "interpretative", or "explanatory" turn. The academic Kevin Barnhurst wrote that elite journocrats assumed they had a duty to explain how the world worked to the mass of people who lacked the qualifications and time to analyze things for themselves. Thus, the desire to, "make sense of a world too complex for average citizens to understand led inexorably to the expansion of explanatory news." Barnhust traced the explanatory turn to the Boomer generation noting that during the 1970s, "interpretation had become widespread in American news... as movements to make news more explanatory pressed on mainstream journalism from all sides."[13] The journalism scholar John Pauly agreed, pointing out that the Boomer generation of journalists, "were ethical in a way that we have not fully recognized" and that their journalism was marked by the "social construction of moral purpose". The explanatory turn had been an ethical-political turn. The goal of news had become changing and improving the world, not describing it. Journalists were expected to be committed to the, "wider moral purposes they hope their stories will serve."[14]

The Groupthink and Sociodrama
of the Journocracy

The first decade of the 21st Century saw the pendulum continuing its unrelenting swing. The view that journalism should be a force for social change and social justice was widely considered normal and obvious, barely worth stating — the unconscious bias of professional journalists. In 2004, the American writer Dave Berman was not saying anything controversial when he suggested the,

"Classic tenets of journalism call for objectivity and neutrality. These are antiquated principles no longer universally observed... We must absolutely not feel bound by them. If we are ever to create meaningful change, advocacy journalism will be the single most crucial element to enable the necessary organizing."[15]

Boomer Journalism evolved methodologies to reflect its increasing reliance on consensus narratives. The trend was noted by the historian Eric Alterman who coined the word "punditocracy" to refer to it. Writing in 1999, Alterman explained that the punditocracy was a,

"Tiny group of highly visible political pontificators who make their living offering 'inside political opinions and forecasts' in the elite national media. And it is their debate, rather than any semblance of a democratic one, that determines the parameters of political discourse in the nation today."[16]

Alterman said contemporary journalism was characterized by an "explosion of the punditocracy" — a self-sustaining feedback loop in which journalists interviewed selected pundits who repeated and amplified the pre-existing, official narrative. The opinions of these pundits created a reassuring feeling of consensus, as well as fresh material that could itself be reported as news. Pundits reacting to the analysis and opinions of other pundits supplied an endless cycle of content to feed hungry news machines. The British academic Brian McNair agreed, referring to an "interpretative moment in the news cycle". Borrowing from Alterman, McNair observed that the output of the "punditocracy" was occupying an, "ever greater proportion of output as a whole, in both the print and broadcast sectors". McNair wrote uneasily that the deluge of opinion and narrative, much of it presented as fact, was cheapening public discourse and "undermining the quality of the public sphere."[17]

Boomer Journalism was also revealing itself to be highly vulnerable to groupthink. This Orwellian-sounding word was coined by the American psychologist Irving L. Janis in 1972. According to Janis, groupthink is a tribal phenomenon that occurs when group members came to value the goal of the prestige and success of their group above all else. The political scientist Paul't Hart summarizes,

> "To preserve the clubby atmosphere, group members suppress personal doubts, silence dissenters, and follow the group leader's suggestions. They have a strong belief in the inherent morality of the group, combined with a decidedly evil picture of the group's opponents. The results are devastating: a distorted view of reality, excessive optimism producing hasty and reckless policies, and a neglect of ethical issues".[18]

The word was new, but the concept was old. John Milton had written about it in 1644, describing truth as a "streaming fountain" which ought to constantly flow lest it become stagnant. In his famous call for freedom of the press he wrote, "If her waters flow not in a perpetual progression, they sicken into a muddy pool of conformity and tradition."[19] The American philosopher Thomas Chamberlin wrote about the same phenomenon in 1890, referring to the "ruling theories" constructed by experts who regarded them as their "intellectual offspring". Once these speculative narratives had been agreed, what inevitably followed was the "unconscious pressing of the theory to make it fit the facts, and a pressing of the facts to make them fit the theory." This led, Chamberlin observed, to a tribal consensus that could not be challenged,

> "The theory then rapidly rises to the ruling position, and investigation, observation, and interpretation are controlled and directed by it. From an unduly favored child, it readily becomes master, and leads its author whithersoever it will. The subsequent history of that mind in respect to that theme is but the progressive dominance of a ruling idea."[20]

A major problem for Boomer Journalism was therefore the circular nature of its narratives. In order to protect the professional reputations and prestige of the journocrats who created them, dissenting voices needed to be silenced. This was justified by arguing that alternative narratives were 'wrong'. Hence debate would serve no purpose, other than to confuse audiences with misinformation. To those raised in the tradition of Victorian Liberalism and the Anglo-American Enlightenment, this way of thinking was full of danger. The British philosopher Bertrand Russell contrasted the two ways of knowing as "liberal" and "illiberal",

"The former regards all questions as open to discussion and all opinions as open to a greater or lesser measure of doubt, while the latter holds in advance that certain opinions are absolutely unquestionable, and that no argument against them must be allowed be heard... This point of view cannot be accepted by any man who wishes reason rather than prejudice to govern human action".[21]

In addition to being illiberal and intolerant of dissent, Narrative-Led Journalism was also vulnerable to the type of corruption associated with power. Corruption in this sense, does not mean financial bribery, but refers to any situation in which a journocrat might find himself being lobbied, cajoled, persuaded or influenced. Journalists have their own professional and personal goals, and, like all other human beings, wish to increase their prestige, status, reputation and wealth. Boomer Journalism is particularly vulnerable to this type of corruption because it tolerates pro-social lying. Hence, a one-sided, incomplete or distorted news report can easily be justified on ethical-political grounds, even when it is really motivated, or partly motivated, by other, less altruistic, considerations. As C.S. Lewis observed,

"Of all tyrannies a tyranny sincerely exercised for the good of its victims may be the most oppressive... those who torment us for our own good will torment us without end for they do so with approval of their own conscience."[22]

The French philosopher Albert Camus said much the same thing, noting that the public good is frequently used as camouflage for a wide variety of problematic, ambiguous and self-serving behaviors,

"The welfare of the people in particular has always been the alibi
of tyrants, and it provides the further advantage of giving the
servants of tyranny a good conscience... But in truth, the very
ones who make use of such alibis know they are lies."[23]

In 2007 the British journalist Robin Aitken wrote a book accusing the
BBC of being a case study in groupthink. Choice of news stories, and many
other journalistic decisions, were driven, he said, by the desire to conform
to peer group pressure and the tribal norms of the newsroom. Reflecting
on his own career at the BBC he admitted,

"We reported things as we did because that's how the great
majority of the journalists in the organization saw the world. It
was an institutional deformation, invisible to the people working
there."[24]

Aitken confessed that professional self-interest, and fear of falling out
of favor, were major drivers of unconscious bias and journalistic conformity. He described elite Journocrats as the privileged "lucky few", and
the remainder as the "lower and middle ranks" among whom there is a,

"Constant, sharp-elbowed struggle for advancement; to get that
big assignment, to become the Assistant Editor, to achieve internal
recognition — these lures keep the Darwinian struggle going."[25]

John Humphrys, a prominent BBC journalist, also acknowledged
the existence of institutional bias and groupthink, describing it as a,
"uniformity of news judgements that are made within the confines of
the 'machine'". Humphrys detected an unwritten code among journalists. There was, he said,

"An overall, if implicit, BBC attitude to what makes news. And
there is very little digression from that shared view. In an organization like the BBC nobody wins a prize for straying too far
outside the framework."[26]

Another high-profile insider, TV anchor Peter Sissons, agreed and
wrote scathingly about the BBC's "cultural mindset" which,

"Percolates subtly throughout the organization, most potently through the process of promotions and appraisals which ensures that the careers of those who set themselves at odds with the corporation's perceived wisdom do not advance."[27]

Sissons described how journalists dedicated considerable time and effort to the "dark art of surviving at the BBC". These arts included reluctance to make a decision, taking the credit when things went well, and blaming others when it did not. Above all, journalists sought to be seen as good, loyal members of the tribe,

"No one wants to wreck his or her chances of breaking through the cash and perks ceiling into the promised land on the floors above. The newsroom has many talented journalists of middle rank, who know what's wrong with the organization but who don't rock the boat for fear of blowing their chances of advancement."

Sissons observed that generous rewards awaited those selected to join the ranks of the elite journocracy. For those who "breakthrough into the senior ranks there's now big, big money and a gold-plated pension to be had."[28]

In 2004, another senior BBC journalist, Andrew Marr, confessed that Narrative-Led News and pro-social lying had become the norm, not the exception. "Our problem" he said, "is less direct lying than slimy misrepresentation". The requirement to make the facts fit the desired narrative and make the world a better place was, he wrote, creating a journalism of deception, "How often" he asked, "has the reporter gone through a long interview and stripped out a few words, junking all context and balance, to produce a deliberately misleading effect?"[29]

The psychiatrist Jacob Levy Moreno developed the idea of psychodrama as a form of creative therapy in which a subject acts-out a traumatic event as if he were performing a play. The technique was an exercise in wishful thinking — a remaking of reality in which the subject invented stories to make sense of events and take control of them. Thus, participants were able to play the role of God and replace the world that was, with the world they wanted. As Moreno explained man, "becomes the master... instead of the servant... he is free from the fetters of facts and actuality."[30] Moreno formed groups to create sociodramas — collaborative, shared psychodramas. Sociodramas draw out the "unconscious fantasy of the group" and use its power to construct a new, better reality — what Moreno referred to as "expanded" or "surplus" reality,

> "Surplus (expanded) reality is used to play out how things could or should have happened. It has a healing dimension that replaces the traumatic experience with a new corrective emotional experience, either on the personal level (psychodrama) or on the group level (sociodrama)."[31]

Moreno was fascinated by the power of sociodrama to produce collective fantasies — which he described as the "sociodynamic effect". He noted group members usually shared common aspects of their identity upon meeting. This "fundamental mental matrix" provided the raw material for "an orchestra of atoms" which created something greater than its parts, "Their closer acquaintances and their intimate exchanges are constantly interacting and we can thus see that they form a current, ever moving, ever developing, dynamic matrix."[32] The result was a shared, tribal fantasy — a "group illusion" produced by the consensus; a projection of their collective desires, hopes and anxieties. In this group illusion, "reality and fantasy can be present on the stage simultaneously without being in conflict. On the sociodrama stage, anything is possible."

Moreno developed sociodrama into the concept of the "Living Newspaper". This mixture of reality and make-believe blended the day's news with spontaneous, improvised performances by actors. In the US, Moreno's Living Newspaper was adopted by the Federal Theatre Project under the directorship of Hallie Flanagan during the 1930s. As Sarah Guthu points out, it was hard to know where journalism ended and fantasy took over,

> "Flanagan created a Living Newspaper staff along the lines of an actual printed daily paper, with an editor-in-chief, managing editors, reporters, copyreaders, etc. and paired this staff of reporters and journalists with dramatists. Together, the Living Newspaper staff would... distill a 'dramatic' piece from the facts."[33]

The process closely resembles the narrative-led methodology of Boomer Journalism. Living newspaper participants, just like journalists, have editorial meetings, create lists of prospective stories and ask themselves,

"What news stories shall we create tomorrow? Through such projection of the future perhaps we can take greater control over our lives, prevent some of the bad news, and create more good news."[34]

Therefore, during the early 21st Century, many journocrats found themselves, largely unconsciously, engaging in a form of sociodrama or "realist-factual therapy". In this narrative-led world, journocrats, freed from the task of impartially reporting facts, selectively gather information and rearrange it to form webs of narrative for their own benefit, the benefit of their peers, their news organization and their audience. Their journalism seamlessly blended elements of what is, with what ought to be. It was partly a description of reality and partly a denial of it — a hybrid of fantasy and fact. Some examples of the trend became notorious.

In 2014, for example, *Rolling Stone* magazine published a sensational story about a brutal gang rape at the University of Virginia. The article, entitled A Rape on Campus was, in the words of *ABC News*, an, "explosive, 9,000-word account of alleged institutional indifference to sexual assault survivors and the mishandling of sexual assaults on college campuses".[35] The article, written by Sabrina Rubin Erdely, chronicled the story of 'Jackie' who claimed she had been raped by seven men. Unfortunately for Erdely, her story was untrue, and *Rolling Stone* found itself on the receiving end of a multimillion-dollar lawsuit. A subsequent investigation by the Columbia Graduate School of Journalism concluded that Narrative-Led Journalism, and a desire to make the world a better place, had played major roles in this epistemic disaster.

The report found staff at *Rolling Stone* were sympathetic to the wider ethical-political narrative that women were routinely raped by men, and that university authorities across the US were knowingly turning a blind eye to a "pervasive culture of sexual harassment/rape culture". This broader narrative, that rape is a tool for sustaining a patriarchal system of male power, was an important article of faith of the feminist movement. It was also part of the accepted groupthink of student politics, sustained, according to the report, by a "wave of campus activism". Erdely therefore wanted Jackie's story to be true because, if it were, it would confirm the wider narrative and help the struggle for social and sexual justice. It would also boost Erdely's prestige and status among her peers. As the report noted, "Erdely and her editors had hoped their

255

investigation would sound an alarm about campus sexual assault and would challenge Virginia and other universities to do better."

Revealingly, when it came to fact-checking, Will Dana, the magazine's managing editor, said he had "faith" the facts would confirm the pre-existing narrative. In other words, once the narrative had been adopted by the group and become the Official Truth, it was the job of the reporter to dig around and find evidence to support it. As Dana explained, "I had a faith that as it went through the fact-checking that all this was going to be straightened out." Because Rolling Stone's senior editorial staff were so heavily invested in the narrative, groupthink took over. Like a runaway train speeding downhill, Erdely's story proved impossible to stop. The Columbia report concluded,

> "The problem of confirmation bias — the tendency of people to be trapped by pre-existing assumptions and to select facts that support their own views while overlooking contradictory ones — is a well-established finding of social science. It seems to have been a factor here".[36]

Erdely's story highlighted the dangers inherent in Boomer Journalism and institutional groupthink. However, when journalism embraces narrative and tolerates pro-social lying, it is only one small further step to completely remove all factual accuracy and produce fiction. The temptation to take this final step proved irresistible for Jayson Blair, a 27-year-old reporter working for *The New York Times.*

The Enhanced Reality of Jayson Blair

In 2003, Blair was exposed for having systematically plagiarized and fabricated information in dozens of his articles. Although he claimed to have interviewed people and witnessed events himself, in reality Blair had cut and pasted from other newspapers, or wire services, and spiced-up his reports with imaginary detail. His journalism was therefore an engaging mixture of fact and fiction. His stories were plausible, and the detail he invented perfectly fitted, and supported, the official narrative. Blair was enhancing reality and improving it. Nonetheless, he had strayed over an invisible ethical line and the scandal sent shockwaves through professional journalism. *The Times* disowned Blair's methodology calling it a, "profound betrayal of trust and a low point in the 152-year history of the newspaper." Blair was portrayed as a single bad apple in the journalistic barrel, and his antics were framed as a rare, one-off event. But not all commentators were convinced by this self-serving narrative.

The writer Michael Wolff saw the Blair scandal as indicative of a much wider problem. Wolff pointed to the rise of pro-social lying in journalism and said newsrooms had become dominated by "narrative stylists" who placed a high value on stories enlivened by "colorful, subjective, semi-bogus detail". Wolff said Boomer Journalism sought to create a "better, more interesting" reality designed to support its narratives. This was Boomer Journalism's dirty secret — the methodology which dared not speak its name and which had to be kept hidden from audiences. Lack of impartiality is the respectable face of Boomer Journalism, lack of accuracy — not so much. Fraud and invention lie beyond the boundary of acceptability. Blair's sin was that he had gone too far. He had wandered into forbidden territory and paid a heavy price. He had broken the unwritten code and travelled "to that point on the reality continuum beyond which you self-destruct." Blair had lost the game of "reality chicken". This was an uncomfortable thing to discuss because journalists are not supposed to wash their dirty linen in public. As Wolff explained,

> "It obviously isn't advisable in this climate to try to describe, no less to mark, the line between absolute fact and the instinctual sense of how far over the line of absolute fact it's safe to go, which is more and more the real tradecraft."[37]

But Blair had also broken another, far more important, code — he had forgotten that Boomer Journalism's pro-social lying is only acceptable when it is *pro-social*. In other words, enhancing reality, embellishing and stretching the facts to fit the narrative, are acceptable provided the motive is *arete*, making the world a better place. Blair's motivation, however, was personal — he wanted to further his own reputation and career. He was also lazy. His motive for dishonesty was often simply that he couldn't be bothered to interview people. As he admitted, when asked to travel to Washington to cover the Beltway sniper attacks, "I just didn't want to go. I thought, I'll call the AP correspondent... what does it matter if I'm there."[38] In other words, Blair's sin was not that he distorted the truth, but that he did so for the wrong reasons. Pro-*personal* lying is not the same thing as pro-*social* lying. Blair had come uncomfortably close to exposing the truthophobic epistemology of Boomer Journalism. He had betrayed the tribe. He had told the right lies, but he had told them for the wrong reasons. This was his real crime, but, as Wolff put it, "of this we must not speak".

PART FOUR

A HOUSE DIVIDED. OFFICIAL AND UNOFFICIAL JOURNALISMS

Chapter 22

Prologue. Djokovic's Biggest Match

"In that country, it is considered a good thing to execute an admiral from time to time to encourage the others".

Voltaire. Candide, Ch 23.

The best tennis player in the world was under arrest. Transported to a seedy detention center, he was interrogated throughout the night and deprived of sleep. It was an unsettling experience for an elite athlete trying to prepare for a major tournament. The detention center had previously been described by journalists as "disgusting" — a place notorious for "maggots and moldy food, medical neglect, mistreatment and lack of hygiene."[1]

Novak Djokovic's crime was that he rejected the official narrative about the new Covid vaccines. Having carried out his own research, he doubted their safety and efficacy, and chose to remain unvaccinated. He was fit and healthy and, since he had recently recovered from Covid, he possessed natural immunity — which is why he had been granted medical exemption from vaccination by the tournament's medical team. Nonetheless, the Australian government decided to deport him and so, for twelve days in January 2022, the story of Djokovic's legal and ideological battle was front page news around the world.

The court case was not about whether Djokovic was a medical danger to Australians. The prosecution accepted he "posed a 'negligible' risk of infection of others."[2] Instead, it argued he was a "high-profile unvaccinated individual who has indicated publicly that he is opposed to becoming vaccinated against COVID-19." What was important, said the government, was "how those in Australia may perceive his views on vaccinations." In other words, Djokovic had unintentionally become the poster boy for an unacceptable way of thinking. The government explained,

> "His presence in Australia may foster anti-vaccination sentiment leading to... a reinforcing of the views of a minority in the Australian community who remain unvaccinated."

The judges agreed that Djokovic was obviously capable of influencing others which would lead to a minority opinion becoming more widespread,

> "An iconic world tennis star may influence people of all ages, young or old, but perhaps especially the young and the impressionable, to emulate him. This is not fanciful; it does not need evidence."

Djokovic lost the case. His visa was revoked and he was deported on 16th January.

At the heart of the courtroom drama was a contest between Victorian Liberalism with its belief in the primacy of the individual, and the Boomer Ideology with its belief in the primacy of the group. According to the great philosopher of liberalism John Stuart Mill, questions about health are fundamentally questions about individual liberty. For Mill, freedom meant the freedom for individuals to decide their own best interest,

> "The only freedom which deserves the name, is that of pursuing our own good in our own way, so long as we do not attempt to deprive others of theirs, or impede their efforts to obtain it. Each is the proper guardian of his own health, whether bodily, or mental and spiritual."[3]

For Mill, the only justification for interfering with an individual's liberty was when his behavior harmed someone else. As he famously explained,

> "The sole end for which mankind are warranted, individually or collectively, in interfering with the liberty of action of any of their number, is self-protection. That the only purpose for which power can be rightfully exercised over any member of a civilized community, against his will, is to prevent harm to others."[4]

In reaching its verdict, the court extended Mill's 'harm principle' to argue that Djokovic's choice would hurt ordinary Australians by encouraging them to defy public health policy. In this view, all independent, critical thinking becomes harmful — because 'harm' is defined as thinking differently to the consensus. The court's decision was therefore a reversal of the spirit of Mill's philosophy — a denial of the doctrine that each individual is the proper guardian of his own health. Underpinning the court's reasoning were the unstated assumptions that Covid vaccines were safe and effective, and that it was therefore a good thing to encourage as many people as possible to be vaccinated. Hence, the legal and ethical-political considerations rested on epistemic foundations. The court's judgement about what was *right*, depended on the judge's beliefs about what was *true*. However, these beliefs were the very things Djokovic was questioning. Ultimately, the ruling was a vindication of Boomer values, and a blow to the pre-Boomer idea that individuals should be free to think for themselves and take responsibility for their own choices.

The philosopher Isaiah Berlin, distinguished between 'positive' and 'negative' liberties. Positive liberty, he explained, was the freedom to behave however one wanted; while negative liberty was the right to be free from the consequences of other people's behavior. The eternal problem for human society, Berlin said, was knowing how to strike the right balance between the two. It was, he said, a process of incessant "haggling" because one person's freedom is another person's slavery,

> "A frontier must be drawn between the area of private life and that of public authority. Where it is to be drawn is a matter of argument, indeed of haggling. Men are largely interdependent, and no man's activity is so completely private as never to obstruct the lives of others in anyway. `Freedom for the pike is death for the minnows'; the liberty of some must depend on the restraint of others."[5]

Berlin was deeply suspicious about positive liberty. He argued it was open to abuse and was at times, "No better than a specious disguise for brutal tyranny." Berlin explained that when people assume they know best and believe they possess certain, infallible knowledge, they will feel entitled to impose their will on other people to prevent them 'harming' themselves. This improper extension of the 'harm principle' was, he said, a recipe for evil which makes it,

> "Easy for me to conceive of myself as coercing others for their own sake, in their, not my interest. I am then claiming that I know what they truly need better than they know it themselves... Once I take this view, I am in a position to ignore the actual wishes of men or societies, to bully, oppress; torture them in the name, and on behalf, of their 'real' selves"

Berlin warned that the only way to avoid violent conflict was to respect diversity of opinion, acknowledge the possibility that we are all fallible, and draw the frontier as far as possible in the direction of individual choice and personal liberty. Berlin described the desire for consensus and tribal unity as, "a craving for the certainties of childhood or the absolute values of our primitive past." Intolerance of dissent was, he concluded, symptomatic of "moral and political immaturity." Using Berlin's formula, Djokovic can be seen as seeking the negative liberty to protect himself from harm because he believed the view of the majority was wrong. His case was an intensely complex clash between the right of an individual to protect himself from harm, and the right of the majority to protect themselves from his right to protect himself from harm. These tangled, vexed questions are, as Berlin explained, subject to constant "haggling" from one generation, and one culture, to the next.

The question — which is more important; the rights of the individual, or the rights of the group, was central to the thinking of the doctors and lawyers who drew-up the famous Nuremberg Code in 1947. The Code was written following the trail of Nazi doctors and nurses who performed medical experiments on Jews and other concentration camp prisoners. In their defense, the Nazis said they were justified in sacrificing a small number of individuals to obtain results that would benefit society as a whole. However, their inhumane, collectivist argument was firmly rejected at Nuremberg in favor of the principles of Victorian Liberalism. Consequently, the Code stressed the sanctity of the individual and the principle of 'informed consent' which rested on the availability of impartial, high-quality information,

> "The voluntary consent of the human subject is absolutely essential. This means that the person involved should have legal capacity to give consent; should be so situated as to be able to exercise free power of choice, without the intervention of any element of force, fraud, deceit, duress, overreaching, or other ulterior form of constraint or coercion; and should have sufficient knowledge and comprehension of the elements of the subject matter involved as to enable him to make an understanding and enlightened decision."[6]

The Nuremberg Code therefore presumes an ethical hierarchy at the top of which is the right of individuals to make choices for themselves and defy the will of the majority. As the Yale law professor Jay Katz summarizes, the Code enshrines the liberal principle that the advancement of science and the public good must,

> "Bow to a higher principle: protection of individual inviolability. The rights of individuals to thoroughgoing self-determination and autonomy must come first. Scientific advances may be

impeded, perhaps even become impossible at times, but this is a price worth paying."[7]

What the Djokovic saga reveals therefore is how far the ideological frontiers were redrawn by the Boomer and Millennial generations during the late 20th and early 21st Centuries and how far they moved away from the rights of the individual. The victory of the Australian government was a victory for the Boomer Ideology over Victorian Liberalism, and for the positive concept of liberty over the negative. The defeat of Djokovic was the defeat of the right of an individual to decide his own best interest and be free from the will of the tribe — a winding-back of the ideological clock towards pre-Enlightenment values.

The Djokovic saga also illustrated a coarsening of public discourse. To most commentators and journalists, all these delicate and complex points of political philosophy were completely invisible. All they saw was a self-ish individual who had stepped out of line — a troublemaker refusing to conform. In this crude narrative, the philosophy of Victorian Liberalism was reduced to a caricature and Djokovic was cast as a rich, privileged celebrity who thought he was better and smarter than everyone else. Jemele Hill writing in *The Atlantic*, accused Djokovic of, "trying to bend the rules — thereby showing that, besides COVID, the other sickness the world is fighting is selfishness". For Hill, duty to the tribe far outweighed consideration of individual liberty, "Even more despicable" she wrote, was that Djokovic "seems so comfortable exploiting his immense privilege to endanger the health and safety of others." Hill concluded the first duty of a celebrity must be to demonstrate conformity to shared values and if necessary sacrifice himself for the greater good,

> "Sacrificing is what caring communities do—and it's something Djokovic knows nothing about. As the top player in men's ten-nis, Djokovic has a responsibility to be a good ambassador for his sport. But that, like Australia's COVID rules, is just another requirement that he's failed to meet."[8]

In the *New York Post*, Johnny Oleksinski unleashed a torrent of abuse at, "the entitled, whiny, rich, loathsome Novak Djokovic". It was selfish and unethical, he wrote, for an individual to question the official narra-tive, therefore,

"The real Djokovic is a pathetic man who complains and attempts to manipulate politicians to bend to his selfish whims in order to pet his insatiable ego. Well done, Australian government, for having the guts to say "No" to Novak."[9]

The sports journalist Sam Fels detected an insolent ideological challenge hidden in Djokovic's stance and called for severe punishment to serve as an example to others who might be tempted to think independently and heretically. What Fels' analysis lacked in philosophical insight, it made up for in profanity,

> "The problem here is that these selfish fucksticks think not only of themselves, but that they shouldn't have to face any ramifications for their damaging theories and ways... Australia decided to boot his ass, not because of the danger he posed in a closed atmosphere of the tournament, but because of what he represented... Hopefully the ATP follows suit and keeps him on ice for a long while. Djokovic may find out that even though he's the best player of all-time, the game doesn't actually need him."[10]

The British writer Josie Appleton was one of a small minority who defended Djokovic and who was troubled by the illiberal assault on the rights of the individual. The world, she said, was collapsing back into pre-Enlightenment ways of knowing and behaving characterized by superstition, conformity and deference to authority. She argued that vaccination had become a form of public, ritual purification equivalent to baptism — a process that made people clean and entitled them to join the tribe,

> "The vaccine is being treated as a mystical state or collective substance that incorporates people into the collective body. Vaccination now is like a sacrament, a transubstantiation ritual; through the vaccine we are receiving the body of the state into our body and therefore joining the community."[11]

A primitive tribalism, Appleton said, had replaced the Victorian Liberal tradition of independent, critical thinking and respect for dissenting individuals,

"You can only have rights (enter society) once you have done your duty (been vaccinated). The idea that duties come before rights means, at base, that the state comes before the citizen: the citizen only takes his place in society at the behest of the state."

The Italian philosopher Giorgio Agamben was also troubled by the case and saw a quasi-theological, totalitarian impulse at work. The human herd, he said, was stampeding in panic. The rights of individuals were being jettisoned in the face of a perceived threat to the group,

"The transformation we are witnessing today operates through the introduction of a sanitation terror and a religion of health. What, in the tradition of bourgeois democracy, used to be the right to health became, seemingly without anyone noticing, a juridical-religious obligation that must be fulfilled at any cost."[12]

Thinking for oneself had become 'selfish'. Going in a different direction to the herd had become a crime. In the process, a primitive tribalism and visceral intolerance had been rekindled. As the former US President Ronald Reagan succinctly put it, "Majority rule becomes mob rule unless there is a set of ground rules protecting the individual."[13]

Banished from the Australian Open, Djokovic paid a heavy price. He could only watch forlornly as his vaccinated rival Rafael Nadal won the title.

Chapter 23

The Post-Affluent Age. The Boomer Ideology in Crisis

"A new, humorless generation is now arising, It takes in deadly earnest all we received with laughter."

Czeslaw Milosz

L ike a brick thrown through a window, the global financial crisis of 2008 shattered the Boomer's world. Like a clanging alarm clock rousing someone from a long peaceful sleep, it signaled the material reality underpinning the Boomer Ideology had profoundly changed. The crisis of 2008 was the visible part of a matrix of transformations which had been slowly taking place during the late 20th and early 21st Centuries. The trend towards globalization, the de-industrialization of the West, a growing dependence on debt to fund Western lifestyles, the rise of China as a manufacturing, economic, political and military superpower, demographic transformation, falling birth rates, the aging and retirement of the Boomers and mass immigration into Western nations were all ingredients in a complex broth of change.

As the shockwaves of 2008 began to ripple out during the second decade of the 21st century, increasing numbers of people began to notice they were becoming less, not more, affluent. It was a realization that produced a torrent of anguished analysis and commentary as people sought explanations and solutions. The academic Stanley Stasch wrote that the West's addiction to an easy life, and to a supply of cheap imported goods, had produced self-destructive, unintended consequences,

"As U.S. trade with China increased year by year after 2000, so also did unemployment in the U.S. manufacturing sector. From 2000 to 2010, employment in the manufacturing sector declined by some 33-34 percent. Many of those who lost high-paying jobs in the manufacturing sector had to settle for lower-paying jobs in the service sector, or worse."[1]

As an official UK government report summarized, the new reality was not the Utopian, progressive Age of Aquarius anticipated by the Boomers. The paper pointed to, "geopolitical and geo-economic shifts such as China's increasing power and assertiveness internationally" and warned of the intensification of,

"Competition between states and with non-state actors, manifested in: a growing contest over international rules and norms; the formation of competing geopolitical and economic blocs of influence and values that cut across our security, economy and the institutions that underpin our way of life."[2]

Instead of Boomertopia, in which the human race would sing in perfect harmony, the report described a type of competition that in previous ages would have resulted in war, but which, in the early 21st Century, was war by other means, "the testing of the boundary between war and peace, as states use a growing range of instruments to undermine and coerce others". Stasch observed that not everyone was equally affected by these structural changes. Wealth, he pointed-out, had been transferred "from the middle and lower classes to the top 0.1% of earners". Instead of a gentle spectrum, society was dividing into sharply delineated groups of winners and losers. Stasch concluded that between 1980 and 2010, prosperity "for the nation's ordinary people and their families" had dwindled leading to the "destruction of the great American middle class."

A 2020 report by the Rand Corporation reported falling affluence and rising inequality, noting that "incomes for those without a college degree have not increased more than inflation over the last forty years". The authors said steady collapse in affluence coincided with the period during which Boomer hands had been on the levers of power,

"The three decades following the Second World War saw a period of economic growth that was shared across the income distribution, but inequality in taxable income has increased substantially over the last four decades."[3]

The journalist Sarah Jaffe put it more vividly. In a 2018 article entitled, *The Struggle to Stay Middle Class*, she painted a picture of, "slashed wages, disappearing pensions, and second jobs to make ends meet." 2008, she wrote, burst a bubble and "led millions of Americans to realize that their 'middle-class' lives were just a pay-check or two from evaporating." There was, she said, widespread anxiety and insecurity as the age of affluence went into reverse, "as people had to work more and harder to keep up their lifestyles, what Barbara Ehrenreich memorably called the 'fear of falling'... tightened its grip."[4]

The analyst Aaron Renn described families struggling to deal with "serious trauma". He wrote of the,

"'Middle-class shame' of half of Americans being unable to come up with $400 in an emergency. A recent Pew Research Center study found the middle class in decline in almost nine out of 10 metro areas. And there is increasing talk of an America in which the upper 20 percent are doing well, while middle-income Americans, like lower-income ones, are under intensifying economic pressure."[5]

It was essential, he said, to acknowledge there were,

"Very hard problems out there that need to be faced, that the solutions aren't obvious and that the issues are so big that the accumulated number of losers simply can't be ignored."

The journalist Michael Snyder analyzed US wage statistics for 2014 and found them shocking. "As a nation", he said, "we are flat broke and most of us are living paycheck to paycheck." It was, he believed, yet more evidence that the middle class in American was "dying",

"In many families, both the husband and the wife are working as hard as they can, but it is still not enough. With each passing day, more Americans are losing their spots in the middle class and this has pushed government dependence to an all-time high. According to the U.S. Census Bureau, 49 percent of all Americans now live in a home that receives money from the government each month."[6]

By 2020, Snyder said things had got worse. Spiraling debt and money-printing had concealed the truth and maintained the illusion of affluence. But now the illusion could no longer be maintained, "Our economic system is in the process of imploding", he wrote angrily,

"For decades, the greatest debt bubble in the history of the world allowed us to enjoy a level of debt-fueled prosperity that was far greater than we actually deserved. Now the party is ending, and our society is going to experience an enormous amount of pain as everything changes."[7]

Many commentators likened the global financial regime to a gigantic Ponzi scheme, a form of investment fraud which transfers wealth from the future to the present. Ponzi schemes create the illusion of affluence in the short term and attempt to postpone the catastrophic consequences that always follow. The writer Mitch Feierstein referred to,

"Planet Ponzi — the massive build-up of debt, the total loss of political transparency — had caused multiple casualties across the world. The failure of banks, the huge rise in government debt, the failure of business, the loss of jobs, the pressure on real incomes — all these things stem from the same dark causes."[8]

Feierstein blamed an ideology that was both, "insane" and "ethically, financially, and socially wrong". It would, he predicted, lead to worse disasters than the crisis of 2008, "Everyone's borrowing, no one's paying. And one day, the merry-go-round will stop." The blogger Egon von Greyerz agreed, claiming the Boomer Ideology has led Western Civilization into a dead end. Populations were therefore horribly unprepared to cope with the new reality. Ingenious forms of debt and money-printing, he said, had not created Boomertopia — but the illusion of Boomertopia,

"We are now at the end of an era of economic and moral decadence in a debt infested world built on false values, fake money and abysmal leadership. All hell will break loose... It is the build up of a massive debt mountain which has given the Western world a false comfort based on false values."[9]

According to von Greyerz, the Boomers had erected a huge tower of self-delusion resting on dreams and hubris. It was, he said, about to collapse,

"Even a monkey would understand that if you print $10s of trillions and keep interest rates at zero or negative for years, the end result will be spectacular inflation... What is coming next is the inevitable perfect storm."

The demographer and scholar Joel Kotkin said the new economic reality was driving profound social change. As the middle class was obliterated, Kotkin argued, a new type of feudal society was emerging to replace it. This "neo-feudal" world was characterized by social polarization and the existence of two distinct blocs: the "highly educated and affluent", and the "expanding serf class". The new world would be segmented and hierarchical. At the top would be a small aristocracy of the super-rich, beneath it, and supporting it, a sprawling "clerisy" of university-educated technocrats,

"The new class structure resembles that of Medieval times. At the apex of the new order are two classes—a reborn clerical elite, the clerisy, which dominates the upper part of the professional ranks, universities, media and culture, and a new aristocracy led by tech oligarchs with unprecedented wealth and growing control of information."[10]

Kotkin argued that the middle class had played a pivotal role in the success of Western civilization and the rise of individual liberty and Liberal Democracy since the 18th Century. However, that remarkable epoch of social mobility and opportunity had been the exception, not the norm. Society was now slipping back into a pre-Enlightenment, hierarchical structure in which the majority were not property owners, but were dependent on the state for survival, "Rather than acquiring property and gaining a modicum of self-sufficiency, workers can now expect a serf-like future of rented apartments and frozen prospects."[11]

The scholar Peter Turchin predicted the dawn of a new age of "bitter struggle" as individuals competed for dwindling resources. As the ship of affluence sank, there would not be enough room in the lifeboats. There would be, he forecast, too many people trying to climb up into the elite category. Like crabs in a bucket they would scramble over each other to escape being at the bottom. It was a phenomenon he labelled "elite overproduction" and he foresaw widespread "social turmoil",

"Elite overproduction generally leads to more intra-elite competition that gradually undermines the spirit of cooperation, which is followed by ideological polarization and fragmentation of the political class. This happens because the more contenders there are, the more of them end up on the losing side. A large class of disgruntled elite-wannabes, often well-educated and highly capable, has been denied access to elite positions."[12]

Soaring fuel prices and inflation, which began to be apparent by early 2022, led to alarm among politicians and prompted calls for state intervention. Senator Chuck Schumer of New York called for an increase in the Home Energy Assistance Program saying, "No family should have to choose between heating their home or putting food on the table. But that's what a lot of people, particularly seniors, have to do." Schumer added,

"No senior has to choose between shivering or purchasing medication that they desperately need."[13] The situation was worse in Europe. According to Euronews,

> "More than 35 million Europeans are unable to afford to keep their homes warm this winter. That's the equivalent of the entire populations of Greece, Portugal, Hungary and Ireland combined having to decide between heating and putting food on the table."[14]

In the UK, rising energy bills prompted people to look for imaginative alternatives to switching on the heating. *The Guardian* reported,

> "Britain's cost of living crisis has another potent symbol: Elsie, a 77-year-old woman who found the cheapest way to keep warm was to switch the heating off, leave home and ride the buses all day."[15]

The American writer Jeffrey Tucker summarized the gathering economic storm as a "mark of civilizational decline". It was, he said, the result of denying reality for decades and believing that wealth could be magically created out of thin air,

> "Historians of the future, if there are any intelligent ones among them, will surely be aghast at our astounding ignorance. Congress enacted decades of spending in just two years and figured it would be fine. The printing presses at the Fed ran at full tilt... Now we face terrible, grim, grueling, exploitative inflation, at the same time we are plunging into recession again, and people sit around wondering what the heck happened. I will tell you what happened: the ruling class destroyed the world we knew. It happened right before our eyes. And here we are."[16]

Tucker predicted new ways of thinking and a new system of values would be the inevitable consequence of the death of the age of affluence,

> "No more charity. No more kindness. No more doing something for nothing. In inflationary times, everyone becomes more grasp-

ing. Morality takes a back seat and generosity is no more. It's every man for himself. This can only get more brutal."

The new reality of the 2020's seemed to resemble the hardship and poverty of the 1930's, not the endless abundance on which the Boomers had been weaned. Writing in 1981, the British sociologist Bernice Martin had reflected that the Boomers were able to,

"Afford an expressive extravaganza because it seemed to most Western people in that decade [the 1960s] that a never-ending economic expansion and rise in standards of living was one of the givens of life."[17]

Since the Boomer Ideology was "the luxury product" of "effortless affluence", she wondered whether a "traumatic world recession" might derail it and lead to its demise. Martin's reflection was prophetic. By the 2020's the age of affluence was over. The post-affluent age had begun.

Generational Change – From Boomers to Millennials

At the same time that material reality was dramatically changing for hundreds of millions of people, a process of generational change and replacement was beginning. In 2008, most Boomers were over the age of sixty and starting to retire. John Lennon, had he lived, would have been sixty-eight. Power was shifting to the Boomer's children — the Millennial generation.*

The Millennials soaked-up the values and folklore of the Boomer Ideology which enveloped them during their youth and formative years. Millennial children were raised by Boomers. They were taught by Boomer teachers in schools using Boomer-designed text-books and curricula. They learned the Boomer version of history. They attended universities that were factories of the Boomer Ideology. They were surrounded by, and saturated in the cultural narratives contained in Boomer

---

* I use the label 'Millennial' to refer to the children of the Baby Boomers and/ or those who grew up in a world shaped by their values. In crude demographic terms, Millennials were born between approximately 1970-1995.

movies, pop music, art and TV shows. The journalism they consumed was Boomer Journalism. When they began to explore the new online and mobile world, the same set of values was imprinted upon them.

To Millennials, the Boomer Ideology was therefore the normal, taken-for-granted set of assumptions that ordinary, decent people shared. The Boomer Ideology did not appear as something radically new constructed by their parents. In other words, the Millennials were the first generation for more than three hundred years not to be raised in the tradition of the Anglo-American Enlightenment and/or Victorian Liberalism. As they grew up, Millennials absorbed the Boomer way of knowing and the Boomer Epistemology. They tended to understand truth as Tribal Truth or Official Truth — the consensus of the opinions of benevolent, college-educated people like themselves. The Victorian Liberal Epistemology — which understood truth as the provisional, fallible product of debate and disagreement — seemed weird, uncomfortable and wrong.

Suckled on a mixture of hedonism and Utopian idealism, the Millennials were intolerant of imperfection, both in their own lives and in the wider world. Millennials felt entitled to a comfortable, affluent life, free from danger, risk, toil, injustice and unfairness. The American psychologist Jean Twenge observed that, "Millennials are the children of baby Boomers, who are also known as the Me Generation, who then produced the Me Me Me Generation." Twenge said Millennials were victims of an unrealistic, Utopian world view inherited from their Boomer parents. The collision between their expectations and reality made them feel they were inadequate if their lives were not perfectly perfect. Millennials, she concluded, have the,

> "Highest likelihood of having unmet expectations with respect to their careers and the lowest levels of satisfaction with their careers at the stage that they're at... It is sort of a crisis of unmet expectations."[18]

The Boomer's rejection of the Victorian virtues of responsibility, self-control, restraint and denial, and their hedonistic belief that desire should be gratified instantly, was bequeathed to their children as normal and healthy. Twenge, and her colleague Keith Campbell, saw it as an increased emphasis on, "material wealth, physical appearance, celebrity worship, and attention seeking." They noted a,

> "Fivefold increase in plastic surgery and cosmetic procedures in just ten years, the growth of celebrity gossip magazines, Americans spending more than they earn and racking up huge amounts of debt, the growing size of houses, the increasing popularity of giving children unique names, polling data on the importance of being rich and famous, and the growing number of people who cheat."[19]

All these things were the result of the Boomer's Utopian cosmology which insisted it was possible to have it all and take more out of the system than you put in. However, in the post-affluent age, this philosophy of life was becoming harder and harder to sustain. It was, Twenge and Campbell wrote,

> "A fantasy in which the world owes you more than you contribute. You can feel entitled to a flat-screen TV without earning the money to pay for it. You can park in the handicapped space because you are in a rush. You can graduate from college and expect to get a fulfilling job with a six-figure salary right away."

To be useful, an ideology must align with economic, social and political reality. Indeed, the stunning success of the Boomer Ideology during the last third of the 20th Century was due to the fact the huge Boomer tribe perceived its interests and aspirations were no longer served by the ideology of Victorian Liberalism. To the Boomers, Victorian Liberalism was an anachronism — a hangover from a time when life for many was a struggle to survive. As The Boomer prophet Charles Reich explained in 1970, the urgent task for the Boomers was to prepare to live in the new world of abundance, prosperity and plenty,

> "Older people learned how to live in a different world... In the world that now exists, a life of surfing is possible, not as an escape from work, a recreation or a phase, but as a life – if one chooses. The fact that this choice is actually available is the truth

that the younger generation knows and the older generation cannot know."[20]

Reich's statement that Boomers could spend their lives surfing if they wanted to, reflected the underlying belief that reality itself had changed in a fundamental way. Reich described it as a, "new head – a new way of living". He added that, "It requires man to create a reality — a fiction based on what can offer men the best hope of a life that is both satisfying and beautiful." [21]

The Boomer Ideology was therefore a map to help the Boomer tribe navigate the reality in which they believed they were living. But after 2008, reality changed. The map, once again, no longer fitted the terrain. Just as the ideology of the 1860's had become inappropriate for the reality of the 1960's; so the ideology of the 1960's was becoming increasingly inappropriate for the reality of the 2020's. The Boomer Ideology was fast decaying into a luxury belief system — as obsolete and irrelevant in its turn as Victorian Liberalism had appeared to the Boomers back in 1968.

As the Boomers transmitted their culture to their children during the late 20th Century, what was lost was the *context* which had made it possible for that culture to take root and flourish in the first place. For example, a major feature of the Boomer Ideology had been its truculent, rebellious playfulness. Part of its function was to subvert and undermine the authority of the War Generation and assert the independence and dominance of Boomer youth. The Boomer Ideology was, in other words, the ritual banter of the Boomer tribe. It was deliberately intended to outrage the War Generation and offend the mores of Victorian Liberalism. However, by the early 21st Century, the War Generation had vanished. In this altered context, many Boomer virtues no longer made sense. For example, in the 2020's, the Boomers taught their children a rebellious ideology from which all the rebelliousness had been removed. Paradoxically therefore, Millennials were expected to uncritically accept their parent's ethical-political values, not rebel against them. Millennials therefore absorbed the Boomer Ideology with a deadly seriousness.

It is extremely dangerous to uncritically transfer a folklore, or mythology, to a new group which does not recognize the context for which it was designed. The peril is that newcomers will fail to understand the playful nature of it and take it seriously. The linguist William Labov studied the language and rituals of gang members in the U.S. and used the phrase "ritual sounding" to describe the verbal sparring between members. For example, one member would tell another, "Your father eats shit", or "Your mother looks like Flipper".** This highly offensive banter, Labov noted, was not intended to be taken literally or seriously. A novice gang member who failed to understand the context, might make the disastrous mistake of responding to the jokes with incomprehension and violence. As Labov put it, the danger of sounds being misinterpreted "cannot be overstated."[22]

In the same way, when the Boomers transmitted their values and ideology to their children, much essential context was lost. The Millennials filtered out the cheeky rebelliousness and game-playing element, and distilled the Boomer Ideology into an intensely serious, quasi-religious tribalism. For example, the Boomer's rebellious contempt for the values of their parents, was transformed, in the minds of the Millennials, into a form of ethical-political absolutism in which the world prior to the 1960s was objectively a dark age of bigotry, sexism, racism, selfishness and hate. Unquestioning faith in this narrative about the pre-Boomer era was obligatory. Uncritical acceptance of the Boomer Ideology as morally good, implied that whatever contradicted it must be evil. If Boomer hedonism, progressivism and Utopianism were correct; then the values of the Anglo-American Enlightenment, and of Victorian Liberalism, must, logically, be wrong. As the process of cultural transmission continued during the early 21st Century, much was lost in translation. If the Boomer Ideology, and belief in Boomer Exceptionalism, were, at least in part, ritual jokes; they were jokes that were entirely lost on the Millennials.

** Flipper was a dolphin featured in the 1960s TV show of the same name.

Chapter 24

Official Ideology v Unofficial Ideology

Welcome to the Culture Wars

As the Boomers faded from the scene during the second decade of the 21st Century, and as the conditions of material reality continued to deteriorate, a period of intense ideological turmoil began. During this period of flux and realignment, two broad, mutually antagonistic ideological positions emerged. One set of assumptions and values coalesced into an 'Official Ideology'. The other set formed into an 'Unofficial Ideology'. The bitter clash between them was widely referred to as the 'culture wars'.

The American social analyst Michael Lind argues that the two ideologies evolved to serve the interests of the two different social blocs. One for the "college-educated managerial-professional overclass minority, and one for the non-college-educated working-class majority of all races."[1] According to the British political commentator Nick Timothy, the Official Ideology is the belief system of the elite "liberal technocrats" who occupy positions of power and authority in the expressive professions and the establishment. It is the ideology of the new ruling class the, "civil service, the media, business, courts, quangos and universities", among whom "there is a remarkable uniformity of opinion that has shaped our country and the decisions of our governments for the past few decades."[2]

In the US, former Congressional aide Mike Lofgren uses the phrase "Deep State" to refer to the "Washington consensus" which believes its mission is to rule over the masses,

> "Its governing philosophy profoundly influences foreign and national security policy and such domestic matters as spending priorities, trade, investment, income inequality, privatization of government services, media presentation of news, and the whole meaning and worth of citizens' participation in their government."[3]

According to Lofgren, the etiquette of the Deep State demands its ideology must be invisible. The Official Ideology is simply the normal, correct way of thinking and behaving. Members of the Deep State believe their own world view is objectively the only correct one and so are,

> "Careful to pretend that they have no ideology. Their preferred pose is that of the politically neutral technocrat offering well-considered advice based on profound expertise. Expertise is what they sell."

Lofgren sees commitment to the Official Ideology as a form of group-think responsible for guiding the decisions of professionals in a wide range of sectors ranging from journalism to the judiciary. However, according to Lofgren, it can also be understood as a form of corruption,

> "Corruption does not always require an immediate cash nexus. Justices of the Supreme Court, who have lifetime tenure and fixed salaries, receive no bribes from corporate America to rule in its favor. They do so because they believe in a certain ideology with dogmatic faith, and accordingly backfill their rulings with

281

whichever legal arguments more or less hang together. It is not corruption so much as bias confused with principle."

The Official Ideology shares the ethical-political Utopianism of the Boomer Ideology and sees the need for radical social change to create a better world. To make this happen, benevolent, educated experts must be given the power and authority to solve humanity's problems. For example, in 2020 the influential German economist Klaus Schwab called for a "Great Reset". He said,

> "We are now at a crossroads. One path will take us to a better world: more inclusive, more equitable and more respectful of Mother Nature. The other will take us to a world that resembles the one we just left behind."[4]

Schwab, who founded the *World Economic Forum* in 1971, argues that the "looming challenges" faced by the human race are too complex and confusing to be understood by the mass of ordinary people. They are, he says, beyond the capacity of Victorian Liberal Democracy to solve. They can only be solved by teams of elite policy makers,

> "Although they are complex, the policy solutions do exist and broadly consist in adapting the welfare state to today's world by empowering people and by responding to the demands for a fairer social contract."

Schwab argues that the Covid-19 pandemic presented an opportunity to "build back better" and transform civilization. "The pandemic" he predicted, "will mark a turning point by accelerating this transition. It has crystallized the issue and made a return to the pre-pandemic status quo impossible."

The Official Ideology therefore can be understood as the logical evolution of the Boomer Ideology. It is Utopian and intolerant of the imperfections of Liberal Democracy. It sees a future in which college-educated experts make decisions for the common good, and strive to create a more perfect world, unhindered by the shortsighted concerns of ordinary people. However, paradoxically, despite its rhetoric of radical social change, the Official Ideology is inherently conservative because it seeks to preserve the ideological status quo of the late 20th Century and defend it from change.

The Unofficial Ideology, on the other hand, represents the interests of those who are deeply suspicious of the future that the elite tribe is preparing for them. The Unofficial Ideology is hostile to the idea that technocratic experts know what is best and should be trusted with unlimited power. Instead, it promotes the pre-Boomer, Enlightenment belief that informed individuals are the best judges of their own self-interest. As the academic James Woodhuysen puts it, the Unofficial Ideology rejects the belief that,

> "The public no longer consists of rational decision-making beings, but of half-conscious, half-baked creatures who need to be subtly guided in what experts deem to be the right direction."[5]

The Australian commentator Maurice Newman attacks Schwab's "Great Reset" as an attempt to introduce a type of "fascism" – authoritarian rule by an unelected cartel of global technocrats allied to the state,

> "Stripped of the propaganda, the Great Reset is not new. It's another fascist experiment being pushed by controlling elitists. Economic growth and social mobility must be subordinate to the collective. Connections will be institutionalized and privilege perpetuated. History demonstrates the children of the elites will receive preferential access to higher education and elite positions. 'Inclusion' and 'fairness'? Forget it. Think inequality, serfdom and misery."[6]

The Unofficial Ideology is anti-Utopian and pragmatic. It embraces reality as it is, not how it ought to be. It is especially hostile to the Utopian schemes of the elite technocrats. The Unofficial Ideology assumes that simple, perfect solutions to complex problems do not exist and are dangerous, sinister illusions. As the journalist Irving Kristol put it, technocrats are wrong to believe the world is full of "problems" which must be "solved",

> "The world isn't full of problems; the world is full of other people. That's not a problem, that's a condition. Politics exist precisely

because the world is full of other people. These other people have ideas, different ways of life, different preferences, and in the end, there is no 'solution' to the existence of other people. All you can do is figure out a civilized accommodation with them."[7]

Those who subscribe to the Unofficial Ideology are often skeptical of the rhetoric of social and environmental justice which they see as a form of trickery to gain power over them, and a disguise for tribal self-interest. As Michael Lind puts it they,

"Mock 'political correctness,' the artificial dialect devised by leftist activists and spread by university and corporate bureaucrats that serves as a class marker distinguishing the college-educated from the vulgar majority below them."[8]

The Unofficial Ideology offers a common-sense approach to help people survive in the harsh reality of the Post-Affluent Age. As the journalist Damian Wilson explained in 2020, this "brave new world" will be,

"Far leaner, far meaner animal than it was this time last year, there will be no room for passengers... Success will be difficult, and it will take street smarts and opportunistic cunning to make it."[9]

Wilson urged young people to reject the strategy of seeking "worthless" university degrees and instead prepare themselves to be, "industrious, energetic, entrepreneurial people" able to "back their own judgement, learn from their mistakes and get on with the next plan." The author and commentator Mark Steyn described the Official Ideology as a form of social signaling designed to serve the interests of the rich and powerful. "They understand" said Steyn, "they're in a world in which striking attitudes which preserve their own power base is more important than anything else." Steyn argued that the Official Ideology's focus on social, racial and environmental justice was fraudulent,

"The whole point is to create a world in which there's an elite at the top and a vast mass underneath, and the escalator to get from the bottom to the top is running ever slower with fewer people able to get on it."[10]

The comedian and author Andrew Doyle agreed. He created Titania McGrath, a character who pretends to care, but whose humanity is a blatantly insincere affectation masking authoritarian instincts. In Doyle's satire, the fashionable rhetoric of social justice is exposed as a way of signaling allegiance to, and gaining status within, the elite tribe. As McGrath explains,

"Anyone can be an activist. By simply adding a rainbow flag to your Facebook profile, or calling out an elderly person who doesn't understand what 'non-binary' means, you can change the world for the better. Indeed, social media has now made it possible to show how virtuous you are without having to do anything at all."[11]

Doyle lampooned the epistemology of the Official Ideology, its love of Tribal Truth and its distaste for impartial, evidence-based enquiry. McGrath tells her followers,

"Feelings don't care about your facts. This is how social justice works. If you feel something to be true, then it is true. For those of you who are skeptical on this point, I would simply ask that you defer to my superior wisdom. I have neither the patience nor the inclination to explain myself in full."

McGrath concludes that the epistemology of Victorian Liberalism is obsolete because it places a higher value on seeking truth, than on doing what is ethically-politically correct. As McGrath puts it, truth should be avoided because "facts are routinely deployed in order to spread hate." This form of virtue signaling is striking similar to the public morality of pre-Victorian society. For example, the historian Ben Wilson describes late 18th Century England as a place, "governed by specious sophistry and smooth-talking charlatans". Public discourse, he says, was marked by, "the 'cant of virtue' — a kind of moralizing verbiage that sounded virtuous but was really empty". Wilson's description of this era sounds uncannily like early 21st Century Anglo-American society in which people vie with one another to appear fashionably virtuous on social media in order to gain approval and prestige. As Wilson continues,

"People were encouraged to talk of virtue and to judge each other by outward appearances of respectability and public rectitude which had nothing to do with inner morality. The 'mere cant of words' was not just irritating but the manifestation of a deep moral illness: the British were becoming censorious and small-minded, vindictively pursuing people for petty things while letting more serious crimes go unmentioned and unpunished. The lies that society told itself and the jargon that upheld dogma had been in circulation for so long and had become so widely repeated that people had stopped noticing hypocrisy and injustice."[12]

The Unofficial Ideology, on the other hand, tends to scorn virtue signalling and seeks inspiration in the values of Victorian Liberalism. It recognizes the importance of the individual and offers ordinary people the opportunity to build a better life through their own talent and hard work. Paradoxically therefore, the Unofficial Ideology is radical and disruptive because it seeks to overturn the established Boomer consensus of the late 20th Century, even though its values reflect the pre-Boomer past. Hence, in the early 21st Century, the meaning of the labels 'conservative' and 'radical' have become strangely reversed. The rhetoric of the Official Ideology calls for radical social change, yet seeks to preserve Boomer values. Whereas the rhetoric of the Unofficial Ideology praises the values of the Anglo-American Enlightenment, and in doing so seeks radical change.

The political landscape of the 2020s is therefore a confused and confusing place in which self-proclaimed 'radicals' are really reactionaries who seek to defend the status quo; while self-proclaimed 'conservatives' seek radical, ideological change. The labels 'left wing' and 'right wing' are equally confusing and unhelpful. 'Left' refers simply to those who embrace the Official Ideology and want to defend it; while 'right' is generally used as a term of abuse by those on the 'left' to identify and demonize the tribal enemy. In summary, the Post-Affluent Age is a period of turmoil and flux as different groups, and alliances of groups, compete for the power to shape the future. In this unsettled world, as the tectonic plates of economics, global politics and culture shift, there is a widespread feeling that Western society stands at an ideological crossroads facing, "an emergent epochal crisis" marked by "feelings of loss, mourning and the search for identity."[13] The journalist John Avlon put it more bluntly,

"Polarization is killing our country. It is weakening our political and social bonds, separating our economic fortunes and driving bitter cultural divides. Hyper-partisanship is poisoning our politics, making our democracy seem increasingly dysfunctional. A fixation on our differences is fracturing us into warring tribes, threatening to turn our country into little more than a collection of grievance groups who believe that folks on the other side of the divide are the ones really tearing our nation apart."[14]

Modernizing Truth. Smith-Mundt and the Leveson Report

When times are hard, having a firm grasp on reality is vital. Epistemology becomes a matter of life and death. Luxury ideologies that disrespect and deny reality are extravagances that can no longer be afforded. They become burdens that must be jettisoned. In times of scarcity and increased competition, when the goal is survival, knowledge of what is, becomes more valuable that dreaming of what ought to be. The epistemology of the War Generation trumps the Boomer Epistemology. The classic text *The Art of War*, written two thousand years ago by the Chinese warrior philosopher Sun Tzu, stresses the importance of deceiving, whilst avoiding being deceived. As Sun Tzu puts it,

"All warfare is based on deception. Hence, when we are able to attack, we must seem unable; when using our forces, we must appear inactive; when we are near, we must make the enemy believe we are far away; when far away, we must make him believe we are near... A good merchant hides his treasures and appears to have nothing... In martial arts, it is important that strategy be unfathomable, that form be concealed, and that movements be unexpected, so that preparedness against them be impossible... Sages hide in unfathomability."[15]

The central theme of *The Art of War* is therefore epistemic. It is studded with advice about how to manipulate the beliefs of competitors, for example by creating confusion, "A military operation involves deception. Even though you are competent, appear to be incompetent. Though effective, appear to be ineffective."[16] At the same time, the book warns of the danger of gullibility and offers advice about how to read the enemy's epistemic tricks, "If they ply you with expensive gifts and sweet talk, they are up to something."[17]   Human conflict is seen, first and foremost, as an epistemic struggle. To control the enemy, you must first control what he believes to be true. Depriving your opponents of the ability to think critically, and encouraging them to believe fantasies, will help your side win. Hence, Sun Tzu includes advice on how to distract and confuse,

> "Seduce them with the prospect of gain... have rhetoricians use fast talk... cause rifts between the leadership and their followers, or between them and their allies; cause division, and then take aim at them."[18]

What Sun Tzu describes, is an epistemic struggle during which one group attempts to impose its reality on another. The goal is to get the other side to believe what you want them to believe. A major theme of *The Art of War* is therefore the art of controlling the narrative. Klaus Schwab echoes both Sun Tzu and Plato in recognizing the importance of narrative control. In a 2022 book entitled *The Great Narrative* he explains the need for a neo-Platonic "noble lie" to inspire people and persuade them to accept the Official Ideology. Narratives, he says,

> "Underpin the perceptions that shape our 'realities' and in the process form our cultures and societies. Through narratives, we explain how we see things, how these things work, how we make decisions and justify them, how we understand our place in the world and how we try to persuade others to embrace our beliefs and values. To sum up: narratives shape our perceptions, which in turn form our realities and end up influencing our choices and actions."[19]

Schwab explains how narrative can be used to lead the mass of ordinary people towards a glorious Utopian future, "Let's muster our collective capacity of imagination to elaborate a set of hopeful futures and map out the various pathways that would lead towards them." Victorian Liberal Democracy, he says, is incapable of leading us to Utopia because it encourages independent critical thinking. This leads to inconclusive debates and to the imperfect compromises and horse-trading of parliamentary and congressional politics. As Schwab puts it, radical change is, "particularly problematic in liberal democracies as they are subject to the vagaries of the electoral cycle." The answer, he says, is to use the bewitching power of narrative to inspire and persuade, and thereby manufacture consent for a new world order,

> "The solutions we find and the decisions we take to make the world a better place – more resilient, more equitable and more sustainable – depend on our willingness to enact positive change. In turn, this propensity depends on our collective capability to develop a set of narratives that instill hope."

The journalist Caitlin Johnstone also sees narrative as a powerful tool, but disapproves of its cynical use by the, "murderous oligarchic forces that are steering us into destruction". Like Sun Tzu, she recognizes that those who control the narrative, have enormous power to manipulate our emotions, beliefs, thoughts and behavior,

> "For as long as there has been human language, humans have been using it to manipulate one another. The fact that it is possible to skillfully weave a collection of symbolic mouth noises together in such a way as to extract favors, concessions, votes and consent from other humans has made manipulation so common that it now pervades our society from top to bottom... Understand the fact that humans are storytelling animals, and that whoever controls the stories controls the humans."[20]

Early 21st Century journalism is marked by a freefall back into narrative. From an historical perspective, as we have already seen, the power of narrative was precisely what the Anglo-American Enlightenment, and Victorian Liberalism, sought to restrain. Victorian Liberal Journalism, with its strict distinction between fact and opinion, aimed to neutralize the seductive lure of emotional storytelling, and replace it with impartial enquiry based on evidence and reason. To the Enlightenment philosophes of the 18th Century, narrative was a gateway drug leading humanity back to the world of superstition, intolerance and sectarian warfare from which it had only recently emerged.

During the early 21st Century, as society fragmented into mutually hostile tribal groups, each with their own guiding narratives; the safeguards introduced by earlier generations to protect citizens from the danger of narrative were systematically removed. In the US, the 1948 Smith-Mundt Act was "modernized" in 2012. Smith-Mundt was a ban on domestic propaganda which ensured that no government funds could be used to "influence public opinion in the United States." It was introduced to preserve diversity of opinion, stimulate debate and facilitate Liberal Democracy. However, when President Barack Obama signed the Smith-Mundt Modernization Act into law in January 2013, these legislative restraints were removed. As the legal scholar Weston Sager explains, "The sixty-four-year-old domestic dissemination ban was suddenly and unceremoniously abolished."[21] Sager was horrified the federal government now had a green light to use taxpayer dollars to persuade and influence taxpayers and shape their thoughts. The risk, he said, was that, the state would "disseminate stories that cover only those issues that advance the federal government's stance, thereby painting an incomplete picture of the issue."

The US seemed to be moving rapidly towards the concept of state-funded, Official Truth. As the academic Mark LeVine explained,

"The US government could routinely lie to citizens about policies which are themselves based on or involve misleading — in Pentagon-speak, 'influencing' — the population, creating a vicious circle of lies and manipulation."[22]

Citizens were now stripped of protection and are, "as vulnerable as people around the world already are to the long arm of American disinformation. The author Kathleen McCarthy warned the repeal of Smith-Mundt meant "the media cartel has a government-sanctioned license to lie." She predicted the rise of a new type of journalism which she christened 'newz'. The role of 'newz', she said, would be to curate and communicate the official narratives of the Federal government,

"Traditional 'news,' based on reliable, verifiable fact-based evidence is slowly giving way to 'newz' – an ersatz form of information dissemination via broadcasting and/or publishing that enjoys specialized immunity for libel, misinformation, false or fraudulent information, misrepresentation, and anything else

290

previously prohibited… Revoking the restrictions once enforced under Smith-Mundt has opened the floodgates."[23]

In 2022, when the entrepreneur Elon Musk bought Twitter, he released internal documents showing the extent to which these predictions had come true. The documents, dubbed the 'Twitter Files' revealed widespread interventions by federal agencies, including the FBI and CIA, to limit free speech and control the information available to U.S. citizens. The story was treated as a major scandal by Unofficial Journalists, but largely ignored by mainstream outlets. Unofficial journalist Matt Taibbi, who was given access to the documents, concluded,

"The files show the FBI acting as doorman to a vast program of social media surveillance and censorship, encompassing agencies across the federal government – from the State Department to the Pentagon to the CIA."[24]

According to the Twitter Files, the FBI persuaded Twitter executives to censor an explosive *New York Post* story accusing the Biden family of corruption in the run-up to the 2020 presidential election. According to the story, Joe's son Hunter was appointed to the board of the Ukrainian energy company Burisma and paid $50,000 a month in return for arranging a meeting between his father, who was then Vice President, and a Burisma executive. Evidence of the corruption was detailed in emails found on a laptop Hunter left in a repair shop. Acting on advice from the FBI, Twitter froze the *New York Post*'s account. Other social media companies also censored the story. The Twitter Files also revealed the FBI requested censorship of jokes hinting at voter fraud and election irregularities during the 2020 election. It also urged Twitter to delete posts questioning the official narrative about the conflict between Ukraine and Russia. Federal agencies also, "pressured Twitter to elevate certain content and suppress other content about Covid-19 and the pandemic."[25]

As Taibbi reported,

"The government was in constant contact not just with Twitter but with virtually every major tech firm. These included Facebook, Microsoft, Verizon, Reddit, even Pinterest, and many others…

There were so many government requests, Twitter employees had to improvise a system for prioritizing/triaging them."[26]

Federal agencies claimed they were only "flagging-up" possible breaches of Twitter's guidelines — not giving Twitter "specific instructions" what to do. But Taibbi was unimpressed by the FBI's protestation of innocence. It was, he said, a "master-canine" relationship. As the journalist Victoria Marshall summarizes,

"The internal documents disclosed in these reports show that FBI agents flagged specific information and individuals for Twitter employees to censor. Twitter employees would then comply, allowing U.S. intelligence agencies to manipulate public discussions and political outcomes, as well as restrict Americans' constitutional right to free speech in the public square."[27]

Unofficial journalist Michael Shellenberger, who had access to the original documents, noted the FBI paid Twitter more than $3.4 million of taxpayer's money to subsidize its domestic propaganda campaign. As Shellenberger reported,

"The FBI's influence campaign may have been helped by the fact that it was paying Twitter millions of dollars for its staff time. 'I am happy to report we have collected $3,415,323 since October 2019!' reports an associate of Jim Baker in early 2021."[28]

The FBI defended its behavior claiming, in a statement, it was merely protecting US citizens from harmful misinformation,

"The correspondence between the FBI and Twitter show nothing more than examples of our traditional, longstanding and ongoing federal government and private sector engagements, which involve numerous companies over multiple sectors and industries... The men and women of the FBI work every day to protect the American public. It is unfortunate that conspiracy theorists and others are feeding the American public misinformation with the sole purpose of attempting to discredit the agency."[29]

This was an extraordinary admission and reveals the extent to which the Boomer and Millennial generations changed what was considered normal and ethical. Prior to the abolition of Smith-Mundt in 2013, what the FBI was boasting about — using tax dollars to control what information US citizens were allowed to see — would have been criminal. When Smith-Mundt was introduced in 1948, it would also have been considered un-American, undemocratic and totalitarian. By the 2020's however, ethical-political norms had changed, ideology had changed, the concept of truth had changed, and so to had journalism. It was the Boomer generation that changed them. The 'modernization' of Smith-Mundt therefore opened the gates to a new era of collusive journalism in the US. This type of journalism, because it abandoned the epistemology and methodology of Victorian Liberal Journalism, was essentially pre-Victorian in nature. It's reliance on simple, ethical-political narratives meant it resembled the partisan American journalism of the antebellum era. As we have seen, the historical roots of this journalism lay in the journalism of 18th Century England and colonial America. It was a tribal journalism which received generous subsidies from the state, and from the rich and powerful, to direct attention towards official narratives, and suppress inconvenient facts and opinions.

The Leveson Report. Restating Journalism's Ethical-Political Responsibilities

At the same time US lawmakers were dismantling Smith-Mundt's restraints on state propaganda, policy-makers in the UK were sending a strong message that journalism's first loyalty must be to making the world a better place, not telling the truth regardless of the consequences. This was the truthophobic take-away from the Leveson Inquiry of 2012. Lord Leveson's inquiry was set-up following revelations that journalists from the tabloid *News of the World* newspaper had illegally eavesdropped on cell phone voice messages. The inquiry was tasked with examining both the scandal and the wider, "culture, practices and ethics of the press." Much of the inquiry focused on whether news organizations were justified in publishing stories that were true, but not ethical. Leveson concluded that truth was not sufficient justification — ethics should be the dominant priority. Lord Justice Leveson was remarkably dismissive of the importance of Journalistic Truth. Born in 1949, he shared many of the epistemic assumptions of his generation. For example, following the doctrine of Tuchmanism and other theorists of the 1970s, he took it for granted that Journalistic Truth was a relative construct,

> "We want the truth, but we understand that there are many versions of the truth, and incompleteness in all versions. Notwithstanding the emphasis put by both the industry and its critics on the difference between 'fact' and 'comment' these are by no means distinct and watertight categories. The very act of describing a fact is to comment on it. All forms of recording are selective."[30]

Leveson often appeared contemptuous of Journalistic Truth which he equated with the public's "right to know". This, he argued dismissively, was little more than a prurient or "vicious curiosity". It was, he said, a concept that was, "puzzling and problematic for many reasons",

> "The fact that people have a vicious curiosity clearly does not entail a right to know those things, nor does it automatically excuse those who breach other norms in the service of that curiosity."[31]

Leveson added, there was, "no ethical duty at all to provide audiences with whatever they want, even if there are good economic reasons for doing so."[32] Hence, for Leveson, *aletheia*, the search for Journalistic Truth was a dubious, grubby motive, stained with commercialism and a vicious desire to know. Instead of truth, Leveson argued that ethics should be journalism's supreme guide. He said the words "ethical" and "public interest" were synonymous, and called for the creation of a code of journalistic ethics to "explain what ethical (or, as it is sometimes described, 'public interest') journalism is".[33]

Leveson quoted with approval the opinion of the British philosopher Onora O'Neill who called for "ethically reflective" journalism guided by an "aspirational" ethical code. In practice, said O'Neill, this would require elite journocrats to generate the correct ethical-political news narratives to guide those lower down the hierarchy,

> "A code by itself is not worth the paper it is written on unless it is a lived code. To make a code a lived code, media organizations

need to attend to the critical factors that can bring about an ethical organization, or promote integrity in an organization. These factors include tone from the top (or leadership)."[34]

Leveson criticized news stories that were true, but served no ethical-political, or public interest, purpose. For example, he attacked stories that insolently revealed facts about the private lives of celebrities such as the comedian and actor Steve Coogan,

> "No clear public interest justification has been offered for the many stories published about Mr. Coogan's sex life. The stories are mere tittle-tattle. But as Mr. Coogan noted, such gossip is not necessarily harmless and, even when true, can be extremely damaging to the parties involved, as well as innocent third parties."[35]

However, although he demanded ethical journalism, Leveson was not able to define it. Instead, he gave examples of unethical reporting which included, "discriminatory, sensational or unbalanced reporting in relation to ethnic minorities, immigrants and/or asylum seekers". Leveson added that good journalism should be factually accurate, but also careful not to, "exacerbate community divisions or increase resentment."[36]

The significance of the Leveson Report was to stamp Boomer Journalism with the authority of the state. The take-away from Leveson was that journalists should see themselves, first and foremost, as ethical-political actors aware of the consequences of their news reports. Leveson was therefore the British equivalent of the US Supreme Court's verdict in *New York Times* v Sullivan. Both sent a strong message that, when they clashed, the goal of doing what was ethically-politically correct must take priority over the goal of telling the truth.

Leveson's thinking also echoed the attitude of those in power and authority during the abdication crisis. Then, the British media had self-censored because it believed the public's right to know should bow to a higher ethical-political purpose. In 1936, protecting the reputation of the Royal Family was considered the moral priority. Therefore, news of Edward VIII's affair with Wallace Simpson was censored. The *Morning Post* newspaper justified this truthophobic approach explaining it was, "no part of the function of the press to publish gossip possibly injurious to such an institution as the monarchy".[37]

Leveson's vison was for a journalism in which official, ethical-political narratives would be constructed by elite journocrats and then communicated to the wider population. Truth was a secondary consideration. What was most important was making the world a better place. Although the British government did not implement Leveson's recommendations, his report had important consequences. *The News of the World*, which had been published since 1843, was closed by its owners. It had fallen into disgrace, not because it had failed to tell the truth, but because it had transgressed against the new ethical-political code of Boomer Journalism. *The News of the World* was the product of an age in which it was considered journalistically acceptable to use sneaky, deceitful, even dishonest methods to get the story. Journalists were not afraid to get their hands dirty. Spying on people, or rummaging through trash for evidence, were all permissible. If the story was true, the ends justified the means. However, by the early 21st Century, the ideological landscape had changed. What mattered now was having a benevolent ethical-political motive. Pursuit of the truth no longer justified immoral, let alone illegal, practices such as phone tapping. As a result, *The News of the World* found itself stranded and vulnerable — an epistemic dinosaur unable to adapt to society's new, nobler standards. Announcing its closure, James Murdoch, chairman of News International, apologized, signalled his conversion to the new ethical values and expressed contempt for the old Victorian Liberal formula of undisguised truth-telling and profit-seeking,

> "While we may never be able to make up for distress that has been caused, the right thing to do is for every penny of the circulation revenue we receive this weekend to go to organizations... that improve life in Britain and are devoted to treating others with dignity. We will run no commercial advertisements this weekend. Any advertising space in this last edition will be donated to causes and charities that wish to expose their good works to our millions of readers."[38]

The News of the World, which occupied a special place in Boomer hell for its persecution of Mick Jagger in 1967, had paid the ultimate price for pursuing Journalistic Truth regardless of consequences. It had sinned against the Boomer Ideology and the Boomer Epistemology. It died a martyr's death, sacrificed on the altar of *arete*.

Politics – Ideology's Periscope

Politics makes ideology visible. Political policies and affiliations are the periscopes signaling the presence of ideological submarines just beneath the waves. Hence, the Brexit referendum vote in the UK in 2016, the election of Donald Trump, and the gilets jaunes protest movement in France during 2018-2019, all represented, not just disagreement about political choices, but rebellion against the Official Ideology. As Nick Timothy put it these political events, "drove a wrecking ball through the assumptions of the liberal technocrats."[39] Chastened and horrified by insurrection, and by the threat to their power and wealth, the elite tribe counter-attacked fiercely. Political rhetoric therefore intensified sharply after 2016 as two ideologies clashed over whose vision of the future would prevail, and whose map of reality should guide society.

The British journalist Andrew Anthony, writing in *The Guardian*, listed a number of bitter public disputes, over issues such as the toppling of statues in the UK and the US in 2020, which he noted were, "vividly symbolic... skirmishes in a larger and ongoing series of battles: the culture wars." There was little doubt, he concluded that these, "symbolic issues and questions of identity occupy a larger and more antagonistic position in the general culture than they did 10 or 20 years ago."[40]

The sociologist Frank Furedi agreed the political skirmishes were the visible signs of a much deeper social instability. Like subterranean seas of boiling lava which vent explosively through cracks in the ground, Furedi argued there was an, "'all or nothing' struggle against some of society's most important values and achievements." It was, he said, "an existential struggle over who we are." Furedi noted both ideological positions seemed to be works in progress rather than clearly stated, coherent theories. Unlike the religious wars of the past, they were based on unwritten, tribal instincts, not written doctrine. He observed, "The main protagonists do not express their beliefs systematically. They do not promote an explicit philosophy or ideology."[41]

In 2019, *The Guardian* labelled the Unofficial Ideology "populism" and deplored a, "two-decade surge in populist rhetoric that has upended the global political landscape". The Official Ideology was portrayed as normal and reasonable, whereas populism was defined as a poisonous doctrine which perversely frames, "politics as a Manichean battle between the will of ordinary people and corrupt, self-serving elites."[42] *The Guardian* drew on the work of the influential Dutch political scientist Cas Mudde who defined populism as a blinkered, fanatical world view in which there were only either "friends or foe". It was, he said, a pathological doctrine which,

> "Considers society to be ultimately separated into two homoge-neous and antagonistic groups, 'the pure people' versus 'the corrupt elite', and which argues that politics should be an expression of the *volonté générale* (general will) of the people."[43]

However, if the Unofficial Ideology stood accused of being a threat to social harmony, the Official Ideology often appeared equally divisive and tribal. For example, during her Presidential campaign, Hilary Clinton famously told a rally in New York,

> "You could put half of Trump's supporters into what I call the basket of deplorables. Right? They're racist, sexist, homophobic, xenophobic, Islamophobic — you name it. And unfortunately there are people like that. And he has lifted them up."[44]

The journalist Ta-Nehisi Coates went further. Writing in 2017, he described supporters of President Trump, not as political opponents whose views should be rationally debated, but as wicked people. He accused them of espousing a poisonous ideology of "white tribalism" and "systemic bigotry". Trumpism, he said, was, "white supremacy, in all its truculent and sanctimonious power — the same philosophy that inspired murderous lynch mobs of the Ku Klux Klan era." According to Coates, non-college educated, white Americans threatened the Official Ideology and were therefore a dangerous mob to be despised and feared, "The salt-of-the-earth Americans whom we lionize in our culture and politics are not so different from those same Americans who grin back at us in lynching photos."

By the beginning of the 2020's, Western society was divided into two ideological blocs — each increasingly intolerant of, and quick to demon-ize, the another. At election time, each bloc voted for the candidate that appeared to share its own assumptions, norms and values.

Chapter 25

Trumpism, The Unofficial Ideology in the White House

D onald Trump is the personification of the Unofficial Ideology – the alternative worldview that arose in the wake of the 2008 Global Financial Crisis to meet the needs of the non-elite half of society. Instead of seeking a Utopian world of equality and social justice run by powerful elites, Trumpism stresses personal qualities such as being smart, tough and resilient. Although Donald Trump rarely talks explicitly about ideology, his speeches and social media posts are suffused with ideological references and warnings of a neo-feudal future in which ordinary people are ruled by authoritarian technocrats. As he told an election rally in Florida in 2016, "The Washington establishment and the financial and media corporations that fund it exist for only one reason: to protect and enrich itself." These people, he said,

"Don't have your good in mind. Our campaign represents a true existential threat like they haven't seen before. This is not simply another four-year election. This is a crossroads in the history of our civilization."[1]

At an election rally in Georgia in 2020, he told the crowd that, if the Democrats won, "Everything you care about will be gone, your whole philosophy is going to be gone". Those who shared his ideology he said, "believe in America, they believe in our values and all that we stand for", adding that his opponents represented a movement that, "hates America and wants to erase our history and everything that we hold dear — they want to rip down our statues."[2]

Donald Trump denounced the Official Ideology, labelling it the philosophy of 'Critical Race Theory'. It was, he said, a "twisted web of lies" and an attempt to, "bully Americans into abandoning their values, their heritage, and their very way of life." The Official Ideology, he said, preached a warped gospel of gross distortions disguised as American history. It was, "toxic propaganda, ideological poison that, if not removed, will dissolve the civic bonds that tie us together. It will destroy our country."[3] At a rally in Alabama in 2021, he continued his attack on the Official Ideology – this time labelling it "wokism". He played a movie clip of George C. Scott's version of General Patton's rousing wartime speech and asked,

"Do you think that General Patton was woke? I don't think so, he was the exact opposite. You know what woke means? It means you're a loser. Everything woke turns to shit."[4]

To roars of approval, he continued his ideological message,

"Our movement is up against some of the most sinister forces and entrenched interests that anyone can even imagine.... This nation does not belong to them, this nation belongs to you. This is your home. This is your heritage and our magnificent American liberty is your God-given right... We are descended from the heroes and the patriots, the pioneers and the legends who tamed the great wilderness, who settled this vast continent and who laid down the railroads, raised up the skyscrapers and poured out their blood, sweat and tears to build this country into the greatest nation in the history of the world, and we are not going to let it be taken away from us under any circumstances."

In February 2022, speaking about the invasion of the Ukraine by Vladimir Putin's Russia, he said that under his leadership the US had been, "powerful, cunning and smart". Now, under the leadership of Joe Biden, a "weak and incompetent President", the US had become a "stupid country." Trump continued, "The problem is not that Putin is smart, of course, he's smart. The real problem is that our leaders are dumb. Dumb. So dumb."[5]

Behind the obvious party-political point-scoring was an ideological message reflecting a fundamental difference between the Official and Unofficial Ideologies. The ideology of the Boomers was built on the Rousseauesque assumption that human nature is fundamentally benign, and that left alone, different nations will live in peace, harmony and brotherhood. In this view, progress towards Boomertopia is natural and inevitable. All that is required to make the lion lie down beside the lamb is goodwill and kindness. The only thing preventing it, is the corrupting influence of modern capitalism and the selfishness of a small number of individuals.

The Unofficial Ideology however, rejects this view as dangerously naïve or "dumb". Instead, it draws on the Enlightenment assumption that human beings are rational actors motivated by their own self-interest. Consequently, Donald Trump sees global politics as competition between rivals for power and domination. In this Darwinian struggle, only the tough and the smart will survive. If the lamb is foolish enough to lie down beside the lion, it will be killed and eaten. Peace does not come from goodwill, but from balancing power with equal power. In the Trumpist worldview, the denial of this reality is not a triumph of ethical-political idealism, it is dangerous stupidity and weakness.

301

Trumpism, Andrew Jackson and the American Dream

Trumpism seeks inspiration from the ideology of the pre-Boomer age, and especially from the folklore of the American Dream. The American Dream is a broad ideology which inspired generations of Americans. It recognizes innate differences between individuals and calls for a level playing field so the race of life can be run honestly and fairly. Writing in 1833, the journalist and economist William Gouge, described this as the, "natural and just order" of the universe. Wealth and success, he wrote, were the reward for, "industry, frugality, skill, prudence, and enterprise; and poverty the punishment of few except the indolent and prodigal."[6]

This cosmology was fiercely rejected by the Boomer generation because it produced imperfect, unequal outcomes. To the Boomers, the American Dream was cruel and unfair — it favored the strong over the weak, encouraged competition at the expense of cooperation, encouraged selfish self-interest and produced a hierarchy of winners and losers. As the activist Abbie Hoffman explained in 1968, the Boomers required something better than the American Dream because, "The institutions and values of imperialism, racism, capitalism and the protestant ethic do not allow young people to experience authentic liberation."[7] However, from the perspective of the American Dream, it is the Boomer Ideology that is unfair because it takes wealth and power from those who have earned it and gives it to those who have not. It denies reality by seeking to reward the lazy, the weak and the unproductive, and punish the hard-working, the tough and the smart. The American Dream is not the dream of a land in which everyone has the same amount of wealth and success, but, as the historian James Truslow Adams explains, a land,

> "With opportunity for each according to his ability or achievement. It is a difficult dream for the European upper classes to interpret adequately... a dream of a social order in which each man and each woman shall be able to attain to the fullest stature of which they are innately capable, and be recognized by others for what they are, regardless of the fortuitous circumstances of birth or position."[8]

The American Dream inspired millions of peasants to flee poverty and suffocating lack of opportunity in Europe and emigrate to the US during the 19th Century. In the old country, ordinary people had little chance of improving themselves. Their destiny was to live their lives toiling for the elite who owned the land. In America, as Truslow-Adams explains, things were different,

> "One man might own fifty acres and another fifty thousand, but there was no sharp line anywhere between them... the man with fifty hoped that some day by a lucky stroke he might own a thousand."[9]

Anyone — with hard work, enterprise and a little luck — could haul himself to the top. The most important qualities were determination and true grit. A man born in poverty might even one day be President. As Adams pointed out,

> "Lincoln was not great because he was born in a log cabin, but because he got out of it – that is, because he rose above the poverty, ignorance, lack of ambition, shiftlessness of character, contentment with mean things and low aims which kept so many thousands in the huts where they were born."[10]

In the moral universe of the American Dream, there is no such thing as a free lunch. Wealth and success must be earned. In the American Dream, the idea of getting something for nothing is a dangerous illusion which leads to corruption, cheating and stealing. At the philosophical core of the American Dream is a belief in the importance of the individual. Writing in 1922, Herbert Hoover described American Individualism as a compassionate philosophy quite different to a system of pure laissez faire. It was not, he said, the law of the jungle, because it gave everyone the same opportunity to compete,

> "While we build our society upon the attainment of the individual, we shall safeguard to every individual an equality of opportunity to take that position in the community to which his intelligence, character, ability, and ambition entitle him."[11]

Hoover dismissed woolly Utopian schemes that wanted to make everyone equal. They were, he said dishonest, seductive fantasies that would lead eventually to tyranny,

> "We in America have had too much experience of life to fool ourselves into pretending that all men are equal in ability, in character, in intelligence, in ambition. That was part of the clap-trap of the French Revolution. We have grown to understand that all we can hope to assure to the individual through government is liberty, justice, intellectual welfare, equality of opportunity, and stimulation to service."[12]

The English philosopher John Locke is widely regarded as the ideological father of the American Dream. Locke argued that all human beings have a natural right to behave with "perfect freedom". Individuals are, he said, responsible for their own decisions, and are entitled to keep what they earn through their own talent and hard work. Consequently, the state has no right to restrict any honest individual's liberty. As he wrote in 1690,

> "To understand political power right, and derive it from its original, we must consider, what state all men are naturally in, and that is, a state of perfect freedom to order their actions, and dispose of their possessions and persons, as they think fit, within the bounds of the law of nature, without asking leave, or depending upon the will of any other man."[13]

Locke was the guiding inspiration for generations of liberal theorists including Adam Smith and John Stuart Mill. As the American academic Richard Ebeling explains,

> "John Locke's ethical and political individualism served as a cornerstone for the great American experiment in self-government, both in the sense of individual freedom and constitutional restraint."[14]

The American Dream is therefore closely related to the ideology of British Victorian Liberalism. Both grew from the same roots and share a common spirit. As President Woodrow Wilson once remarked, "We

304

deemed ourselves rank democrats, whereas we were in fact only pro-gressive Englishmen."[15]

A more modern version of the philosophy of the American Dream can be found in the work of the Russian-American writer Ayn Rand. The ideological link between Rand and Donald Trump has been pointed out by a number of commentators including Cass Sunstein who argues "The age of Trump can be seen as the age of Rand... If we want to un-derstand Trump we should focus on Rand whose presence haunts the spirit of our time".[16] Rand's philosophy of the individual is the polar opposite of the Boomer Ideology and is deeply triggering to modern sen-sibilities. According to Rand, competition, and the desire to get ahead, produce good results for all in the long run. In her provocatively titled *The Virtue of Selfishness*, she defines self-interest simply as "man's desire to live". Consequently, those who criticize it are guilty of criticizing life itself which, she says, is a form of evil. Rand attacked modern theories of social justice arguing they were built on a false understanding of al-truism. The worship of altruism, she said, led to "appalling immorality", "chronic injustice" and "grotesque double standards" because it justified evil in the name of helping others,

"So long as that beneficiary is anybody other than oneself, anything goes.... A dictator is regarded as moral, since the unspeakable atrocities he committed were intended to benefit "the people," not himself."[17]

Rand argued the concept of the "common good" was a trick used by "altruist-collectivists" to transfer welath from others to themselves and thereby get something for nothing. Those who shouted loudest about social justice, she said, were in reality selfish hypocrites, "man's well-being is not their goal."

"It is morally obscene to regard wealth as an anonymous, tribal product and to talk about "redistributing" it... America's abun-dance was not created by public sacrifices to "the common good," but by the productive genius of free men who pursued their own personal interests and the making of their own private fortunes."[18]

Historically, Trumpism reflects a schism in US politics that can be traced back to the competing views of Thomas Jefferson and Alexander Hamilton during the late 18th Century. Jefferson put his trust in the honesty and good sense of the common man, and was suspicious of sophisticated city life which he believed would lead to moral decay and corruption. He argued that the best government is that which governs least. In order to facilitate popular democracy, he believed citizens should be well-informed, well-educated and capable of independent, critical thinking. As he explained in 1787,

> "I think our governments will remain virtuous for many centuries; as long as they are chiefly agricultural...When they get piled upon one another in large cities, as in Europe, they will become corrupt as in Europe. Above all things I hope the education of the common people will be attended to; convinced that on their good sense we may rely with the most security for the preservation of a due degree of liberty."[19]

Hamilton, on the other hand, believed the great mass of humanity was incapable of rational self-government because human beings would always be ignorant, selfish and ruled by their emotions and delusions. The people, he once remarked, was a "great beast". Hamilton wanted to create a powerful, industrialized America that could compete with the European powers. To achieve this, he sought to help bankers, financiers and manufacturers to prosper. Instead of hoping to educate the mob, Hamilton called for an educated elite of policy makers to rule over the common people for their own good,

> "It is the duty of the persons whom they have appointed to be the guardians of those interests, to withstand the temporary delusion, in order to give them time and opportunity for more cool and sedate reflection."[20]

Trumpism therefore, reflects this old division in American politics. It is rooted in Jeffersonian ideals. It supports the interests of the common man, and rejects Hamiltonian doctrine with its elitist overtones. However, Trumpism's most obvious antecedent is the political doctrine, spirit and style of Andrew Jackson who was President between 1829 and 1837. Donald Trump made no secret of his admiration for Jackson. He hung 'Old Hickory's' portrait in the Oval Office and laid a wreath on Jackson's tomb in Tennessee.* As one journalist commented, "Trump has embod-

---

* The portrait was symbolically removed by President Biden in 2021.

ied the populist spirit of Jackson. And while Jackson was wealthy, like Trump, he stood up to moneyed interests and Washington elites."[21] The academic Walter Russell Mead also notes the similarity between Trump and Jackson, pointing out that Donald Trump sensed the surging force in American politics was "Jacksonian populist nationalism",

> "Jacksonian America felt itself to be under siege, with its values under attack and its future under threat. Trump, flawed as many Jacksonians themselves believed him to be, seemed the only candidate willing to help fight for its survival."[22]

According to Mead, Trump's supporters, like Jackson's, were concerned about the threat posed by, "powerful forces in the American elite, including the political establishments of both major parties, in cahoots against them."

Jackson was an unashamed populist. He attacked corporate privilege and government corruption, and appealed to a wide range of people who felt the race of life was unfairly rigged against them. As Truslow Adams explains, during the 1820s and 1830s, the common man had watched,

> "With growing resentment what seemed to him the closing of doors upon him, the rise of privileged classes, and the increasing difficulty or inability for himself to reap profit and benefit from his toil… He sought a leader of his own sort."[23]

Originally, American democracy — like the British model on which it was based — was reserved for the owners of property. However, during the 1820s and 1830s, the number of people permitted to vote dramatically increased. States discarded the freehold requirement, and the taxpaying qualification was also removed. Jackson's election in 1828 therefore reflected a battle between two rival visions of America's future. Would it be a land that offered the newly enfranchised average families independence and opportunity? Or would it be one geared towards the interests of wealthy landowners, big businesses, newspaper editors, industrialists and financiers? As the historian Harry Watson says, "On the symbolic level, at least, the election of 1828 pitted these two viewpoints against each other."[24]

The Jacksonian era, like the Trump era, was a time of vicious, partisan journalism and fake news. During the 1828 election, Jackson found himself accused of being a war criminal, a murderer and an adulterer by a bitterly partisan press. Newspapers supporting his opponent John Quincy Adams, promoted the narrative that Jackson was a dangerous, mentally deranged man unfit to be President. Pro-Jackson newspapers were equally vitriolic, hurling abuse at Adams. However, despite furious press hostility, Jackson won. As President, Jackson's most significant political act was to veto plans to recharter the federal bank – the Bank of the United States. For Jacksonians, the bank symbolized the forces of elite wealth and power. It was, he said a, "many headed monster" and an engine of moral and financial corruption. In his Bank Veto Message of 1832, Jackson said the US financial system was a crooked game rigged in favor of the rich — a way of legally stealing from hard-working ordinary folk,

"It is to be regretted that the rich and powerful too often bend the acts of government to their selfish purposes. Distinctions in society will always exist under every just government. Equality of talents, of education, or of wealth cannot be produced by human institutions. In the full enjoyment of the gifts of Heaven and the fruits of superior industry, economy, and virtue, every man is equally entitled to protection by law; but when the laws undertake to add to these natural and just advantages artificial distinctions, to grant titles, gratuities, and exclusive privileges, to make the rich richer and the potent more powerful, the humble members of society - the farmers, mechanics, and laborers - who have neither the time nor the means of securing like favors to themselves, have a right to complain of the injustice of their Government."[25]

In his farewell address of 1837, Jackson again attacked the powerful elites who benefitted most from the existence of the federal bank. He attacked the bank's ability to print paper money and summon wealth into existence *ex nihilo*. This he described as a social "evil" whose "mischievous consequences" would, "engender a spirit of speculation injurious to the habits and character of the people." Printing paper money, he argued, created the illusion of wealth and distracted citizens from honest, productive economic activity. It seduced citizens into believing in the possibility of "wealth without labor" and corrupted them to,

308

"Withdraw their attention from the sober pursuits of honest industry. It is not by encouraging this spirit that we shall best preserve public virtue and promote the true interests of our country."[26]

Once the population was addicted to the printing of paper money, other forms of corruption — financial and political — would, said Jackson, inevitably follow,

"The temptation to obtain money at any sacrifice will become stronger and stronger, and inevitably lead to corruption, which will find its way into your public councils and destroy at no distant day the purity of your Government."

The end result, Jackson argued, would be the destruction of liberty and democracy, and rule by an elite of the wealthy and powerful. Jackson famously warned that freedom and democracy were fragile, and were constantly threatened by man's insatiable craving for shortcuts to wealth and power. "You must remember" he said, "that eternal vigilance by the people is the price of liberty, and that you must pay the price if you wish to secure the blessing."

Trumpism's repudiation of the Boomer worldview and all its philosophical assumptions, and its reassertion of the values of individualism and the American Dream, triggered a spectacular journalistic reaction — a far-reaching mobilization of effort to defend the status quo and the Official Ideology. As the figurehead of the movement, Donald Trump found himself the target of attacks just as extreme as those faced by Jackson. Chauncey Devega for example, writing in *Salon*, described Trump, and those who voted for him, as "evil",

"He is evil. By implication, Trump's policies and those who enact and support them are stained by his evil. The cruelty, the violence, the greed, the selfishness, the racism, the sexism, the nativism, the bigotry, the destruction, the lying, the assault on reality, the contempt for human dignity and civil rights, rejection of the rule of law and democracy, the summoning and mainstreaming of chaos and nihilism and a panoply of other social pathologies are more than the absence of good. They are evil."[27]

The academic Gini Graham Scott agreed, asking in the *HuffPost*, "Can one compare Trump to the most evil monster of all — the devil or demon in his many forms? Certainly, it would seem that one can." She called on members of the elite class to remove him from office,

> "Who will take him on? Who will throw him out of heaven for good? Perhaps it's time for writers, politicians, government officials, and others working towards a better future to find a way to open the door and say, 'Get him outta here,'"[28]

The American academic Gary Leupp, writing in *CounterPunch*, developed the Satanic theme referring to President Trump as the "Antichrist". Leupp described Trump supporters as uneducated fanatics, "Much of the false prophet's base is extremely ignorant, religiously so... Many actually believe in Satan." Leupp labelled Trumpists as white supremacists and racists to whom Trump had given, "greater space to spread their hate proudly". He called on Trump followers to admit, "Trump who seemed like God was actually the Antichrist all the time", adding that those who had voted for him were in fact "Satan-possessed".[29]

To those who subscribed to the Official Ideology, Trumpists were the tribal "other" — demons who should be labelled: Populists, Racists, White Supremacists, Alt Right, Extreme Right, Neo-Nazis, Cultists, Spreaders of Misinformation and Conspiracy Theorists. To journocrats suckled on the codes of Boomer Journalism, a President in the Oval Office who rejected their entire world view was both an existential threat and an unbearable incitement. Boomer Journalism, dedicated to pursuing social justice and making the world a better, more Boomer-friendly place, and armed with the weapons of narrative and pro-social lying, found itself with an urgent ethical-political mission — to rid the world of this deplorable President.

Chapter 26

Russiagate; Journalism's Ideological War with Donald Trump

"It was Napoleon, I believe, who said that there is only one figure in rhetoric of serious importance, namely, repetition. The thing affirmed comes by repetition to fix itself in the mind in such a way that it is accepted in the end as a demonstrated truth."

Gustave Le Bon, The Crowd.

Official Journalism launched its attack on Donald Trump ten days before his official inauguration in January 2017. The weapon used against him became known as the 'Russiagate' scandal — the repeated accusation that the new President, despite his fierce patriotism, was, in reality, a Russian agent. The opening shots were fired on 10 January when the news website *Buzzfeed* published pages from a dossier which made sensational claims, including the accusation that, during a trip to Moscow, Donald Trump had indulged in activities such as,

> "Hiring the Presidential suite of the Ritz Carlton Hotel, where he knew President and Mrs Obama (whom he hated) had stayed on one of their official trips to Russia, and defiling the bed where they had slept by employing a number of prostitutes to perform a 'golden showers' (urination) show in front of him."[1]

Buzzfeed claimed the orgy had been secretly filmed by Russian intelligence who were using it to blackmail the President to do their bidding. Having published the allegations, Buzzfeed added a qualifier admitting that the claims were, "unverified, and potentially unverifiable".[2] The dossier, it later emerged, had been commissioned and paid for by the Hillary Clinton 2016 presidential campaign. It contained a series of scurrilous accusations and titbits of gossip described by *The Washington Post* in 2021 as, "unconfirmed tips from unidentified sources".[3] Publication of the dossier by *Buzzfeed* unleashed a feeding frenzy of media coverage, opinion and speculation — much of it presented as fact. For example, MSNBC's Rachel Maddow told audiences there had been a, "Russian election attack" during which sinister Russian operatives had, somehow, manipulated the minds of US citizens and persuaded them to vote for Donald Trump. What made it worse, she said, was that the Trump campaign knew exactly what was going on and "colluded" with the Russians. This was not a trivial thing Maddow explained, "The allegation of collusion is very, very, very, serious. It's sort of as serious as it gets."[4] The dossier, she said, was self-verifying. Its author would not have made the accusations in the first place unless they were true,

> "The Trump campaign was in on it! Little checkable pieces of that have been falling into place almost every day now, and clearly the author of this dossier thought that he was onto something."[5]

After four months of relentless media coverage, the Attorney General appointed former FBI Director Robert Mueller as a Special Counsel to investigate if there had been any improper links or coordination, "between the Russian government and individuals associated with the campaign of President Donald Trump." The Mueller investigation provided fresh meat to feed the narrative. Each twist and turn was leaked, dissected and analyzed by pundits and politicians while audiences awaited the final report. When it came, it found no evidence that Donald Trump had colluded with Russia to win the 2016 election. In Mueller's own words, "The evidence was not sufficient to charge that any member of the Trump Campaign conspired with representatives of the Russian government to interfere in the 2016 election."[6]

But whether the accusations were true or untrue was largely irrelevant. The existence of an official enquiry had justified a tsunami of media coverage and provided innumerable opportunities to repeat the false allegations. Russiagate then, was a weapon used by journalists to inflict reputational damage on Donald Trump and help neutralize Trumpism. According to the unwritten code of Boomer Journalism, pro-social lying was acceptable in the crusade against the figurehead of a movement that threatened the Boomer worldview. From a technical point of view, Russiagate was also an example of a "wrap up smear" — a political tactic described by Democrat Congresswoman Nancy Pelosi as the creation of a feedback loop of slander stamped with the authority of professional journalism. If the media can be persuaded to report a false accusation, then politicians can use the media coverage as evidence that the rumor must be true. The media can then report the reactions and opinions of politicians and pundits which in turn generates content for the next news cycle. The result is a spiral of self-sustaining, self-referential rumor, hearsay and gossip which feeds off itself to create the psychological illusion of truth. As Pelosi explained,

"You smear somebody with falsehoods and then you merchandise it. And then *you* [gesturing to journalists] write it and then they say, 'See, it's reported in the press that this, this, this, and this'. So they have that validation that the press reported the smear, and it's called the wrap-up smear. Now I'm going to merchandise the press reports of the smear that we made. It's a tactic and it's self-evident."[7]

The psychologist David Bell refers to "venomous innuendo" as a tactic where the motive is to "smear the target of the innuendo" while disguising the intention behind a mask of truth-seeking.[8]   Therefore, a news report describing how Donald Trump cavorted with Russian prostitutes, followed by the qualifier 'this is unverified' will lead audiences to understand that the qualifier is not sincerely meant — as if it had been delivered with a knowing look, a nod and a wink. In other words, the audience assumes the news organization would not have reported the story in the first place unless it had reason to believe it was true. Another psychologist, Lynn Hasher, has noted that the constant repetition of an accusation creates the illusion of truth in the minds of the audience. She observes,

"Humans are profoundly sensitive to frequency... That is, the more often you hear that 50,000 people live in Greenland, even if you do so in contexts that are explicitly ambiguous or equivocal, the more certain you will become that indeed they do."[9]

One of Hasher's most interesting findings is that, even when people are told that a much-repeated statement is untrue, they still tend to remember and believe it. In other words, qualifiers generally have little or no effect on the strength of belief. What counts is *repetition*. Hasher called it the "illusory truth effect". The repetition of venomous innuendo with qualifiers became the defining journalistic feature of Russiagate.

Media coverage of Russiagate was so extensive that it is impossible to measure it. A Google search for "Trump Russia" in August 2021 found 126 million results of which 25.3 million were in the news section, but even this fails to capture the endless hours of TV and radio coverage. In the UK, the BBC even amended its editorial guidelines to help facilitate its truthophobic reporting of Donald Trump. In October 2020, it released an extraordinary document which granted its North America Editor Jon Sopel, unique permission to express his personal opinions about Donald Trump's motives. The document stated,

"Specialist correspondents and senior editors may have the licence to use their professional judgement and make evidence-based assessments as part of BBC content… For example, the North America Editor may be able to ascribe motive to the President of the United States based on information or evidence they have gathered and using their professional experience to assess the situation. But this permission will not apply generally and depends

314

on seniority and experience. These evidence-based judgements should not be confused with expressions of personal opinion or personal prejudices."[10]

Despite its protestations to the contrary, the document uniquely permitted elite journocrats to report their own personal opinions as fact. Although it said these "judgements" should not be confused with "personal prejudices", it did not explain *how* they were different, nor how senior journocrats would be able to acquire the psychic powers necessary to read Donald Trump's mind and divine his true motives. The fact that this dispensation specifically targeted just one person — Donald Trump — made the document even more astonishing. Just how significant it is, can be sensed by comparing it with the BBC's editorial guidelines of the pre-Boomer era. For example, the BBC's *1957 Handbook* states that news must be a,

> "Fair selection of items impartially presented... there is no room in a BBC bulletin for the personal views of the editors or sub-editors. Their duty is to give the facts so that listeners may form their own opinions."[11]

This is a world away from the BBC's 21st Century approval of personal opinions, provided they are generated by elite journocrats and provided the target is Donald Trump. In 1957, the distinction between fact and opinion was considered sacred. By 2020, it had become legitimate to report personal speculation as fact — provided the goal was to make the world a better place.

An example of the sort of journalism produced by this methodology was broadcast by the BBC on its flagship news and current affairs show *Today* on 10 November 2020. The item asked, "Should we pity Donald Trump?" It dealt with the President's claims that there had been irregularities in the 2020 election. Although there was *prima facie* evidence of irregularities and questionable practices in several states,[12] the BBC's narrative demanded the President could not possibly be the victim of election fraud. The narrative decreed he must be a bad loser — a madman unable to face reality. The BBC did not therefore take the allegations seriously, or discuss them farily and impartially. Instead, *Today* presenter Justin Webb (also a former North America Editor) introduced the pundit

Natalie Haynes and Michael Dobbs, author of the political thriller House of Cards. Webb began by explaining, "He's reported to be eating too many hamburgers, refusing to accept the inevitable."[13] Haynes gave his opinion that, "Absolute power is a very risky thing to get out of", adding, "I think we're all probably thinking a little bit of the Emperor Nero aren't we?... He is forced to take his own life... it really reminds me of the post-election White House." Haynes laughed at the suggestion that the President resembled the Greek hero Achilles, and suggested Agamemnon was a better fit because he was,

> "Incredibly petulant, enormously ineffectual, other people have to do all the decision making because he just stands there helplessly stamping his foot and demanding things."

Haynes said the Emperor Caligula was killed by his own bodyguard and suggested there were contemporary parallels, "I saw on the BBC only over the weekend, they're saying that if the President doesn't leave on the given day, he'll be taken out of there by the secret service." Haynes returned to the most infamous of Roman tyrants, "My favorite I'm afraid is Nero who has to kill himself, but he can't bear to because he's too cowardly."

This piece of journalism is remarkable and would certainly have been unimaginable during the era of impartial, Victorian Liberal Journalism. It was not factual reporting, nor was it analysis. It is best described as sociodrama — the fusion of narrative and wishful thinking and the production of a morally and emotionally satisfying fantasy. The BBC was describing the reality it believed ought to be, not the reality that actually was. There was no attempt to report facts impartially, nor to objectively scrutinize the evidence relating to election fraud. In the world of narrative-led journalism, narrative reigns supreme.

A year later, in another remarkable journalistic moment, BBC News quietly published an article admitting the Russiagate allegations were untrue. The report detailed the arrest of one of the dossier's main sources of information Igor Danchenko and referred to, "baseless claims that Mr Trump colluded with Russia to win the 2016 election." The BBC, making no reference to its own extensive role in promoting this false narrative, explained the dossier was,

"Held up by Democrats to paint Mr Trump as a Russian puppet, a narrative amplified in a feedback loop by most US media for much of the president's four years in office."[14]

The BBC article concluded the dossier had, "made unsubstantiated claims linking Donald Trump to the Kremlin". The narrative the BBC had assiduously promoted for four years, turned out to have been, by its own admission, fake news — a lie, a deception, a monstrous conspiracy theory. Yet there was no soul-searching, no recognition the BBC had done anything wrong, no regret, no apology, no remorse. When the goal of telling the truth clashed with the higher goal of promoting the Boomer Ideology and making the world a better place, *arete* trumped *aletheia*. Hence, according to its own values, the BBC had done nothing wrong. Its lies had been pro-social lies. It had nothing for which to apologize.

From Boomer Journalism to Official Journalism.

Donald Trump was not content to passively play the role of Boomer Journalism's punchbag. He counter attacked vigorously arguing that professional journalists were producing something that looked like journalism, but which in reality was a counterfeit, bogus product. What they manufactured, he said, was not real news; it was "fake news". As he told an election rally in Florida in 2016,

> "The corporate media in our country is no longer involved in journalism. They are a political special interest, no different than any lobbyist or other financial entity with an agenda... For them, it is a war – and for them, nothing is out of bounds."[15]

What Donald Trump had detected was the transformation of impartial Victorian Liberal Journalism into Boomer Journalism, a narrative-led genre conscious of its ethical-political responsibilities and tolerant of pro-social lying. For Trump, 'real' news was journalism that privileged its truth-telling role and scrupulously followed the methodology of Victorian Liberal Journalism. 'Fake news' was truthophobic Boomer Journalism. By early 2017, with the Russiagate conspiracy theory dominating the news

317

agenda, he was regularly using the phrase 'fake news'. For example, in February he Tweeted,

"The fake news media is going crazy with their conspiracy theories and blind hatred. @MSNBC & @CNN are unwatchable."[16]

Journalists, he said, had forgotten their duty to provide balanced, objective reports. Instead, they were misleading the public and deceiving them. Consequently, the news media were undermining democracy by creating a misinformed population,

"The FAKE NEWS media (failing @nytimes, @NBCNews, @ABC, @CBS, @CNN) is not my enemy, it is the enemy of the American People!"[17]

The following year he mockingly 'honored' eleven examples of Boomer Journalism with his "Fake News Awards", saying,

"2017 was a year of unrelenting bias, unfair news coverage, and even downright fake news. Studies have shown that over 90% of the media's coverage of President Trump is negative."[18]

By 2019, he was convinced he was engaged in a bitter war against a genre of journalism that was fundamentally dishonest, ideologically opposed to his Presidency and hostile to the values of those who had elected him,

"The Fake News Media has NEVER been more Dishonest or Corrupt than it is right now. There has never been a time like this in American History. Very exciting but also, very sad! Fake News is the absolute Enemy of the People and our Country itself!"[19]

The problem of "fake news" had become the hot issue of the day, as the journalist James Carson observed,

"'Fake news' was not a term many people used 18 months ago, but it is now seen as one of the greatest threats to democracy, free debate and the Western order... it has been named the word of the year, raised tensions between nations, and may lead to regulation of social media. And yet, nobody can agree on what it is, how much of a problem it is, and what to do about it".[20]

Many fair-mined observers were disturbed by the blatant lack of impartiality in media coverage of Donald Trump. By trying to undermine public confidence in him, had journalism merely succeeded in undermining public confidence in itself? Two days after news broke that the President was not guilty of colluding with Russia *The Wall Street Journal's* Sean Davis reflected, under the headline "A Catastrophic Media Failure",

"Robert Mueller's investigation is over, but questions still abound. Not about collusion, Russian interference or obstruction of justice, but about the leading lights of journalism who managed to get the story so wrong, and for so long."[21]

The journalist and author Justin Raimondo branded Russiagate, "a very messy narrative" which had clearly been a, "fraud, a setup, and really a criminal conspiracy to take down a sitting US President on the basis of a gigantic lie."[22]

The scholar Oliver Boyd-Barrett detected a moral panic among journalists and a desire to paint Vladimir Putin and Donald Trump as folk devils. Media coverage of Russiagate, he said, was a collective fantasy — a modern morality play in which emotions were,

"Enflamed by obfuscations, exaggerations, and outright lies and deceptions concerning the alleged role of Russia in "subverting US democracy" by means of actions that allegedly favored the electoral chances of Donald Trump."[23]

Matt Taibbi, in a 2020 article entitled, *The American Press Is Destroying Itself,* argued that Donald Trump had provoked mainstream journalism into a suicidal frenzy of pro-social lying,

"The instinct to shield audiences from views or facts deemed politically uncomfortable has been in evidence since Trump became a national phenomenon... I listened to colleagues that summer of 2016 talk about ignoring poll results, or anecdotes about Hillary's troubled campaign, on the grounds that doing otherwise might 'help Trump'."[24]

Taibbi recognized the overriding objective of professional journalism had become the neutralization of Trumpism. To achieve this ethical-political goal, pro-social lying had become, not merely acceptable, but compulsory,

"It's been learned in these episodes we may freely misreport reality, so long as the political goal is righteous. It was okay to publish the now-discredited Steele dossier, because Trump is scum."

Taibbi lamented the demise of Victorian Liberal Journalism in which, "We showed you everything we could see, good and bad, ugly and not, trusting that a better-informed public would make better decisions." The journalist Howard Kurtz also detected the dominance of narrative and pro-social lying. The mask of impartiality he said, had been discarded by reporters who believed it was their sacred ethical-political duty to destroy Trumpism,

"Too many journalists and media executives, dwelling in a bubble of like-minded opinion, became convinced that they had a solemn duty to oppose Trump. The normal rules of balance and attempted objectivity were suspended, dismissed as a relic of a calmer time. And they justified the new approach by telling themselves and the world that they had a duty to push back — perhaps even push out — a president they viewed as unqualified, intemperate, and insistent on pursuing harmful policies."[25]

Kurtz said that, for most professional journalists, the goal of changing society and making the world a better place by destroying the ideology of Trumpism, outweighed the goal of telling the truth. But, he warned, the use of pro-social lying on such a massive scale, was a terrible mistake,

"A common refrain among Trump's antagonists in the press is that they must resist normalizing his presidency. But in the process, they have abnormalized journalism."

Kurtz concluded something important had changed, perhaps forever, "My greatest fear is that organized journalism has badly lost its way in the Trump era and may never fully recover." The historian Victor Davis Hanson agreed. The Russiagate dossier was, he said,

"A mishmash concoction of half-baked fantasies and outright lies, sloppily thrown together by the grifter and has-been ex-British spy and Trump hater, Christopher Steele—all in the pay of Hillary Clinton, the original architect of the collusion hoax... Most of those who had seeded the dossier around Washington now either agree it was fake, or 'partially' false, or remain silent in embarrassment."[26]

Hanson concluded,

"The Russian collusion hoax will go down in history as one of the most shameful examples of Washington, D.C. mass hysteria, and of a concentrated effort to destroy an elected president, in modern American political history."

Boomer Journalism's ideological crusade against Trumpism, and Donald Trump's aggressive counter-attacks, created a perfect storm. Each side inciting the other to ever-more intense assaults, and each blaming the other for the consequences. The journalist Marc Hetherington, for example, claimed Donald Trump was responsible for, "destroying trust in the media, science, and government",

"He called the media 'absolute scum' and 'totally dishonest people.' As president, he has called news organizations 'fake news' and 'the enemy of the people' over and over. The examples are endless."[27]

Supporters of Donald Trump however, challenged the narrative of the 'Trump Effect'. The author Steve McCann said Trump Effect theory reversed cause and effect. According to McCann, Donald Trump did not *cause* the problem, he just drew attention to it,

"Among the more notable accomplishments of the watershed Trump presidency was exposing and marginalizing the mainstream media. Donald Trump's damn the torpedoes mindset in taking on and exposing them... has finally begun to awaken the American people."[28]

It is hard to judge who is more responsible for undermining public trust in journalism — Donald Trump, or mainstream journalism itself. It is noteworthy however that trust in journalism had been in decline prior to the Trump Presidency. The real correlation was between the rise of Boomer Journalism and the rise of distrust. For example, in 2003 the media scholar Yariv Tsfati, wrote,

> "In the past three decades communication researchers have become preoccupied with the increasingly negative attitudes audiences hold about the news media... The discovery that people mistrust the media gave rise to journalistic and academic discourse that tried to explain the drop in audience trust."[29]

Tsfati referred to the decline in trust as "media skepticism" which he defined as a,

> "Feeling of alienation and mistrust toward the mainstream news media. For example, media skepticism is the feeling that journalists are not fair or objective in their reports about society and that they do not always tell the whole story."

It was certainly easier and more comfortable for journalists to blame Donald Trump for the decline in trust than to examine their own role. But the decline was real. Successive opinion polls confirmed it. In 2021 Gallup reported,

> "Americans' trust in the media to report the news fully, accurately and fairly has edged down four percentage points since last year to 36%, making this year's reading the second lowest in Gallup's trend... 29% of the public currently registers 'not very much' trust and 34% have 'none at all.'"[30]

Another 2021 survey reported that most respondents believed professional journalists were,

> "Purposely trying to mislead people by saying things they know are false. The global infodemic has driven trust in all news sources to record lows with social media (35 percent) and owned media

(41 percent) the least trusted; traditional media (53 percent) saw the largest drop in trust at eight points."[31]

The report concluded, "This is the era of information bankruptcy... We've been lied to by those in charge, and media sources are seen as politicized and biased. The result is a lack of quality information and increased divisiveness." The highly-respected 2022 *Reuters Digital News Report* noted the phenomenon of "selective news avoidance" — audiences abandoning mainstream journalism because it seemed to have become a sermon repetitively preaching a predictable agenda of ethical-political narratives. According to the report, "Many people are becoming increasingly disconnected from news — with falling interest in many countries, a rise in selective news avoidance, and low trust."[32] In the UK, the report said selective avoidance of mainstream journalism had doubled,

"Many respondents say they are put off by the repetitiveness of the news agenda... A significant proportion say they avoid news because they think it can't be trusted."

As one woman told the survey's authors, "I don't like to dwell too much on the mainstream news. I find sometimes it can be repetitive and negative." In the US the picture was the same. The report detected a deep-seated belief that journalism was not motivated by a desire to report the truth. One American woman told researchers it required hard work to decode the news narratives and work out what was really going on, "A lot of the time" she said, "mainstream news can be very biased or politically motivated. This makes it hard to decipher its credibility."

Donald Trump was the catalyst for something very important in the history of journalism. He represented an ideological threat that Boomer Journalism could not ignore. However, in its willingness to use one-sided narratives, and embrace pro-social lying, professional journalism paid a heavy price. During its four-year war against Trumpism, Boomer Journalism lurched along the spectrum of truth in the direction of propaganda. The movement was unmistakable. The Trump Presidency was therefore a watershed moment during which journalism changed. It became more brazen, more shameless — prouder than ever of its ethical-political responsibilities. It abandoned the last trappings of its impartial, Victorian Liberal heritage. Narrative and pro-social lying were normalized. Like

a beetle emerging from its chrysalis, Boomer Journalism had metamor-
phosed into something visibly different. It had become Official Journalism,
designed to defend and promote the Official Ideology.

Chapter 27

Two Epistemic Worlds. Official v Unofficial Journalisms

B y the time Donald Trump left office in January 2020, two rival epistemic worlds existed in which rival journalisms offered rival facts
and opinions to sustain rival beliefs, world views and ideologies.
Official Journalism presented official narratives representing the values
and way of knowing of the Official Ideology, while Unofficial Journalism
represented the values and epistemology of the Unofficial Ideology. The
more Official Journalism omitted certain facts and opinions, the more
Unofficial Journalism put them back in. The more Official Journalism
attempted to nudge audiences in a single direction, the more Unofficial
Journalism rebelliously showed them alternatives. The more Official Journalism promoted official, ethical-political narratives, the more Unofficial

Journalism questioned them. The rise of Unofficial Journalism was, above all, a protest against the Boomer way of knowing, because, in the eyes of Unofficial Journalism, the material conditions in which the Boomers grew up no longer existed and their ideology had become a dangerous liability. Official Journalism, with its elite journocrats, official narratives and embrace of pro-social lying, was leading liberal democracy towards the edge of a cliff. As the manifesto of one website explained,

> "For years, we watched the power-brokers posing as democratic governments around the world tighten regulation in the name of 'freedom', tighten the censorship of opinions that contradict their agenda... and feed the public 'news' that seems invented solely to manipulate, control and instill fear and division... We offer information that we think will help people to live better, see through the lies, and break down the old ways of thinking and being that no longer serve our society."[1]

The unofficial journalist Charles Smith also argued the ideology of the late 20th Century had passed its sell-by date. The 2020s, he said, are fundamentally different. Robotically applying Boomer solutions to contemporary problems was simply adding fuel to the fire,

> "Instability is being accelerated by doing more of what worked in the previous era, in the mistaken belief that the 2020s are simply an extension of the eras that began 40 and 30 years ago... We've entered a new era, and so the fixes and incentives that worked in the past 40 years no longer work... It may turn out that all the lessons we learned in the past 40 years will not only be useless in this new era, they will be disastrously counter-productive."[2]

The Rise of Unofficial Journalism

'Unofficial', 'alternative' or 'independent' journalism grew rapidly in the fertile soil of the online world, producing innumerable blogs, websites, newsletters and social media posts. As the academic Stephen Cushion puts it, there has been a dramatic growth of,

"New alternative online and social media platforms challenging the long-held hegemony of traditional mainstream media. With this greater choice and market competition, there is evidence of rising public disaffection with mainstream media in many advanced Western democracies."[3]

The central complaint of Unofficial Journalism is that it is impossible to find out what is really happening in the world because Official Journalism only produces emotional, one-sided narratives — pro-social lies designed, not to inform, but to influence, manipulate and persuade. The Unofficial Journalist Mark Petrakis accuses Official Journocrats of using the power of narrative to bewitch audiences. News narratives, he argues, are, "constructed by skilled media professionals and put in place to overwhelm our critical thinking and that of millions of others from seeing what's really going on." These beguiling narratives are, he says, "sugar water bullshit" that make citizens "easy to control" because they find themselves, "ensnared in mind-numbing opinions and outrages". According to Petrakis, Official Journalism is the propaganda wing of elite "technocratic-fascism",

"That is why a growing number of people have given up on the media's crudely fictional depiction of reality, and are instead trying to figure out how to thrive and to reconnect energetically with others – and with truths that can only exist OUTSIDE the reach of the propaganda spectacle."[4]

The veteran *Guardian* columnist John Pilger noticed a "seismic shift" in journalism and a dramatic retreat from impartial, objective reporting during the late 20th Century. He says the type of journalism which replaced it is both intolerant and censorious. "The spaces allotted to independent journalists" he says, "have vanished. The dissent that was tolerated, even celebrated when I arrived in Fleet Street in the 1960s, has regressed to a metaphoric underground." According to Pilger, contemporary journocrats have become the new priesthood tasked with, "policing the new groupthink" and promoting, "its politics and hypocrisies, its omissions and fabrications while pursuing the enemies of the new national security state." Pilger calls for greater awareness of how audiences are now routinely misled and deceived by Official Journalism,

"Journalism students need to study this urgently if they are to understand that the true source of the contrivance known as 'fake news' is not merely social media, but a liberal 'mainstream' self-anointed with a false respectability that claims to challenge corrupt and warmongering power but, in reality, courts and protects it, and colludes with it."[5]

The Unofficial Journalist Lance Morrow also highlights the dominance of narrative and factinion which, he says, creates a misinformed, ignorant public and makes critical reflection impossible,

"News is laid before the citizen's mind so packaged and tarted up with a narrative line that the simple facts are often impossible to discern. This is not honest reporting but garish, partisan fabulation. Its object is not to inform, or to encourage reflection, but to stimulate feelings. Let not the listener or viewer or reader be detained by thought but instead move briskly on to emotions."[6]

The Canadian journalist Alexandra Kitty launched an outspoken attack on Official Journalism describing it as a, "sewer of lies and fake news" driven by, "presumptuous attempts at social engineering". Kitty said the methodology of pro-social lying had, "destroyed the industry with arrogance, deceit, and immaturity". Addressing the journocrats responsible for manufacturing ethical-political narratives, she wrote,

"You are working in a dead profession that you all had a part in killing. You have confused running a Bedlam with being journalists, rigging coverage with loaded language, distorted videography, and selective reportage... all while trying to pretend you extol something that resembles progressive values. Stop believing your own hype. It is as fake as your concern for humanity."[7]

Matt Taibbi also deplored the changed epistemic landscape, the rise of truthophobic news and the demise of Victorian Liberal Journalism. He complained the,

"Traditional liberal approach to the search for truth, which stresses skepticism and free-flowing debate, is giving way to a reactionary movement that Plato himself would have loved, one that believes knowledge is too dangerous for the rabble and must be tightly regulated by a priesthood of 'experts.'"[8]

Taibbi refers to the dominance of Narrative-Led Journalism as the "Sovietization" of news. It produces, he said, a homogenous news agenda with predictable narratives and binary casts of heroes and villains. Journocrats are promoted to senior positions according to their talent for conformity and sycophancy. They are, he says, "people with the digestive systems of jackals or monitor lizards, who can swallow even the most toxic piles of official nonsense without blinking." Those who resist Official Truth, and who think independently and critically, will be sidelined or forced out. Official Journalism, he glumly concludes, has a totalitarian intolerance of dissent and quietly carries out, "purges of the politically unfit."[9]

One journalist purged from *The New York Times* was senior editor Bari Weiss who left the paper in July 2020. Her letter of resignation accused *The Times* of slavish adherence to Official Truth and editorial groupthink. News stories, she said, were, "molded to fit the needs of a predetermined narrative". These ethical-political narratives were constructed by senior journocrats and treated as unquestionable facts. Hence, Journalistic Truth at *The New York Times* had become an, "orthodoxy already known to an enlightened few whose job is to inform everyone else." According to Weiss, pro-social lying and self-censorship were viewed as legitimate journalistic practices because the "ultimate goal is righteous."[10]

Another victim of Official Journalism's 'purges' was the American journalist Glenn Greenwald who resigned from his own online journal *The Intercept* in October 2020 after one of his articles was altered. Greenwald hit out at the, "pathologies, illiberalism, and repressive mentality that led to the bizarre spectacle of me being censored by my own media outlet." The assumptions, values and prejudices of the Official Ideology, he said, were widespread. They were the, "viruses that have contaminated virtually every mainstream center-left political organization, academic institution, and newsroom."[11]

The Unofficial Journalist Jacob Siegel accuses Official Journalism of being a secular church delivering ideological sermons to the masses. Elite journocrats, he says, believe in their own ethical-political infallibility and are driven by a sense of moral mission that,

"Releases adherents from the normal bounds of reason. The arguer-commander is animated by a vision of secular hell... Those in possession of this vision do not offer the possibility of redemption or transcendence, they come to deliver justice."[12]

Unofficial Journalism's biggest complaint is therefore that Official Journalism has abandoned the impartial search for truth. Instead, it has become a factory that manufactures simplistic fairy tales in which good fights evil. As the American political commentator Brian Kennedy summarized in 2022, "today we are living in the age of political narratives that are nothing more than lies told to serve some political end."[13]

As a result of growing disatisfaction with Narrative-Led news, many Unofficial Journalism manifestos promise to reject narrative and restore the facts and opinions which Official Journalism slyly omits. For example, the *Epoch Times* stresses its commitment to a pre-Boomer epistemology. "We are", it asserts,

"Nonpartisan and dedicated to truthful reporting... our goal is to bring our readers accurate information so they can form their own opinions about the most significant topics of our time... we use our principles of Truth and Tradition as our guiding light."[14]

The news website *Zerohedge* also pledges to supply information which Official Journalism suppresses. *Zerohedge* promises to, "liberate oppressed knowledge, to provide analysis uninhibited by political constraint, to facilitate information's unending quest for freedom."[15] The Unofficial news organization *Project Veritas* says its goal is truth, not manipulation,

"Truth is paramount. Our reporting is fact based with clear and irrefutable video and audio content. Truth is paramount. We never deceive our audience. We do not distort the facts or the context. We do not 'selectively edit.' We do not manufacture content."[16]

The Unofficial Journalist Caitlin Johnstone argues that the role of Unofficial Journalism is "waking up" people and alerting them to what's really happening,

"Trust in the mass media is at an all-time low and humanity's ability to network and share information is at an all-time high, which means we've got a one-time shot at breaking public trust in the mass media using our unprecedented information-sharing abilities and waking people up to the fact that they're being propagandized. Propaganda only works if you don't know it's happening, so we have to wake people up to the reality that it is happening."[17]

Steve Bannon, the broadcaster and former advisor to Donald Trump, describes it as an informational war with journalism in the front line. Bannon, who accuses Official Journalism of being the "opposition party", told an audience in Arizona,

"This is what they fear. They fear, not just an electorate that is informed, but an electorate that says no longer are we going to just sit there and take it. You are an awakened army!"[18]

In the UK, the *Conservative Woman* website also offers to fill the informational void created by Official Journalism. Its website promises to challenge the narratives of the, "virtue-signalling, intolerant and self-interested elites". These narratives, it claims dominate,

"The news media (most worryingly the licence fee-funded BBC), entertainment and academia, destroying independent and critical thought in the attempt to control how we speak and think. Whether on climate, gender, relations between the sexes or race, it can feel as if we are entering a new Dark Age of anti-reason."[19]

The Daily Sceptic offers, "skeptical articles by disaffected journalists and academics" to resist the, "new climate of Maoist intolerance that is sweeping through our most important institutions". *The Sceptic* vows to,

"Challenge the new powerful class of government scientists and public health officials – as well as their colleagues in universities, grant-giving trusts, large international charities, Silicon Valley and the pharmaceutical industry – that have emerged as a kind of secular priesthood."[20]

The *UK Column* claims to offer a pre-Boomer approach to news, rejecting the concept of simple, tribal truth. Its website asks, "Why should I trust the *UK Column*? Put simply, you shouldn't. The question of whether or not to trust a news organization is a false choice." Instead of a lazy dependence on narrative, UK Column challenges its audience to engage in effortful, critical thinking,

> "We ask you not to trust us. Instead, view everything published here with a critical eye. Where possible, primary source material is made available for everything we publish: check it; make up your own mind."[21]

The British politician, turned broadcaster, Nigel Farage proclaimed, on the newly launched *GB News* TV channel, "We need to change the landscape of British broadcasting". Farage set out a manifesto of a new journalistic epistemology inspired by the methodology of Victorian Liberal Journalism. "I will", he promised, "have guests on that disagree with me",

> "The point is we want open, free democratic debate conducted in a civilized manner. You will, I promise you, get both sides of every argument, including my own position and my own view, and you then can make your own minds up."[22]

Unofficial Journalism therefore claims its mission is to supply audiences with the evidence and dissenting opinions necessary for audiences to think for themselves and resist the Official Truths of Official Journalism. The model Unofficial journalist is hard-nosed and thick-skinned. He does not shy away from reporting facts — even if they are uncomfortable or painful. Underlying this is the philosophical assumption that people are mature, rational individuals capable of independent thought. In the collective mind of Unofficial Journalism, the audience cries out; "Let me decide things for myself. I realize life is complex and uncertain, but I'm prepared to spend time and effort attempting to figure things out. Give me all the facts as honestly and fully as you can. Don't pollute them with opinions and theories. Don't infantilize me — don't keep me ignorant for my own good. Let me hear both sides equally and let me be responsible for my own beliefs and choices."

Official Journalism Bites Back

Official Journalism was enraged by the insults and insolence of Unofficial Journlism and responded with a vigorous campaign to delegitimize it. The arguments it employed were however based on an entirely different set of assumptions and values. Whereas Unofficial Journalism demanded more truthful journalism and an end to pro-social lying, Official Journalism demanded more ethical journalism and an end to reckless, irresponsible impartiality. For example, the journalist Vickram Singh accused Unofficial Journalism of publicizing "fascist ideas" and "polluting vulnerable minds". Singh said Unofficial Journalism provided a platform for, "unsavory, misinformation spreaders" who were infecting audiences with "dangerous conspiracy theories." Unofficial Journalism, he wrote, was guilty of, "giving radical ideologies a platform to spew misinformation and hatred". Because of Unofficial Journalism he claimed, "Lies are spreading across the internet at an alarming rate. In the internet age, radicalization is running rampant on social media."[23]

The journalist Nesrine Malik accused Unofficial Media of abusing freedom of speech to spread "abhorrent views" including,

> "Rising anti-immigration sentiment and Islamophobia. Free-speech-crisis advocates always seem to have an agenda. They overwhelmingly wanted to exercise their freedom of speech in order to agitate against minorities, women, immigrants and Muslims."

The consequence, she claimed, was, "the rise in far-right or hard-right political energy, as evidenced by anti-immigration rightwing electoral successes in the US, the UK and across continental Europe". Malik argued that Unofficial Journalism had no ethical-political right to express opinions that disturbed social tranquility and caused harm,

> "There are those who abuse free speech, who wish others harm, and who roll back efforts to ensure that all citizens are treated with respect. These are facts – and free-speech-crisis mythology is preventing us from confronting them."[24]

The BBC also attacked Unofficial Journalism on ethical-political grounds. The corporation cited research by the broadcast regulator Ofcom which portrayed the internet as a jungle stalked by peddlers of "hateful content" and "potentially harmful material." The message was that straying from Official Truth and official narratives was dangerous,

"One in three people spotted hate speech in online video platforms in the past three months, a report by Ofcom found. Racist content was most frequently seen, but religious discrimination, transphobic and homophobic content were also common, it said."[25]

The BBC's Disinformation and Social Media Reporter Marianna Spring agreed, suggesting that censorship was needed to protect the public. She noted with approval that the UK government's new Online Safety Bill will compel social media sites to, "protect users from online harm", including, "harmful disinformation on social media."

"I've spent the past year investigating the very real-world harm myths and conspiracy theories shared online - about the pandemic, vaccines, and elections - can cause offline. Under the proposals, social media sites will be required to act on harmful content like this — even when legal. Otherwise, they'll find themselves at risk of fines or even criminal action from regulator Ofcom."[26]

In the *New Yorker*, Anna Wiener said Unofficial Journalism was unreliable because it was produced by small groups, or lone wolves, who lacked the resources to research facts and provide trustworthy news. Wiener argued that journalism was best left in the hands of large teams of well-resourced official journalists,

"A robust press is essential to a functioning democracy, and a cultural turn toward journalistic individualism might not be in the collective interest. It is expensive and laborious to hold powerful people and institutions to account, and, at many media organizations, any given article is the result of collaboration between writers, editors, copy editors, fact checkers, and producers."

Wiener accused Unofficial Journalism of creating a dangerous world, "The Internet is flooded with disinformation and conspiracy theories. Amazon's self-publishing arm has become a haven for extremist content."[27]

The journalist Olivia Solon described Unofficial Journalism as an, "alternative influence network" responsible for encouraging undesirable ethical-political views. She described unofficial journalists as, "broadly united by their reactionary position: an opposition to feminism, social justice and left-wing politics". These rogue voices, she said, "present themselves as an underdog alternative to the mainstream media." Solon noted that Unofficial Journalism's home was the internet, social media and video sharing sites such as *YouTube*. Hence, in their videos, "members of the network frequently use a live debate format, with multiple speakers arguing for hours on topics such as race, immigration and feminism." Solon called for censorship of these "harmful" belief systems, arguing that, by permitting them to be heard, social media sites had "allowed racist, misogynist, and harassing content to remain online."[28]

The philosophical assumptions and arguments of Official Journalism are therefore completely different to those of Unofficial Journalism. Official journalists take the view that audiences are not composed of rational individuals who should be encouraged to research things for themselves. The model Official journalist is able to judge the ethical-political consequences of telling the truth and knows when to self-censor. Like the model academic described by the American educator Clark Kerr, the ideal official journalist should be, "firm, yet gentle; sensitive to others... a seeker of truth where the truth may not hurt too much."[29] Official Journalism understands the audience as a herd which needs to be led, which craves simple, explanatory narratives and which recoils from the idea of epistemic effort and personal responsibility for knowing. In the collective mind of Official Journalism, the audience cries out, "Tell me what to think and what to do. Protect me from uncertainty and from harmful, wrong ideas. Economics and politics are complicated and boring. I want to spend my spare time living the good life and having fun. I want to be a good person and I want others to think of me as a good person. I am a loyal member of the tribe and I delegate my responsibility for knowing to you. Please be my epistemic parent and my guide. Give me news that makes me feel good about myself. Help me — tell me what I should believe and what it is safe for me to know."

Chapter 28

Aggressive Impartiality and Both-Sidesism

"By virtue of position, certain individuals in our society are accorded the privilege of stating as fact what, in the nature of things, is unknowable... Those privileged as prophets are permitted to identify salvation with the action which at the moment they find most expedient."

J.K. Galbraith.

Those who have lost trust in Official Journalism often find themselves asking: Do mainstream journalists really believe the narratives they produce? Why is Official Journalism so one-sided — why does it so often ignore or suppress the other side of the argument? and, Are official journalists conscious of their bias — is it deliberate or unintended? Official journalists understandably bristle at these questions which they interpret as questioning their honesty and integrity. To try to answer them, it is useful to consider the work and thoughts of two senior journocrats — Jon Sopel, the BBC's former North America Editor, and his colleague Emily Maitlis, a high-profile news anchor. Sopel and Maitlis both worked on the BBC's popular *Americast* podcast. Together, they were highly influential in shaping the British public's perception of Donald Trump.

In his 2019 book, *A Year at the Circus: Inside Trump's White House,* Sopel describes in detail how he constructed his Donald Trump narrative. In his first attempt, he likens Trump to the stereotypical baddie from a James Bond movie. He wonders whether the President should be a,

"Bond villain, stroking a white pussycat, while carefully figuring out every move that will ultimately deliver him world domination. But there are other times when this presidency is more Austin Powers than Ernst Blofeld."[1]

Sopel decides therefore not to cast Donald Trump as an evil psychopath. He explains he wants to make the President an object of ridicule, so he considers casting him as Dick Dastardly, the cartoon baddie from the 1960s TV show *Wacky Races.* Sopel is attracted to the idea of Trump as a comedy villain who combines malice and incompetence in equal measure,

"The Dick Dastardly *de nos jours* careering along some mountain road, crashing into other vehicles, brakes failing, the wheels about to fall off, body parts crumpled, the engine about to seize, black smoke belching out of the exhaust pipe... out steps Donald Trump, hair unruffled and that half smile, half smirk firmly in place."[2]

However, Sopel is still not satisfied. Dick Dastardly is ultimately a harmless, almost likeable, buffoon. The narrative Sopel is constructing requires a character capable of causing real harm. He is trying to manufacture, he says, a, "well-staged drama" in which there will be, "intriguing sub-plots and twists, with a cast of characters that is every bit as unbelievable as the President himself." The supporting cast will be made up of, "deeply flawed individuals — amateurs, grifters, weaklings, convicted and unconvicted felons". Sopel says he wants the "central guiding narrative" to be a "battle between a president who sees himself as the all-powerful ringmaster; and those around him."[3] Finally inspiration strikes, Sopel decides to cast Donald Trump as the notorious showman and circus owner P.T. Barnum — a man known to history for his arrogance, vulgarity, narcissism, showmanship and dishonesty. As Sopel contentedly summarizes, "Barnum liked creating his own hoaxes and designing his own reality."[4]

Having cast Donald Trump as a charlatan and hoaxer, Sopel's next task is to collect an assortment of anecdote and hearsay to legitimize the narrative. For example, he repeats a "glorious story", from a book by Omarosa Manigault, that Donald Trump swallowed a piece of paper in the Oval Office to prevent anyone reading it. Sopel says the paper *may* have contained information about, "a former porn star who wanted to sell her story of an alleged affair with Donald Trump."[5] Sopel includes the anecdote, not because it is true, but because it supports his narrative. It is an example of venomous innuendo and Sopel adds the qualifier that the story has, "been denied. Michael Cohen said it did not happen. The White House said the book was riddled with lies."

Aggressive Impartiality

Jon Sopel rejects the idea news has become narrativized, and is indignant at the suggestion that he constructs news narratives. "I don't buy your analysis" he says, "I just don't buy where your questions are going. I disagree."[6] He says he reported news about Donald Trump accurately and so did the BBC, "I think you're trying to say that there was an anti-Trump narrative at the BBC. I think that's bullshit" he asserts firmly. "I absolutely believe in impartiality, but I believe you can be quite *aggressive* in that impartiality". Sopel explains that "aggressive impartiality" means that if Donald Trump makes a statement that is inaccurate, it is the duty of journalists to expose the falsehood, "We're not going to say 'he says', 'she says' — we're going to say it's not true. And I think that's good journalism." In the case of Donald Trump, Sopel is adamant, "He lied quite frequently" therefore he deserved to be called out for it. "I'm absolutely, firmly of the view that it's my job is to hold people in power to account" he says. How does Sopel justify the process of narrative construction? How does he justify likening Donald Trump to Blofeld, Dick Dastardly and P.T. Barnum? What sort of journalism is it? Is it even journalism at all? "It's a book", he says, "it's not a news report. And in a book I've got more room to expand. And analysis forms a central part of what I do, it's not just a recitation of facts."

Sopel is urbane and eloquent, however his spirited defense is not entirely convincing. What he refers to as "aggressive impartiality" is a very ambiguous concept. In practice, it is an aggressive *incuriosity* because it does not allow audiences to hear both sides of the argument. Instead, it starts by assuming guilt and then aggressively proceeds to punishment. A similar approach was taken by the Queen of Hearts who proclaimed, in *Alice's Adventures in Wonderland*, "Sentence first — verdict afterwards". Sopel's aggressive impartiality is certainly aggressive, but it is hard to see how it is impartial. Sopel's biggest problem however is epistemic — Narrative-Led News requires audiences to accept that senior journocrats possess supernatural powers to know with certainty things which are, in reality, unknowable. Sopel's argument is plagued by relentless circularity — how can he be sure that Donald Trump frequently lied? It is perfectly possible for people to disagree about what has been established as fact. This does not mean one of them is lying. Part of the problem is that contemporary journalism erases the distinction between fact and opinion, and replaces them with narrative. As a result, it labels information that contradicts the official, frequently-repeated narrative, as 'lies'. Ultimately, those who believe the ethical-political narratives of Official Journalism have to accept them as articles of faith. Only then does everything make sense and fall into place. In other words, Donald Trump is only like P.T. Barnum if you begin by assuming he is a charlatan and a fraud. If you reject this starting position, then Donald Trump is not like P.T. Barnum. Finally, Sopel describes what he is doing as "analysis" which he says is, "not just a recitation of facts." But this seems to be stretching the meaning of the word 'analysis' to breaking point. Here, journalistic 'analysis' has become indistinguishable from unrestrained fantasy and narrative-construction.

Both-sidesism v One-sideism

While Sopel is reluctant to accept he is a manufacturer of ethical-political narratives, his colleague Emily Maitlis is far less squeamish. Contradicting Sopel, she argues journalists *should* take sides and produce news that is aware of its ethical-political responsibilities. Impartiality, she says bluntly, is a distraction that gets in the way.   Maitlis set out her views at the prestigious Edinburgh TV Festival in the summer of 2022. Her lecture was, she said, "the result of thoughts that have been circulating in my brain for years".[7] Journalism, she argued, must discard once and for all the outdated, Victorian Liberal notions of objectivity and impartiality which she scathingly labelled "both-sidesism". Both-sidesism, she said was a "myopic style of journalism" which "reaches a superficial balance whilst obscuring a deeper truth". Being impartial, she argued, should not be a journalist's prime goal, "Sometimes we tie ourselves in knots over the both-sidesism balance." According to Maitlis, trying to achieve good ethical-political outcomes is more important than the old, truthful type of reporting, "Is it enough", she asked, "to report things that might radically change the very fabric of our democracies and our societies as if they were merely a weather update?" Instead of reporting factual information, she said, the duty of a senior journocrat should be to "interpret and explain what is going on" and "lift the curtain on why things happen."   Like Sopel, Maitlis believes analysis is journalism's most important function.

To illustrate her argument, Maitlis referred to media coverage of the FBI's raid on former President Donald Trump's home at Mar-a-Lago in August 2022. The correct way to report the story, she said, was to portray it simply as the execution of a search warrant, and thus as a straightforward law enforcement operation. It should not be portrayed, she explained, as a politically-motivated act,

> "We should beware the 'parallel that is not remotely parallel.'
> The FBI search on Trump's house at Mar-a-Lago this month was
> re-imagined by Trump for his supporters as equivalent to Richard
> Nixon's burglary of the Watergate office building. It wasn't. It
> is a trope. See false equivalence!"

Instead of wasting time and energy reporting both sides of the argument, Maitlis said journalists should concentrate on their real role — "holding power to account" by fighting populism in all its forms,

> "Populism — make no mistake — is not a traditional "ism" of
> ideology. It's not Marxism or Reaganism — it has no adherence

to a set belief or policy... It's not an ideology. It is a means to achieve and retain power."

The audience, she said, was like a pot of frogs being slowly boiled to death. It was the ethical-political responsibility of journalists to alert them to the danger they faced from the Unofficial Ideology, rouse them to action and save them. There was no place here for objective, impartial reporting,

"We do not have to be campaigners, nor should we be complacent, complicit onlookers. Our job is to make sense of what we are seeing and anticipate the next move. It's the moment, in other words, the frog should be leaping out of the boiling water and phoning all its friends to warn them. But by then we are so far along the path of passivity, we're cooked."

Emily Maitlis is passionate about the ethical-political mission of Official Journalism. However, much of her argument does not stand up to critical scrutiny. Her use of the Mar-a-Lago/Watergate example seems confused and uninformed. For example, one of the charges levelled at President Nixon was, "using federal agencies to attack the President's political opponents".[8] Nixon was accused of weaponizing both the Internal Revenue Service (IRS) and the FBI for "his political advantage". The investigating committee found, "The surveillance and investigations served no lawful purpose" and had, "no national security objective, although he [Nixon] falsely used a national security pretext to attempt to justify them".[9] Specifically, Nixon sought to use the IRS tax records of his political opponent Governor George Wallace to make him look bad and sabotage his chances of being elected in the 1970 Alabama gubernatorial primary.[10]

In the Mar-a-Lago raid, the accusation was the same — that the Biden administration weaponized the FBI and the National Archives and Records Administration (NARA) to attack Donald Trump for political advantage. In both cases it was alleged a sitting President inappropriately politicized federal agencies. Maitlis however seems aggressively incurious about this. But the bigger, more important point, is that the judgement about whether Mar-a-Lago and Watergate are equivalent, is a matter of *opinion*, not a statement of *fact*, and opinions are neither true nor false. However, according to Maitlis' understanding of journalism, this distinction is irrelevant. Modern Official Journalism asks, 'which narrative benefits our side and damages the other side?' What is true is whatever is most ethically-politically useful. The Watergate analogy is therefore not true because it shows our side in a bad light. No factual evidence or logical argument is required to make this calculation. It is not necessary to consider both sides and it is ethically-politically wrong to do so. As Maitlis summarizes, when a narrative is useful, "Let's not turn ourselves inside out wondering if it's true".[11] Instead, she says, the other side's argument should be written-off as "absurd". Discussing it, she says, risks "normalizing" it. And, Maitlis stresses, above all else, "We have to stop normalizing the absurd".

The opposite of 'both-sidesism' is, logically, 'one-sideism'. Maitlis is therefore passionately pleading for one-sided journalism. Recognizing this helps understand the naïve, circular reasoning which lies at the heart of the Official Epistemology. One-sideism argues it is not necessary to hear the other side, because we already possess infallible knowledge of what is good and evil and what is true and false. This is like arguing that a woman accused of witchcraft should not be allowed to defend herself because we already know she is a witch. Listening to her side of the story would only create doubt and confusion, embolden other witches and help the devil. The possibility that the woman is not a witch should be rejected because it is absurd. The correct ethical-political thing to do is to be aggressively incurious about her side of the story and burn her.

Because one-sided journalism is not a form of evidence-based, rational enquiry, the unofficial journalist and blogger C.J. Hopkins refers to it as 'gaslighting'. Official Journalism is, he says, a sermon intended to tell the faithful what they ought to believe. It communicates the approved narrative to audiences via daily bulletins of, "official scripts, talking points, and thought-terminating clichés". It creates its own ethical-political reality, hence millions of people, he says,

"Have been systematically conditioned to believe a variety of patently ridiculous assertions, assertions based on absolutely nothing, repeatedly disproved by widely available evidence, but which have nevertheless attained the status of facts. An entire fictitious history has been written based on those baseless and ridiculous assertions."[12]

One-sideism is what the scientist and author Carl Sagan referred to as the, "celebration of ignorance". In the eyes of the Victorian Liberal Epistemology, it is fundamentally a religious, theocratic way of knowing. It is truthophobic and bypasses the error-correcting mechanism baked into impartial, objective enquiry. It replaces what is, with what ought to be. It is wishful thinking. As Sagan put it, "When we are self-indulgent and uncritical, when we confuse hopes and facts, we slide into pseudo-science and superstition."[13]

Both Sopel and Maitlis are sincere and passionate about their journalistic mission to "speak truth to power" and "hold power to account". However, they understand truth in ethical-political terms and assume they possess infallible knowledge of what is true and false, good and bad. Neither believe they are doing anything wrong. On the contary, they both believe they are doing precisely what is expected of them — and doing it well. When the dominant goal is to make the world a better place, what matters are the *consequences* of journalism and the *consequences* of impartiality. If reporting both sides fairly would harm the Official Ideology and embolden populists, then self-censorship, aggressive incuriosity, one-sideism, and other forms of pro-social lying become acceptable and desirable. In Boomer Journalism, first comes the verdict, then comes evidence to justify it. In this truthophobic world, journalism becomes a form of ethical-political lynching.

Chapter 29

Fact Checking, Conspiracy Theories, Misinformation and other Heresies

The Problem with Fact Checking

A curious feature of the journalistic landscape of the early 21st Century is the rise of fact-checking websites and their widespread use by Official Journalism and social media organizations. Many fact-checkers designed computer algorithms to help them identify truth and falsehood. So how do fact-checkers know what is true? Are their

344

fully-automated fact-checking algorithms really able to distinguish fact from fiction, and if so, how do they do it?

The prominent fact-checker *Full Fact* distinguishes between "bad" information and "good" information, not information that is "true" or "false". The choice of words, with its obvious ethical-political overtones, is significant. *Full Fact* explains, "Bad information ruins lives. It harms our communities, by spreading hate through misleading claims."[1] *Full Fact* says its algorithms automatically scan thousands of "publicly available" online sources to search for good information and filter out bad information. *Full Fact* uses the word "correct" interchangeably with "good" as in, "Our technology can automatically match with significantly more data to identify whether it's correct." What *Full Fact* is doing therefore, is programming its algorithm to detect consensus belief, i.e., the opinion of the majority. The more popular an opinion, the more more 'correct' it will be. By sampling large amounts of data, the algorithm will be better able to measure the consensus. However, *Full Fact* explains that not all sources of information are equally "good". More weight must be given to "trusted" sources, while "untrustworthy" sources should be disregarded. As the website puts it, when it comes to information, "a trusted source is your safest option."[2] In other words, the algorithm is programmed to place its finger on the scales and give more weight to 'trusted' sources. But how does the algorithm know which sources to trust?

Full Fact does not explain the criteria it uses for distinguishing between trustworthy and untrustworthy sources, but it does say, if its fact-checkers require clarification, they "speak to relevant experts for advice." However, what makes someone a "relevant expert" is not explained. Finally, having identified the consensus of "trusted" sources, and double-checked it with the opinion of "relevant experts", *Full Fact* labels statements either "true" or "false". *Full Fact* is therefore an excellent example of the Boomer Epistemology in action. What it generates is Tribal Truth, or Official Truth — the opinion of the consensus of tribal experts after "untrustworthy", or dissenting, voices have been removed. This is indistinguishable from pre-Renaissance ways of knowing. The only difference is the use of modern computer algorithms to automate the process. Hence, in the 2020s, the Boomer way of knowing combines the technology of the future with the epistemology of the distant past.

Other fact checkers understand the concept of truth in much the same way. They use the same epistemology and, unsurprisingly, obtain the same results. For example, *Snopes* explains it uses expert opinion and news articles to help assess whether a claim is true or false. *Snopes* says it contacts,

> "Individuals and organizations who would be knowledgeable about, or have relevant expertise in, the subject at hand, as well as searching out printed information (news articles, scientific and medical journal articles, books, interview transcripts, statistical sources) with bearing on the topic."[3]

Once again, what *Snopes* understands as truth is the consensus of expert opinion. In this view, truth reduces to officially sanctioned belief — Official Truth. But this is a self-referential, circular epistemology which relies heavily on confirmation bias. Which "news articles" does *Snopes* consult? Which experts does *Snopes* contact? Does *Snopes* seek out dissenting opinion, or does it exclude it? It is also an extremely fragile epistemology. Experts are not infallible. No matter how impressive their credentials, they remain human and therefore subject to groupthink and other psychological and emotional biases. Above all, it is logically fallacious to assert that belief, even widespread belief, makes something true. Therefore, seen from the perspective of Victorian Liberal Epistemology, contemporary fact checking is simply an appeal to authority. Scholars of the 18th or 19th Centuries would have dismissed this methodology as a form of superstition. They would have recognized it, in the words of Edward Gibbon, as the, "triumph of barbarism and religion" characteristic of the pre-scientific era. To the Victorians, *Full Fact*'s "facts" are not facts at all. They are an uncertain cocktail of fact, interpretation and opinion, heavily seasoned with groupthink, and stamped with the approval of those in positions of power and authority.

The poverty of the epistemology on which early 21st Century fact-checking rests was illustrated during a 2021 court case. When *Facebook* labeled two climate change videos by the journalist John Stossel "misleading", Stossel sued for libel. *Facebook* defended itself by arguing that its fact checkers were merely expressing their opinion. As *Facebook* put it, "The labels themselves are neither false nor defamatory; to the contrary, they constitute protected opinion."[4] *Facebook* said its fact checking was simply a "personal perspective" — a, "judgment call, one that is 'not capable of verification or refutation by means of objective proof.'" To add further epistemic ambiguity, *Facebook* also argued its opinions about what was true and false were based on facts that had been checked. In making this argument, *Facebook* was trying to both have its cake and eat it. If *Facebook*'s verdicts were opinions, then why were the offending videos not also opinions? What the court filings reveal is the tangled, arbitrary thinking of the Boomer Epistemology and its slippery, equivocal use of key words and concepts. As the political scientists Joseph Uscinski and Ryden Butler observe, "Fact checkers often attempt to check statements that are not facts and cannot be verified as true or false".[5] This reflects a much wider confusion about how truth is understood in contemporary society. As the researchers conclude there is a, "naïve political epistemology at work in the fact-checking branch of journalism" which reveals the unhappy and muddled state of epistemology in, "journalism at large, and in politics." This epistemic confusion is, in simple terms, the result of the truthophobia of the Boomers, and especially the way they recklessly erased the old distinction between fact and opinion.

The economist Jonas Herby and his colleagues were dismayed to find themselves on the receiving end of this "naïve political epistemology" when they published an analysis of public health statistics and reached the conclusion that mask-wearing and lockdowns, "in the spring of 2020 had little to no effect on COVID-19 mortality". Their research was attacked by *Snopes* and other fact checkers who reasoned that evidence contradicting the official narrative must be wrong because it contradicted the official narrative. According to *Snopes*, "Ordering people to stay at home... decreases disease transmission." Hence, "a study purporting to prove the opposite is almost certain to be fundamentally flawed."[6] Troubled by the absurdity of this circular reasoning, Herby responded by fact checking the fact checkers and concluded, "The new cottage industry called 'fact checking' has arguably become highly politicized",

> "As a result, there is not much fact checking, but rather opinions about whether the so-called fact checkers agreed or disagreed with the policy implications or conclusions of what they are supposed to be fact checking. So, for the most part, fact checkers were not engaged in fact checking, but were engaged in publishing opinion and narrative. By hiding behind the shroud of 'facts'

and 'fact-checking', they have attempted to cast doubt, in our case, via innuendo."[7]

The Unofficial Journalist Anthony Watts agrees and sees the entire fact-checking enterprise as a cynical attempt to legitimize official narratives and suppress dissent. According to Watts, fact-checking is "media activism" in disguise. He condemns it as a form of censorship designed to "suppress free speech" and limit "open discussion".[8]

Official Truth Goes to War.
The BBC's Trusted News Initiative

Another example of the Boomer Epistemology in action is the BBC's Trusted News Initiative (TNI) which was set up to, "protect audiences and users from disinformation, particularly around moments of jeopardy, such as elections."[9] The TNI is a collaboration between a broad network of international news organizations including,

"AP, AFP; BBC, CBC/Radio-Canada, European Broadcasting Union (EBU), *Facebook, Financial Times, First Draft, Google/YouTube, The Hindu*, Microsoft , Reuters, Reuters Institute for the Study of Journalism, *Twitter, The Washington Post*."[10]

The TNI uses the same epistemology as the major fact checking organizations. Information is either "good" or "bad" according to whether or not it conforms to the official, tribal consensus. Hence, the BBC's Disinformation Lead Rebecca Skippage, describes a binary world in which there are two ethical-political blocs — one good and one bad. The "bad guys", she says, "build like-minded communities which rally together through mistrust of authority to disparate but emotively-expressed causes." In order to "combat" the bad tribe, Skippage calls for the building of, "collaborations with like-minded providers and platforms to produce and seed appropriate material throughout native and external content streams." The aim, she explains, is to build a group of people, "who share your values". According to Skippage, journalism is a brutal, Darwinian struggle between rival narratives. To win it, Skippage recommends constructing simple, persuasive stories and repeating them over and over again until audiences accept them unquestioningly.

"The more easily we are able to process information, the more likely we are to believe it is true. This phenomenon — known as "fluency" — is why repetition is so powerful; if our brain is familiar with something, we find it easier to absorb... Those promoting good information can learn from this: keep it simple, put it where you know your audience will find it, and repeat."[11]

Skippage says audiences are "consumers" and suggests the role of journalism is to sell consumers "good" narratives and protect them from "harmful" ones. She recommends delegitimizing dissenting points of view using a process known as "nudging". As Skippage puts it, "Prebunking select stories and exposing consumers to general tools for inoculation — such as 'nudges' — have been proven to be effective." "The fight against disinformation, to win trust and report truth" she warns, "has only just started". It will be a fight, she predicts, "for the audience — all the audience — as a whole".

Project Origin is another BBC collaboration — this time with Microsoft. Its aim is to develop software capable of automatically distinguishing between good and bad information. Project Origin's methodology is to inject digital watermarks into officially approved media content. Media lacking the watermark will automatically be recognized as harmful misinformation and removed from search results and social media feeds to protect "consumers" from "information disorder".[12]

Skippage quotes with enthusiasm the work of the Spanish fact checking organization *Maldita* which adopts an aggressively militant stance inspired by the Spanish historical memory. Maldita's approach, for example, resonates with the philosophy of the Reconquista (the crusade by Catholic Spain against Islam during the 15th Century) and the sectarian mindset of the Spanish Civil War of the 1930s. In both cases, bitter conflict stemmed for the desire to achieve ideological hegemony and stamp-out diversity of belief. As one famous Spanish historian explained, the desire to create a single, cohesive ideology to unite the Spanish people is deeply ingrained, "Spain, evangelizer of half the world. Spain, hammer of heretics... That is our greatness and our unity, we have no other."[13]

According to Maldita, it is the moral duty of members of "our tribe" to root out false belief and impose our narratives on "their tribe". Clara Jimenez Cruz, CEO of Maldita, describes journalists as "soldiers" who are part of an, "army of superpower warriors to fight disinformation". Using an overtly military vocabulary, Cruz talks about a battle in which "truth disseminators" must target social media feeds to "fight in those private spaces" and "complete our mission". In this crusade to control what audiences believe, Cruz recommends using weapons such as automated bots, simple, often-repeated narratives, slogans and even comic books. "If you want to fight a battle" she says bluntly, "you need an army".[14]

The mindset of Cruz and Skippage, with their desire to "fight a battle" and sell their narratives to consumers, is a world away from the epistemology of Victorian Liberalism with its notions of balance, tolerance and impartiality in which dissent, debate and independent critical thinking are encouraged and celebrated. Seen from this perspective, the BBC's epistemology is both naïve and totalitarian. As Joseph Uscinski points out,

"The subject matter of politics is often complex, ambiguous, and open to a variety of conflicting interpretations, even when empirical claims are being made. Therefore, people may genuinely disagree about the truth. The fact that a politician disagrees with a fact checker about the facts does not make the politician a liar any more than it makes the fact checker a liar."[15]

Uscinski notes that the obliteration of the distinction between fact and opinion and the rise of Narrative-Led News, has resulted in a dangerously immature way of thinking that is both incapable of recognizing, and fearful of, complexity. The American medical researcher and blogger Robert Malone agrees, criticizing the TNI's epistemology for its reliance on a simplistic, tribal model of truth. Malone argues that knowledge is a delicate, imperfect thing that requires constant challenge in order to reach a "working approximation" of truth. Consequently, he says, the TNI is an "intellectual obscenity" that,

"Purports to be able to discern and enforce scientific 'truth' by defining truth as that which established public health bureaucracies (and singularly autocratic public health 'leaders') say it is."[16]

Malone says the TNI is a "monstrosity" waging a war on alternative points of view. It aggressively employs, he says,

"Both globally coordinated media and the tools of modern big technology to censor, demean, de-platform, delegitimize and de-license all others who seek to document, advance or discuss alternative versions of officially endorsed reality. The trusted news initiative has functionally morphed into Orwell's predicted ministry of truth."

Unofficial Journalists working for *The Liberty Beacon* take a similar view and accuse the TNI of being a "a shadowy global censorship network" attempting to establish a, "monopoly of legitimate information". The *Liberty Beacon* says the notion that audiences should be protected from information is "infantilizing" and part of a wider move towards dismantling, "the free speech culture that perhaps peaked in the 20th Century."[17] Free speech advocate Robert F. Kennedy accused TNI members of forming a restrictive cartel and launching a "group boycott" to crush rivals. According to Kennedy, the TNI is an unlawful attempt by Official Journalism to put Unofficial Journlism out of business. It was motivated, he said, by economic and ideological self-interest,

"While the 'Trusted News Initiative' publicly purports to be a self-appointed 'truth police' extirpating online 'misinformation,' in fact it has suppressed wholly accurate and legitimate reporting in furtherance of the economic self-interest of its members... The TNI is thus a paradigmatic antitrust violation: a horizontal agreement among competitor firms to cut off from the market upstart rivals threatening their business model. Every news company has the right to decide for itself what to publish, but they have no right to combine together to restrict what their rivals can publish."[18]

The clash of mindsets between of the TNI and its critics vividly illustrates the two different epistemologies that support Official and Unofficial Journalisms. According to Official Journalism, dissent from Official Truth causes division, disharmony and confusion. It is therefore the ethical-political duty of loyal members of the tribe to stamp it out. Those who spread misinformation are malicious actors who want to harm the tribe and help its enemies. Such people deserve to be punished. This is the inevitable consequence of a type of journalism that privileges *arete* over *aletheia*. As the American psychologist Cory Clark summarizes, Official Truths become the "sacred values" of the tribe. Hence, "defending and promoting them are particularly important for one's prestige within a coalition". Clark says those who offer alternative points of view will be demonized because anyone,

> "Who rejects a sacred value is advertising that he or she is not a loyal member of the tribe that holds it and appears intentionally to be transgressing a hallowed moral principle".[19]

The journalist Will Storr refers to this tribalism as the "evil truth" about humans. We are, he says, unconsciously in the grip of deeply-ingrained forces — the product of tens of thousands of years of evolution. As a result, we are slaves to the power of tribal narrative,

> "We willingly allow highly simplistic narratives to deceive us, gleefully accepting as truth any tale that casts us as the moral hero and the other as the two-dimensional villain. We can tell when we're under its power. When all the good is on our side and all the bad on theirs, our storytelling brain is working its grim magic in full. We're being sold a story. Reality is rarely so simple. Such stories are seductive because our hero-making cognition is determined to convince us of our moral worth. They justify our primitive tribal impulses and seduce us into believing that, even in our hatred, we are holy."[20]

Unofficial Journalism, on the other hand, draws on the Victorian Liberal Epistemology. According to this approach, tribal narratives must be restrained, while dissent should be encouraged as much as possible as a corrective to pro-tribe bias, groupthink and the numerous other emotional and psychological prejudices that cloud our thinking. The goal of journalism therefore becomes the impartial search for truth, not the promotion of tribal narratives. Hence, freedom of thought and freedom of expression are essential. Open-minded skepticism and reasonable doubt are epistemic virtues in the endless quest for truth. As John Stuart Mill wrote, it is important to recognize,

> "Mankind are not infallible; that their truths, for the most part, are only half-truths; that unity of opinion, unless resulting from

the fullest and freest comparison of opposite opinions, is not desirable, and diversity not an evil, but a good."[21]

The acceptance of human fallibility, and the fragility of our claims to knowledge, also form the basis of the scientific method. Hence, Victorian Liberal Journalism and scientific enquiry are both methodologies designed to encourage disbelief. The American physicist and philosopher Richard Feynman memorably defined science simply as the right to doutbt,

> "We must recognize our ignorance and leave room for doubt. Scientific knowledge is a body of statements of varying degrees of certainty — some most unsure, some nearly sure, but none absolutely certain... Our freedom to doubt was born out of a struggle against authority in the early days of science. It was a very deep and strong struggle: permit us to question — to doubt — to not be sure."[22]

Feynman famously added that, "Science is the belief in the ignorance of experts", and that, ordinary citizens,

> "Have as much right as anyone else, upon hearing about the experiments (but we must listen to all the evidence), to judge whether a reusable conclusion has been arrived at... The experts who are leading you may be wrong."[23]

Experts are not simply fallible and prone to error, they are also corruptible. In the case of science, this means they may, in some cases, produce research that is fraudulent. For example, an investigation by the *Better Science* blog in 2020, exposed the existence of "paper mills" operating in China. These lucrative businesses produce scientific papers in return for payment, and churn out, "masses of 100% fabricated, never performed science which only exists in Photoshop." Many of these papers are peer reviewed and published in respectable western journals, after which they pass into the canon of scientific literature and are cited in good faith by other researchers. After exposing the scandal, the authors were contacted by a remorseful Chinese researcher who explained emotionally,

> "Without papers, you don't get promotion; without a promotion, you can hardly feed your family... You expose us but there are

thousands of other people doing the same. As long as the system remains the same and the rules of the game remain the same, similar acts of faking data are for sure to go on."[24]

This form of corruption is not limited to China, it is believed to be a widespread global phenomenon. Richard Smith, former editor of the *British Medical Journal*, agrees part of the problem is the business model of scientific journals which,

> "Depends on publishing, preferably lots of studies as cheaply as possible. They have little incentive to check for fraud and a positive disincentive to experience reputational damage — and possibly legal risk — from retracting studies."[25]

Smith concludes,

> "The problem is huge, the system encourages fraud, and we have no adequate way to respond. It may be time to move from assuming that research has been honestly conducted and reported to assuming it to be untrustworthy until there is some evidence to the contrary."

Research can also become corrupted when researchers seek to please the organization that employs and pays them. The American writers Jon Jureidini and Leemon McHenry point out that, in the 21st Century, medical research is generally funded by a, "small number of very large pharmaceutical companies". Because these companies control the flow of money, they are able to influence, albeit subtly, research findings — such as the efficacy of their latest drugs. In effect, they are able to "mark their own homework". The result is the pharmaceutical industry,

> "Suppresses negative trial results, fails to report adverse events, and does not share raw data with the academic research community. Patients die because of the adverse impact of commercial interests on the research agenda".[26]

Jureidini and McHenry argue that universities, hungry for research funding, "become instruments of industry" and, "agents for the promotion of commercial product." The writers conclude that,

354

"Instead of acting as independent, disinterested scientists and critically evaluating a drug's performance, they become what marketing executives refer to as 'product champions'."

In other words, gullibility and uncritical trust in experts are not epistemic virtues. Trust, in these cases, often arises from people's ignorance of the ignorance of the experts. Consensus belief is ultimately therefore little more than belief in what is currently fashionable. However, fashions change. Indeed, history teaches that many beliefs held in one era, will be shown to be unfounded in the next. As the American philosopher Willard Van Orman Quine shrewdly pointed out,

"We must recognize that there are almost certain to be many items of today's so-called common knowledge, some springing directly from science and some not, that will illustrate the follies of our age in the next century's textbooks... The lesson is one not of despair, but of humility."[27]

The psychologist Daniel Kahneman agrees that our confidence in experts is often little more than a lazy epistemic shortcut and a comforting illusion. The fact that many credentialled experts believe something, does not mean it is true,

"Subjective confidence in a judgement is not a reasoned evaluation of the probability that this judgement is correct... declarations of high confidence mainly tell you that an individual has constructed a coherent story in his mind, not necessarily that the story is true."[28]

Experts, including elite journocrats, do not therefore possess supernatural powers of infallibility. They are prone to the same prejudices and biases that affect us all. As Kahneman puts it, they are, "just human in the end. They are dazzled by their own brilliance and hate to be wrong."

Misinformation and Heresy

In March 2020, Jacinda Ardern, New Zealand's Prime Minister, was asked to comment about rumors of an imminent Covid lockdown. She replied by explaining how citizens could distinguish between misinformation and truth, "Remember, unless you hear it from us, it is not the truth... we will continue to provide everything you need to know." According to Ardern's epistemology, truth is simply official information issued by those in positions of power and authority, as she put it,

"We will share with you the most up to date information daily, you can trust us a source of that information. You can also trust the Director General of Health and the Ministry of Health... otherwise dismiss anything else. We will continue to be your single source of truth; we will provide information frequently... everything else you see; a grain of salt!"[29]

What Ardern did not explain was the source of the government's information, and why it should be regarded as certain and infallible. The US government went even further by suggesting in 2022 that unauthorized, non-official news was "mis-dis-and mal-information" and that spreading it should be considered an act of domestic terrorism. The Department of Homeland Security (DHS) warned of an,

"Online environment filled with false or misleading narratives and conspiracy theories, and other forms of mis-dis-and mal-information (MDM)... These threat actors seek to exacerbate societal friction to sow discord and undermine public trust in government institutions to encourage unrest."[30]

Two months later, in April 2022, the DHS announced it was setting-up a federal Committee on Public Information — a body quickly dubbed the "Ministry of Truth" by critics such as the journalist David Harsanyi who viewed it as a sinister development. Making belief in the 'wrong' facts and opinions a matter of national security was, he said, a horrible idea, "While the state putting an imprimatur on 'truth' is dangerous to freedom, it is also laughable in practice". Harsanyi argued that allowing people to believe things that might be untrue was the lesser of two evils compared with introducing official state censorship,

"It is by any liberal ideal of open discourse preferable to allow lies to seep into the information stream than to allow a panel nomenklatura to start dictating the veracity of what we read and hear. First, and foremost, because it's authoritarian. Second, because those who take the job can't be trusted."[31]

In the face of widespread opposition, the Disinformation Governance Board was shut down just three weeks after its launch. *The Washington Post* described it as a "disastrous rollout", but reported the board's purpose had been "grossly mischaracterized". The DHS said it had never intended to, "Police speech... quite the opposite, its focus is to ensure that freedom of speech is protected."[32]

When truth is understood as Official Truth, then 'misinformation' and 'heresy' become synonymous. The word heresy derives from the Greek word *hairesis* meaning choice. Heresy therefore implies personal choice in matters of belief. Throughout history, people who carried out their own research, and who reached their own conclusions, were judged to be guilty of heresy — especially when their opinions contradicted official religious doctrine. Writing around 200 A.D., the Christian theologian Tertullian condemned the personal pursuit of truth as wicked and declared, "We want no curious disputation after possessing Christ Jesus, no inquisition after enjoying the gospel! With our faith, we desire no further belief."[33] Similarly, in 1546 at the Council of Trent, the Catholic Church forbade unauthorized interpretations of the Bible in response to the rise of "heretical" Protestant narratives. Catholics were instructed not to interpret sacred texts,

> "Contrary to that sense which holy mother Church, to whom it belongs to judge of their true sense and interpretation, has held and holds... Those who act contrary to this shall be made known to ordinaries and punished."[34]

The Baptist preacher Charles Haddon Spurgeon argued that heresy was the "parent" of all other evils. Refusing to believe the official narrative was, he thundered,

> "The monarch sin, the quintessence of guilt; the mixture of the venom of all crimes; the dregs of the wine of Gomorrah; it is the A1 sin, the master-piece of Satan, the chief work of the devil... it

is the egg of all crime, the seed of every offence; in fact everything that is evil and vile lies couched in that one word — unbelief."[35]

Heresy was the principal target of the Catholic Inquisition which burned hundreds of thousands of stubborn heretics along with their books and pamphlets. Indeed, capital punishment for heresy was still being recommended by the Catholic Church as late as the beginning of the 20th Century. As one manual of church law explained,

"The death sentence is a necessary and efficacious means for the Church to attain its end when rebels act against it and disturbers of the ecclesiastical unity, especially obstinate heretics and heresiarchs, cannot be restrained by any other penalty from continuing to derange the ecclesiastical order and impelling others to all sorts of crime... When the perversity of one or several is calculated to bring about the ruin of many of its children it is bound effectively to remove it, in such wise that if there be no other remedy for saving its people it can and must put these wicked men to death."[36]

Nor is hatred of heresy confined to Christianity. The author Salman Rushdie discovered the perils of heresy when he was accused of spreading 'misinformation' about Islam in his novel *The Satanic Verses*. In 1989 a fatwa calling for his execution was proclaimed by Iran's Ayatollah Khomeini. The fatwa referred to his book as, "a text written, edited, and published against Islam, the Prophet of Islam, and the Qu'ran". Khomeini targeted Rushdie and his publishers, "I call on all valiant Muslims wherever they may be in the world to kill them without delay, so that no one will dare insult the sacred beliefs of Muslims henceforth."[37] Thirty-three years later, in August 2022, Rushdie was attacked while giving a talk in New York. He was fortunate to survive after being stabbed repeatedly in the neck, face and body.

The clash between Official and Unofficial Journalisms is therefore an age-old clash of epistemologies. It is the clash between a scientific, evidence-based way of knowing, and a theological, or magical, way of knowing. In the 21st Century, the boundary between these epistemologies has become hopelessly blurred. For example, large numbers of people sincerely claim to venerate science. However, as the blogger Iain Davies points out, upon closer inspection, their epistemic process is much closer to theology. Scientism is the name given to the superstitious worship of the pronouncements of scientists. According to Davies, it leads people to believe that science is not a methodology of doubt and skepticism, but a canon of settled doctrine which it is wrong to question. Those who worship at the altar of scientism delude themselves into thinking they are critical thinkers, but in reality they are embracing a fanatical tribalism. They believe,

> "Undertaking independent research or thinking for yourself is dangerous. Primarily because that is what they have been told to think. They accept all statistics as reported to them by the MSM but rarely, if ever, go to the sources themselves and look at the statistics."[38]

Scientism creates the illusion of reason yet remains a profoundly faith-based way of knowing intolerant of heresy. Davies observes that followers of scientism,

> "No longer recognize the need to think for themselves. Rather they see themselves as the defenders of the official truth as they consider unquestioning obedience to authority to be the only rational position."

Heresy threatens to split and divide the herd. It is therefore the ultimate tribal crime because human beings have evolved over thousands of years to fear the fragmentation of the group knowing that it exposes members to danger. For most people, the safest course of action is to try to remain near the center, away from the periphery where the risk of becoming prey is highest. As the evolutionary biologists Denni Chao and Simon Levin write,

> "Herd members can realize a variety of benefits by joining large groups, many of which relate to protection from predation and reduction of search time for patchy resources."[39]

The behavior of the tribe is a "large-scale phenomenon" which arises out of innumerable "local interactions" i.e., decisions by individuals and micro groups. Thus, heretical views, such as those which threaten to take the tribe in a different direction, are both contagious and destabilizing. As Chao and Levin put it, "Herding animals typically react to a small subset of their neighbors."

Heresy presents a paradox. Its disruptive force is initially feared, resisted and punished. However, if its message persists and spreads, then it will be adopted by the majority. If the new direction of travel turns out to be beneficial to the tribe, then it will become the new orthodoxy and a new equilibrium will be established. In a herd of cattle, heretics are those who see greener grass and want to move towards it, or who spot a threat and want to take the herd away from it. In tribes of humans, heretics are those who call for new beliefs and behaviors to take advantage of new opportunities, or protect the herd from perceived threats. In such cases, access to accurate, reliable information will play a major role in correctly assessing the presence of threat or opportunity. Invariably, the process will also be marked by disagreement, disequilibrium and stress.

Political theorists have long argued that Victorian Liberal Democracy cannot exist without the steady flow of controversial new ideas and debate. Therefore, they argue for the maximum possible degree of freedom of expression and thought. As the champion of individual liberty Friedrich Hayek warned, the suppression of dissent from Official Truth logically leads to,

> "The stagnation, if not the decay of civilization. Advance consists in the few convincing the many. New views must appear somewhere before they can become majority views. There is no experience of society which is not first the experience of a few individuals… It is always from a minority acting in ways different from what the majority would prescribe, that the majority in the end learns to do better."[40]

Because dissent is so important to Liberal Democracy, the stigmatization of minority opinion as 'misinformation' amounts to the rejection of Liberal Democracy itself. The war on mis, dis and mal-information therefore implies tacit support for the Boomer version of democracy — a form of post-democracy based on the domination of the majority. This crude, tribal understanding of democracy draws heavily on the Utopian longing of the Boomer generation for a regime in which everybody shares the same core ethical-political values. From the perspective of Victorian theorists, Boomer democracy is an illiberal democracy.

The Truth About Fake News

The fake news phenomenon of the early 21st Century is highly confusing due to the existence of two different, incompatible journalisms, based on two different, incompatible epistemologies. The concept of fake news cannot make sense unless there is first agreement about which journalism is genuine. Official Journalism draws on the Boomer Epistemology. Its goal is *arete* — making the world a better place. It is aware of its ethical-political responsibilities and sees itself as a higher, more evolved form of journalism. For those who embrace the Official Ideology, its epistemology and narratives, this is genuine journalism. Unofficial Journalism, on the other hand, seeks inspiration in the epistemology of Victorian Liberal Journalism. Its goal is *aletheia* — the impartial search for truth regardless of ethical-political and tribal consequences. For those who embrace the Unofficial Ideology and its values, this is genuine journalism.

In summary, 'fake news' is simultaneously both genuine and fake — depending on which epistemology one uses. The label 'fake news' signals which journalism one regards as legitimate. This, in turn, signals one's position in the wider epistemic and ideological battle. Therefore, the fake news debate is not an innocent, technical dispute of interest only to students of journalism. It is the visible sign of a wider struggle for economic, cultural and political power with implications for how society should be organized and what system of government should prevail. It is a contest for what we should believe, how we should think and how we should lead our lives. Ultimately, what we label 'fake news' tells us more about ourselves and our ideological convictions, than about what is objectively true or false.

Chapter 30

The
Covid Pandemic.
A Case Study in
Contemporary
Journalism

The Covid pandemic was the first major news story of the post-Trump era. To make the world a better place, Official Journalism deployed the same techniques it had used in its war against Trumpism. These were: the repetition of simple, official narratives; the suppression of evidence that contradicted them; the reporting of opinion as fact; and the labelling of dissent as fake news, conspiracy theory, or misinformation. Covid was also the battleground for a bitter conflict between Official Journalism and Unofficial Journalism, with each accusing the other of deceiving and misleading the public. It was a conflict between two ways of knowing and two different types of journalism.

The World Health Organization declared a global pandemic on 11th March 2020 and, by the end of the year, pharmaceutical companies including Pfizer, Moderna and AstraZeneca, had produced vaccines which they claimed offered protection against severe illness. The vaccines were novel, gene-based therapies using mRNA technology to instruct healthy human cells to produce the spike protein characteristic of the SARS-CoV-2 virus, in order to stimulate an immune system response. The vaccines were rolled-out in a fraction of the time normally allowed for vaccine development. The US government chose the name Operation Warp Speed to highlight the accelerated pace of its vaccination program. However, a consequence of the rapid roll-out was that no medium or long-term safety data was available for the new products. Hence, it was impossible for individuals to make accurate assessments of benefit and risk.

The key questions were not therefore medical, they were epistemic and ideological — how could anyone know whether the vaccines were safe and beneficial? Should individuals take responsibility for deciding whether or not to accept them, or should they unquestioningly trust the expert consensus and follow official advice? In the UK, the Medicines and Healthcare products Regulatory Agency (MHRA) awarded temporary authorization for the new vaccines on 2nd December 2020 and mass vaccination began on 8th December. In the US, the Food and Drug Administration (FDA) granted emergency use authorization to the Pfizer–BioNTech vaccine on 10th December and mass vaccination began the following week.

One significant feature of the pandemic was that it disproportionately threatened the Boomer generation. Covid was essentially a Boomer plague. As Mark Woolhouse, one of the world's leading epidemiologists pointed out in 2022, Covid was a, "very discriminatory virus. Some people are much more at risk from it than others. People over 75 are an astonishing 10,000 times more at risk than those who are under 15." Woolhouse concluded that public health policies, such as lockdowns, harmed young people far more than elderly Boomers. These policies,

"Did serious harm to our children and young adults who were robbed of their education, jobs and normal existence, as well as suffering damage to their future prospects, while they were left to inherit a record-breaking mountain of public debt."[1]

As a 2020 medical study explained, non-Boomers were very unlikely to be harmed by Covid. Those under the age of sixty-four,

"Have very small risks of COVID-19 death even in pandemic epicenters and deaths for people <65 years without underlying predisposing conditions are remarkably uncommon."[2]

Unknown, long-term harms may therefore have been inflicted on the young for the sake of protecting the elderly Boomer generation. For example, one UK government report noted that large numbers of infants were finding it unusually difficult to learn to speak and that, "babies have struggled to respond to basic facial expressions, which may be due to reduced social interaction during the pandemic." The report also observed, "delays in babies learning to crawl and walk", and pointed out that some children had, "regressed in their independence and self-care skills".[3] As one blogger bluntly summarized, lockdowns, mask wearing and social distancing meant the young stayed home to save the lives of the Boomer generation,

"Thousands lost jobs. Millions of lives were put on hold... Schooling and university teaching was axed for months, then implemented in a pale imitation of its former self via video calls. Human social interaction was criminalized. Little of this was for the personal benefit of the young, who, even in March 2020, were much less likely to be hospitalized or die from Covid. Young compliance with these unprecedented measures was for the selfless protection of the elderly in society, not for the self."[4]

The politics of Covid was therefore shaped by demographics and presented the spectacle of the Boomer generation asking their healthy children and grandchildren to sacrifice themselves by, amongst other things, injecting themselves with experimental gene-based vaccines. It was, on the face of it, an astonishing reversal of the attitude of the Boomers who, when they were young, had demonized old people proclaim-

364

ing, "Kill your parents!", "Don't trust anyone over thirty"and singing, "Hope I die before I grow old". Amongst other things therefore, Covid revealed the self-serving nature of the Boomer Ideology and its core of Boomer Exceptionalism. The Boomers regarded old people as the tribal enemy when they were young, and the young as the tribal enemy when they were old. Boomers, such as the British celebrity journalist Andrew Neil, were among the most severe critics of those who, "through fear, ignorance, irresponsibility or sheer stupidity refuse to be jabbed." Neil called for the unvaccinated to be punished arguing,

"It is simply selfish not to be vaccinated. We all have a responsibility to act in ways that don't just protect our own health but also that of others… If they contract Covid, it is they who will put the biggest strain on the NHS, denying the rest of us with serious non-Covid ailments the treatment that is our right."[5]

Official Journalism in the Age of Covid

Two weeks after the pandemic was declared, UK government advisors published a document recommending the use of fear as a tactic to manipulate the beliefs and behavior of the population for the collective good. The report, written by the Scientific Pandemic Influenza Group on Behaviour (SPI-B), argued that manufacturing a sense of mass panic was the best way to get the public to obey public health policies. The report explained,

"A substantial number of people still do not feel sufficiently personally threatened; it could be that they are reassured by the low death rate in their demographic group… The perceived level of personal threat needs to be increased among those who are complacent, using hard-hitting emotional messaging."[6]

Ofcom, the organization that regulates broadcast journalism in the UK, reacted quickly. The following day, 23 March, it issued a warning to TV and radio journalists that they would face fines or other regulatory enforcement, if they published information contradicting the Official Truth. Ofcom said the, "Dissemination of accurate and up-to-date information to audiences will be essential" and warned of the, "significant potential harm that can be caused by material relating to the Coronavirus." Ofcom did not distinguish between truthful and untruthful information, only to "harmful" information which it said must be avoided. This information, it said, might include, "health claims related to the virus which may be harmful. Medical advice which may be harmful" and, "misleadingness in programmes in relation to the virus or public policy regarding it." Ofcom made it clear that journalists should only report Official Truth explaining, "All organizations will need to follow Government advice", and that compliance would be policed, "Ofcom will consider any breach arising from harmful Coronavirus-related programming to be potentially serious."[7]

It is impossible to judge the impact of Ofcom's guidance on Official Journalism in the UK. However the unofficial journalist Laura Dodsworth says it provided important regulatory justification for narrative-led journalism and prosocial lying,

> "Ofcom's decision may have chilled the inclination of the media to explore theories which were counter to government advice. The state broadcaster, the BBC, refused to challenge state orthodoxy, which is the sort of thing we criticise other countries for… There is a word for only sharing information which is biased and is used to promote a political cause: propaganda."[8]

Whatever the impact of the Ofcom guidance, Official Journalism embraced its role of purveyor of official narratives and Official Truth during the pandemic with zeal. In a report entitled, *How do we know Covid vaccines are safe?* BBC News' Online Health Editor Michelle Roberts noted, "The Oxford-AstraZeneca vaccine has been linked to very rare cases of blood clots", however despite this, she dismissed safety fears and reassured audiences by describing the testing process used by drug companies,

> "Safety trials begin in the lab, with tests and research on cells and animals, before moving on to human studies. The principle is to start small and only move to the next stage of testing if there are no outstanding safety concerns. All of the work and findings are checked and verified independently. The Covid vaccine trials happened at breakneck speed, but they didn't skip any steps - they

were able to move faster because so many people were involved and other projects were put aside."[9]

Roberts continued,

"Approval is only given in the UK if the regulator is happy that a vaccine is safe and effective... Independent experts on the Joint Committee on Vaccination and Immunization decide how best to use a vaccine and who should get it."

She concluded, "Experts stress the benefits of vaccination outweigh the risks for the vast majority of people." Here, Roberts was relying on the Boomer Epistemology in which the existence of expert consensus justifies believing something to be true. It is not an epistemology designed to facilitate effortful, individual enquiry. On the contrary, it is designed to make it easy for those in positions of power and authority to steer the population in the right direction. In her report, Roberts did not feel it was necessary to provide any clinical data, nor explain how the experts arrived at their conclusions. She did not explain the distinction between the different phases of clinical safety trials, nor did she provide a balancing, counter argument. Indeed, she attacked those who were skeptical, warning audiences that, "Anti-vaccine stories are spread online through social media. These posts are not based on scientific advice (or blend facts with misinformation)."

Official Journalism's reliance on the Boomer Epistemology can also been seen in a revealing article by the journalist Fiona Fox. Writing in *The Guardian,* Fox defended the authority of experts, and their computer models, to predict the future trajectory of the pandemic. She explained, "If models show a range of between 40 and 4,000 deaths a day, the truth will probably be somewhere in the middle." Here, Fox is defining truth as a super-consensus — the consensus of the consensus. Fox argues that consensus belief is reliable because it is the result of,

"Hundreds of researchers throughout the UK working collaboratively to constantly reassess data, refine methodology, challenge assumptions, and compare and debate results to reach a scientifically sound consensus. The whole point of Sage and the Spi-M-O advisory group is that we don't rely on individual models or views but develop a consensus of what the science is telling us which can be useful to policymakers."[10]

What is noteworthy is that Fox does not explain why the consensus of expert opinion should be true — she simply defines truth as the consensus of expert opinion. In other words, according to Fox, a statement is not the consensus because it is true, it is true because it is the consensus. Using the same logic, if experts were to say there were between 40 to 4,000 witches in England, then the truth would be somewhere in the middle — around 2,000. In the Boomer Epistemology, questioning the consensus is the same thing as questioning the truth, and this, Fox asserts, is ethically and politically wrong, "Encouraging the public not to trust experts who revise their data and correct themselves is anti-science and anti-intellectual."

The philosopher Martin Heidegger referred to this way of knowing as one based on "idle talk". Idle talk, he said, does not require evidence or logical thinking. On the contrary, it "covers up" genuine understanding with a powerful shared illusion,

"Idle talk, which anyone can pick up, dispenses us from the task of genuine understanding. One can talk along and be taken seriously in idle talk. This free-floating interpretation, which belongs to everyone and no one, dominates everydayness."[11]

Heidegger said the repetition of idle talk leads to the illusion of knowledge. By distilling the consensus, Official Truth can be made to appear magically out of Tribal Truth,

"Even if all the speakers who thus speak their minds have understood little of the matter, one is of the opinion that the cumulation of this lack of understanding will nevertheless eventually generate an understanding."

Official Journalism during the Covid pandemic often blamed sinister conspiracies for causing people to doubt Official Truth. For example, BBC News reported a, "mysterious marketing agency secretly offered to pay social media stars to spread disinformation about Covid-19 vaccines."

The BBC darkly hinted that this conspiracy was funded by evil Russian agents, and interviewed a politician whose opinion was,

"Bad-mouthing vaccines in the West undermines trust in our democracies and is supposed to increase trust in Russia's vaccines, and there is only one side that benefits and that is the Kremlin."[12]

In another report, the BBC probed the minds and motives of those who doubted and questioned. Its specialist disinformation reporter Marianna Spring wrote approvingly, "*Facebook* is now removing groups and pages that discourage people from getting vaccines." The big social media corporations were, she said, heroically "grappling" with "the anti-vaccine movement". Spring interviewed Dave who had fallen into "some dark places" after having been exposed to Unofficial Journalism,

"'I wasn't in a good place,' he says, sitting on his leather sofa at home. He explains how he spent hours watching *YouTube* videos made by anti-vaccine activists".

Spring explained that Dave finally turned away from the "dark places" where Unofficial Journalism lurked, he accepted the vaccine and returned to a normal, healthy family life, "'I'm in a better place,' he says. 'I'm in a proper home environment now, I've got rugrats running around my feet again.' His face lights up as he speaks of his grandchildren."[13]

A BBC News video entitled, "Escaping the anti-vax conspiracy rabbit hole" told a similar story. The film introduced Catherine who,

"Used to be an ardent believer in conspiracy theories, including thinking that vaccines are part of a sinister global plot to make millions ill. Now she spends her time trying to convince others to climb out of the online rabbit hole that she was once down."[14]

Catherine said she was brainwashed by Unofficial Journalism and compared the experience to being inducted into a "cult". She said she was led astray by, "Hundreds of *YouTube* videos, *Facebook* videos, memes, articles and clips that would catch your attention in the news feed." The video ended happily with Catherine abandoning her old beliefs. The final scene celebrated Catherine's conversion to the official narrative, "Now" asked the presenter, "Would you have the vaccine?" "Yes, absolutely!" Catherine replied joyously as the film faded to black.

A striking feature of this news report, and this style of journalism, is the absence of any clinical data, rational argument, or debate about vaccine efficacy or safety. The goal of the journalism is simply to influence and persuade. It is, essentially, a theological argument which stresses the need for faith. The story also implies it is not possible to read Unofficial Journalism critically or discriminatingly. To do so is to dance with the devil and turn to the dark side. The film tells the story of the battle for Catherine's soul, and her progress from "conspiracy theorist" via confession and repentance to redemption. The video also illustrates how labelling someone a "conspiracy theorist" stigmatizes them and can be used to close down an argument without having to win it with superior evidence or logic. Branding one's opponent a conspiracy theorist is therefore a highly manipulative strategy that makes people too afraid to question or challenge. It is, as the American scholar Ginna Husting explains, a tactic of intimidation and intellectual terrorism,

> "If I call you a 'conspiracy theorist,' it matters little whether you have actually claimed that a conspiracy exists or whether you have simply raised an issue that I would rather avoid... Using the phrase, I can symbolically exclude you from the imagined community of reasonable interlocutors... In fact, I have done even more. By labeling you, I strategically exclude you from the sphere where public speech, debate, and conflict occur."[15]

There is also a deep irony in the spectacle of someone attributing lack of belief to the existence of a conspiracy. This is because those who accuse others of being conspiracy theorists, are themselves, by definition, conspiracy theorists. Instead of contemplating the possibility of their own error, they blame disagreement on the existence of a conspiracy. If it wasn't for this sinister conspiracy, they argue, there would be no disagreement, and everyone would believe the same thing.

Unofficial Journalism

To hear the other side of the argument, it is necessary to cross the epistemic divide and enter the world of Unofficial Journalism. Here, different facts and opinions were presented. For example, writing for the *UK Column* in 2021, Iain Davis argued that the official narrative exaggerated the threat from Covid because the PCR tests, commonly used to diagnose the illness, were unreliable,

> "Currently, the UK Government claim they have conducted 209 million PCR tests, of which 4.8 million were positive, representing 2.3% of tests. The UK Scientific Advisory Group for Emergencies (SAGE) estimated the RT-PCR false positive rate to vary between 0.8% and 4.0%, with a mean false positive rate of 2.3%. Therefore, at the lower estimate, 1.7 million of the alleged 4.8 million "cases" could be false positives. As we approach the mean, it is possible that none of the claimed cases are based upon genuine positives."[16]

Here, Davis is following the epistemology of Victorian Liberal Journalism which is skeptical of the authority of experts, and which insists on scrutinizing the original data. Using this methodology, it is the evidence that counts, not the status and prestige of those presenting it. Davis also acknowledges that reality is complex and our knowledge uncertain. However, understanding his article and mathematical calculations requires substantial cognitive effort. It is far more difficult to digest than the simplified, seductive narratives of Official Journalism. Unofficial Journalism also reported the views of renegade experts who dissented from the consensus. For example, the American cardiologist Peter McCullough refered to the vaccines as "poisonous". They are, he claims, radically new genetic treatments that can cause blood clots and are "alarmingly dangerous". McCullough told the Unofficial Journalist Stew Peters that mass vaccination, "will go down as the most dangerous biological medicinal product rollout in human history", adding, "This is far and away the most lethal, toxic, biologic agent ever injected into a body in American history,"[17]

In the UK, Michael Yeadon, former Chief Scientist of Pfizer's allergy and respiratory research unit, came to a similar conclusion, claiming the vaccines were unnecessary, ineffective and unsafe. Yeadon accused those promoting them of deliberately distorting the truth, "I'm afraid everything our government and scientific advisors have told us over the last 18 months are lies. All lies. They're telling untruth deliberately and we call that lying."[18] Yeadon criticized the return of pre-Victorian ways of knowing based on superstition, blind faith and obedience to authority. Governments, he said, should not,

> "Vaccinate millions of fit and healthy people with a vaccine that hasn't been extensively tested on human subjects…. The 'scientific method' is what separates us from pre-renaissance peoples, who might tackle plagues with prayer."[19]

However, these counter arguments remained unavailable to audiences whose only source of information was Official Journalism. As the Unofficial Journalist Mark Steyn asked in frustration in 2022, "Why, two years in, is the media still so invested in the official narrative and only that?" Steyn pointed to an increasing number of reputable scientific studies suggesting the vaccines suppress the human immune system and may cause long-term harm. These studies, he said, were omitted from mainstream reporting,

> "We say, basically, 'Everybody on the planet has to get this stuff injected into their arm' – including people who are at no risk whatsoever, such as people in young middle-age, in the flower of youth, or even primary school children. So, we insist that all of those people have to get jabbed with this stuff. And there is a discernible uptick in excess mortality and yet we're not permitted to talk about it."[20]

The British TV executive Mark Sharman, formerly Head of News at ITV and Director of Broadcasting at Sky, also expressed exasperation with Official Journalism. Sharman said what remained of old-fashioned, impartial journalism was being squeezed to death by a two-pronged pincer movement,

"I feel as though freedom of speech, the impartiality of reporting and honest debate are all under attack. I feel as though it's a pincer movement. On the one hand you've got big tech through *YouTube, Facebook* and *Twitter,* they're cancelling people and they're using these terrible terms; 'misinformation' 'conspiracy theorists' just to dismiss anything that doesn't fit the narrative... Mainstream media is the other side of the pincer movement. They're also only telling one side of the story over Covid. There appears to be a worldwide narrative and mainstream media has signed up to it. They're acting as government cheerleaders, and that's not the role of mainstream media or any journalist."[21]

It was not only the voices of rebellious virologists, immunologists and media executives that were silenced by Official Journalism. Victims of the harmful side effects of the mRNA vaccines also found themselves suddenly invisible. Caroline Pover suffered disabling pain after her vaccination and was dismayed to be treated with disbelief, indifference and hostility,

"The lack of compassion I have seen during the past fourteen months, as I look at the world through the lens of a vaccine-injured person, has greatly disturbed me. What has happened to our compassion?"[22]

What Pover had discovered is that compassion is reserved for loyal members of the tribe and withheld from those who question its sacred myths. The official narrative insisted vaccines were safe and beneficial, therefore, claiming to be injured by them does not signal misfortune — it signals heresy, disloyalty and mendacity. Pover's experience was a challenge to the wider, accepted framework of belief. As she sadly reflected, "The vaccine-injured do not fit in the new Covid world... the Covid world has pushed people into camps that do not allow space for anyone in pain. It doesn't even allow you your own pain."

The Return of Pre-Victorian Business Models

A striking feature of Official Journalism during the Covid pandemic was the return to a pre-Victorian business model based on state subsidy and private patronage. For example in the US, Covid was the first major news story to be bank-rolled by the federal government. Without the restrictions of the Smith-Mundt Act, which had been removed in 2012, the road was open for Washington to pay news organizations to promote its Covid narrative and suppress dissent.

The investigative journalist Chris Pandolfo believes that up to $1 billion of state funding was used during 2021 and 2022 to bribe news organizations to report Covid vaccines in a positive light. The money was funneled via the Department of Health and Human Services which purchased advertising from major news networks including ABC, CBS, and NBC, as well as cable TV news stations Fox News, CNN, and MSN-BC. Newspapers, including *The New York Post*, *The Los Angeles Times*, and *The Washington Post* along with digital media companies such as *BuzzFeed News* and *Newsmax* as well as hundreds of local newspapers and TV stations were also paid as part of a "comprehensive media campaign".

> "These outlets were collectively responsible for publishing count-less articles and video segments regarding the vaccine that were nearly uniformly positive about the vaccine in terms of both its efficacy and safety."[23]

According to Pandolfo, "Congress appropriated $1 billion in fiscal year 2021 for the Secretary of Health to spend on activities to 'strengthen vaccine confidence in the United States.'" Although some of the resulting media content was paid advertising, some was presented as unbiased reportage. In many cases it was a confusing mixture of both. For example, highly emotional,

> "Fear-based vaccine ads from HHS featuring 'survivor' stories from coronavirus patients who were hospitalized in intensive care units were covered by CNN and discussed on ABC's 'The View' when they were unveiled last October."

Unofficial journalist Emerald Robinson accused Official Journalism of blatant corruption. For two years, she said, professional news orga-nizations pocketed money from the federal government to promote the official vaccine narrative. Robinson described it as the most extensive propaganda campaign in the history of the world,

"The largest and most comprehensive breach of journalistic ethics that has ever occurred. Almost everybody took the money. Almost everybody lied about the vaccines (knowingly or unknowingly). Almost everybody refused to report anything negative about the vaccines — because they were paid to close their eyes. Almost everybody is implicated."[24]

However, state subsidy was not the only form of funding that shaped media coverage of Covid. The investigative reporter Tim Schwab described how the Bill and Melinda Gates Foundation gifted hundreds of millions of dollars to news organizations including the BBC, *The Guardian*, *The Financial Times*, *Medium* and *Le Monde*. Schwab said the precise extent of Gates' funding is unknown. However, he says it touched all aspects of Official Journalism including training and education,

"Gates-backed think tanks turn out media fact sheets and newspaper opinion pieces. Magazines and scientific journals get Gates money to publish research and articles. Experts coached in Gates-funded programs write columns that appear in media outlets from *The New York Times* to *The Huffington Post*, while digital portals blur the line between journalism and spin."[25]

In the UK, Laura Dodsworth observed a similar shift to a new journalistic business model. Dodsworth noted the decline in commercial advertising revenue during the pandemic and how state funding was replacing it,

"There was a 48% decline in traditional advertising spend in the UK in the lockdown period 23 March to 30 June. Public Health England became the UK's largest advertiser, and the government the sixth biggest advertiser, during this time. The chancellor, Rishi Sunak, announced in April 2020 that the UK would spend £35 million on the 'All in, All together' advertising campaign in national and regional newspapers. Did that set the tone for editorial coverage at the outset of the epidemic?"[26]

In other words, the Boomer generation's desire to abandon impartiality and return to a pre-Victorian model of journalism, had, by the 2020's, found its natural corollary — a pre-Victorian business model. Ironically therefore, Official Journalism's rejection of impartiality and its tolerance of self-censorship and pro-social lying led it, via a series of inevitable steps, back towards the corrupt, mercenary journalism of the 18th Century. This is because ethical-political narratives can be easily influenced and shaped. Therefore, when journalism adopts an epistemology in which facts follow narrative, then control of the narrative becomes supremely important. Whoever controls the narrative, also controls which facts will be heard, and which suppressed. The scientist and writer Guy Hatchard argues that, during the Covid pandemic, many official journalists, perhaps unwittingly, danced to the tune of a matrix of interests with the power and money to shape the narrative to serve its own interests,

> "As we exit the pandemic, it is apparent that the promoters of pharmaceutical biotech dreams and fantasies have a bulging public relations war chest. There is a lot of money, prestige, and political capital riding on an officially sanctioned A+ rating for the Covid pandemic response. Part and parcel of this is the adjustment of fact to fit the genetic vaccine safety narrative."[27]

This is essentially the methodology of 18th Century journalism applied to the early 21st Century. It is a methodology where facts follow narrative, narrative is determined by what is deemed ethically-politically good, and what is deemed ethically-politically good is shaped by what is lucrative, rewarding and profitable. This is precisely the truthophobic type of journalism the Victorians despised and replaced with a form of journalism based on objective, impartial reporting.

Social Media and Censorship

The second half of Sharman's pincer comprised the giant social media corporations which also promoted Official Truth during the pandemic and choked off access to unofficial information and opinion. *Facebook*, for example, announced it would censor views that contradicted the expert consensus,

> "We do not allow false claims about the vaccines or vaccination programmes which public health experts have advised us could

lead to COVID-19 vaccine rejection. This includes false claims about the safety, efficacy, ingredients, development, existence or conspiracies related to the vaccine or vaccination programme."

For *Facebook*, as for Official Journalism, truth was understood as Official Truth — the advice of "public health experts". Dissent from the consensus was misinformation. Hence, *Facebook* announced it would not tolerate "claims that COVID-19 vaccines kill or seriously harm people."[28]

Twitter took a similar approach warning users, "You may not use *Twitter*'s services to share false or misleading information about COVID-19 which may lead to harm." The company explained, "We've observed the emergence of persistent conspiracy theories, alarmist rhetoric unfounded in research or credible reporting, and a wide range of false narratives and unsubstantiated rumors."[29] *Twitter* defined misleading information as "claims contrary to health authorities" and said it would suppress,

"False or misleading information regarding the safety or science behind approved or authorized COVID-19 vaccines, such as: The vaccines will cause you to be sick, spread the virus, or would be more harmful than getting COVID-19."

YouTube's vaccine misinformation policy adopted the same epistemology and announced it would not permit users to post videos that questioned Official Truth,

"*YouTube* doesn't allow content that poses a serious risk of egregious harm by spreading medical misinformation about currently administered vaccines that are approved and confirmed to be safe and effective by local health authorities and by the World Health Organization (WHO). This is limited to content that contradicts local health authorities' or the WHO's guidance on vaccine safety, efficacy, and ingredients."[30]

These policies demonstrate the viciously circular nature of Official Truth. When scrutinized, it reduces to the following formula: "Covid vaccines are safe and effective, therefore those who disagree are spreading misinformation. We know they're spreading misinformation because we know the vaccines are safe and effective". The same self-confirming logic was even applied to cases involving knowledgeable virologists, epidemiologists and immunologists where the argument ran, "We know the vaccines are safe and effective because that is the expert consensus. Experts who disagree with the consensus are spreading misinformation. We know they're spreading misinformation because they disagree with the consensus." Self-referential, circular reasoning is the curse of the Boomer Epistemology, and, during the pandemic, it silenced the voices of many eminent scientists. The US researcher Robert Malone was banned by *Twitter* despite being an important figure in the development of mRNA technology and hence a respectable and authoritative commentator. Malone became a vocal critic of the decision to vaccinate children arguing,

"Children risk severe, adverse events from receiving the vaccine. Permanent physical damage to the brain, heart, immune and reproductive system associated with SARS-CoV-2 spike protein-based genetic vaccines has been demonstrated in children... Unfortunately, the topic has become highly politicized, and active censorship by legacy media outlets has made it difficult for parents and stakeholders to obtain access to the actual data required for the full informed consent"[31]

Because he contradicted the official narrative, Malone was banned from *Twitter* in December 2021. He said he was disappointed, but not surprised,

"We all knew it would happen eventually. Today it did. Over a half million followers gone in a blink of an eye. That means I must have been on the mark, so to speak. Over the target. It also means we lost a critical component in our fight to stop these vaccines being mandated for children and to stop the corruption in our governments, as well as the medical-industrial complex and pharmaceutical industries."[32]

The following week, Malone echoed Sharman's observation that there existed an Orwellian pincer movement made up of Official Journalism and the big social media corporations.

"We have also been living through the most massive, globally coordinated propaganda and censorship campaign in the history of the human race. All major mass media and the social media technology companies have coordinated to stifle and suppress any discussion of the risks of the genetic vaccines."[33]

In the UK, *Twitter* threatened an award-winning epidemiologist with a similar fate when he questioned the official Covid narrative. The highly credentialled Professor Carl Heneghan, director of the University of Oxford's Centre for Evidence-Based Medicine, found his account temporarily frozen after suggesting the death toll from Covid may have been overstated. Heneghan was told he was,

"Violating the policy on spreading misleading and potentially harmful information related to Covid-19… content that goes directly against guidance from authoritative sources of global and local public health information."[34]

The irony was that Heneghan was himself an authoritative source of public health information.

Although dismissed by Official Journalism as dangerous conspiracy theorists, Malone and Sharman proved to be remarkably accurate. The big social media corporations *were* supressing facts and opinions that didn't fit the official narrative. In late 2022, *Twitter*'s new owner Elon Musk, released internal documents which revealed the extent of the censorship. The unofficial journalist David Zweig was given access to the documents and explained,

"HOW TWITTER RIGGED THE COVID DEBATE:
- By censoring info that was true but inconvenient to U.S. govt. policy.
- By discrediting doctors and other experts who disagreed.
- By suppressing ordinary users, including some sharing the CDC's own data."[35]

Reviewing *Twitter*'s internal emails and records, Zweig discovered,

"Many medical and public health professionals who expressed perspectives or even cited findings from accredited academic journals that conflicted with official positions were also targeted. As a result, legitimate findings and questions about our Covid policies and their consequences went missing... Dissident yet legitimate content was labeled as misinformation, and the accounts of doctors and others were suspended both for tweeting opinions and demonstrably true information."[36]

Twitter was not alone in censoring information and opinion that dissented from the official Covid narrative. Court papers released in early 2023 showed *Facebook* and other organizations changed their algorithms in response to pressure from the US government. As *The Wall Street Journal* reported,

"Newly released documents show that the White House has played a major role in censoring Americans on social media. Email exchanges between Rob Flaherty, the White House's director of digital media, and social-media executives prove the companies put Covid censorship policies in place in response to relentless, coercive pressure from the White House — not voluntarily."[37]

According to unofficial journalist Joy Pullmann, the revelations proved the US government was using CIA-style "regime-change tactics" on US citizens. The information contained in the new documents, "reinforces and enlarges shocking conclusions about the corruption of American government", and illuminate how the U.S. bureaucracy pushed communications monopolies to, "shut down discourse that undermines the administrative state." Pullman noted that even search engines were involved in manipulating what the public believed by changing their algorithms to make dissenting voices disappear, "The emails also showed *Google* employees confirming to the White House that they are algorithmically killing the reach of speech."[38]

Journalism and Systems of Government

The Covid pandemic marked the final evolution of journalism into Official Journalism — a form of public communication whose role is to promote and defend Official Truth. The American attorney and author Robert F Kennedy Jnr says it is a form of journalism made possible by the existence of ,"credulous journalists who do not ask critical questions" and who accepted during the pandemic that, "the science was what the regulators declared it to be." With few exceptions he said,

> "It is a media populated by journalists who don't even attempt to understand the science. These journalistic interpreters of those they label scientists are pawns in the hands of authorities in long-sleeved, white laboratory coats."[39]

Kennedy described impartial, Victorian Liberal Journalism as an, "artifact of an expired era... a quaint relic of a time when editors and producers still permitted their reporters and correspondents to express skepticism." Kennedy also noted that Official Journalism is not designed to support individual decision making and independent, critical thinking. Hence, it is not designed to support Victorian Liberal Democracy. Instead, it is suited to life in Boomertopia where citizens would live in a form of post democracy — liberated from the tedious, effortful businesses of researching things for themselves and able to concentrate on gratifying their personal desires. Kennedy argued therefore that the Covid pandemic marked, not just the final demise of Victorian Liberal Journalism, but also of Victorian Liberal Democracy. It was being replaced, he said, by the illiberal rule of an elite aristocracy of unelected, technocrats who had,

> "Pulled off the ultimate coup d'état: some 250 years after America's historic revolt against entrenched oligarchy and authoritarian rule, the American experiment with self-government was over. The oligarchy was restored, and these gentlemen and their spymasters had equipped the rising technocracy with new tools of control unimaginable to King George or to any other tyrant in history."

Kennedy's assessment echoed that of the political scientist Samuel Huntington who described the rise of a post-democracy ruled by a global elite of, "dead or dying souls". This elite,

> "Labeled 'Davos Men', 'gold-collar workers' or . . . 'cosmocrats'... includes academics, international civil servants and executives in global companies, as well as successful high-technology entrepreneurs."[40]

Members of the new elite, said Huntington, "abandon their commitment to their nation and their fellow citizens and argue the moral superiority of identifying with humanity at large." He identified a strong generational element in this worldview. It was, he said, the product of the Boomer Ideology. For example, in colleges and universities, "the radical students of the 1960s have become tenured professors, particularly in elite institutions."

In the UK, the historian and former British Supreme Court Judge Jonathan Sumption, reached a similar conclusion, warning that government was falling into the hands of a technocratic caste of experts which believed itself to be both benevolent and infallible. Whereas Kennedy singled out Anthony Fauci, the Chief Medical Advisor to the President for special criticism, Sumption took aim at his British counterpart, the influential Sir Jeremy Farrar, accusing him of having a fanatical faith in his mission,

"He is terrifyingly sincere and really does have the interest of mankind at heart. Therein lies the problem. There are few more obsessive fanatics than the technocrat who is convinced that he is reordering an imperfect world for its own good."[41]

Sumption said that Farrer was, "convinced he's right and the Government should listen to no one else", disagreement was a "hurdle" which "just gets in his way". Sumption argued that the technocratic class was composed of, "frustrated autocrats" — pitiless individuals who opposed personal freedom and who were zealous for lockdowns and other restrictions,

"Entirely missing from Farrar's worldview is any conception of the complexity of the moral judgments involved. Of course public health matters, but it is not all that matters. Interaction with other human beings is a fundamental human need. Criminalising it is a sustained assault on our humanity. Doing so without assessing the wider consequences is irresponsible folly."

The Covid pandemic vividly illustrated the continued, rapid evolution of Anglo-American journalism into two competing journalisms powered by two incompatible, mutually-hostile epistemologies and ideologies. These

382

journalisms are designed to facilitate two very different types of democracy. The clash between the two journalisms was further sharpened by the next major news story of the 2020's — the conflict between Russia and the West over Ukraine.

Chapter 31

Russia Invades Ukraine and the Rise of Authoritarian Journalism

"I beseech you, in the bowels of Christ, think it possible you may be mistaken."
Oliver Cromwell.

The Russian invasion of Ukraine in February 2022 did not occur in a vacuum. As the foreign affairs expert Angela Stent summarizes, "The current crisis between Russia and Ukraine is a reckoning that has been 30 years in the making".[1] According to the influential American foreign policy expert John Mearsheimer, the single biggest cause of the fighting was the West's disregard of Russian strategic interests. Mearsheimer argues the West provoked Russia by seeking to bring Ukraine into NATO and making it an anti-Russian state. The consequences, he says, were entirely predictable,

> "Those who believe in facts and logic will quickly discover that the United States and its allies are mainly responsible for this train wreck... The tragic truth is that if the West had not pursued NATO expansion into Ukraine, it is unlikely there would be a war in Ukraine today… Washington played the central role in leading Ukraine down the path to destruction. History will judge the United States and its allies with abundant harshness for its remarkably foolish policy on Ukraine."[2]

Mearsheimer also observes, "It is widely and firmly believed in the West that Putin is solely responsible for causing the Ukraine crisis" because he has "imperial ambitions". However, although this narrative is, "repeated over and over in the mainstream media and by virtually every western leader", Mearsheimer concludes there is little or no evidence to support it.

In war, it is often said, truth is the first casualty. It is standard operating procedure to portray your adversaries as blood-soaked murderers; inhuman monsters who take pleasure in slaughtering innocent civilians, women and children. One's own side, on the other hand, are never portrayed as committing atrocities or war crimes. We fight honorably and fairly, and only in self-defense. Writing in the 1950s, Walter Lippmann described this age-old formula. When military conflict breaks out, he said, the population has to be "drugged by propaganda" into believing the enemy is "altogether evil" and our side "nearly perfect". According to this simplistic narrative, the destruction of the enemy will lead, somehow, to a better world for all. It is necessary to promote this fantasy because people would be reluctant to support war, and pay for it, unless they were incited by the state to, "paroxysms of hatred and to Utopian dreams". Thus the need for propaganda designed to stir up a mixture of, "envenomed hatred and furious righteousness".[3]

When the invasion began, Russia was therefore unsurprisingly cast in the role of evil villain by Official Journalism. *Time* magazine described Putin as a vampire who wanted to rape Ukraine and drink its blood,

> "Vladimir Putin is an old man scared of death trying to turn back time. Ukraine and Ukrainians are as his blood sacrifice. His invasion of their country is his attempt to forestall his personal, inevitable demise."[4]

Putin, the article continued, wanted to, "return to the past: take Ukraine back to the 19th century, to the Soviet Union, to his youth. He rambles menacingly about restoring the glories of the Russian Empire."

The *Guardian*'s Luke Harding compared Putin to Hitler and Stalin, and portrayed him as a tyrant disconnected from reality, "Putin has been living in an alternative reality for a long time... It's what you might call 'dictator syndrome'." Harding reduced the conflict in the Ukraine to a simple narrative in which a ruthless psychopath, "decided he's going to annihilate a country and its people." Putin, said Harding, should be understood as a brutal thug who enjoyed assassinating opponents and who had turned Russia into a "mafia state". Putin was a gangster who wanted everyone to know, "All enemies of Putin will die in a very terrible way."[5]

Writing in *The Hill*, Alexander Motyl also compared Putin to Hitler, "The striking similarities between Vladimir Putin's Russia and Adolf Hitler's Germany are not accidental." Since Putin and Hitler were so similar, Motyl prophesied Putin would suffer the same fate, "Hitler committed suicide in his bunker... Fittingly, Putin reportedly also resides in a bunker. In all likelihood, that's where he, too, will meet his end."[6]

The commentator David Ignatius told MSMBC's Joe Scarborough that Putin was a mad dictator cut off from the world, dreaming blood-thirsty dreams of conquest,

> "He's a man out of time and a man out of touch. He sits in the Kremlin isolated. The circle of advisors around him, I'm told, has shrunk and shrunk until it's just a handful of people... Nobody sees him, people can't even get in to talk to him. Remember

those crazy pictures of him at a long table. What kind of leader has a table like that? Like a bowling alley table! That's Putin!"[7]

According to MSNBC, Putin is driven by a pathological hatred of modernity and progress — someone who wants to turn the clock back to dark ages of traditional, Christian values, "He resents he way Ukrainians are becoming Western, modern people. He doesn't like it. He wants things to be like they were in the old days."

These media narratives were generally indistinguishable from the official narratives of Western governments. Official Journalism revealed itself therefore to be highly collusive — sharing a common worldview and set of values with politicians and policy makers. For example, the British Prime Minister Boris Johnson also reduced the conflict to a simple struggle between good and evil,

"It is a conflict that has no moral ambiguities or no gray areas. This is about the right of Ukrainians to protect themselves against Putin's violent and murderous aggression... It is about Ukrainian democracy against Putin's tyranny. It is about freedom versus oppression. It is about right versus wrong. It is about good versus evil."[8]

Another feature of the journalistic landscape was Western censorship of Russian media which made it harder for audiences to access facts or opinions that contradicted Official Truth. *Russia Today*, the Russian-government-controlled news network, was removed from the schedules of DirecTV and Roku, the largest U.S. pay-tv providers. At the same time, the big social media corporations were also suppressing Russian voices. As unofficial journalists at *Consortium News* reported, "DirecTV's move comes hours after *Facebook, YouTube* and other social networks announced plans to limit access to Russian state-controlled media outlets RT and *Sputnik* across Europe".[9] The European Commission President Ursula von der Leyen announced a similar move to silence Russian broadcasters,

""We will ban the Kremlin's media machine in the EU. The state-owned *Russia Today* and *Sputnik*, and their subsidiaries, will no longer be able to spread their lies to justify Putin's war," she said. "We are developing tools to ban their toxic and harmful disinformation in Europe."[10]

In the UK, the regulator Ofcom followed suit and revoked RT's license to broadcast. Ofcom said it, "recognised that RT is funded by the Russian state, which has recently invaded a neighbouring sovereign country."[11] Western censorship of Russian media prompted Russia to respond in kind. Kremlin spokesman Dmitry Peskov said, "Of course, we will take similar measures of pressure on Western media that operate in our country." "RT has been blocked and cannot operate in Europe". Europeans, he added, are, "Trampling on their own ideals."[12]

The veteran media theorist Noam Chomsky described the level of censorship as "unprecedented". Contemporary Western journalism, he said, seemed to be designed to produce misinformed citizens,

"Censorship in the United States has reached a level beyond anything in my lifetime. Such a level that you are not permitted to read the Russian position. Literally. Americans are not allowed to know what the Russians are saying. Except, selected things... If the Russians make an offer for a negotiation, you can't find it. That's suppressed... I have never seen a level of censorship like this."[13]

The celebrated war correspondent John Pilger took a similar view, pointing out there are always two sides to every conflict, but Official Journalism was only reporting one,

"Nothing should be trusted unless you're going to sit in front of your television and deconstruct what you see – actually check it and try to verify it as much as you can, and if you can't, then discard it. Well, most people don't have the time to do that."[14]

The Unofficial Journalist Jim Rickards accused Official Journalism of reporting only information that supported the official narrative. Facts that contradicted it, he said, were omitted. "Almost everything you heard about the war in Ukraine from U.S. media" Rickards said, "was a lie."

"You heard that Putin was losing the war. You heard that Russians had poor training and low morale and were deserting in droves. You heard that Ukrainians were destroying Russian armor in large numbers to blunt the Russian advance. None of this was true... It's not that I'm pro-Russian — I'm not. I'm pro-truth. And I don't defend the Russian invasion in any way (although I do understand it)."[15]

The Unofficial Journalist Arta Moeini said the, "establishment's Manichean narrative" relied on the constant repetition of accusations of war crimes against the Russians, while the Ukrainians were cast either as helpless civilians, or brave, noble warriors. It was journalism, he said, designed to provoke an emotional response,

"Not only has the Ukraine coverage been highly charged, morally self-righteous, and plainly political, it actively demands a collective suspension of disbelief as it cultivates and redirects a natural reaction of sympathy felt by all into a moral outrage that insists on certain retaliation."

Official Journalism, he said, had become, "narrative control and information warfare targeting domestic audiences". He accused official journalists of claiming a monopoly over truth and attempted to marginalize and neutralize dissenters by branding them, "appeasers, apologists, and/or outright traitors." Simply pointing out there are always "at least two sides to a conflict" was, "now tantamount to championing tyranny."[16]

Journalism's New Role: Policing the Narrative

Another characteristic of Official Journalism's coverage of the Ukraine conflict was its militant intolerance of alternative points of view. Hence, the war marked a further step in journalism's evolution — from reporting news, to actively stamping out dissent and demonizing impartiality. For example, BBC News' award-winning current affairs documentary series *File on 4* dedicated an entire episode to attacking two British academics because they called for independent, critical thinking. Dr Justin Schlosberg, Reader in Journalism and Media at Birkbeck University in London, and Professor Tim Hayward, a philosopher at the University of Edinburgh,

389

both expressed doubt about the completeness and truthfulness of Official Journalism's reports.

Both were careful to avoid taking the Russian side. For example, referring to events in the town of Bucha in April 2022, Schlosberg Tweeted, "TO BE CLEAR: a civilian massacre may well have occurred for which Russia should be held responsible and accountable, on top of other heinous war crimes".[17]

However, he also Tweeted disapproval of uncritical anti-Russian reporting which he said was little more than journalists parroting government propaganda. Western media, he said, must avoid becoming, "stenographers of their governments rather than anything that could remotely be considered independent journalism."[18] Schlosberg and Hayward's skepticism and lack of zeal for Official Truth, plus the fact they were active on social media, soon attracted the attention of Official Journalism.

The BBC documentary ominously told the audience, "Welcome to a parallel reality, where facts are batted away and conspiracies abound." The voice-over explained, "A number of people here in Britain" were happy to believe and repeat "Russian stories of false attacks and staged massacres." "Most worrying of all" the narration continued, some of those sharing Russian disinformation were university academics, "responsible for shaping young minds and influencing the way the next generation understands the world they live in."[19] The documentary featured the voices of several British officials, such as Minister for Education Nadhim Zahawi who said,

"Putin and his cronies are a malign influence on anyone in this country buying their false narrative. And I have to repeat, it is a false and dangerous narrative, and we will crack down on it hard."

James Roscoe, UK Ambassador to the UN General Assembly, explained that questioning Official Truth was dangerous because it created doubt and undermined certainty among the audience,

"What they hear is, 'this fact is disputed' and that's the critical thing, I think, in all of this. They hear that there are two sides to this story, and they're not in a position to make a decision one way or the other."

Marianna Spring, the BBC's specialist disinformation and misinformation reporter, explained those who wanted to hear both sides of the argument were guilty of "distorting the narrative", while journalist and commentator Paul Mason said those repeating the Russian version of events were *ipso facto* supporting it, "They're actively promoting the talking points and disinformation of the Kremlin. I think that is objectively being pro-Putin." Mason also argued it was dangerous to point out that some statements of fact were contested, or poorly supported by evidence, "The degradation of facts into 'maybes'" he said, "is really important."

The documentary failed to mention the Tweet in which Schlosberg stated Russia may well have committed "heinous war crimes". By omitting it, *File on 4* gave audiences the impression Schlosberg was uncritical of Russia. The omission was, Schlosberg concluded, "a deliberate attempt to mislead."[20] For the BBC to manipulate audience perception in this way, especially in a show about disinformation was, he said, "beyond shameful."[21]

The BBC also sent an email to Schlosberg's employer Birkbeck University, provocatively asking, "Is the university aware that Justin Schlosberg is sharing articles containing disinformation about the war in Ukraine and about Coronavirus?" This, says Schlosberg, was a deliberate and sinister attempt by the BBC to denounce and punish him for questioning the consensus narrative. It is a tactic, he says, that has become disturbingly common,

> "I have been subject to repeated formal complaints submitted to my university by journalists. One journalist from *The Times* submitted repeated, outrageous complaints which were all rejected out of hand. It's a troll campaign to get me fired. So, the way the BBC contacted my employer was actually disturbingly reflective of these kinds of attacks... It's quite astonishing really".[22]

Schlosberg believes, "Something has shifted in newsroom culture." The narrative is today seen simplistically as either absolutely true, or else a lie. Contemporary journalism, he says, has a problem dealing with the,

"Messiness and uncertainty of truth. It presents things as a black and white binary. It says in effect 'there are only facts and lies' and we tell you facts, while they tell you lies. Whereas, what we're really dealing with here is controversy and conflicting claims and perspectives which we may never have sufficient evidence to determine one way or the other. The inevitable gray area of uncertainty that hangs around a lot of controversies has been lost. We have created the illusion of certainty and we have eradicated uncertainty. We have lost the ability to say 'we don't know'".

Tim Hayward, who was also accused by the documentary of helping Russia in its disinformation efforts, agrees journalism has changed. It has become narrativized and intolerant of dissent,

"This new style of journalism seems to be underpinned by the view that, 'there are not two sides — there is only one side and we're going to tell you what it is'. But there *are* two sides, or there wouldn't be conflict! For most of my career, pointing that out would have been a banal thing to say. Now it's controversial. That is extraordinary!"[23]

The documentary reveals the extent to which journalism has changed. The spectacle of BBC journalists attempting to publicly humiliate academics, and contacting their employers to intimidate them, for the crime of encouraging independent critical thinking would have been regarded as grotesque by Victorian Liberal journalists. For example, Desmond Taylor, Editor of BBC TV News in the pre-Boomer era, described responsible journalism as "disinterested journalism". It was the duty of journalists, he said, to be as detached and as neutral as humanly possible. As he explained, "We suppress our views and it is an effort." This way of thinking was, of course, based on the epistemology of the Anglo-American Enlightenment. Since journalists could not possess God-like knowledge of what was true and false, their function was limited to reporting facts as accurately and honestly as possible. Because they were as ignorant as everyone else, and could not know the truth with certainty, journalists had to behave with epistemic humility and report both sides. As Taylor put it, a journalist,

"Must have the same attitude to his raw material that an employee of a bank has to its money — it isn't his. He is handling it on behalf of other people, he must preserve it scrupulously, never convert it to his own use. He must not try to change people's minds, or confirm their beliefs; he must give them the untainted information they need to make up their own minds. He cannot aim to move events, from however worthy a motive and for however worthy an end."[24]

Responding to Boomer pressure for more active, committed journalism, Taylor said it would be irresponsible to assume journalists possessed superior, certain knowledge. Journalists were not, he said, entitled to use journalism as a tool for solving complex political problems,

"It would be arrogant and insupportable if we tried to take a hand in solving them ourselves and strayed outside the strictly journalistic role. Provided we stick to that, and do our job well, society is not hurt. The effect of journalism is, in the long run, to heal."

We might call this 'Taylor's Law'. It states that honesty is the best policy for journalists. Honest, impartial journalism may provoke quarrels between people in the short term; but — in the long run — it promotes understanding and leads to better outcomes. Ethical-political journalism, on the other hand, which encourages pro-social lying, may create the comforting illusion of consensus and agreement in the short term, but — in the long run — causes anger and division. Modern, Official Journalism therefore, although it aspires to make the world a better place, does so by stamping out dialogue and debate. In the process, it breeds resentment and inflames conflict. Official Journalism reverses Taylor's Law. It does not heal society's wounds, it keeps them open and unhealed.

The need for frank, honest discussion was widely recognized during the pre-Boomer era. The American jurist Murray Gurfein, for example, said the expression of different, opposing views served as a vital safety valve for society. Therefore, the long-term benefit of allowing them to be voiced, outweighed the short term pain of having to listen to views which we might find uncomfortable, or with which we might strongly disagree,

"A cantankerous press, an obstinate press, a ubiquitous press must be suffered by those in authority to preserve the even greater values of freedom of expression and the right of the people to know... There is no greater safety valve for discontent and cynicism about the affairs of Government than freedom of expression in any form. This has been the genius of our institutions throughout our history."[25]

Modern, Official Journalism rejects Taylor's Law and Gurfein's mature wisdom. It craves something better and more perfect than disagreement, uncertainty and endless quarreling. It is Utopian and aspires to the creation of a world in which everyone agrees and sings the same song in perfect harmony.

Authoritarian Journalism

The type of journalism which *File on 4* exemplifies is described by the Unofficial Journalist Glenn Greenwald as 'Authoritarian Journalism'. It is recognizable, he says, by its methodology of, "censorship and the destruction of reputations." Its goal is not the impartial search for truth, but to root out and punish those who question the consensus, and who undermine Official Truth. It is the opposite of Victorian Liberal Journalism — the "very antithesis of journalism" as Greenwald puts it. In a scathing denunciation, he says authoritarian journalists,

> "Cannot abide the idea that there can be any place on the internet where people are free to speak in ways they do not approve. Like some creepy informant for a state security apparatus, they spend their days trolling the depths of chat rooms... to find anyone — influential or obscure — who is saying something they believe should be forbidden."[27]

Having identified their targets, authoritarian journalists conduct defamatory, *ad hominem* attacks to silence those who dissent from their informational hegemony, "They do it" says Greenwald, "out of hubris: the belief that their worldview is so indisputably right that all dissent is inherently dangerous 'disinformation.'" According to Greenwald, these tactics have become widespread and are an accepted part of the, "prevailing ethos in corporate journalism". Those who plead for impartiality, who are skeptical of the official narrative and who want to hear the other side of the argument become targets for authoritarian journalists who hunt them down and accuse them of,

"Any kind of bigotry that casually crosses your mind — just smear them as a racist, misogynist, homophobe, transphobe, etc. without the slightest need for evidence — and it will be regarded as completely acceptable."

Authoritarian Journalism attempts to intimidate dissenters into silence. Its methodology is to manufacture the illusion of consensus by bullying. How many people, Greenwald asks, are,

"Intimidated into silence and conformity. They know if they express views these Stasi agents and their bosses dislike, their reputations can be instantly destroyed. So they remain silent or pliant out of necessity."

Greenwald's verdict is that contemporary authoritarian journalists deserve nothing but "intense scorn."

Authoritarian Journalism is not an extraordinary or unexpected phenomenon. It is simply the logical outcome of the Boomer way of knowing and how the Boomers changed the concept of truth. It is what happens when the impartial search for truth is shifted to second place behind the well-meaning desire to make the world a better place. It is what happens when journalists come to believe they possess certain knowledge about what is true and false, and what is ethically-politically good and bad. It is what happens when truth is understood as the consensus of 'people like us' — as the narrative constructed by the benevolent experts of our tribe — journocrats and politicians in positions of power and authority. When this happens, it becomes the ethical-political duty of journalists to self-censor and use forms of pro-social lying for the benefit of the community. Facts and opinions that contradict the official narrative serve no useful purpose and are viewed as misinformation. Those who spread them become the modern equivalent of 17th Century witches. Their Tweets and social media posts are spells that trick us, confuse us, fill us with doubt and further the work of the devil. Hence, it becomes legitimate for journalists to hunt these people down and expose them. Shaming them becomes part of journalism's social function. Thus does Official Journalism become Authoritarian Journalism. Thus, does a pre-Renaissance epistemology beget a pre-Renaissance form of journalism.

Chapter 32

The Pornification
of Journalism

Pornography is often referred to as 'dehumanizing' — not because its subject matter is obscene, but because it paints a dishonest picture of human beings and human nature. Seen through pornography's distorting lens, men and women are degraded into beasts, objects for each other's gratification. Driven only by their primitive urges and lusts, they cease to be complex, thinking creatures capable of creativity, self-control, love, sacrifice, loyalty and affection. Pornography's lens sees only a single aspect of our humanity and exaggerates it, blurring and excluding all others. It strips human beings of agency and depicts them as helpless creatures at the mercy of blind, implacable forces. As Duncan Williams put it, to do this is to dehumanize,

"To emphasize man's primitivism, to ignite his baser passions, to question his capacity for sympathy and empathy, in short to depict him as merely a trousered ape, is not only a form of literary, aesthetic and philosophic dishonesty. It is a sin against life itself, a crime against humanity."[1]

Contemporary, Narrative-Led Journalism is also, in its own way, dehumanizing. It seduces audiences with the visceral power of narrative. It prevents them seeing the other side of the argument because, in Narrative-Led Journalism, there is no other side of the argument worth seeing. Those who disagree are not just wrong, they are bad. Seen through the lens of modern Official Journalism, dissenters cease to be complex human beings with feelings and opinions as valid as our own. Instead, they are objectified and become receptacles for our hatred, anger, fear and prejudice. They are the tribal other who threaten us with disturbing heresies and whose voices must be stilled. Like porn, Official Journalism's one-sidedness inflames our feelings and passions. It incites us to act. It limits our ability to think, reason and debate. It closes the door to understanding. *Homo sapiens*, the thinking individual, is reduced to *homo narrans*, the slave of narrative. As the journalist Will Storr puts it, narrative assigns to the opposing group purely selfish motives,

"It hears their most powerful arguments in a particular mode of spiteful lawyerliness, seeking to misrepresent or discard what they have to say. It uses the most appalling transgressions of their very worst members as a brush to smear them all. It takes its individuals and erases their depth and diversity. It turns them into outlines; morphs their tribe into a herd of silhouettes. It denies those silhouettes the empathy, humanity and patient understanding that it lavishes on its own. And, when it does all this, it makes us feel great, as if we're the moral hero of an exhilarating story."[2]

The narrativization of journalism during the late 20th Century was designed to help the Boomer generation change the world and make it a better place. In the process, journalism was pornified.

The toxic legacy of this shift is visible in the 2020s as a coarsening of public discourse. For example, in 2021 former President Barack Obama launched a scathing attack on Steve Bannon, the unofficial journalist and former Chief Strategist to Donald Trump. Obama likened him to Vladimir Putin. Both, he said, were agents of evil who spread dangerous misinformation,

> "People like Putin and Steve Bannon understand it's not necessary for people to believe this information in order to weaken democratic institutions. You just have to flood a country's public square with enough raw sewage. You just have to raise enough questions, spread enough dirt, plant enough conspiracy theorizing, that citizens no longer know what to believe. Once they lose trust in their leaders, in mainstream media, in political institutions, in each other, in the possibility of truth, the game's won."[3]

By portraying Bannon as a dirty creature flooding the country with "raw sewage", Barack Obama was not merely disagreeing with his point of view, he was monsterizing and dehumanizing him. Obama's rhetoric transforms Bannon into a menace to health — a spreader of disease. No evidence is provided. The audience is not told what Bannon said, nor why the former President believed it was misleading. The visceral nature of the attack is reinforced by the phrase , "People like Putin and Steve Bannon" which implies the existence of a dangerous minority group seeking to harm the majority. By arousing our sense of disgust, Obama is tapping into an ancient, tribal emotion. As Will Storr explains, we have evolved to fear the deadly pathogens and diseases that come from contact with dirt,

> "Exposure to carriers of pathogens — in faeces, say, or rotten food — naturally activates feelings of disgust and revulsion... Tribal propaganda exploits these processes by representing enemies as disease-carrying pests such as cockroaches, rats or lice."[4]

In the same speech, Barack Obama also referred to the modern understanding of truth as something which comes from a shared ethical-political intuition. Obama told his audience truth is something that good people *feel*,

"It is a chance for all of us to fight for truth, not absolute truth, not a fixed truth, but to fight for what, deep down, we know is more true; is right."

The former President called for new laws to censor voices like Bannon's. Regulation, he said, "has to be part of the answer".

In 2022, President Biden followed Barack Obama's example and denounced his political opponents as a deviant tribe threatening to drag American back to the pre-Boomer era. They were, he said, abnormal,

"Too much of what's happening in our country today is not normal. Donald Trump and the MAGA Republicans represent an extremism that threatens the very foundations of our republic."[5]

Donald Trump's Make America Great Again movement, said Biden, threatened the "very soul of this country" because it rejected the Boomer consensus and sought to resurrect pre-Boomer values, "MAGA forces" said President Biden, are determined to take this country "backwards",

"MAGA Republicans have made their choice. They embrace anger. They thrive on chaos. They live not in the light of truth but in the shadow of lies. But together — together, we can choose a different path. We can choose a better path. Forward, to the future. A future of possibility. A future to build and dream and hope."

Former President Donald Trump responded to the attack equally aggressively, describing President Biden as an "enemy of the state",

"This week, Joe Biden came to Philadelphia to give the most vicious, hateful and divisive speech ever delivered by an American president, vilifying 75 million citizens… as threats to democracy and as enemies of the state. He's an enemy of the state,"[6]

The public discourse of the early 21st Century is marked by the absence of debate, courtesy, compromise and toleration. Instead of these things, we see the resurgence of narrative and the return of superstition, tribalism and unreason. It was these forces Victorian Liberal Journalism attempted to restrain. It was these forces the Boomers rediscovered and released.

The New Censorship

When a society views deviance and non-conformity as evil, censorship follows. Restraint and moderation become ethical-political sins. Intolerance becomes a virtue. Previous eras burned books to stamp out heresy; contemporary censorship operates differently, but just as effectively. For example, in 2022 the popular online payment system PayPal suspended the accounts of several unofficial journalists and organizations. As Matt Taibbi reported,

> "In the last week or so, the online payment platform PayPal without explanation suspended the accounts of a series of individual journalists and media outlets, including the well-known alt sites *Consortium News* and *MintPress*."[7]

According to Taibbi, *Consortium* was targeted because it had been, "critical of NATO and the Pentagon and a consistent source of skeptical reporting about Russiagate." We were witnessing, he said, censorship by stealth and the creation of a new world in which,

> "Having the wrong opinions can result in your money being frozen or seized. Going after cash is a big jump from simply deleting speech, with a much bigger chilling effect. This is especially true in the alternative media world, where money has long been notoriously tight, and the loss of a few thousand dollars here or there can have a major effect on a site, podcast, or paper."

In September 2022, PayPal took similar punitive action against the *Daily Sceptic*, a popular British unofficial journalism website. PayPal accused the *Sceptic* of violating its Acceptable Use Policy by promoting, "hate, violence or racial intolerance" — although the company did not provide any evidence to support its accusation. The *Sceptic*'s Editor Toby Young said the move was part of a wider trend towards censorship — book burning for the digital age, "This is the new front in the ongoing war against free speech: the withdrawal of financial services from people and organizations that express dissenting opinions." According to Young, the *Daily Sceptic* was targeted, not because it promoted 'hate', but because it regularly published articles questioning the most sacred narratives of the Official Ideology,

> "There are five issues in particular where it's completely verbo-ten to express sceptical views and if you do you can expect to be cancelled, not just by PayPal but by *YouTube, Facebook, Twitter, Instagram*, etc.: the wisdom of the lockdown policy and asso-ciated Covid restrictions, the efficacy and safety of the mRNA vaccines, Net Zero and the 'climate emergency', the need to teach five year-olds that sex is a social construct and the war in Ukraine. Dissent from the prevailing orthodoxy in any of those areas is no longer permitted."[8]

PayPal's behavior alarmed a group of British Members of Parlia-ment who said it was hard to, "avoid construing PayPal's actions as an orchestrated, politically motivated move to silence critical or dissenting views on these topics".[9] Following the political outcry, PayPal reversed its decision and reinstated the *Daily Sceptic*'s account.

The dominant epistemological approach of the early 21st Century has returned us to a world in which we are guided by Tribal Truth and Official Truth. In this world, we are prepared to believe almost anything if we think the majority of our tribe believes it, and if those in positions of power and authority tell us it is true. We have rediscovered the power of narrative and myth and are falling spellbound back into their warm, comfortable embrace. But we have also fallen in love with a cruel episte-mology — one which the historian Peter Gay observes, was responsible for the religious wars of the past — for bitter fighting between rival, im-placable sects, "all claiming possession of infallible truth and denouncing their adversaries as fools or agents of the devil."[10]

Luxury Beliefs

When a society's guiding ideology no longer fits reality, people will make bad decisions. Although well-intentioned, these can prove ruinous and self-destructive. Society will resemble a group of people lost in the desert whose map is wrong. Believing they are walking towards an oasis, every step they take is in fact leading them further into the wilderness. As the eminent economist John Kenneth Galbraith explained, when reality shifts, we find we are led by, "ideas that are relevant to another world; and as a further result we do many things that are unnecessary, some that are unwise and a few that are insane." [11] As our guiding ideology becomes more and more untethered from reality, our decisions appear more and more irrational. The economist Philip Pilkington argues, for example, that Western energy policies based on obsolete, Utopian thinking are causing a devastating global depression. The road to ruin, he says, has been paved with a series of well-intentioned, but suicidal choices,

> "The decisions made that led to the great European energy war of 2022 will likely go down in history as some of the greatest economic and geopolitical miscalculations in the history of mankind. They will join the Treaty of Versailles and the tariff wars of the 1930s in the basket of policy pariahs that future generations will be taught to avoid at all costs. How did we get here? How have such poor decisions been made on our behalf? I will leave it to future historians to work that out."[12]

Henry Kissinger, the veteran former secretary of state and national-security adviser, was similarly perplexed by the West's foreign policy decisions which he said were incomprehensible, "We are at the edge of war with Russia and China on issues which we partly created, without any concept of how this is going to end or what it's supposed to lead to."[13] To save us from ourselves, and from our outdated assumptions, the international relations expert Philip Cunliffe argues that the 2020s will require new theoretical frameworks, new ways of seeing and new ways of knowing,

> "As power continues to diffuse from the unipolar USA, we can expect a multipolar world to be more complex and multi-layered... Such a world will require more careful reference to systemic forces and political competition."[14]

According to Cunliffe, many of our most cherished narratives will inevitably appear to future generations as obsolete "theoretical flourishes" produced by the, "ideological hubris of a past unipolar system". Writing in 2022, the unofficial journalist and blogger Michael Snyder also saw profound change and the emergence of a new, harsher reality,

> "All of our lifestyles are about to change in a major way, but the vast majority of the population still does not understand what is coming... The artificially-inflated lifestyles that we were able to enjoy for decades are now disappearing, and there is a tremendous amount of pain on the horizon."[15]

The blogger Eric Peters believes the post-World War Two era which shaped the Boomer mind was an, "historical anomaly, utterly extraordinary. And it is ending." Every world leader on the planet, he says, "knows this now. Even those who desperately cling to the hope that this is not so." The values and rules for living manufactured by the Boomers are increasingly obsolete and irrelevant. "We must" Peters concludes, "unanchor ourselves from a past that is no longer and proceed with open minds."[16]

In summary, we see the world through the eyes of the Baby Boomer generation. We think Boomer thoughts and we feel with Boomer hearts. Our values, assumptions, hopes, fears and prejudices — our entire ideology and worldview were constructed by the Boomers. Our knowledge of history, our understanding of truth and our journalism were all shaped by the Boomer tribe. Writing in 1969, the journalist Christopher Booker penetratingly observed that the ideology of his generation was based on a, "kind of all-encompassing make-believe". The defining characteristic of the Boomers, he said, was their ability to fantasize,

> "When one is caught up in such a fantasy, like an adolescent infatuation, it can seem more real than anything else in the world. Viewed from the outside, such fantasies can be seen to shape people's thoughts and behaviour to a far greater extent than we commonly recognise... until they work up to a self-destructive catastrophe."[17]

The passage of time allows us to view the Boomer Ideology and its journalism "from the outside" and see them for what they were — rebellions against the imperfections of reality and an attempt to replace what is, with what ought to be. But the Boomers bequeathed a toxic legacy. The Official Ideology cannot provide answers and solutions to the challenges of the 2020s because it was designed as a guide for living during an age of endlessly increasing affluence when the biggest problem was learning how to enjoy life. The ideology constructed by the Boomers offers no way of solving human disagreement and conflict, because it naively assumed that, in Boomertopia, there would be no disagreement or conflict. It is an ideology contemptuous of producing wealth, because it assumed that in Boomertopia there would be an abundance of wealth — one would simply have to redistribute, or print it. Its epistemology discouraged skepticism, because it assumed that perfect knowledge was simply the consensus opinion of benevolent experts of the tribe. The Vortex of Immaturity, in short, produced a luxury belief system which no longer fits the realities of life. As the geo-political and geo-economic tectonic plates shift, the map no longer fits the terrain. The matrix of values and beliefs that guide us — the Utopian fantasies of the Boomers — seem to be increasingly generating irrational decisions and leading us further into the desert.

Why it is Wrong to Blame the Boomers

The Boomers broke Victorian Liberal Journalism. They replaced *aletheia* with *arete* and truth with truthophobia. They erased the distinction between fact and opinion. They changed the way truth and legitimate knowledge were understood. They created Boomer Journalism — a committed, narrativized form of news intended to change the world and make it a better place. They legitimized pro-social lying and freed individuals from the tedious, effortful business of having to take responsibility for their own beliefs. Instead, responsibility for knowing passed to benevolent, elite journocrats. The Boomers, like any successful group, adapted to exploit their habitat. They harvested the fruit that previous generations had grown and planted little themselves because it seemed to them that abundance would last forever. As one Boomer anthem from 1968 perceptively put it,

> "Those were the days, my friend,
> We thought they'd never end,
> We'd sing and dance forever and a day,

We'd live the life we choose,
We'd fight and never lose,
For we were young and sure to have our way."[18]

As the lens of time slowly turns, it brings the Boomer Ideology into historical focus. It enables us to see Boomer values, not as eternal and fixed, but as part of an ever shifting continuum — a set of values appropriate for their time. But this insight does not entitle us to blame them. It is not the fault of the Boomers they developed new ways of seeing and knowing to fit the world they inhabited. It is the right of every generation to change the ideology it inherits. Failure to do so leads to stagnation and decay. It is not the fault of the Boomers that they changed everything — but it will be the fault of subsequent generations if they change nothing. The generational challenge of the Millennials and their children is to avoid becoming unthinking replicas of the Boomers and uncritical defenders of their ideology in a rapidly-changing world. By the same logic, the truthophobic Official Journalism of the 2020s, developed by the Boomers, is fast becoming anachronistic. The political cartoonist and unofficial journalist Bob Moran is one of those who calls for an end to committed, ethical-political news and a return to impartial truth seeking on the Victorian Liberal model,

"We need journalists who seek the truth above all else and upon finding it, however unpleasant or inconvenient it may be, give it to the people without hesitation. We need them now more than ever."[19]

But this is easier said than done.

Most contemporary journalists are attracted to the idea of telling the truth, but they understand it as Tribal Truth — something that can be known intuitively without listening to both sides of the argument. For example, a recent survey of seventy-five journalists entitled *Beyond Objectivity* calls for journalism to, "move beyond accuracy to truth". The report attacks Victorian Liberal notions of objectivity and impartiality referring to them as "outmoded". "Journalistic 'objectivity' or 'balance'" it says, leads to "'bothsides-ism' — a dangerous trap when covering issues like climate change." The report suggests there is something ethically-politically questionable about impartial journalism and hints it may even be racist,

"A growing number of journalists of color and younger white reporters, including LGBTQ+ people, believe that objectivity has become an increasingly outdated and divisive concept that prevents truly accurate reporting informed by their own backgrounds, experiences and points of view."[20]

What the report reveals is that when truth is understood as the consensus of the in-group, 'telling the truth' becomes an exercise in finding different voices from within the group to say the same thing in different ways. What this understanding of diversity lacks however, is diversity of thought and opinion. Only the official narrative is allowed because truth is Official Truth. For example, as the report makes clear, "issues like climate change" cannot be questioned.

In the 17th Century, Galileo invited philosophers to look through his telescope and see for themselves evidence that the Earth moved around the sun, and not the other way round. To his dismay, these eminent, highly-educated men refused to look because they were terrified of what they might see. They feared that looking at the evidence, might undermine their entire worldview and cause it to collapse. This, in turn, would force them to challenge the authority of the Church and become dissident thinkers. They chose ignorance over heresy. In Bertolt Brecht's version of the story, Galileo's goal is to discover truth, so he argues, "I would suggest that as scientists it is not for us to ask where the truth may lead us". But the philosophers have different goals and protest panic-stricken, "The truth may lead us to absolutely anything"![21]

When the primary goal of journalism is to protect the narrative, then searching for truth, questioning orthodoxy and impartially weighing the evidence become dangerous. Hence contemporary Official Journalism goes to great lengths to avoid looking through the telescope for fear of what it might see. There are also powerful psychological and social forces that prevent journalists questioning the official consensus. When a society's myths and fantasies collide with reality, powerful shock waves are produced. As Brecht put it,

"Terrible is the disappointment when men discover, or think they discover, that they have fallen victims to an illusion... that the 'facts' are against them and not for them... Then, things are

407

not merely as bad as before, but much worse because people have made immense sacrifices for their schemes and have lost everything; they have ventured and are now defeated."[22]

There are also numerous personal motives which lock journalists into the institutional groupthink and deter them from stepping out of line. The economist Jeffrey Tucker argues this groupthink is fuelled by the internal power structures of news organizations, by careerism and by simple self-interest. Journalists understand that rocking the boat and telling their colleagues they might be wrong, is a recipe for workplace unpopularity and professional suicide. Journalists know their,

"Career paths absolutely require compliance with prevailing narratives. Any deviation could lead to potential doom for them. The spirit of going along is the driving force of everything they do."[23]

Even if they wanted to, most journalists would be incapable of challenging the consensus simply because, despite the theatre of news reporting, the truth is they are ignorant about what is really going on. But Official Journalism is increasingly not about facts, nor about distinguishing reality from fantasy. It is increasingly about nudging people to be good members of the tribe. In the words of the author Michael Crichton, "It's about whether you are going to be a sinner, or saved. Whether you are going to be one of the people on the side of salvation, or on the side of doom. Whether you are going to be one of us, or one of them."[24]

Official Journalism shows little sign of changing, or even recognizing the need for change. On the contrary, in the face of attacks from Unofficial Journalism, its instinct is to circle the wagons and vigorously defend itself. As the author Casey Chalk summarizes,

"In truth, corporate media is so deeply compromised by its ideological biases that there is little hope for its renewal as a source of trusted, unbiased news."[25]

Reconnecting with the concept of impartial, objective journalism regardless of the ethical-political consequences, seems highly unlikely anytime soon. An entire way of thinking has been lost. The meanings of basic words such as 'truth', 'impartial' and 'objective' have become hazy and fuzzy. These fundamental epistemic concepts now appear to us only indistinctly, like ghosts in the twilight. It is naive to think journalism can be fixed unless the epistemology on which it rests is fixed first. Until this happens, what counts as legitimate knowledge will increasingly be the product of the theological, faith-based way of knowing rediscovered by the Boomers.

The Boomers steered journalism away from epistemic humility, towards tribal certitude and intolerance of dissent. Tragically, in their desire to create Utopia and fight evil, they overlooked the fact that ignorance is perhaps the greatest evil of all. Reversing the damage is a Herculean task. From the viewpoint of the early 2020s, it is a long way back up the hill. How can we hope to know what is true if we don't know what is meant by 'truth'? The gloomy 1995 prophesy of the scientist Carl Sagan rings true,

"I have a foreboding of an America in my children's or grandchildren's time... when the people have lost the ability to set their own agendas or knowledgeably question those in authority; when, clutching our crystals and nervously consulting our horoscopes, our critical faculties in decline, unable to distinguish between what feels good and what's true, we slide, almost without noticing, back into superstition and darkness."[26]

The year is 2022. This is where our story ends. It is where we get off the bus. It is the end of the Elizabethan era. As we look around us, we see our Official Journalism is the tribal journalism created by the Boomer generation. Having faith in its narratives is what good people do. Doubting them signals deviance and that one has turned to the dark side. Our journalism cannot change until and unless our epistemology changes. And this will not change unless our society feels the need to change it. Do we want to change it? Or are we happy to continue our addiction to narrative? Ultimately, we get the ideology, the epistemology and the journalism we deserve.

Writing at the very end of the 1960's, the art critic and public intellectual Kenneth Clark likened the cognitive nihilism of the Boomer generation to the mindset of the barbarians who destroyed Rome. *Civilization*, his famous TV documentary series, was both an impassioned defense of the pre-Boomer era and a warning. Although he tried to be positive about the future, he could not shake off a feeling of impending doom. He ended the final episode with melancholy words that do not seem out of place in the 2020s. One can choose to be optimistic, he said, "but one can't exactly be joyful at the prospect before us."[27]

Glossary of Terms

In this book I use several unfamiliar words, including some which I have invented. For the sake of clarity, I explain here how I intend these words to be understood.

✌ ✌ ✌

Aletheia. (pronounced al-*ee*-thia) In journalism, the goal of wanting to discover the truth regardless of the ethical-political consequences. Hence, an objective, quasi-scientific, quasi-legal methodology of impartial enquiry. *Aletheia* was the dominant goal of Victorian Liberal Journalism. Contrasts with *Arete.*

American Dream. An ideology based on Enlightenment values which stresses individual responsibility, opportunity and liberty. It holds that all citizens are entitled to improve themselves through their own hard work and ability. It is a meritocratic creed which says that people should be allowed to profit from their own toil and good fortune. It accepts life's race will produce both winners and losers. Suspicious of big government and the power of elites, it is especially associated with Thomas Jefferson and Andrew Jackson. Its emphasis on individual responsibility and its acceptance of unequal outcomes were widely rejected by the Boomer generation. See also; Victorian Liberalism.

Arete. In journalism, the goal of wanting to make the world a better place. Having an awareness of journalism's ethical-political responsi-

411

bilities. When *arete* is the dominant goal, journalists are permitted, and expected, to self-censor and engage in forms of subtle pro-social lying to help promote the overriding objective of social, environmental, or racial justice. The journalism of *arete* tends to be narrative-led.

Boomer. A member of the Baby Boomer generation born approximately between 1940–1955. Numerically dominant, they grew up during a period of rapidly increasing prosperity. Idealistic and Utopian, they regarded Victorian Liberalism as imperfect and rejected it because they wanted something better, more relevant and more useful to their values and dreams.

Boomer Epistemology. The way of knowing and seeing preferred by the Boomer generation. Based on shared feelings and tribal intuition. Suspicious of, and hostile to, reason, logic and the epistemology of the Enlightenment. Knowledge and truth are understood as the consensus opinions of elite, benevolent Boomers — what the majority of people 'like us' believe. What we believe people whom we admire would believe. Because it is based on a shared tribal faith, it is fundamentally a theological, magical or superstitious way of knowing, rather than one based on evidence and reason.

Boomer Journalism. Journalism based on the Boomer Epistemology which rejects objectivity and impartiality, and replaces them with commitment, attachment and *arete* — the desire to make the world a better place. It appeared as the Underground Journalism of the 1960s and became the dominant form of mainstream journalism by the end of the 20th Century. In the hands of the Millennial generation, it is simply 'journalism', or Official Journalism — the normal, taken for granted form of journalism.

Boomertopia. The vaguely-imagined better world that would spontaneously come into existence if the suffocating restraints of Victorian Liberalism and the American Dream were removed. A new age of peace, fairness, equality and personal fulfilment that would come about as a result of Boomer exceptionalism. A future in which want would be replaced by abundance, and in which competition would be replaced by harmonious co-operation. To construct Boomertopia, it was first necessary to destroy the old world order. Hence the cognitive nihilism of the Boomers — their intolerance of imperfection, their hatred of alienation and their hostility to the values and achievements of the Anglo-American Enlightenment.

Epistemology. How we see the world and how we understand the concepts of truth and knowledge. Our foundational beliefs about what constitutes legitimate knowledge and what does not. These concepts change over time and are shaped by social and generational forces in ways that are hard, or impossible, to see. The study of different, technical understandings of truth such as judicial, scientific and Journalistic Truth.

Factinion. A complex blend of fact and opinion presented as simple fact by journalists. Ambiguous, unknowable assertions — often involving forecasts or subjective analysis — that are simplified, packaged and used as axioms to justify new conclusions. Factinions play a major role in the creation of circular arguments and Official Truth. Factinions are regarded as legitimate (i.e. true) because they are stamped with the authority of the consensus of elite experts.

Journalistic Truth. A technical form of truth comparable to the concept of judicial or legal truth. For example, in Victorian Liberal Journalism, it was understood as an account that was both accurate and impartial. In Boomer Journalism, it is understood as an ethical-political narrative that corresponds to the beliefs of the consensus of experts.

Journocrat. A senior, elite journalist working in Official Journalism whose main role is to shape the official news narratives which junior staff will maintain and promote. Journocrats are influential, senior figures within news organizations. Often designated by the title "correspondent" or "editor", journocrats sit at the apex of the hierarchy of Official Journalism and are permitted to create factinions. Ordinary journalists defer to their knowledge and authority.

News Narratives. The wider, explanatory frameworks into which individual news stories fit. News narratives are simplified scripts with casts of morally good and bad actors. News narratives are understood by journalists, but rarely explicitly stated. News narratives help make sense of events and embrace the psychological and emotional power of story-telling which Victorian Liberal Journalism strove to restrain.

Narrative-Led Journalism. Journalism which selectively reports information to nourish, sustain and protect its guiding News Narratives. Information is reported prominently when it supports the narrative, and played-down or omitted when it does not. Boomer Journalism and Official Journalism are Narrative-Led genres. In Narrative-Led Journalism, the narrative determines the news agenda.

Official Journalism. Also known as mainstream media (MSM) or corporate media. The professional journalism of the early 21st Century. It is the logical development of Boomer Journalism and exaggerates its core features. It is aware of its ethical-political responsibilities and tolerates pro-social lying in pursuit of social and environmental justice. It rejects the impartiality of Victorian Liberal Journalism which it refers to dismissively as 'both-sidesism', or 'false equivalence'.

Official Truth. Tribal Truth after it has been officially adopted by elite members of the group. Knowledge that bears the stamp of authority. Questioning Official Truth implies questioning the wisdom, honesty or integrity of the consensus of those in positions of power and authority.

Paltering. A form of pro-social lying. It is a technique which selectively stresses some facts while playing-down others. It tells the truth to mislead by making statements that are factually accurate, but incomplete. Paltering creates a false impression by not telling the whole truth.

Pro-social lying. Journalistic self-censorship, or other form of deception that is ethically-politically justified. For example, withholding certain facts that might inflame hatred, or lead people towards morally or politically undesirable conclusions. Pro-social lying uses many different techniques including; framing, agenda-setting, repetition of innuendo, the blurring of fact and opinion, use of factinions, paltering and the widespread use of narrative. It can be understood as a type of 'morally good lying'.

Tribal Truth. The shared belief of a group. The beliefs and opinions of the consensus. What most people in a group believe, or believe other group members believe. Hence, what good, loyal members of the group *ought* to believe. What it is safe to believe within a given community. Consequently, those who do not believe the tribal truth, signal they are outsiders — weird, disloyal, heretical dissenters and potentially dangerous tribal enemies.

Truthophobia. In journalism, the logical consequence of *arete*. When the dominant goal of journalism is social, environmental and racial justice, then pro-social lying is tolerated and encouraged. Hence, impartial enquiry comes to be feared because it might lead to ethically-politically unwanted conclusions and outcomes. Journalists are truthophobic when their dominant goal is *arete*. Truthophobia is having something other than truth as one's prime goal.

Unofficial Journalism. An alternative type of journalism hostile to Official Journalism and which emerged in opposition to it. It seeks to put back the facts and opinions which Official Journalism removes. Reviled by Official Journalism, which often accuses it of spreading conspiracy theories, hate speech and misinformation. A competitor to Official Journalism.

Victorian Liberalism. A development of the Anglo-American Enlightenment. Its philosophy was made explicit by theorists such as John Stuart Mill and James Fitzjames Stephen. Victorian Liberalism stresses realism, individual liberty, free speech, the maximum toleration of dissent, reason, logic and minimal government interference. It is closely related to the concepts of Liberal Democracy and the American Dream. Victorian Liberalism was despised by the Boomer generation who viewed it as obsolete because its gritty realism imposed restraints on their dreams, desires and aspirations.

Victorian Liberal Epistemology. A rejection of the faith-based, theological way of knowing and superstition of the pre-Enlightenment era. An evidence-based, scientific process which sees the world as complex, mankind as fallible and knowledge as uncertain. It demands epistemic humility, reasonable doubt, impartiality, objectivity, critical thinking, free speech and debate. It is designed to act as a brake on our emotional and psychological biases, on narrative, and on our tribal impulses.

Victorian Liberal Journalism. Developed in England during the 19th Century, it became the dominant form of journalism until it was replaced by Boomer Journalism. Adopted in the US towards the end of the 19th Century, it relied on the Victorian Liberal Epistemology. It aspires to Journalistic Truth and to present an accurate and impartial account of events. It separates fact from opinion and values objectivity above emotional, Narrative-Led reporting. It evolved to support Victorian Liberal Democracy in which individuals are required to think independently for themselves, and who must therefore have access to honest, truthful journalism to enable them to be well-informed, responsible voters.

Vortex of Immaturity. The perfect storm of environmental, demographic, psychological, economic, cultural and social conditions that existed in the US and the UK during the post-World War Two era. Not a single factor, but a complex, self-reinforcing feedback loop — a unique combination of forces that created, nourished and sustained the Boomer Ideology and the worldview of the Boomer generation.

Notes and References

INTRODUCTION

1. Sperber, D. et al. (2010) Epistemic Vigilance. Mind & Language, 25: 359-393. 360.

2. Bagdikian, B. (1971) The Information Machines. Harper & Row. New York (xii) .

3. Butterfield, G. (1931) The Whig Interpretation of History. London. G. Bell.

4. The Problem of Journalism History. In; James Carey; A Critical Reader. Ed. Eve Munson. (1997) University of Minnesota Press. Minneapolis. 88.

5. Atwood, R. (1978) New Directions for Journalism Historiography. Journal of Communication Inquiry, 4(1), pp. 3–14. doi: 10.1177/019685997800400101.

6. Boyce, G. (1978) The Fourth Estate: the Reappraisal of a Concept. In G. Boyce, J. Curran and P. Wingate, eds. 1978. Newspaper History from the Seventeenth Century to the Present Day. London: Constable. 19-40.

7. Elliott, G. (1978) Professional Ideology and Organisational Change: The Journalist Since 1800. In G. Boyce, J. Curran and P. Wingate, eds. 1978. Newspaper History from the Seventeenth Century to the Present Day. London: Constable. 172-191.

8. Smith, A. (1978) The Long Road to Objectivity and Back Again: The Kinds of Truth we get in Journalism. In G. Boyce, J. Curran and P. Wingate, eds. 1978. Newspaper History from the Seventeenth Century to the Present Day. London: Constable. 153-171.

9. Curran, J., Seaton, J. (1997) Power Without Responsibility: The Press And Broadcasting In Britain. 5th Edition. London, Routledge. Front matter.

10. Williams, K. (1998) Get Me a Murder a Day! Hodder Arnold. London. 29.

11. Flynt, H. (1975) Blueprint for a Higher Civilization. Milan. Multhipla.

12. Flynt. 18-19.

13. Flynt. 23.

14. Flynt. 188.

15. Madison Kaleidoscope. Vol 2 (7). 8 April 1970. 11.

16. Gilley, Bruce. 2020. An Academic Responds To His Cancellers. American Conservative. 9 October 2020. http://www.web.pdx.edu/~gilleyb/An%20 Academic%20Responds%20to%20his%20Cancellers.pdf

CHAPTER TWO

1. Mannheim, K. (1952). The problem of generations. In K. Mannheim & P. Kecskemeti (Eds.), Essays on the sociology of knowledge (pp. 276–322). London: Routledge and Kegan Paul. 291.

2. Martin, B (1981) A Sociology of Contemporary Cultural Change. Blackwell. Oxford. 1.

3. Andrews, Helen. 2021. Boomers: The Men and Women Who Promised Freedom and Delivered Disaster. Penguin. London.

4. Goldberg, D. (2017) In Search of the Lost Chord. New York. Akashic. 2.

5. Ali, T; Watkins, S. (1998) 1968; Marching in the Streets. Free Press. London. 215.

6. Ali, op cit. xi.

7. Arain M, Haque M, Johal L, et al. Maturation of the adolescent brain. Neuropsychiatr Dis Treat. 2013. 9. 449–461. 449.

8. Arnett, J. J. (2003). Conceptions Of The Transition To Adulthood Among Emerging Adults In American Ethnic Groups. New Directions For Child And Adolescent Development. 100, 63-75.

9. Almeida, F. et al (2019) Immature Personality Disorder: Contribution to the Definition of this Personality. Clinical Neuroscience & Neurological Research International Journal. 2,2. 15.

CHAPTER THREE

1. Jones, L. (1980) Great Expectations: America and the Baby Boom Generation. Ballantine. New York. 92.

2. Keniston, K. (1969) Notes on Young Radicals. Change in Higher Education. (1) 6.

3. Wild in the Streets (1968) Dir. Barry Shear. American International Pictures.

4. Hobsbawm, E. (1995) Age of Extremes. Abacus. London. 261 & 328.

5. Packard, V. (1961). The Status Seekers. Penguin. Harmondsworth. 11.

6. Booker, C. (1992) The Neophiliacs. Pimlico. London. 133-4.

7. Mazur, P. (1953) The Standards We Raise. Harper & Brothers. New York. 162.

8. Galbraith, J, K. (1958) The Affluent Society. Pelican. London. 14.

9. Galbraith, 227.

10. Galbraith, op cit 276.

11. Galbraith, op cit 274.

12. Hobsbawm, E. (1995) Age of Extremes. Abacus. London. 259.

13. BBC. (1985) We Were the Lambeth Boys. Dir. Rob Rohrer.

14. Polybius. Histories. Book 6, section 9.

15. Vico, G. (2013) New Science. Penguin. London. 98.

16. Vico, op cit 487.

17. Megill, K. (1970) The New Democratic Theory. The Free Press. New York. 119.

18. Seidman, M. (2004) The Imaginary Revolution. Berghahn Books. New York. 18.

19. Martin, op cit. 25.

20. Beckett, op cit. 38.

21. Booker, op cit. 134.

22. Jones, L. (1980) Great Expectations: America and the Baby Boom Generation. Ballantine. New York. 142.

23. The Lone Ranger. (1956) Opening monologue. Dir. Stuart Heisler. Warner Brothers.

24. Ewen, S. (1988) All Consuming Images: The Politics of Style in Contemporary Culture. Basic Books. New York. 265.

25. Rubin, J. (1970). Do It! Scenarios of the Revolution. Simon and Schuster. New York. 79.

26. Bodroghkozy, A. (2001) Groove Tube: Sixties Television and the Youth Rebellion. Duke University Press, Durham NC. 22.

27. Andrew, A. (2013) A history of television, the technology that seduced the world – and me. The Observer. 7 September 2013. https://www.theguardian.com/tv-and-radio/2013/sep/07/history-television-seduced-the-world .Accessed 7 June 2020

28. Gibney. Op cit. 20.

29. Packard, V. (1962) The Hidden Persuaders. Penguin. Harmondsworth. 133.

30. Veerkumar, V. (2015) Impact of Television Advertisement on Purchases Made for the Children. Anchor Academic Publishing. Hamburg. 30.

31. Veerkumar, 135.

32. Booker, 265.

33. Schlafly, P. (1975) TV Violence. Syndicated newspaper column. 22 August 1975. https://www.phyllisschlafly.com/family/tv-violence/

34. Thompson, B. (2012) Ban This Filth! Letters From the Mary Whitehouse Archive. Faber & Faber. London. 34-35.

CHAPTER FOUR

1. Allyn. D. (2016) Make Love, Not War: The Sexual Revolution: An Unfettered History. Routledge. Abingdon. 5.

2. Neville, R. (1971) PlayPower. Paladin London. 60.

3. Moorehead, K. (2016) Haight-Ashbury: The Hippie Epicenter. Groovy History. 29 November 2016. https://groovyhistory.com/haight-ashbury-the-hippie-epicenter

4. Goldberg, op cit. 260.

5. Legman, G. (1967) The Fake Revolt. Breaking Point. New York. 18.

6. Williams, D. (1971) Trousered Apes; A Study in the Influence of Literature on Contemporary Society. Churchill Press. Enfield. 11.

7. Jones, op cit. 206.

8. Ortiz-Ospina, E.; Roser, M. (2020) Marriages and Divorces. Our World In Data. https://ourworldindata.org/marriages-and-divorces.

9. Marripedia. Effects of Fatherless Families on Crime Rates. http://marripedia.org/effects_of_fatherless_families_on_crime_rates

10. Leary, T. (1990) The Psychedelic Experience. Citadel Press. New York. 13.

11. Fine, J. (2002) Harrison. Simon and Schuster. London. 145.

12. Lennon, J.; McCartney, P. (1967) Strawberry Fields Forever. Sony/ATV Music Publishing.

13. Neville, op cit. 9.

14. Wells, S. (2011) Butterfly on a Wheel; The Great Rolling Stones Drugs Bust. Omnibus Press. London. 72.

15. Gould, J. (2007) Can't Buy Me Love: Beatles, Britain and America. Portrait. New York. 8.

16. Donovan. (1966) Queen Magazine.

17. Clark, R. (2020) Interview with author. 24 June 2020.

18. Pinker, S. (2012) The Better Angels of Our Nature: Why Violence Has Declined. Penguin. New York.

19. Salvatierra, P. (2016) The Second Golden Age of the Serial Killer. Science Leadership Blog. 2 November 2016. https://scienceleadership.org/blog/the_second_golden_age_of_the_serial_killer

20. Booker, op cit.

21. Daily Express. 19 May 1964. Quoted in Cohen 27.

22. Hamblett, C.; Deverson, J. (1964) Generation X. Tandem Books. London.

23. Cohen, S. (2011) Folk Devils and Moral Panics; The creation of the Mods and Rockers. Routledge. London. 11.

24. Cohen, 5.

25. Cohen, 232-3.

26. Erich H.; Heinemann, E. (1967) Credit Cards: Instant Affluence Is on Rise. New York Times. 1 August 1967, 41.

27. Zumello, C. (2011) The "Everything Card" and Consumer Credit in the United States in the 1960s. The Business History Review. 85 (3). 557.

28. Smith, A. (1776) The Wealth of Nations. Book 1. Ch 5.

29. Galbraith, op cit. 172.

CHAPTER FIVE

1. Harris, J, R. (1995) Where Is the Child's Environment? A Group Socialization Theory of Development. Psychological Review. 102 (3) 458–4895.

2. Blakemore, S.; Robbins, T. (2012) Decision-making in the adolescent brain. Nat Neurosci 15, 1184.

3. Shulman, E. P. et al. (2016). The dual systems model: Review, reappraisal, and reaffirmation. Developmental Cognitive Neuroscience, 17, 114.

4. Malone, T. (1968) In: Revolution. Dir. Jack O'Connell. MGM.

5. Mead, M. (1972) Culture and Commitment; A Study of the Generation Gap. Panther Books. Frogmore. 68-69.

6. Goodenough, A et al. (2017) Birds of a feather flock together: Insights into starling murmuration behaviour revealed using citizen science. PLOS ONE, 19 June 2017. 12 (6) e0179277.

7. Levin, B. (2003) The Pendulum Years: Britain in the Sixties. Icon Books. London. 9.

8. Booker, op cit. 135.

9. Hobsbawm, op cit. 325.

10. Levin, op cit. 7.

11. Thompson, op cit. 70.

12. Tyler, R. (2006) Psychological Perspectives on Legitimacy and Legitimation. Annual Review of Psychology. 57, 1. 378.

13. Kelman, H. C. (2001). Reflections on social and psychological processes of legitimization and delegitimization. In J. T. Jost & B. Major (Eds.), The psychology of legitimacy. Cambridge University Press. 69.

14. Eagleton, T. (1991) Ideology, An Introduction. Verso. London.

15. Feldman, D. (1984). The Development and Enforcement of Group Norms. The Academy of Management Review, 9 (1), 47-53.

16. Haidt, J. (2001) The Emotional Dog and Its Rational Tail: A Social Intuitionist Approach to Moral Judgements. Psychological Review. 108, 4. 814.

CHAPTER SIX

1. Beharrell, P; Philo, G (ed). (1977) Trade Unions and the Media. Macmillan. London.

2. Gibney, B, C. (2017) A Generation of Sociopaths. Hachette Books. New York. 72.

3. Farr, A. (2019) Herbert Marcuse. The Stanford Encyclopedia of Philosophy. Summer 2019. Edward N. Zalta (ed.) https://plato.stanford.edu/archives/sum2019/entries/marcuse.

4. Marcuse, H. (1986) One Dimensional Man; Studies in the ideology of advanced industrial society. Ark Paperbacks. London. 1.

5. Marcuse, op cit. 7.

6. Marcuse, op cit. 18.

7. Marcuse, op cit. 143.

8. Marcuse, op cit. 144.

9. Marcuse, op cit. 127

10. Marcuse, op cit. 134.

11. Marcuse, op cit. 65.

12. Hume, D. (2007) Enquiry Concerning Human Understanding. XII, 3. Oxford. Oxford. 120.

13. Orwell, G. (1950) Shooting an Elephant and Other Essays. Secker and Warburg. London.

14. Kellner, D. (2007). In: Marcuse, Herbert (1964, 2007) One-Dimensional Man: Studies in the ideology of advanced industrial society. Routledge, Abingdon. xi.

15. MacMullen, R. (1984) Christianizing the Roman Empire A.D.100-400, Yale University Press. 95.

16. Marcuse, H. (1965) Repressive Tolerance. In; A Critique of Pure Tolerance. (1969) Jonathan Cape. London. 137.

17. Marcuse,H. (1966) Eros and Civilization. A Philosophical Inquiry into Freud. Beacon Press. Boston. 149-150.

18. Marcuse, op cit. 15.

19. Marcuse, op cit. 16.

20. Marcuse, op cit. 17.

21. Marcuse, op cit. 40.

22. Marcuse, op cit. Xxii.

23. Marcuse, op cit. Xxvi.

24. Marcuse, M. (1967) Liberation from the Affluent Society. In: David Cooper (ed.), The Dialectics of Liberation. (1968) Harmondsworth/Baltimore: Penguin. 175-192.

25. Horkheimer, M. (1968) Critical Theory; Selected Essays. Continuum. New York. vii.

26. Horkheimer, M. (1972) Critical Theory: Selected Essays (1972) Trans. Matthew J. O'Connell. New York. Herder and Herder. viii.

CHAPTER SEVEN.

1. Levitas, R. (2007) Looking for the Blue: The Necessity of Utopia, Journal of Political Ideologies, 12:3, 289-306. 290.

2. Chen, A. (2011) The Concept of 'Datong' in Chinese Philosophy as an Expression of the Idea of the Common Good. University of Hong Kong Law Research Paper No. 2011/020. 11 November 2011. http://dx.doi.org/10.2139/ssrn.1957955

3. Popper, K. (2011) The Open Society and Its Enemies. (6). Routledge. Abingdon. 102.

4. McGrath, T. (1967). International Times (10). in. Nuttall, J. (1968/2018) Bomb Culture. Strange Attractor Press. London. 219.

5. Disney, W. (1966) E.P.C.O.T Florida Film. The Walt Disney Company.

6. Mosley, L. (1990) The Real Walt Disney. Scarborough House, Lanham. 289.

7. Roth, M. (1996) The Lion King; A short history of Disney-fascism. Jump Cut. (40) March 1996, 15-20. https://www.ejumpcut.org/archive/onlinessays/JC40folder/LionKing.html?sfns=mo

8. Lennon, J. (1971) Imagine. Sony/ATV Music Publishing.

9. Gilmore, M. (2005) Lennon Lives Forever. Twenty-five years after his death, his music and message endure. Rolling Stone.

10. Cook, R. et al. (1971) I'd Like to Teach the World to Sing. Polydor/Elecktra.

11. Zanger, D. (2015) Coca-Cola: Behind the scenes of its most celebrated advert 'Hill Top'. The Drum. 10 July 2015. https://www.thedrum.com/news/2015/07/10/coca-cola-behind-scenes-its-most-celebrated-advert-hill-top

12. Hobbes, T. (1965) Leviathan. Oxford University Press. London. 97.

13. Maddison, J. (1787) Notes of Debates in the Federal Convention. 6 June 1787.

14. Hamilton, A. (1787) Alexander Hamilton's Notes. 18 June 1787. US National Archives. https://founders.archives.gov/documents/Hamilton/01-04-02-0098-0002

15. Mill, J, S. (1859) On Liberty. Chapter 1.

16. Rousseau, J. (1755). Discourse on the Origin and Basis of Inequality Among Men. Part Two.

17. Reich, C. 1970 (1974). The Greening of America. Penguin, Harmondsworth. 190.

18. Reich, op cit. 111.

19. Reich, op cit. 131-134.

20. Reich, op cit. 185.

21. Neville, op cit. 214.

22. Neville, op cit. 222.

23. Neville, op cit. 213.

24. Ibid.

25. Neville, op cit. 218.

26. Neville, op cit. 273.

27. Neville, op cit. 221.

28. Neville, op cit. 227.

29. Loeser, H. (2022) Interview with author. 29 April 2022.

30. Bhagwan, S, R. (2018) In: Wild, Wild Country. TV Documentary. Netflix. Dir. Chapman Way. Part One.

31. Ibid.

CHAPTER EIGHT

1. Mead, op cit. 108.

2. Hayden, T. (1962) Port Huron Statement of the Students for a Democratic Society. https://www.ssc.wisc.edu/~wright/929-utopias-2013/Real%20 Utopia%20Readings/Port%20Huron%20Statement.pdf

3. Hanisch, C. (1969) The Personal Is Political. February 1969. Carol Hanisch website. http://www.carolhanisch.org/CHwritings/PIP.html

4. Keniston, K. (1968) Young Radicals: Notes on Committed Youth. Harcourt, Brace and World. New York. 16-17.

5. Keniston, op cit. 8.

6. Keniston, op cit. 143

7. Keniston, op cit. 10.

8. Keniston, op cit. 31.

9. Keniston, op cit. 238.

10. Keniston, op cit. 262.

11. Hall, S. (1980) Culture, Media, Language: Working Papers in Cultural Studies, 1972-79. Hutchinson. London. 17.

12. Engels, F. (1880) The Development of Utopian Socialism. In: Marx/Engels Selected Works, Volume 3, p. 95-151. Progress Publishers. 1970. London. https://www.marxists.org/archive/marx/works/download/Engels_Socialism_Utopian_and_Scientific.pdf

13. Marx, K.; Engels, F. (1875) Critique of the Gotha Programme. Marx/Engels Selected Works, Volume Three, p. 13 - 30. Progress Publishers, Moscow, 1970. https://www.marxists.org/archive/marx/works/download/Marx_Critque_of_the_Gotha_Programme.pdf

14. Jackson, L. (1991). The Poverty of Structuralism: Literature and Structuralist Theory. Routledge. 3.

15. Sedgwick, P. (1964) The Two New Lefts. International Socialism (1) 17. August 1964.15.

16. Socialist Standard. (2004) Hippies: An Abortion of Socialist Understanding. In: Socialism or Your Money Back. SPGB. London. 201.

17. Campbell C. (2018) The Puzzle of Modern Consumerism. In: The Romantic Ethic and the Spirit of Modern Consumerism. Cultural Sociology. Palgrave Macmillan, Cham. 131.

18. Neville, op cit, 10.

19. Wolfe, T. (1970). Radical Chic: That Party at Lenny's. New York Magazine. 8 June 1970. https://nymag.com/news/features/46170/index15.html

20. Grogan, E. (1974) Ringolevio: A Life Played for Keeps. Panther. St Albans. 372.

21. Grogan, op cit. 372.

22. Grogan, op cit. 373-374.

23. Nuttall op cit. 110.

24. Lennon, J.; McCartney, P. (1968) Revolution. Sony/ATV

25. Hoyland, J. (1968) An Open Letter to John Lennon. The Black Dwarf. 13 (7) 27th October 1968.

26. Lennon, J. (1969) A Very Open Letter to John Hoyland from John Lennon. Black Dwarf. 13 (9) 10th January 1969.

27. Hoyland, J. (1969) John Hoyland Replies. Black Dwarf. 13 (9) 10th January 1969.

28. Fire (SDS), Volume 1, issue 2, 15 November 1969. https://voices.revealdigital.org/

29. Jackson, R. (1946) Nuremberg Trial Proceedings Volume 19. 26 July 1946. https://avalon.law.yale.edu/imt/07-26-46.asp   427.

30. Tusa, A.; Tusa, J. (2010) The Nuremburg Trial. Skyhorse Publishing. New York.

31. Jackson, R. H. (1945) Opening address for the United States of America. Department of State Bulletin. 25 November 1945 (335) XIII. 2432. Washington: US Government Printing Office. p. 850-860.

32. Ibid.

33. Jackson, (1946) op cit. 424.

34. Meerloo, J. (2009) The Rape of the Mind: The Psychology of Thought Control, Menticide, and Brainwashing. Progressive Press. 88.

35. Meerloo, op cit. 126.

36. Lewis, H. (2020) Our Big Fight Over Nothing: The Political Spectrum Does Not Exist. Hetrodox Academy. 12 June 2020. https://heterodoxacademy.org/blog/social-science-political-spectrum/

37. Andrews, H. (2021) Boomers: The Men and Women Who Promised Freedom and Delivered Disaster. Penguin. London.

38. Agnew, S. (1969) The Dangers of Constant Carnival. Address at Pennsylvania Republican Dinner Harrisburg, 30 October 1969. https://wps.prenhall.com/wps/media/objects/108/111235/ch29_a4_d2.pdf

39. Williams, D. (1971) Trousered Apes; A Study in the Influence of Literature on Contemporary Society. Churchill Press. Enfield. 86.

40. Williams, op cit. 124.

CHAPTER NINE

1. Monsarrat, N. (2009) The Cruel Sea. London. Penguin. 208.

2. Ibid.

3. Monsarrat, op cit. 206-213.

4. Monsarrat, op cit. 10.

5. Stephen, J. F. (1993) Liberty, Equality, Fraternity. Indianapolis. Liberty Fund. 205.

6. Hobhouse, L. (1911) Liberalism. London. Everyman. 108.

7. Morley, J. (1877) On Compromise. London. Chapman and Hall. 107.

8. Morley, op cit. 60.

9. Morley, op cit. 111-113.

10. Russell, B. (1940) Power; A New Social Analysis. London. Basic Books. 312.

11. Stebbing, S. (1939) Thinking to Some Purpose. Pelican. Harmondsworth. 221.

12. Stephen, op cit. 231.

13. Kersh, G. (1941) They Die With Their Boots Clean. London. William Heinemann. 197-198.

14. Kersh, G. (1946) Clean, Bright and Slightly Oiled. London. William Heinemann. 35.

CHAPTER TEN

1. Scott, C.P. (2017) A Hundred Years. The Guardian. 23 October 2017 (May 1921). https://www.theguardian.com/sustainability/cp-scott-centenary-essay

2. Stephen, op cit. 351.

3. Newton, I. (1672) Mr. Newton's Answer to the foregoing Letter of Ignace Pardies. Philosophical Transactions of the Royal Society, No. 85. 15 July 1672. pp. 5014-5018. https://www.newtonproject.ox.ac.uk/view/texts/diplomatic/NATP00029

4. Buckle, H. 1906 (1861). History of Civilization in England. London. Henry Frowde. Vol 3. 281.

5. Conan Doyle, A. (1891). A Scandal in Bohemia. Strand Magazine. https://en.wikisource.org/wiki/Talk:The_Strand_Magazine/Volume_2/A_Scandal_in_Bohemia

6. Rattigan, T. (2000) The Winslow Boy. Nick Hern Books. London.

CHAPTER ELEVEN

1. Fukuyama, F. (2006) The End of History and the Last Man. New York. Free Press.

2. Horne, T. (1980) Politics in a Corrupt Society: William Arnall's Defense of Robert Walpole. Journal of the History of Ideas, 41(4), 601–614. https://doi.org/10.2307/2709276

3. Roberts, W. (1888) Grub Street and its Journal. The Bookworm: An Illustrated Treasury of Old-time Literature. 1 January 1888. London. 20-27.

4. Johnson, S. (1757) The London Chronicle, January. In: The Works of Samuel Johnson, A New Edition in Twelve Volumes. 1820. Ed.Arthur Murphy. 204. Available at Google Books.

5. Pettegree, A. (2014) The Invention Of News: How The World Came To Know About Itself. New Haven. Yale University Press. 316.

6. Savage, R. (1729) An Author to be Let. London. Available at Google Books. https://www.google.co.uk/books/edition/An_author_to_be_let_etc/qR5kAAAAcAAJ?hl=en&gbpv=1

7. Hecht, J, J. (1956) The Domestic Servant Class in Eighteenth-Century England. London, Routledge and Kegan Paul. 200.

8. Johnson, S. (1888) Lives of the English Poets; Addison, Savage, Swift. Cassell. London. Chapter on Savage. Available at Project Gutenberg. https://www.gutenberg.org/files/4679/4679-h/4679-h.htm

9. Bowdler, J. (1797) Reform Or Ruin: Abridged: In which Every Man May Learn the True State of Things at this Time: and what that Reform Is, which Alone Can Save the Country! London. Hatchard. 5. Available at Google Books.

10. Jefferson, T. (1807) Letter to John Norvell, June 11, 1807. In; Ed. Ford, P, L. (1904). The Works of Thomas Jefferson in Twelve Volumes. Federal Edition. New York. Putnam.

11. Mott, F, L. (1942). American Journalism; A History Of Newspapers In The United States Through 250 Years 1690 to 1940. New York. Macmillan.

12. Lindsay, D.; Washington, E. (1956) A Portrait of Britain Between the Exhibitions 1851-1951. London. Oxford University Press. 71.

13. Hudson, D. (1943) Thomas Barnes of the Times. Cambridge University Press. Cambridge. 30.

14. Hudson, op cit. 36.

15. The Times. (1939) The history of The Times : Vol. 2 - The tradition established. London. The Times. 120.

16. Schlesinger, M. (1853) Saunterings In And About London. Nathaniel Cooke. London. Ch 7.

17. Lindsay, op cit. 79.

18. King, E. (2007) British Newspapers 1860-1900. British Library Newspapers. Detroit. Gale.

19. Leupp, F, E. (1918) The Waning Power of the Press. in; Bleyer, W, G. 1918. The Profession of Journalism. The Atlantic Monthly Press. Boston. 39.

20. Cooper, J, F. (1838) The American Democrat. In: Eds. Birzer, B; Wilson, J (2001) The American Democrat and Other Political Writings. Washington. Regnery.

21. Scribner's Monthly, June, 1872. In: Mott, op cit. 412.

22. Stone, M, E. (2017). Fifty Years a Journalist. Miami. HardPress.

23. Stone, op cit. 235.

24. Lindsay, op cit. 165.

25. Connery, T, B. (1893) A Famous Newspaper Hoax. Harper's Weekly. 3 June 1893. 534-535.

26. Glackens, L, M (1910). The Yellow Press. Cartoon for Puck magazine. 12 October 1910. https://upload.wikimedia.org/wikipedia/commons/9/97/The_Yellow_Press_by_L.M._Glackens.jpg

27. Davis, E, H. (1921) History of the New York Times, 1851-1921. New York Times, New York. 194.

28. Mencken, H. L. (2006) 1918. The Public Prints. Menckeniana, 180, 1–5. http://www.jstor.org/stable/26484844

29. Harger, C, M. (1918) Journalism as a Career. in; Bleyer, W, G. (1918) The Profession of Journalism. The Atlantic Monthly Press. Boston. 166.

30. Welles, O. (1941) Citizen Kane. RKO Radio Pictures.

31. Johnson, G. (1946) An Honorable Titan; A Biographical Study of Adolph S. Ochs. New York. Harper & Brothers. 147.

32. ASNE. (1923) American Society of Newspaper Editors. Code of Ethics or Canons of Journalism. https://ethics.iit.edu/ecodes/node/4457

33. Coblentz, E. (1968) Newsmen Speak. Journalists on their Craft. Freeport, New York. Books for Libraries Press. 41.

34. Bleyer, W, G. 1918. The Profession of Journalism. The Atlantic Monthly Press. Boston. 14. Available online at: https://www.gutenberg.org/files/61982/61982-h/61982-h.htm

35. Villard, O, G. (1918) Press Tendencies and Dangers. In; Bleyer, W, G. 1918. The Profession of Journalism. The Atlantic Monthly Press. Boston. Avail-

able online at: https://www.gutenberg.org/files/61982/61982-h/61982-h.htm 34.

36. Coblentz, op cit. 13.

37. Coblentz, op cit. 71.

38. Coblentz, op cit. 82.

39. Coblentz, op cit. 67.

40. Coblentz, op cit. 61.

41. Coblentz, op cit. 48.

42. Lippmann, W. (2010) Liberty and the News. Mineola, New York. Dover. 43.

43. Lippmann, op cit. 4.

44. Ibid.

45. In: Luckhurst, T. (2023) Reporting the Second World War: The Press and the People 1939-1945. London. Bloomsbury. 10.

46. Robinson, N. (2013). Live from Downing Street: The Inside Story of Politics, Power and the Media. London. Random House. 146

47. Luckhurst, T. op cit. 23.

CHAPTER TWELVE

1. Kersh, G. (1941) Not So Dusty! Daily Herald. 2 June 1941. In: Private Life of a Private. (2020) Ed. Paul Duncan. London. Wordsmith.

2. Orwell, G. (1943) Looking Back on the Spanish War. New Road. June 1943. https://www.orwellfoundation.com/the-orwell-foundation/orwell/essays-and-other-works/looking-back-on-the-spanish-war

3. Ibid.

4. Gilbert, G. (1947), Nuremberg Diary. New York, Signet.

5. Orwell, G. (1972) Politics and the English Language. In: Inside the Whale and Other Essays. Middlesex. Penguin. 143–157.

6. Royal Commission on the Press. (1949) Cmd. 7700. H.M.S.O. London. 155.

7. Royal commission, op cit. 154.

8. Royal commission, op cit. 127

9. Royal commission, op cit. 108.

10. Royal commission, op cit. 150-151.

11. Hutchins, R, M. (1947) A Free and Responsible Press. University of Chicago Press. Chicago. 1.

12. Hutchins, op cit. 2

13. Hutchins, op cit. 3

14. Hutchins, op cit. 21

15. Hutchins, op cit. 22

16. Ibid.

17. Hutchins, op cit. 11

18. Hutchins, op cit. 132.

19. Siebert, F.; Peterson, T.; Schramm, W. (1956/1963). Four Theories of the Press: The Authoritarian, Libertarian, Social Responsibility, and Soviet Communist Concepts of What the Press Should Be and Do. Illini Books. University of Illinois Press. Chicago. 1.

20. Siebert, op cit. 2.

21. Siebert, op cit. 11.

22. Siebert, op cit. 116.

23. Mott, op cit. 822.

24. Qualter, T. (1962) Propaganda and Psychological Warfare. New York. Random House. 122.

25. Armstrong, M. (2008) Talking about the Principles of Smith-Mundt. MountainRunner.us 15 March 2008. https://mountainrunner.us/2008/03/talking_about_the_principles_s/

26. Congressional Record of the 99th Congress, 1st Session, June 7, 1985 (legislative day of June 3, 1985).

27. FCC. (1949) Editorializing by Broadcast Licensees. June 8th1949. Docket 8516, 13 FCC 1246.

28. Baker, R. (2018) Former BBC newsreader Richard Baker dies aged 93. BBC News Video. 17 November 2018. https://www.bbc.co.uk/news/entertainment-arts-46246049

29. Coblenz, op cit. 162.

30. Weaver, D. (1961) Mansfield's Complete Journalist. Pitman. London. 267-8.

31. Weaver, op cit. 271.

32. Coblenz, op cit. 192.

33. Coblenz, op cit. 193.

34. Mott, op cit. 835.

CHAPTER THIRTEEN

1. Willsher, K. (2014) How the BBC brought hope to occupied France. The Guardian. 3 May 2014. https://www.theguardian.com/world/2014/may/03/d-day-bbc-occupied-france-letters

2. Luckhurst, op cit. 201.

3. Haley, W. (1954) The Central Problem of Broadcasting. In: Three Essays on Broadcasting. (1954) BBC. London. 9.

4. Haley, op cit. 15-16.

5. Haley, W. (1948) The Responsibilities of Broadcasting. Lewis Fry Memorial Lecture. 12th May 1948. In: Three Essays on Broadcasting. (1954) BBC. London. 5.

6. Haley, op cit. 31.

7. Haley, op cit. 24.

8. Haley, op cit. 5.

9. Greene, H, C. (1969) The Third Floor Front: A View of Broadcasting in the Sixties. Bodley Head. London. 26.

10. Greene, op cit. 21.

11. Booker, op cit. 187.

12. Booker, op cit. 216.

13. Greene, op cit.127.

14. Greene, op cit.128.

15. Greene, op cit. 133.

16. Curran, op cit. 206.

17. Greene. op cit. 93-94.

18. Ibid.

19. Greene, op cit. 101.

20. Greene, op cit. 100.

21. Greene, op cit. 129.

22. Greene, op cit. 106.

23. Fiddick, P. (1976) Why the Beeb Boss is Bowing Out. The Guardian. 14th October 1976. 13.

24. Curran, C. (1979) A Seamless Robe: Broadcasting Philosophy and Practice. Collins. London. 107.

25. Curran, op cit. 110.

26. Curran, op cit. 91.

27. Curran, op cit. 114.

28. Curran, op cit. 95.

29. Curran, op cit. 100.

30. Curran, op cit. 126.

31. Curran, op cit. 115.

CHAPTER FOURTEEN

1. Ali, T.; Watkins, S. (1998) 1968: Marching in the Streets. The Free Press. New York. 7.

2. Goldin, R. et al. (2013) A comparison of tantrum behavior profiles in children with ASD, ADHD and comorbid ASD and ADHD. Research in Developmental Disabilities. 34 (9) 2013. 2669-2675.

3. Fraser, R. (1988) 1968; A Student Generation in Revolt. London. Chatto & Windus. 10.

4. Fraser. op cit. 8.

5. Fraser. op cit. 12.

6. Fraser. op cit. 317.

7. Charrière, C. (1968) Le Printemps des enragés. Feyard. Paris. 44-45.

8. Burrough, B. (2015) Days of Rage: America's Radical Underground, the FBI, and the Forgotten Age of Revolutionary Violence. New York. Penguin. ebook.

9. Burrough, op cit.

10. Seidman, M. (2004) The Imaginary Revolution. Berghahn Books. New York. 18.

11. Loeser, op cit.

12. Bright, M. (2002) Look back in anger. The Observer. 3 February 2002. https://www.theguardian.com/theobserver/2002/feb/03/features.magazine27

13. Burrough, op cit.

14. Seidman, op cit. 276.

15. Hare, T. (1859) A Treatise on the Election of Representatives, Parliamentary and Municipal. London. Longman, Brown, Green, Longmans & Roberts. 111.

16. Hare, T. (1860) Representation in Practice and in Theory. Fraser's Magazine. February 1860. Google Books. 201.

17. Saunders, R. (2016) Democracy and the Vote in British Politics, 1848-1867: The Making of the Second Reform Act. Routledge. London. 169.

18. Jefferson, T. (1820) Letter from Thomas Jefferson to William Charles Jarvis. 28 September 1820.

19. Mill, J, S. (1861) Considerations on Representative Government. Chapter 10.

20. Mill, J, S. (1859) On Liberty. Chapter 1. Introductory.

21. Stephen, op cit. 137.

22. Jefferson, T. (1779) Diffusion of Knowledge Bill. FE 2:221, Papers 2:526.

23. Jefferson, T. (1816) Thomas Jefferson to Charles Yancey. ME 14:384.

24. Franklin, B. (1773) Letter to Jane Mecom. 1 November 1773. Founders Online website. https://founders.archives.gov/documents/Franklin/01-20-02-0246#BNFN-01-20-02-0246-fn-0002

25. Thomas Carlyle (1859). On Heroes, Hero-worship, and the Heroic in History: Six Lectures. Sterling Edition. Lect. V: "The Hero as Man of Letters". https://www.gutenberg.org/files/1091/1091-h/1091-h.htm

26. Ibid.

27. Collins, V. (1969) Representation of the People Bill. House of Lords debate. 6 February 1969. Hansard. vol 299. 213-96 https://api.parliament.uk/historic-hansard/lords/1969/feb/06/representation-of-the-people-bill

28. Ibid.

29. Cellar, E. (1967) In; John Chamberlain, "These Days. . . Should 18-Year-Olders Vote?" Washington Post. 1 May 1967. A18.

30. Cellar, E. (1954) New York Times. 8 January 1954. 11.

31. Atlanta Constitution. 8 January 1954, 11.

32. Reich, op cit. 24.

33. Rockoff, H.; Bordo, M. (1995) The Gold Standard as a 'Good Housekeeping Seal of Approval'. Working Paper, No. 1995-28, Rutgers University, Department of Economics.

34. Prentice, B. (2020) WTF Happened in 1971? The1millionproject. 3 July 2020. Medium. https://medium.com/@t1mproject/wtf-happened-in-1971-acff27741e9d

CHAPTER FIFTEEN

1. Wells, S. (2011) The Great Rolling Stones Drugs Bust. London. Omnibus. 269.

2. Maclean, I. (2019) Behind Open Doors; From the CIA to the Beautiful People. London. Resonance Books. 268.

3. Wells, op cit. viii.

4. Wells, op cit. 216.

5. Rees-Mogg, W. (1967) The Times. Leader. 1 July 1967.

CHAPTER SIXTEEN

1. Goldberg. op cit. 90.

2. Goldberg, op cit. 96.

3. Berkeley Barb. No Peace for Fuzz as Disaster Strikes. Vol 7. Issue 9. September 6-12, 3.

4. Neville, op cit. 120.

5. Neville, op cit. 127.

6. Ibid.

7. Freedomways, Volume 7, issue 2, Spring (Second Quarter) 1967, Edition 02.

8. Dreyer, T.; Smith, V. (1969) The Movement and the New Media. Liberation News Service. 1 March 1969. http://www.nuevoanden.com/rag/newmedia.html

9. Ibid.

10. Ibid.

11. Ibid.

12. Los Angeles Free Press. 5, (201) 24 May 1968. 5.

13. Los Angeles Free Press. Volume 6, issue 258, June 27 - July 4, 1969.

14. Liberation News Service, issue 94. 26 June 1968. 30.

15. The Paper. Vol 2. (10). 12 August 1966. 1-2.

16. Muhammad Speaks. Issue Vol. 5 No. 15, 31 December 1965. 21.

17. The Activist, Volume 7, issue 3, Spring 1967. 13.

18. The Seed. Volume 3, issue 8. January 3, 1969. 12.

19. Black Dwarf. 22 May 1968.

20. Los Angeles Free Press, Volume 4, issue 28 (156), July 14-20. 1967.

21. RAT Subterranean News. 22 March – 4 April 1968.

22. Berkeley Barb. Volume 6, issue 17(141), 26 April – 2 May, 1968. 5.

23. Loeser, op cit.

24. Black Dwarf. Vol 13. 7. 27 October 1968.

25. Fire (SDS), Volume 1, issue 2, 15 November 1969. https://voices.revealdigital.org/

26. Rubin. Do it! 221.

27. Wolfe, T. (1972) Why They Aren't Writing the Great American Novel Anymore. A treatise on the Varieties of Realistic Experience. Esquire. December 1972. https://www.esquire.com/lifestyle/money/a20703846/tom-wolfe-new-jounalism-american-novel-essay/

28. Hahn, M. (1997) Writing on the Wall. The Atlantic. 26 August 1997. http://www.theatlantic.com/past/docs/unbound/graffiti/hunter.htm

29. Thompson, H, S. (1970) The Kentucky Derby is Decadent and Depraved. Scanlan's Monthly. June 1970.

30. Macdonald, D. (1965). Parajournalism, or Tom Wolfe & His Magic Writing Machine. The New York Review of Books. 26 August 1965.

CHAPTER SEVENTEEN

1. Kruglanski, A. W.; Szumowska, E. (2020) 'Habitual Behavior Is Goal-Driven', Perspectives on Psychological Science, 15(5), pp. 1256–1271.

2. Levine, E. E.; Schweitzer, M. E. (2015). Prosocial Lies: When Deception Breeds Trust. Organizational Behavior and Human Decision Processes, 126. 88-106.

3. Gunia, B. C.; Levine, E. E. (2019). Deception as competence: The effect of occupational stereotypes on the perception and proliferation of deception. Organizational Behavior and Human Decision Processes, 152, 122-137.

4. Plato. (2007) The Republic. Trans. Desmond Lee. London. Penguin. 115.

5. Gaspar, J. et al. (2019) Fifty Shades of Deception: Characteristics and Consequences of Lying in Negotiations. Academy of Management Perspectives, 33 (1) 62-81.

6. Fisher, C. (2016) Ten shades of truth: A study of Australian journalists' shift to political PR. Public Relations Review, Volume 42, Issue 4. 665-672.

7. Rogers, T. et al. (2017) Artful paltering: The risks and rewards of using truthful statements to mislead others. J Pers Soc Psychol. 2017; 112 (3): 456-473.

8. Frankfurt, H, G. (1988) On Bullshit; The Importance of What We Care About. Cambridge: Cambridge University Press. pp. 117–133.

9. Wolff, J. (2018) An Introduction to Moral Philosophy. New York. W. W. Norton & Company. 4.

10. Greene, M. (1998) Introduction: Teaching for Social Justice. In: Teaching for Social Justice, eds. by William Ayers, xxvii-xlvi. New York: Teachers College Press. xlv.

11. Rizvi, F. (1998) Some Thoughts on Contemporary Theories of Social Justice. In: Action Research in Practice: Partnerships for Social Justice in Education, eds. Bill Atweh et al. 47-56. London. Routledge. 47.

12. Kent State University. (2021) The Five Principles of Social Justice. 30 July 2020. https://onlinedegrees.kent.edu/political-science/master-of-public-administration/community/five-principles-of-social-justice. Accessed 27 May 2021.

13. Miller, D. (1999) Principles of Social Justice. David Miller. Cambs. Harvard University Press. 1.

14. O'Neill, B. (2011) The Injustice of Social Justice. Mises Institute. 16 March 2011. https://mises.org/library/injustice-social-justice

15. Plato. (1956). Protagoras and Meno. WKC Guthrie Ed. London: Penguin Classics. 124 & 142.

16. Bloom, P. (2005) Descarte's Baby; how Child Development Explains what Makes Us Human. London. Arrow Books. 100.

17. Greene, J. (2015) Moral Tribes: Emotion, Reason, and the Gap Between Us and Them. London. Atlantic. 26

18. Greene, op cit. 102.

19. Cai, C.W. (2020) Nudging the financial market? A review of the nudge theory. Account Finance, 60: 3341-3365.

20. Bernays, E. L. (1947) 'The Engineering of Consent', The ANNALS of the American Academy of Political and Social Science, 250 (1). 113–120.

CHAPTER EIGHTEEN

1. Snyder, T. (1993) 120 Years of American Education: A Statistical Portrait. Report for US Center for Education Statistics. 6.6.

2. Horowitz, H. (1986). The 1960s and the transformation of Campus Cultures. History of Education Quarterly, 26(1), 1-38. 15.

3. Horowitz, op cit. 34.

4. Turner, G. (1990) British Cultural Studies: An Introduction. Third Edition. Routledge. London. 2.

5. Turner, op cit. 230.

6. Ibid.

7. Hirst, P. (1973) Some Problems of Explaining Student Militancy. In: Brown, R. Knowledge, Education and Cultural Change. Routledge. London. 221.

8. Martin, op cit. 188.

9. Aylesworth, G. (2015) Postmodernism. The Stanford Encyclopedia of Philosophy (Spring 2015 Edition), ed. Edward N. Zalta.

10. Tuchman, G. (1972) Objectivity as Strategic Ritual: An Examination of Newsmen's Notions of Objectivity. American Journal of Sociology. 77 (4) January 1972. 660.

11. Tuchman, op cit. 336.

12. Tuchman, op cit. 664.

13. Tuchcman, G. (1980). Making News: A Study in the Construction of Reality. Free Press. New York. 5-6.

14. Tuchman, op cit. 88.

15. Tuchman, op cit. 100.

16. Tuchman, op cit. 86.

17. Berger, P,; Luckmann, T. (1991) the Social Construction of Reality. A Treatise in the Sociology of Knowledge. London. Penguin. 14.

18. Berger, P. L. (1992) Reflections On The 25th Anniversary Of The Social Construction Of Reality. Perspectives. 15 (2) April 1992. 2.

19. Tuchman (1972) op cit. 667.

20. Shibutani, T. (1966) Improvised News; A Sociological Study of Rumor. Bobbs-Merrill. 42.

21. Shibutani, op cit. 43.

22. Shibutani, op cit. 45-46.

23. Tuchman, G. (1978), Professionalism as an Agent of Legitimation. Journal of Communication, 28: 112.

24. Belsey, C. (1980). Critical Practice. London. Methuen.

25. Hall, S., et al. (2013) Policing the Crisis: Mugging, the State and Law and Order. London: Macmillan. 1.

26. Bødker, H. (2016) Stuart Hall's encoding/decoding model and the circulation of journalism in the digital landscape. Critical Studies in Media Communication, 33:5, 409.

27. Hall, S. (1980) Encoding/Decoding. In; Durham and Kellner eds. Media and Cultural Studies Keyworks. (2001) Blackwell. London. 172-173.

28. Love, P.G.; Guthrie, V.L. (1999) Women's Ways of Knowing. New Directions for Student Services, 1999: 17-27.

29. Watson, B. (2014). Stephen Colbert: Beyond Truthiness. New York: New Word City.

30. Colbert, S. (2006) Stephen Colbert's Blistering Performance Mocking Bush and the Press Goes Ignored by the Media. Democracy Now. 3 May 2006. https://www.democracynow.org/2006/5/3/stephen_colberts_blistering_performance_mocking_bush

31. Clark, C., J.; Winegard, Bo., M. (2020) Tribalism in War and Peace: The Nature and Evolution of Ideological Epistemology and Its Significance for Modern Social Science. Psychological Inquiry, 31:1, 10.

32. Clark, op cit. 22.

33. Marton-Alper, I.Z. et al. (2020). Herding in human groups is related to high autistic traits. Scientific Reports, 10.

34. Watts, I. et al. (2016). Misinformed leaders lose influence over pigeon flocks. Biology letters. 12. 10.1098/rsbl.2016.0544.

35. Le Bon, G. (1895) The Crowd: A Study of the Popular Mind. Book 1. Ch 4.

36. Grossberg, L. (2015) We All Want to Change the World: The Paradox Of The U.S. Left, A Polemic. Lawrence & Wishart. Chadwell Heath. 87.

37. Grossberg, op cit. 173.

38. Hall, S. (1994) Some 'Politically Incorrect' Pathways Through Political Correctness. In: Dunant, S. ed. The War of the Words: The Political Correctness Debate. London: Virago. 164.

39. Hall, op cit. 173.

40. Davis, H. (2004). Understanding Stuart Hall. London: Sage. 66

41. Gartman, D. (2013). Culture, Class, and Critical Theory. New York: Routledge. 33.

42. Bourdieu, P. (1998) On Television. New York. The New Press. 52.

43. Bourdieu, op cit. 41.

44. Bourdieu, op cit. 51.

45. Bourdieu, op cit. 63.

46. Bourdieu, op cit. 65.

47. Bourdieu, op cit. 55.

48. Bourdieu, op cit. 77.

49. Bourdieu, op cit. 55.

50. McNair, B. (1991). Glasnost, Perestroika and the Soviet Media. London: Routledge. 65.

51. Lenin, V.,I. (1918). The Immediate Tasks of the Soviet Government (The Organisation Of Competition). Pravda no. 83 and Izvestia VTsIK no.85, 28 April 1918.

52. McNair, op cit. 23

53. McNair, op cit. 19.

54. McNair, op cit. 21.

55. Bourdieu, op cit. 74.

56. Bourdieu, op cit. 76.

57. Bourdieu, op cit. 75.

58. Bourdieu, op cit. 72.

59. McNair, op cit. 2.

60. Newfield, J. (1967) A Prophetic Minority: The American New Left. London. Anthony Blond. 178.

CHAPTER NINETEEN

1. Birt, J. (2002) The Harder Path. Time Warner Books. London. 47.

2. Birt, J. (2005) John Birt's MacTaggart Lecture 2005. The Guardian. 26 Aug 2005. https://www.theguardian.com/media/2005/aug/26/broadcasting.uknews

3. Birt, (2002) op cit. 112-113.

4. Birt, J. (1975) Can television news break the understanding-barrier? The Times. 28 February 1975.

5. Birt, J. (1975a) Television Journalism: The child of an unhappy marriage between newspapers and film. The Times. 30 September 1975. 12.

6. Birt, J. (1975b) The radical changes needed to remedy TV's bias against understanding. The Times. 1 October 1975. 14.

7. Birt, J. (1976) Why television news is in danger of becoming an anti-social force. The Times. 3 September 1976. 6.

8. Berlin, I. (1969) Two Concepts Of Liberty, in; Four Essays On Liberty. Oxford, England: Oxford University Press, 1969. 30.

9. Gardner, Llew. 1975. The Times. Letters to the Editor. 3 October 1975.

10. Birt, (2002) 146.

11. Heren, L. (1976) The alarming flaws in the case for New Journalism. The Times. 9 September 1976.

12. Birt, (2002) 251.

13. Birt, op cit. 254.

14. Birt, op cit. 146.

15. Birt, op cit. 249.

16. Birt, op cit. 257

17. Birt, op cit. 261.

18. Birt, op cit. 262.

19. Birt, op cit. 263.

20. Birt, op cit. 264.

21. Daily Mail. (2006) P.S. And even (Dame) Polly Toynbee has seen the light. Daily Mail. 10 August 2006. https://www.dailymail.co.uk/news/article-399922/P-S-And-Dame-Polly-Toynbee-seen-light.html

22. Birt, op cit. 265.

23. Tusa, John. 2018. Making a Noise. Weidenfed and Nicolson. London. 168.

24. Birt, op cit. 278.

25. Understanding John Birt (2002). Director: Paul Jenkins. BBC. 4 November 2002. Online at: https://youtu.be/c4_KhuWykaU

26. Tusa, op cit. 269.

27. Born, G. (2005) Uncertain Vision. Birt, Dyke and the Reinvention of the BBC. Vintage. London. 387.

28. Born, op cit. 388.

29. Mills, T. (2015) The end of social democracy and the rise of neoliberalism at the BBC. Interview with Stephen Coulter. Doctoral Thesis. University of Bath. 16 June 2015.

30. Born. op cit. 389.

31. Born. op cit. 397.

32. Born. op cit. 390.

33. Born. op cit. 405.

34. Understanding John Birt (2002). Director: Paul Jenkins. BBC. 4 November 2002. Online at: https://youtu.be/c4_KhuWykaU

35. Birt, op cit. 392.

36. Birt, op cit. 278.

37. Oborne, P. (2008) The Triumph of the Political Class. Pocket Books. London. 259.

38. Oborne, P. (2005) The Rise of Political Lying. Pocket Books. London. 242.

39. Oborne, op cit. 122.

40. Born. op cit. 396.

41. Schudson, M. (1998) Changing Concepts of Democracy. 4 June 1998. http://web.mit.edu/m-i-t/articles/index_schudson.html

42. Crouch, C. (2001). Coping with Post Democracy. Fabian society. https://www.fabians.org.uk/wp-content/uploads/2012/07/Post-Democracy.pdf

43. Birt, (2005) op cit.

44. Born. op cit. 448.

45. Born, op cit. 459.

CHAPTER TWENTY

1. New York Times Co. v. Sullivan, 376 U.S. 254. 1964. At par 6.

2. Nelson, J. (2001) The Civil Rights Movement – A Press Perspective. Human Rights, 28 (4) Fall 2001: 3-6.

3. Young, A (2012) quoted in, Papandrea, Mary-Rose, 2012. The Story of New York Times Co. v. Sullivan. In eds. Garnett, R.; Koppelman, A. 2012. First Amendment Stories. New York. Foundation Press/Thomas Reuters.

4. Morris, A.; Clawson, D. (2005) Lessons of the Civil Rights Movement for building a worker rights movement. Working USA, The Journal of Labor and Society. 8 (6) 683-704.

5. Anderson, D. (2014) Wechsler's Triumph. Alabama Law Review. Vol 66, 2. 229-252.

6. Stern ,S; Wermiel, S. (2010) Justice Brennan: Liberal Champion. Boston. Houghton Mifflin Harcourt. Xiii.

7. Newsweek. 19 January 1998. 62.

8. Kalven, H. Jr. (1964) The New York Times Case: A Note on 'The Central Meaning of the First Amendment'". 1964 Supreme Court Review. 191.

9. Ibid.

10. Epstein, R. (1986) Was New York Times v. Sullivan Wrong? University of Chicago Law Review. 53. 782.

11. US Supreme Court. (1985) Dun & Bradstreet, Inc. v. Greenmoss Builders, 472 U.S. 749.

12. Logan, D. (2020) Rescuing our Democracy by Revisiting New York Times v. Sullivan. 81 Ohio State Law Journal, 759.

13. Stiglitz, J. (2003) The Roaring Nineties. Penguin. London. 89.

14. Stiglitz, op cit. 104.

15. Supreme Court of the United States. (1969) Red Lion Broadcasting v. FCC. 395. No. 717.

16. Supreme Court of the United States. (1972) F.C.C. v. WNCN Listeners Guild. Box 73. Powell Papers. Washington & Lee Uni School of Law. 3.

17. U.S. Reports. (1981) FCC v. WNCN Listeners Guild, 450 U.S. 582.

18. Broadcasting Magazine (1981) March. Vol 100 (13) 23.

19. Ibid.

20. Fowler, M.; Brenner, D. (1982) Marketplace Approach to Broadcast Regulation. Texas Law Review 60 (2) February 1982: 209.

21. FCC. (1985) The Fairness Report. Inquiry into Section 73.1910 of the Commission's Rules and Regulations Concerning the General Fairness Doctrine Obligations of Broadcast Licensees. 23 August 1985. Docket 84-282.

22. FCC. (1949) In the Matter of Editorializing by Broadcast Licensees. Docket No. 8516. 1249.

23. FCC. (1987) Syracuse Peace Council v WTVH Syracuse, New York. Memorandum Opinion And Order. August 4, 1987. Record Volume 2 (17). https://digital.library.unt.edu/ark:/67531/metadc1594/: accessed June 11, 2021

24. Anderson, B. (2006) The Plot to Shush Rush and O'Reilly. City Journal. Winter 2006. https://www.city-journal.org/html/plot-shush-rush-and-o%E2%80%99reilly-12907.html

25. Cronauer, A. (1994) The Fairness Doctrine: A Solution in Search of a Problem. Federal Communications Law Journal. 47 (1) 6.

26. Ibid.

27. Rubin, J.; Hoffman, A. (1985) Jerry Rubin and Abbie Hoffman at Red Deer College on 8 March 1985. Video online at: https://youtu.be/UOFBAJ8BlJs

28. Sunstein, C. (2009) Going to Extremes; How Like Minds Unite and Divide. Oxford University Press. Oxford. 2.

29. Sunstein, op cit. 157.

30. Peacock, A. (1997) The Political Economy of Economic Freedom. Edward Elgar Publishing. Cheltenham. 38.

31. Peacock, op cit. 44.

32. Lippmann, W. (1956) The Public Philosophy. New York. Mentor. 99.

33. Zelizer, J. (2017) How Washington Helped Create the Contemporary Media: Ending the Fairness Doctrine in 1987. In; Media Nation: The Political History of News in Modern America, eds. Zelizer Julian E. and Schulman Bruce J., 176-89. Philadelphia: University of Pennsylvania Press.

34. Boyer, P. (1987) Television, Mark S. Fowler once observed, is really nothing more than "a toaster with pictures." New York Times. 19 January 1987. Section C. 15.

35. Pagano, P. (1987) The Fowler Legacy And Shock Radio facing test of time: at FCC, word is deregulation. Los Angeles Times. 25 April 1987. https://www.latimes.com/archives/la-xpm-1987-04-25-ca-959-story.html

CHAPTER TWENTY-ONE

1. Bell, Martin. 1997. TV News: How far Should we go? British Journalism Review (8) 1.

2. Ward, S. J. (1998) An Answer to Martin Bell: Objectivity and Attachment in Journalism. Harvard International Journal of Press/Politics, 3(3). 121–125.

3. O'Neill, B. (2012) Dangers of the "journalism of attachment". ABC News. 24 February 2012. https://www.abc.net.au/news/2012-02-24/oneill-dangers-of-the-journalism-of-attachment/3850566

4. BBC Radio Ulster (2012). Debating the "journalism of attachment". 4 March 2012. https://brendanoneill.co.uk/post/18794475962/debating-the-journalism-of-attachment

5. Hume, M. (1997) Who's War is it Anyway. The Dangers of the Journalism of Attachment. London. Informinc. 4.

6. Landes, R. (2021) Lethal, Own-Goal War Journalism on the Israeli-Palestinian Conflict. Algemeiner. 13 June 2021. https://www.algemeiner.com/2021/06/13/lethal-own-goal-war-journalism-on-the-israeli-palestinian-conflict/

7. Davis, D. (2002). The BBC is quickly becoming one of the world's 'kosher' purveyors of hate. Jewish World Review. 24 July 2002.

8. Marmari, H. (2002). Digging Beneath the Surface in the Middle East Conflict. Haaretz. 6 June 2002. https://www.haaretz.com/2002-06-06/ty-article/digging-beneath-the-surface-in-the-middle-east-conflict/0000017f-e5ec-df2c-a1ff-fffd6e3d0000

9. Ricchiardi, S. (1993) Exposing Genocide...For What? American Journalism Review. June 1993. https://ajrarchive.org/article.asp?id=1516&id=1516. Accessed 1 June 2021.

10. Mills, K. (1993). Taking It to the Streets. What are the limits of activism for journalists? American Journalism Review. July/August 1993. https://ajrarchive.org/Article.asp?id=1462&id=1462 Accessed 8 February 2022.

11. Ibid.

12. Hume, op cit.

13. Barnhurst, K. (2014) The Interpretive Turn in News. In; Journalism and Technological Change: Historical Perspectives, Contemporary Trends. Eds. Clemens Zimmermann and Martin Schreiber, Frankfurt: Campus Verlag. 118.

14. Pauly, J. (2014) The New Journalism and the Struggle for Interpretation. Journalism 15 (5) 589–604. 601.

15. Berman, D. (2004) Advocacy Journalism, The Least You Can Do, and The No Confidence Movement. Dave Berman. 29 Jun 2004.https://web.archive.org/web/20141020081742/http://publish.indymedia.org/en/2004/06/854953.shtml

16. Alterman, E. (1999) Sound and Fury: The Making of the Punditocracy. Ithaca. Cornell University Press.

17. McNair, Brain. 2000. "Journalism and Democracy: An Evaluation of the Political Public Sphere." London: Routledge. 61.

18. Hart, P. (1991). Irving L. Janis' Victims of Groupthink. Political Psychology. 12(2), 247-278.

19. Milton, J. (2016) Areopagitica; A Speech For The Liberty Of Unlicensed Printing To The Parliament Of England. Project Gutenberg. https://www.gutenberg.org/files/608/608-h/608-h.htm

20. Chamberlin, T. (1965) The Method of Multiple Working Hypotheses. Science, New Series, 148 (3671) 7 May 1965. 754-759.

21. Russell, B. (1965). Freedom and the colleges. In: Why I Am Not A Christian. New York, Simon and Schuster.

22. Lewis, C. S. (1987) The Humanitarian Theory of Punishment. Issues in Religion and Psychotherapy: Vol. 13 (1) 11. 151.

23. Camus, A. (1955) Homage to an Exile. Speech at banquet in honor of Eduardo Santos. 7 December 1955. In; Resistance, Rebellion, and Death. New York. Alfred A. Knopf (1961) 101.

24. Aitken, Robin. 2007. Can We Trust the BBC? Continuum. London. 20.

25. Aitken, op cit. 60.

26. Humphrys, J. (2019) A Day Like Today. London. William Collins.

27. Sissons, P. (2012) When One Door Closes. London. Biteback Publishing. 248.

28. Sissons, op cit. 325-6.

29. Marr, A. (2004) My Trade: A Short History of British Journalism. Oxford. Macmillan. 379.

30. Moreno, J. (1987) The Essential Moreno. Ed. Fox, J. New York: Springer. 11.

31. Blaskó, A., et al. (2021) Glossary. In: Sociodrama; The Art and Science of Social Change. Eds. Galgóczi, K. et al. L'Harmattan. Budapest. 352.

32. Takis, N. (2021) Group Phenomena, Processes And Dynamics In Sociodrama. In: Sociodrama; The Art and Science of Social Change. Eds. Galgóczi, K. et al. L'Harmattan. Budapest. 103.

33. Guthu, S. (2009) Living Newspapers. The Great Depression in Washington State Project. https://depts.washington.edu/depress/theater_arts_living_newspaper.shtml

34. Casson, J. (2000). Living Newspaper: Theatre and Therapy. TDR/The Drama Review. 44: 2 (166), 120.

35. McNiff, E. et al. (2015) How the Retracted Rolling Stone Article 'A Rape on Campus' Came to Print. ABC News. https://abcnews.go.com/2020/deepdive/how-retracted-rolling-stone-article-rape-on-campus-came-print-42701166

36. Coronel, S. et al. (2015). Rolling Stone and UVA: The Columbia University Graduate School of Journalism Report; An anatomy of a journalistic failure. Rolling Stone. 5 April 2015.

37. Wolff, M. (2003) Troubled Times. NY Mag. 16 May 2003. https://nymag.com/nymetro/news/media/features/n_8723/

38. Younge, G. (2004) The man who took the New York Times for a ride. The Guardian. 6 March 2004. https://www.theguardian.com/world/2004/mar/06/usa.pressandpublishing

CHAPTER TWENTY-TWO

1. Shelton, T. (2022) Park Hotel detainees housed alongside Novak Djokovic describe 'disgusting' and 'cruel' conditions. ABC News. 9 January 2022. https://www.abc.net.au/news/2022-01-09/park-hotel-detainee-speak-out/100745456

2. Djokovic v Minister for Immigration, Citizenship, Migrant Services and Multicultural Affairs (2022) FCAFC 3. 20 January 2022. https://www.fedcourt.gov.au/services/access-to-files-and-transcripts/online-files/djokovic

3. Mill, J. (1940) On Liberty, Ch 1. In; Utilitarianism, Liberty and Representative Government. London. J.M. Dent. 75.

4. Mill, op cit. 73.

5. Berlin I. (1958) Two Concepts of Liberty. In: Liberty. Oxford University Press; (2002) Ch 4.

6. Nuremberg Code. (1947) BMJ 1996. 313:1448.

7. Katz J. (1992) The Consent Principle of the Nuremberg Code; Its Significance Then and Now. In: Nazi Doctors and the Nuremberg Code. Human Rights in Human Experimentation. Oxford. Oxford University Press. 236.

8. Hill, J. (2022) The Selfishness of Novak Djokovic. The Atlantic. 15 January 2022. https://www.theatlantic.com/ideas/archive/2022/01/novak-djokovic-vaccine-australia-special-treatment/621270/

9. Oleksinski, J. (2022) Novak Djokovic's Australian Open vaccine exemption is a joke. New York Post. 4 January 2022. https://nypost.

com/2022/01/04/novak-djokovics-australian-open-vaccine-exemption-is-a-joke/

10. Fels, S. (2022) Novak Djokovic is still a selfish jackass. Deadspin. 15 February 2022. https://deadspin.com/novak-djokovic-is-still-a-selfish-jackass-1848539515

11. Appleton, J. (2022) Macron Says, "No Vaxx, No Citizenship" as France Unveils New, Stricter Vaccine Passports. Daily Sceptic. 24 January 2022. https://dailysceptic.org/macron-says-no-vaxx-no-citizenship-as-france-unveils-new-stricter-vaccine-passports/

12. Agamben, G. (2022) Where Are We Now? The Epidemic as Politics. London. Rowman & Littlefield. ebook.

13. Reagan, R. (1966) The Myth of the Great Society. Speech at the Patton Center, NYC. 1966. Ronald Reagan Presidential Library.

CHAPTER TWENTY-THREE

1. Stasch, S. (2018) The Creation and Destruction of the Great American Middle Class (1930-2010). Loyola University Chicago. School of Business.

2. HM Government. (2021) Global Britain in a competitive age; The Integrated Review of Security, Defence, Development and Foreign Policy. March 2021. CP403. 24.

3. Price, C.; Edwards, K. (2020) Trends in Income From 1975 to 2018. Rand. Working paper. September 2020.

4. Jaffe, S. (2018). The Struggle to Stay Middle Class. The New Republic. 26 April 2018. https://newrepublic.com/article/148130/struggle-stay-middle-class

5. Renn, A. (2016) The Rage of Those Left Behind. Manhattan Institute. 5 July 2016. https://www.manhattan-institute.org/html/rage-those-left-behind-9046.html

6. Snyder, M. (2015) Goodbye Middle Class: 51 Percent Of All American Workers Make Less Than 30,000 Dollars A Year. End of the American Dream. 20 October 2015. http://endoftheamericandream.com/goodbye-

454

middle-class-51-percent-of-all-american-workers-make-less-than-30000-dollars-a-year/

7. Snyder, M. (2020) Goodbye Middle Class: Half Of All American Workers Made Less Than $34,248.45 Last Year. Washington Standard. 15 October 2020. https://thewashingtonstandard.com/goodbye-middle-class-half-of-all-american-workers-made-less-than-34248-45-last-year/

8. Feierstein, M. (2012) Planet Ponzi: How the World Got Into This Mess, What Happens Next, How to Save Yourself. Wilmington. Glacier.

9. Von Greyerz, E. (2022) All Hell Will Break Loose For Humanity. Gold Switzerland blog. 22 March 2022. https://goldswitzerland.com/all-hell-will-break-loose

10. Kotkin, J. (2020) The Coming of Neo-Feudalism. Website. https://joelkotkin.com/the-coming-of-neo-feudalism/ Accessed 1 June 2022.

11. Kotkin, J. (2020) The Coming of Neo-Feudalism: A Warning to the Global Middle Class. Encounter Books. New York. 35.

12. Turchin, P. (2013) Blame Rich, Overeducated Elites as Our Society Frays. Bloomberg. 20 November 2013. https://www.bloomberg.com/opinion/articles/2013-11-20/blame-rich-overeducated-elites-as-our-society-frays

13. Discenza, N. (2021) With energy costs rising across N.Y., Schumer pushes for federal relief. WSHU. 15 October 2021. https://www.wshu.org/news/2021-10-15/with-energy-costs-rising-across-n-y-schumer-pushes-for-federal-relief

14. Lloyd, N. (2022) Turning up the heat on Europe's fuel poverty crisis. Euronews. 2 February 2022. https://www.euronews.com/my-europe/2022/01/26/turning-up-the-heat-on-europe-s-energy-poverty-crisis

15. Butler, P. (2022) Woman who rides bus to stay warm is tip of pensioner poverty iceberg. The Guardian. 3 May 2022. https://www.theguardian.com/business/2022/may/03/stories-like-elsies-highlight-pensioners-plight-and-the-inadequate-help

16. Tucker, J. (2022) The Economic Meltdown Has Roots In Lockdown. Zerohedge. 15 June 2022. https://www.zerohedge.com/economics/economic-meltdown-has-roots-lockdown

17. Martin, op cit. 23.

18. Twenge, J. (2013) Millennials: The Me Me Me Generation. Time. 20 May 2013. https://time.com/247/millennials-the-me-me-me-generation/

19. Twenge, J.; Campbell, K. (2009) The Narcissism Epidemic. Free Press. New York.

20. Reich, op cit. 185.

21. Reich, op cit. 24.

22. Labov W. (1997) Rules for Ritual Insults. In: Coupland N., Jaworski A. (eds) Sociolinguistics. Modern Linguistics Series. London. Palgrave

CHAPTER TWENTY-FOUR

1. Lind, M. (2020) The New Class War. New York. Penguin Random House.

2. Timothy, N. (2019) It's time for Boris Johnson to take on Britain's cult of liberal technocrats. Daily Telegraph. 29 December 2019. https://www.telegraph.co.uk/politics/2019/12/29/time-boris-johnson-take-britains-cult-liberal-technocrats/

3. Lofgren, M. (2016) The Deep State: The Fall of the Constitution and the Rise of a Shadow Government. New York. Viking Press. Ebook.

4. Schwab. K. (2020) Covid-19 The Great Reset. Forum Publishing.

5. Woudhuysen, J. (2020) Nudging: an elite disease. Spiked. 18 March 2020. https://www.spiked-online.com/2020/03/18/nudging-an-elite-disease/

6. Newman, M. (2021) Dangerous elites planning 'the Great Reset'; Davos 2021 will launch its own Green New Deal. Be afraid. The Spectator. 10 October 2020. https://spectator.com.au/2020/10/dangerous-elites-planning-the-great-reset/

7. Kristol, I. (1975) Is technology a threat to liberal society? Talk given by Irving Kristol at the Polytechnic Institute of New York in 1975. https://www.nationalaffairs.com/public_interest/detail/is-technology-a-threat-to-liberal-society

8. Lind, op cit.

9. Wilson, D. (2020) UK ditches Blair's 50% university graduate plan. Maybe now we can get the skilled elite we'll need after Covid. RT.com. 10 July 2020. https://www.rt.com/op-ed/494306-uk-education-blair-universities/

10. Steyn, M. (2019) Steyn breaks down why liberals love 'woke billionaires'. Fox News. 1 February 2019. YouTube. https://youtu.be/YBr6wnyixXY

11. Doyle, A. (2019) Woke; A Guide to Social Justice. Titania McGrath. London. Little Brown Books.

12. Wilson, B. (2008) Decency and Disorder; the Age of Cant. 1789-1837. London. Faber and Faber.

13. CESJ. (2021) Brochure for; Britain on the Couch. Centre for the Study of Conflict, Emotion and Social Justice, Bournemouth University. 13 July 2021.

14. Avlon, J. (2019) Polarization is poisoning America. Here's an antidote. CNN. 1 November 2019. https://edition.cnn.com/2019/10/30/opinions/fractured-states-of-america-polarization-is-killing-us-avlon/index.html

15. Sun Tzu. (1988) The Art of War. Boston. Shambhala. Xix.

16. Sun Tzu, op cit. 11.

17. Sun Tzu, op cit. 16.

18. Sun Tzu, op cit. 18.

19. Schwab, K.; Malleret, T. (2022) The Great Narrative. Forum Publishing. e-book.

20. Johnstone, C. (2019) 37 Tips For Navigating A Society That Is Full Of Propaganda And Manipulation. Caitlin Johnstone Blog. 3 June 2019. https://caitlinjohnstone.com/2019/06/03/thirty-two-tips-for-navigating-a-society-that-is-full-of-propaganda-and-manipulation/

21. Sager, W. (2015). Apple pie propaganda? The smith–mundt act before and after the repeal of the domestic dissemination ban. Northwestern University law review. 109. 511-546. 537.

22. LeVine, M. (2012) The high price of 'dark fusion': The US government can already detain citizens as enemy combatants; now it wants to deploy propaganda across the country. Al Jazeera. 4 June 2012. https://www.aljazeera.com/opinions/2012/6/4/the-high-price-of-dark-fusion/

23. McCarthy, K. (2012) The Smith-Mundt Modernization Act of 2012. River Cities' Reader. https://www.rcreader.com/commentary/smith-mundt-modernization-act-2012

24. Taibbi, M. (2022) Twitter Files Thread: The Spies Who Loved Twitter. TK News. 25 December 2022. https://taibbi.substack.com/p/twitter-files-thread-the-spies-who

25. Zweig, D. (2022) How Twitter Rigged the Covid Debate. The Free Press. 26 December 2022. https://www.thefp.com/p/how-twitter-rigged-the-covid-debate

26. Taibbi, M. op cit.

27. Marshall, V. (2022) FBI Admits It Meddles In 'Numerous Companies,' Not Just Twitter. The Federalist. 22 December 2022. https://thefederalist.com/2022/12/22/fbi-admits-it-meddles-in-numerous-companies-not-just-twitter/

28. Shellenberger, M. (2022) Twitter.com. 19 December 2022. 6.36pm. https://twitter.com/ShellenbergerMD/status/1604908670063906817

29. Gibson, J. et al. (2022) FBI responds to Twitter Files disclosures, says it didn't request 'any action' on specific tweets. Fox News. 21 December 2022. https://www.foxnews.com/politics/fbi-responds-twitter-files-disclosures-says-didnt-request-any-action-specific-tweets

30. Leveson, B. (2012) An Inquiry Into The Culture, Practices And Ethics Of The Press. Report by The Right Honourable Lord Justice Leveson. November 2012. Volume 1. London. The Stationery Office. 79.

31. Leveson, op cit. 37.

32. Leveson, op cit. 38.

33. Leveson, op cit. 87.

34. Leveson, op cit. 89.

35. Leveson, op cit. 598.

36. Leveson, op cit. 673.

37. In: Luckhurst, op cit. 10.

38. Murdoch, J. (2011) James Murdoch: News of the World statement in full. BBC. 7 July 2011. https://www.bbc.co.uk/news/uk-14070822

39. Timothy, op cit.

40. Anthony, A. (2021) Everything you wanted to know about the culture wars – but were afraid to ask. The Guardian. 13 June 2021. https://www.theguardian.com/world/2021/jun/13/everything-you-wanted-to-know-about-the-culture-wars-but-were-afraid-to-ask

41. Furedi, F. (2021) The culture war is real and it's getting worse. Spiked. 15 June 2021. https://www.spiked-online.com/2021/06/15/the-culture-war-is-real-and-its-getting-worse/

42. Lewis, P. et al. (2019) Revealed: the rise and rise of populist rhetoric. The Guardian. 6 Mar 2019. https://www.theguardian.com/world/ng-interactive/2019/mar/06/revealed-the-rise-and-rise-of-populist-rhetoric

43. Mudde, C. (2004) The Populist Zeitgeist. Government and Opposition, 39: 541-563. 543.

44. Windsor, M.; Caplan, D. (2016) Clinton's 'Deplorables' Comment Show Disdain for Working People, Trump Camp Says. ABC News. 10 September 2016. https://abcnews.go.com/Politics/hillary-clinton-half-donald-trumps-supporters-basket-deplorables/story?id=41993204

CHAPTER TWENTY-FIVE

1. Trump, D. (2016) Speech at West Palm Beach, Florida. 13 October 2016. National Public Radio. https://www.npr.org/2016/10/13/497857068/transcript-donald-trumps-speech-responding-to-assault-accusations?t=1645535893433

2. Trump, D. (2020) Remarks at rally at Valdosta, Georgia. 5 December 2020. https://youtu.be/Ps1HIzfBbqk

3. Trump, D. (2020) Remarks by President Trump at the White House Conference on American History 17 September 2020. https://www.whitehouse.gov/briefingsstatements/remarks-president-trump-white-house-conference-american-history/

4. Trump, D. (2021) Former President Trump holds a rally in Cullman, Alabama. C-Span. Saturday 21 August 2021. https://www.c-span.org/video/?514187-1/president-trump-holds-rally-cullman-alabama.

5. Trump, D. (2022) Remarks at CPAC Florida 2022. Newsmax TV. 26 February 2022 https://www.youtube.com/watch?v=cev2s7nbmWM

6. Gouge, W. (1968) A Short History of Paper Money And Banking In The United States. New York. Augustus Kelley.

7. Hoffman, A. (1968) Revolution for the hell of it. New York, Dial Press.

8. Adams, J., T. (1932) The Epic of America. Boston. Little Brown. 404.

9. Adams, op cit. 99-100.

10. Adams, op cit. 411.

11. Hoover, H. (1923) American Individualism. New York. Doubleday Page. 13.

12. Hoover, op cit. 19.

13. Locke, J. (1690) Second Treatise of Government. Ch 2.

14. Ebeling, R. (2016) John Locke and American Individualism. Future of Freedom Foundation. 29 August 2016. https://www.fff.org/explore-freedom/article/john-locke-american-individualism/

15. Hofstadter, op cit. 242.

16. Sunstein, C. (2021) This Is Not Normal. New Haven. Yale University Press. 136.

17. Rand, A. (1964) The Virtue of Selfishness. New York. Signet. 6.

18. Rand, A. (1986) Capitalism: The Unknown Ideal. New York. Signet. 27. Jefferson, T. (1787) Letter to James Madison. 20 December 1787.

19. Jefferson, T. (1787) Letter to James Madison. 20 December 1787.

20. Hamilton, A. (1788) The Federalist Papers. No. 71. The Duration in Office of the Executive. 18 March 1788.

21. Thomas. (2017) What a Beautiful Moment. 30 Seconds of Video of President Trump at Andrew Jackson Memorial is Going Viral. Political Insider. 16

March 2017. https://thepoliticalinsider.com/beautiful-moment-30-seconds-of-video-president-trump-andrew-jackson-memorial/

22. Mead, W. R. (2017) The Jacksonian Revolt: American Populism and the Liberal Order. Foreign Affairs 96, no. 2 (March/April 2017) 2-7.

23. Adams, op cit. 172.

24. Watson, H. (2006) Liberty and Power: The Politics of Jacksonian America. New York. Hill and Wang. 94.

25. Jackson, A. (1832) Bank Veto Message. 10 July 1832. https://millercenter. org/the-presidency/presidential-speeches/july-10-1832-bank-veto

26. Jackson, A. (1837) Farewell Address. 4 March 1837. https://millercenter. org/the-presidency/presidential-speeches/march-4-1837-farewell-address

27. Devega, C. (2019) Philosopher Susan Neiman says Trump is evil — and she literally wrote the book. Salon. 24 September 2019. https://www.salon. com/2019/09/24/philosopher-susan-neiman-says-trump-is-evil-and-she-literally-wrote-the-book/

28. Scott, G. (2017) Is Trump the Modern Day Devil? HuffPost. 31 March 2017. https://www.huffpost.com/entry/is-trump-the-modernday-de_b_9579936

29. Leupp, G. (2021) Trump as Antichrist: A Way Out for the Disillusioned Cultist. CounterPunch. 2 April 2021. https://www.counterpunch. org/2021/04/02/trump-as-antichrist-a-way-out-for-the-disillusioned-cultist/

CHAPTER TWENTY-SIX

1. Buzzfeed (2016) US Presidential Election: Republican Candidate Donald Trump's Activities in Russia and Compromising Relationship with the Kremlin. 19 October 2016. https://s3.documentcloud.org/documents/3259984/pages/Trump-Intelligence-Allegations-p2-normal. gif?ts=1607969312412

2. Bensinger, K. et al. (2017) These Reports Allege Trump Has Deep Ties To Russia. Buzzfeed. BuzzfeedNews. 10 January 2017. https://www.buzzfeednews.com/article/kenbensinger/these-reports-allege-trump-has-deep-ties-to-russia

3. Farhi, P. (2021) The Washington Post corrects, removes parts of two stories regarding the Steele dossier. The Washington Post. 12 November 2021. https://www.washingtonpost.com/lifestyle/style/media-washington-post-steele-dossier/2021/11/12/f7c9b770-43d5-11ec-a88e-2aa4632af69b_story.html

4. Maddow, R. (2017) More Pieces Of Donald Trump Russia Dossier Check Out. MSNBC. 8 March 2017. https://www.youtube.com/watch?v=5exiuko3-nQ

5. ibid.

6. Mueller, R. (2019) Report on the Investigation into Russian Interference in the 2016 Presidential Election. US Dept of Justice. March 2019. 9. https://s3.documentcloud.org/documents/5955997/Muellerreport.pdf

7. Pelosi, N. (2017) The Wrap Up Smear. House Minority Leader Weekly Briefing. C-Span. 22 June 2017. https://www.c-span.org/video/?c4674689/user-clip-wrap-smear

8. Bell, D. (1997) Innuendo. Journal of Pragmatics 27: 35–59.

9. Hasher, L., Goldstein, D., & Toppino, T. (1977). Frequency and the Conference of Referential Validity. Journal of Verbal Learning and Verbal Behavior, 16, 107-112. http://bear.warrington.ufl.edu/brenner/mar7588/Papers/hasher-et-al-jvvb-1977.pdf. 108.

10. BBC. (2020) Impartiality - Guidance note. 29 October 2020. https://www.bbc.co.uk/editorialguidelines/guidance/impartiality Accessed 11 August 2021.

11. BBC (1957). BBC Handbook 1957. Number 3400. BBC. London. 63.

12. Cleveland, M. (2022) J6 Committee Focuses On Election Fraud Claims While Ignoring Tactics Used To Rig The 2020 Election. The Federalist. 22 June 2022. https://thefederalist.com/2022/06/22/j6-committee-focuses-on-election-fraud-claims-while-ignoring-tactics-used-to-rig-the-2020-election/

13. BBC Radio 4. (2020) Today. 10 November 2020.

14. BBC News (2021) Trump-Russia Steele dossier analyst charged with lying to FBI. BBC News. 5 November 2021. https://www.bbc.co.uk/news/world-us-canada-59168626

15. Trump, D. (2016) Presidential Candidate Donald Trump at the South Florida Fair Expo Center Rally in West Palm Beach, Florida. 13 October 2016. https://www.c-span.org/video/?416882-1/donald-trump-calls-allegations-absolutely-false

16. Trump, D. (2017) Twitter. 15 February 2017

17. Trump, D. (2017a) Twitter. 17 February 2017

18. Trump, D. (2018) The Highly-Anticipated 2017 Fake News Awards. GOP. com. 17 January 2018. https://web.archive.org/web/20180118010005/https://gop.com/the-highly-anticipated-2017-fake-news-awards/

19. Trump, D. (2019) Twitter. 19 March 2019

20. Carson, J. (2018). Fake news: What exactly is it – and how can you spot it? Daily Telegraph. 28 November 2018. https://www.telegraph.co.uk/technology/0/fake-news-exactly-donald-trump-rise/

21. Davis, S. (2019) A Catastrophic Media Failure. Wall Street Journal. 25 March 2019. https://www.wsj.com/articles/a-catastrophic-media-failure-11553555444

22. Raimondo, J. (2018) Whatever Happened to the Russia-gate 'Scandal'? AntiWar.com. 5 November 2018. https://original.antiwar.com/justin/2018/11/04/whatever-happened-to-the-russia-gate-scandal/

23. Boyd-Barrett, O. (2020) RussiaGate and Propaganda; Disinformation in the Age of Social Media. Routledge. New York. 99.

24. Taibbi, M. (2020) The American Press Is Destroying Itself. TK News. 12 June 2020. https://taibbi.substack.com/p/the-news-media-is-destroying-itself

25. Kurtz, H. (2018) Media Madness; Donald Trump, the Press and the War over the Truth. Regnery. Washington DC.

26. Hanson, V, D. (2022) The Truths We Dared Not Speak in 2021. American Greatness website. 2 January 2022. https://amgreatness.com/2022/01/02/the-truths-we-dared-not-speak-in-2021/

27. Hetherington, M.; Ladd, J. (2020) Destroying trust in the media, science, and government has left America vulnerable to disaster. Brookings. 1 May 2020. https://www.brookings.edu/blog/fixgov/2020/05/01/destroy-

ing-trust-in-the-media-science-and-government-has-left-america-vulnerable-to-disaster/

28. McCann, S. (2021) The Left-Wing Legacy of the Mainstream Media. American Thinker. 7 December 2021. https://www.americanthinker.com/articles/2021/12/the_leftwing_legacy_of_the_mainstream_media_.html

29. Tsfati, Y. (2003). Media skepticism and climate of opinion perception. International Journal of Public Opinion Research, 15(1), 65–82, 67.

30. Brenan, M (2021). Americans' Trust in Media Dips to Second Lowest on Record. Gallup. 7 October 2021. https://news.gallup.com/poll/355526/americans-trust-media-dips-second-lowest-record.aspx

31. Edelman. (2021). 2021 Edelman Trust Barometer Reveals a Rampant Infodemic is Fueling Widespread Mistrust of Societal Leaders. Edelman.com 13 January 2021. https://www.edelman.com/trust/2021-trust-barometer/press-release

32. Newman, N. et al. (2022) Reuters Institute Digital News Report 2022. Reuters Institute for the Study of Journalism. https://reutersinstitute.politics.ox.ac.uk/sites/default/files/2022-06/Digital_News-Report_2022.pdf. 11.

CHAPTER TWENTY-SEVEN

1. Wake Up World. (2014) About Wake Up World. https://wakeup-world.com/about/

2. Smith, C. (2022) It's a New Era. Of Two Minds Blog. 30 December 2022. https://charleshughsmith.blogspot.com/2022/12/its-new-era.html

3. Cushion, S. et al. (2021) Why National Media Systems Matter. Journalism Studies, 22:5, 633-652.

4. Petrakis, M. (2020) The Fatal Attraction of Techno-Fascism. 26 August 2020. https://off-guardian.org/2020/08/26/the-fatal-attraction-of-techo-fascism/

5. Media Lens. (2021). Shocking Omissions: Capitalism's Conscience–200 Years of The Guardian – John Pilger and Jonathan Cook Respond. Media Lens. 19 April 2021. https://www.medialens.org/2021/shocking-omis-

sions-capitalisms-conscience-200-years-of-the-guardian-john-pilger-and-jonathan-cook-respond/

6. Morrow, L. (2020) Before Reporting Became 'Journalism' Writers subdued their egos and encouraged readers to think. Nowadays it's all about arousing emotion. Wall Street Journal. 23 September 2020. https://www.wsj.com/articles/before-reporting-became-journalism-11600879803

7. Kitty, A. (2018) When Journalism Was a Thing. Zero Books, Winchester, UK.

8. Taibbi, M. (2021) Congratulations, Elitists: Liberals and Conservatives Do Have Common Interests Now. TK News. 3 June 2021. https://taibbi.substack.com/p/congratulations-elitists-liberals-6ec

9. Taibbi, M. (2021) The Sovietization of the American Press. TK News. 12 March 2021. https://taibbi.substack.com/p/the-sovietization-of-the-american

10. Weiss, B. (2020) Twitter is editing the New York Times. The Spectator. 14 July 2020. https://spectator.us/bari-weiss-twitter-is-editing-the-new-york-times/

11. Greenwald, G. (2020) My Resignation From The Intercept. Glenn Greenwald website. 29 October 2020. https://greenwald.substack.com/p/my-resignation-from-the-intercept

12. Siegel, J. (2020) The New Truth; When the moral imperative trumps the rational evidence, there's no arguing. Tablet Magazine. 22 June 2020. https://www.tabletmag.com/sections/news/articles/new-truth-rationalism-religion

13. Kennedy, B. (2022) DC Elites Have Opened Americans To Nuclear Attack, So Americans Must Protect Themselves. The Federalist. 7 March 2022. https://thefederalist.com/2022/03/07/dc-elites-have-opened-americans-to-nuclear-attack-so-americans-must-protect-themselves/ Accessed 8 February 2022

14. Epoch Times. (2022) About Us. Epoch Times Website. https://www.theepochtimes.com/about-us

15. Zerohedge. (2022) About. Zerohedge Website. https://www.zerohedge.com/about

16. Project Veritas. (2022) About. Project Veritas Website. https://www.projectveritas.com/about/

17. Johnstone, C. (2021) What I'm About And What I'm Trying To Accomplish Here. Caitlinjohnstone.com. 31 July 2021. https://caitlinjohnstone.com/about/

18. Bannon, S. (2022) Steve Bannon's 2022 AmFest Speech At Turning Point Action. 31 December 2022. Warroom. https://warroom.org/2022/12/31/steve-bannons-2022-amfest-speech-at-turning-point-action/

19. TCW. (2022) Our Mission. TCW Website. https://www.conservativewoman.co.uk/our-mission/

20. Young, T. (2021) The Daily Sceptic. 19 July 2021. https://dailysceptic.org/2021/07/19/the-daily-sceptic/

21. UK Column. (2022) About The UK Column. https://www.ukcolumn.org/about-uk-column

22. Farage, N. (2021) Nigel Farage's first show on GB News in full. GB News YouTube channel. 19 July 2021. https://www.youtube.com/watch?v=NFWs8T1Jc74

23. Singh, V. (2019) The Rise of Alternative Media. HoneySuckle Magazine. 4 November 2019. https://honeysucklemag.com/the-rise-of-alternative-media/

24. Malik, N. (2019) The myth of the free speech crisis. Guardian. 3 September 2019. Guardian. https://www.theguardian.com/world/2019/sep/03/the-myth-of-the-free-speech-crisis

25. BBC. (2021) One in three spot hate speech in online videos. BBC News. 24 March 2021. https://www.bbc.co.uk/news/technology-56513000

26. Spring, M. (2021) Government lays out plans to protect users online. BBC News. 12 May 2021. https://www.bbc.co.uk/news/technology-57071977

27. Wiener, A. (2020) Is Substack the Media Future We Want? New Yorker. 28 December 2020. https://www.newyorker.com/magazine/2021/01/04/is-substack-the-media-future-we-want

28. Solon, O. (2018) YouTube's 'alternative influence network' breeds right-wing radicalisation, report finds. 18 September 2018. https://www.

theguardian.com/media/2018/sep/18/report-youtubes-alternative-influ-ence-network-breeds-rightwing-radicalisation

29. Marginson, S. (2016). The Uses of the University. In The Dream Is Over: The Crisis of Clark Kerr's California Idea of Higher Education (21–27). University of California Press. http://www.jstor.org/stable/10.1525/j.ctt1kc6k1p.8

CHAPTER TWENTY-EIGHT

1. Sopel, J. (2019) A Year At The Circus: Inside Trump's White House. London. BBC Books. 11.

2. Sopel, op cit. 16.

3. Sopel, op cit. 37.

4. Sopel, op cit. 36.

5. Sopel, op cit. 30.

6. Sopel, J. (2022) Interview with author. 22 March 2022. Recording in author's collection.

7. Maitlis, E. (2022) We have to stop normalising the absurd. Transcript of the James MacTaggart Memorial Lecture at the Edinburgh TV Festival. 25 August 2022. https://www.prospectmagazine.co.uk/politics/we-have-to-stop-normalising-the-absurd

8. Rodino, P. (1975) Impeachment of Richard M. Nixon, President of the United States. The Final Report of the Committee on the Judiciary House of Representatives. Bantam. New York. 210.

9. Rodino, op cit. 212.

10. Rodino, op cit. 206.

11. Maitlis, op cit.

12. Hopkins, C.J. (2022) The Gaslighting of the Masses. Consent Factory inc. 16 October 2022. https://consentfactory.org/2022/10/16/the-gaslighting-of-the-masses/

13. Sagan, C. (1997) The Demon-Haunted World: Science as a Candle in the Dark. New York. Ballantine.

CHAPTER TWENTY-NINE

1. Full Fact (2022). About Us. https://fullfact.org/about/automated/

2. Full Fact (2022a). The Full Fact Toolkit. https://fullfact.org/toolkit/

3. Snopes. (2019). What is Snopes' fact-checking process? 30 May 2019. https://www.snopes.com/faq/fact-checking-process/

4. Facebook (2021). Stossel v Facebook. US District Court. San Jose Division. Case 5:21-cv-07385-VKD Document 27. Notice of Motion & Motion to Dismiss. 29 November 2021.

5. Uscinski, J, E.; Butler, R, W. (2013) The Epistemology of Fact Checking. Critical Review, 25:2, 162-180. 163.

6. Evon, D. (2022) Here's What We Know About 'Johns Hopkins Study' on Lockdowns. Snopes. 3 February 2022. https://www.snopes.com/news/2022/02/03/johns-hopkins-study-on-lockdowns/

7. Herby, J. et al. (2022) A Literature Review And Meta-Analysis Of The Effects Of Lockdowns On Covid-19 Mortality. Studies in Applied Economics. 210. May 2022.

8. Watts, A. (2021). BOMBSHELL: In court filing, Facebook admits 'fact checks' are nothing more than opinion. WattsUpWithThat. 9 December 2021. https://wattsupwiththat.com/2021/12/09/bombshell-in-court-filing-facebook-admits-fact-checks-are-nothing-more-than-opinion

9. BBC. (2020) Trusted News Initiative (TNI) to combat spread of harmful vaccine disinformation and announces major research project. 10 December 2020. https://www.bbc.com/mediacentre/2020/trusted-news-initiative-vaccine-disinformation

10. Ibid.

11. Skippage, R. (2020) The role of public service media in the fight against disinformation. Reuters Institute for the Study of Journalism. Journalist Fellowship Paper. December 2020https://reutersinstitute.politics.ox.ac.uk/sites/default/files/2021-02/RISJ_Final%20Report_RebeccaS_2020.pdf

12. IBC. (2020) Multi-Stakeholder Media Provenance Management To Counter Synthetic Media Risks In News Publishing. White Paper. https://drive. google.com/file/d/11c41iTwq7z-nMMMPQLE5GZ6gJmc_llJ1/view

13. Menéndez, P. (2018) In: García-Sanjuán, A., 2018. Rejecting al-Andalus, exalting the Reconquista: historical memory in contemporary Spain. Journal of Medieval Iberian Studies, 10(1), 127-145.

14. BBC Trusted News Initiative. Engaging Hard to Reach Audiences. Video. https://www.bbc.co.uk/beyondfakenews/catchup/enagaginghardto-reachaudiences

15. Uscinski, op cit. 163.

16. Malone, R. (2021). On "Science" and Controversy; Infectious disease outbreaks require constant re-evaluation of accepted truth. Robert Malone blog. 21 December 2021. https://rwmalonemd.substack.com/p/on-science-and-controversy

17. The Liberty Beacon. (2021) COVID-19 & the Shadowy "Trusted News Initiative". 13 August 2021.https://www.thelibertybeacon.com/covid-19-the-shadowy-trusted-news-initiative/

18. Kennedy, R. F. et al (2023) Children's Health Defense et al v The Washington Post, The BBC et al. Complaint. US District Court, Amarillo Division. Case 2:23-cv-00004-Z. 10 January 2023. 12, 22-23

19. Clark, C., J.; Winegard, Bo., M. (2020) Tribalism in War and Peace: The Nature and Evolution of Ideological Epistemology and Its Significance for Modern Social Science. Psychological Inquiry, 31:1, 1-22.

20. Storr, W. (2019) The Science of Storytelling. William Collins. London. 163.

21. Mill, J., S. (1940) On Liberty. Ch 3. In: Utilitarianism, Liberty and Representative Government. London. J.M. Dent. 114.

22. Feynman, R. (1955) The Value of Science. Engineering and Science, 19 (3). 13-15.

23. Feynman, R. (1999) The Pleasure of Finding Things Out: The Best Short Works of Richard Feynman. Perseus Publishing Company. 1999. 187.

24. Schneider, L. (2020) The full-service paper mill and its Chinese customers. For Better Science blog. 24 January 2020. https://forbetterscience. com/2020/01/24/the-full-service-paper-mill-and-its-chinese-customers/

25. Smith, R. (2021) Time to assume that health research is fraudulent until proven otherwise? BMJ Blog. 5 July 2021. https://blogs.bmj.com/bmj/2021/07/05/time-to-assume-that-health-research-is-fraudulent-until-proved-otherwise/

26. Jureidini, J.; McHenry, L. (2022) The illusion of evidence based medicine. BMJ. 16 March 2022.

27. Quine, W, V.; Ullian, J, S. (1970) The Web of Belief. New York, Random House. 39.

28. Kahneman, D. (2012) Thinking Fast and Slow. Penguin. London. 212.

29. Haynes, M. (2021) FLASHBACK: New Zealand PM told public 'we are your single source of truth'. LifeSiteNews. 16 July 2021. https://www.lifesitenews.com/news/flashback-new-zealand-pm-told-public-we-are-your-single-source-of-truth

30. Department of Homeland Security. (2022) National Terrorism Advisory System Bulletin. 7 February 2022. https://www.dhs.gov/sites/default/files/ntas/alerts/22_0207_ntas-bulletin.pdf Accessed 12 March 2022.

31. Harsanyi, D. (2022) Biden's Ministry of Truth. Real Clear Politics. https://www.realclearpolitics.com/articles/2022/04/29/bidens_ministry_of_truth_147538.html

32. Lorenz, T. (2022) How the Biden administration let right-wing attacks derail its disinformation efforts. The Washington Post. 18 May 2022. https://www.washingtonpost.com/technology/2022/05/18/disinformation-board-dhs-nina-jankowicz/

33. Ellerbe, H. (1996) The Dark Side of Christian History. Morningstar & Lark. 11.

34. Finocchiaro, M. 1991. The Galileo Affair. Berkeley. University of California Press. 12.

35. Spurgeon, C. (1855) The Sin of Unbelief. Sermon. 14 January 1855. https://www.spurgeon.org/resource-library/sermons/the-sin-of-unbelief/#flip-book/

36. De Luca, M. (1901) Institutiones Juris Ecclesiastici Publici. 1, 143.

37. Khomeini, R., A. (1989) Fatwa Against Salman Rushdie. Iran Data Portal. 1 April 2013. https://irandataportal.syr.edu/fatwa-against-salman-rushdie

38. Davies, I. (2021) Covidiot or Covid-idiot? Which One Are You? In This Together website. 12 July 2021. https://in-this-together.com/covidiot/

39. Chao, D.; Levin, S. (1999) Herding behavior: The emergence of large-scale phenomena from local interactions. In; S. Ruan, G. S. K. Wolkowicz and J. Wu., editors, Differential Equations with Applications to Biology, Fields Institute Communications 21. 81-95. American Mathematical Society, Providence, RI, 1999.

40. Hayek, F. (2006) The Constitution of Liberty. Abingdon. Routledge. 96.

CHAPTER THIRTY

1. Woolhouse, M. (2022) The Year the World Went Mad: A Scientific Memoir. Dingwall. Sandstone Press.

2. Ioannidis, J. et al. (2020). Population-level COVID-19 mortality risk for non-elderly individuals. Environmental research. 188.

3. Ofsted. (2022) Education recovery in early years providers: spring 2022. Report 4 April 2022. https://www.gov.uk/government/publications/education-recovery-in-early-years-providers-spring-2022/education-recovery-in-early-years-providers-spring-2022

4. James. (2022) The Triumph of Janet; And how boomer entitlement stole your prosperity. Himbonomics Blog. April 2022. https://himbonomics.substack.com/p/-the-triumph-of-janet-

5. Neil, A. (2021) It's time to punish Britain's five million vaccine refuseniks: They put us all at risk. Daily Mail. 9 December 2021. https://www.dailymail.co.uk/debate/article-10294225/Its-time-punish-Britains-five-million-vaccine-refuseniks-says-ANDREW-NEIL.html

6. SPI-B. (2020) Options for increasing adherence to social distancing measures. 22 March 2020. https://assets.publishing.service.gov.uk/government/uploads/system/uploads/attachment_data/file/882722/25-options-for-increasing-adherence-to-social-distancing-measures-22032020.pdf

7. Ofcom. (2020) Note to Broadcasters – Coronavirus. 23 March 2020. https://www.ofcom.org.uk/__data/assets/pdf_file/0025/193075/Note-to-broadcasters-Coronavirus.pdf

8. Dodsworth, L. (2021) A State of Fear: How the UK government weaponised fear during the Covid-19 Pandemic. London. Pinter & Martin.

9. Roberts, M. (2021) How do we know Covid vaccines are safe? BBC News. 10 May 2021. https://www.bbc.co.uk/news/health-55056016

10. Fox, F. (2021) Britain's Covid experts are under attack, but they are just doing their jobs. The Guardian. 8 August 2021. https://www.theguardian.com/world/2021/aug/08/britains-covid-experts-neil-ferguson-sage-are-under-attack-but-they-are-just-doing-their-jobs

11. Heidegger, M. (1985) History of the Concept of Time. Translated by Theodore Kisiel. Indiana University Press. Bloomington. 216.

12. Carmichael, F., Haynes, C. (2021) The YouTubers who blew the whistle on an anti-vax plot. BBC News. 25 July 2021. https://www.bbc.co.uk/news/blogs-trending-57928647

13. BBC Trending. (2021) The volunteers using 'honeypot' groups to fight anti-vax propaganda. BBC. 11 May 2021. https://www.bbc.co.uk/news/blogs-trending-57051691

14. BBC News. (2021). Escaping the anti-vax conspiracy rabbit hole. BBC News. 16 April 2021. https://www.youtube.com/watch?v=09t_7ZgVjLE

15. Husting, G.; Orr, M. (2007) Dangerous Machinery: 'Conspiracy Theorist' as Transpersonal Strategy of Exclusion. Symbolic Interaction 30, 2: 127-50. https://onlinelibrary.wiley.com/doi/pdf/10.1525/si.2007.30.2.127

16. Davis, I. (2021) Why We Must Question Vaccine Efficacy And Safety Claims. UK Column. 2 July 2021. https://www.ukcolumn.org/article/why-we-must-question-vaccine-efficacy-and-safety-claims

17. Peters, S. (2021) Dr. Peter McCullough Issues URGENT VAXX WARNING. The Stew Peters Show. 21 July 2021. https://stewpeters.podbean.com/e/dr-peter-mccullough-issues-urgent-vaxx-warning-clay-clark-asks-questions-implicating-globalists/

18. Yeadon, M. (2021) Dr Mike Yeadon IN HARM'S WAY. Be Afraid of Government Not Covid. The Highwire. 14 June 2021. https://www.bitchute.com/video/8KLmLNzkVD2k/

19. Yeadon, M. (2020) What SAGE Has Got Wrong. Daily Sceptic. 16 October 2020. https://dailysceptic.org/what-sage-got-wrong/

20. Steyn, M. (2022) Mark Steyn Show. GB News. 23 March 2022.https://www.youtube.com/watch?v=wea4ex6x5w0

21. Sharman, M. (2021) Former ITV & Sky News Boss Mark Sharman. YouTube. 31 December 2021. https://youtu.be/WLujtPH-SQU

22. Pover, C. (2022) Life through the lens of the vaccine-injured. TCW. 29 June 2022. https://www.conservativewoman.co.uk/life-through-the-lens-of-the-vaccine-injured/

23. Pandolfo, C. (2022). Exclusive: The federal government paid hundreds of media companies to advertise the COVID-19 vaccines while those same outlets provided positive coverage of the vaccines. 3 March 2022. Blaze Media. https://www.theblaze.com/news/review-the-federal-government-paid-media-companies-to-advertise-for-the-vaccines. Accessed 8 March 2022

24. Robinson, E. (2022) Fox News & Newsmax Took Biden Money to Push Deadly COVID Vaccines To Its Viewers. The Right Way. 5 March 2022. https://emeralddb3.substack.com/p/fox-news-and-newsmax-took-biden-money?

25. Schwab, T. (2020). Journalism's Gates keepers. Columbia Journalism Review. 21 August 2020. https://www.cjr.org/criticism/gates-foundation-journalism-funding.php

26. Dodsworth, op cit.

27. Hatchard, G. (2022) If the Covid facts are inconvenient, alter them. TCW. 3 June 2022. https://www.conservativewoman.co.uk/if-the-covid-facts-are-inconvenient-alter-them/

28. Facebook. (2021) COVID-19 policy updates and protections. https://www.facebook.com/help/230764881494641/

29. Twitter. (2021) COVID-19 misleading information policy. December 2021. https://help.twitter.com/en/rules-and-policies/medical-misinformation-policy

30. YouTube. (2022) Vaccine misinformation policy. https://support.google.com/youtube/answer/11161123?hl=en

31. Malone, R. (2021) Analysis Overview: COVID-19 Genetic Vaccine Safety in Children. Robert Malone Blog. https://www.rwmalonemd.com/mrna-vaccination-in-children

32. Malone, R. (2021a) Permanently suspended on Twitter... and how to find me. Robert Malone blog. 29 December 2021. https://rwmalonemd.substack.com/p/permanently-suspended-on-twitter

33. Malone, R. (2022) What if the largest experiment on human beings in history is a failure? Robert Malone Blog. 3 January 2022. https://rwmalonemd.substack.com/p/what-if-the-largest-experiment-on

34. Powell, M. (2022) Twitter bans Oxford academic who shared this Mail on Sunday article. Daily Mail. 26 March 2022. https://www.dailymail.co.uk/news/article-10655577/Twitter-bans-Oxford-academic-shared-MoS-article-allows-anti-vax-rants.html

35. Zweig, D. (2022) Twitter. 26 December 2022. @davidzweig https://twitter.com/davidzweig/status/1607378386338340867?s=20&t=0xgsbyRpPRKF0abBkEa0QA

36. Zweig, D. (2022) How Twitter Rigged the Covid Debate. The Free Press. 26 December 2022. https://www.thefp.com/p/how-twitter-rigged-the-covid-debate

37. Younes, J.; Kheriaty, A. (2023) The White House Covid Censorship Machine. Wall Street Journal. 8 January 2023. https://www.wsj.com/articles/white-house-covid-censorship-machine-social-media-facebook-meta-executive-rob-flaherty-free-speech-google-11673203704

38. Pullmann, J. (2023) What Spygate Tells Us About The Google, Facebook, And Twitter Files. The Federalist. 9 January 2023. https://thefederalist.com/2023/01/09/what-spygate-tells-us-about-the-google-facebook-and-twitter-files/

39. Kennedy, R, F. (2021) The Real Anthony Fauci. Bill Gates, Big Pharma, and the Global War on Democracy. New York. Skyhorse.

40. Huntington, S. (2002) Dead Souls: The Denationalization of the American Elite. The National Interest. 1 March 20014. https://nationalinterest.org/print/article/dead-souls-the-denationalization-of-the-american-elite-620

41. Sumption, J. (2021) Tyranny of the Covid experts. Daily Mail. 31 July 2021. https://www.dailymail.co.uk/debate/article-9847775/Tyranny-Covid-experts-JONATHAN-SUMPTION.html

CHAPTER THIRTY-ONE

1. Stent, A. (2022) The Putin Doctrine. Foreign Affairs. 27 January 2022. https://www.foreignaffairs.com/articles/ukraine/2022-01-27/putin-doctrine

2. Mearsheimer, J. (2022) The Causes and Consequences of the Ukraine War. 6 June 2022. Lecture at the EUI Robert Schuman Centre. https://youtu.be/qciVozNtCDM

3. Lippmann, W. (1955) The Public Philosophy. New York. Mentor. 26.

4. Pomerantsev, P. (2022) Putin's Attack on Ukraine Is an Attempt to Delay His Own Inevitable Demise. Time. 25 February 2022. https://time.com/6151377/putin-ukraine-attack-dictator/

5. Harding, L. (2022) Putin's Russia: dictator syndrome and the rise of a 'mafia state'. The Guardian. Video. 20 June 2022. https://www.theguardian.com/world/video/2022/jun/20/putins-russia-dictator-syndrome-and-the-rise-of-a-mafia-state-video

6. Motyl, A. (2022) Putin's Russia rose like Hitler's Germany — and could end the same. The Hill. 3 May 2022. https://thehill.com/opinion/national-security/3470515-putins-russia-rose-like-hitlers-germany-and-could-end-the-same/

7. MSNBC. (2022) In attempt to stifle dissent, Putin shows he is a 'man out of time, and a man out of touch'. MSNBC. 25 February 2022. https://www.msnbc.com/morning-joe/watch/in-try-to-stifle-dissent-putin-shows-he-is-a-man-out-of-time-and-a-man-out-of-touch-134024773653

8. Johnson, B. (2022) Prime Minister Boris Johnson's address to the Ukrainian Parliament. 3 May 2022. https://www.gov.uk/government/speeches/prime-minister-boris-johnsons-address-to-the-ukrainian-parliament-3-may-2022

9. Husseini, S. (2022) The Predictable Demise of RT America. Consortium News. 5 March 2022. https://consortiumnews.com/2022/03/05/the-predictable-demise-of-rt-america/

10. Kayali, L. (2022) EU to ban Russia's RT, Sputnik media outlets, von der Leyen says. Politico. 27 February 2022. https://www.politico.eu/article/ursula-von-der-leyen-announces-rt-sputnik-ban

11. Ofcom (2022) Ofcom revokes RT's broadcast licence. 18 March 2022. https://www.ofcom.org.uk/news-centre/2022/ofcom-revokes-rt-broadcast-licence

12. AFP. (2022) Russia Vows to Hinder Work of Western Media After RT France Ban. The Moscow Times. 27 July 2022. https://www.themoscowtimes.com/2022/07/27/russia-vows-to-hinder-work-of-western-media-after-rt-france-ban-a78418

13. Baroud, R. (2022) 'Not a Justification but a Provocation': Chomsky on the Root Causes of the Russia Ukraine War. Counterpunch. 28 June 2022. https://www.counterpunch.org/2022/06/28/not-a-justification-but-a-provocation-chomsky-on-the-root-causes-of-the-russia-ukraine-war/

14. Pilger, J. (2022) 'This is a war of propaganda': John Pilger on Ukraine and Assange. South China Morning Post. YouTube. 9 July 2022. https://youtu.be/u9pEotvlW-s

15. Rickards, J. (2022) Needless Death and Misery. Daily Reckoning. 12 July 2022. https://dailyreckoning.com/needless-death-and-misery/

16. Moeini, A. (2022) How Western elites exploit Ukraine. Unherd. 5 March 2022. https://unherd.com/2022/03/how-western-elites-exploit-ukraine/

17. Schlosberg, J. (2022a) Twitter. 4 April 2022. https://twitter.com/jrschlosberg/status/1510986180397088777

18. Schlosberg, J. (2022b) Twitter. 4 April 2022.https://twitter.com/jrschlosberg/status/1510986182083108864

19. BBC (2022) Ukraine: The Disinformation War. BBC File on 4. 31 May 2022. http://downloads.bbc.co.uk/rmhttp/fileon4/PAJ_4562_PG07_Disinformation_war.pdf

20. Schlosberg, J. (2022c) Twitter. 1 June 2022. https://twitter.com/jrschlosberg/status/1531889814462685190

21. Schlosberg, J. (2022d) Twitter. 1 June 2022. https://twitter.com/jrschlosberg/status/1531890636160475136

22. Schlosberg, J. (2022e) Interview with author. 16 August 2022. Hayward, T. (2022) Interview with author. 9 June 2022.

23. Hayward, T. (2022) Interview with author. 9 June 2022.

24. Taylor, D. (1975) Editorial Responsibilities. BBC Lunch-time Lectures. 10th Series (2). 13 November 1975.

25. Gurfein, M. (1971) U.S. District Court for the Southern District of New York. 19 June 1971. 328 F. Supp. 324 (S.D.N.Y. 1971)

26. Obama, B. (2021) Disinformation Is a Threat to Our Democracy. Barack Obama website. 21 April 2021. https://barackobama.medium.com/my-remarks-on-disinformation-at-stanford-7d7af7ba28af

27. Greenwald, G. (2021) The Journalistic Tattletale and Censorship Industry Suffers Several Well-Deserved Blows. Glenn Greenwald blog. 7 February 2021. https://greenwald.substack.com/p/the-journalistic-tattletale-and-censorship

CHAPTER THIRTY-TWO

1. Williams, D. op cit. 127.

2. Storr, W. (2019) The Science of Storytelling. London. William Collins. 160.

3. Obama, B. (2021) Disinformation Is a Threat to Our Democracy. Barack Obama website. 21 April 2021. https://barackobama.medium.com/my-remarks-on-disinformation-at-stanford-7d7af7ba28af

4. Storr, op cit. 162.

5. Biden, R. (2022) Remarks by President Biden on the Continued Battle for the Soul of the Nation, Independence National Historical Park, Philadelphia. 1 September 2022. White House Press Room. https://www.whitehouse.gov/briefing-room/speeches-remarks/2022/09/01/remarks-by-president-bidenon-the-continued-battle-for-the-soul-of-the-nation/

6. Scully, R. (2022) Trump calls Biden 'an enemy of the state'. The Hill. 4 September 2022. https://thehill.com/homenews/state-watch/3628611-trump-calls-biden-an-enemy-of-the-state/

7. Taibbi, M. (2022) PayPal's IndyMedia Wipeout. TK News. 3 May 2022. https://taibbi.substack.com/p/paypals-indymedia-wipeout

8. Young, T. (2022) PayPal Demonetises the Daily Sceptic. Daily Sceptic. 21 September 2022. https://dailysceptic.org/2022/09/21/paypal-demonetises-the-daily-sceptic/

9. Turner, C. (2022) PayPal urged to release confiscated funds from frozen British accounts. Daily Telegraph. 24 September 2022. https://www.telegraph.co.uk/news/2022/09/24/paypal-urged-release-confiscated-funds-frozen-british-accounts/

10. Gay, P. (1969) The Enlightenment: An Interpretation. Vol 2. New York. Alfred Knopf. 163.

11. Galbraith, J.K. (1962) The Affluent Society. London. Penguin. 14.

12. Pilkington, P. (2022) The next Great Depression? Economic warfare has severe implications. The Critic. 29 September 2022. https://thecritic.co.uk/the-next-great-depression/

13. Secor, L. (2022) Henry Kissinger Is Worried About 'Disequilibrium'. The Wall Street Journal. 12 August 2022. https://www.wsj.com/articles/henry-kissinger-is-worried-about-disequilibrium

14. Cunliffe, P. (2019) Framing intervention in a multipolar world. Conflict, Security & Development. 19:3, 245-250.

15. Snyder, M. (2022) The Era Of Cheap Food And Cheap Gasoline Is Over. The Most Important News blog. 11 October 2022. http://themostimportantnews.com/archives/the-era-of-cheap-food-and-cheap-gasoline-is-over

16. Peters, E. (2022) Hedge Fund CIO: "An Utterly Extraordinary Period Is Ending: Macron Knows This, So Does Xi" ZeroHedge. 24 October 2022. https://www.zerohedge.com/markets/hedge-fund-cio-utterly-extraordinary-period-ending-macron-knows-so-does-xi

17. Boomer, C. (1992) The Neophilics. London. Pimlico. 9.

18. Hopkins, M. (1968) Those Were the Days. Fomin, B.;Raskin, G. Apple Records.

19. Moran, B. (2022) After self-censoring shame over lockdown, how can journalists stay silent on vaccine danger? TCW. 31 August 2022. https://www.

conservativewoman.co.uk/after-self-censoring-shame-over-lockdown-how-can-journalists-stay-silent-on-vaccine-danger/

20. Downie, L.; Heyward, A. (2023) Beyond Objectivity: Producing Trustworthy News in Today's Newsrooms. Walter Cronkite School of Journalism and Mass Communication. 10.

21. Brecht, B. (1963) The Life of Galileo. London. Methuen. 85.

22. Brecht. Op cit. 6.

23. Tucker, J. (2022) Why Did So Many Intellectuals Refuse to Speak Out? Brownstone Institute. 6 October 2022. https://brownstone.org/articles/why-did-so-many-intellectuals-refuse-to-speak-out/

24. Crichton, M. (2003) Environmentalism is a Religion. Speech to The Commonwealth Club in San Francisco. 15 September 2003. www.michael-hoskinson.com/michael-crichton-environmentalism-is-a-religion/

25. Chalk, C. (2022) Hundreds Of Newspapers Work To Bury Opinion As Journalism By Dropping Op-Eds. The Federalist. 17 June 2022. https://thefederalist.com/2022/06/17/hundreds-of-newspapers-work-to-bury-opinion-as-journalism-by-dropping-op-eds/

26. Sagan, C. (1997) The Demon-Haunted World: Science as a Candle in the Dark. New York. Ballantine. 25.

27. Clark, K. (1969) Civilisation; A Personal View. London. BBC & John Murray. 347.

Printed in Great Britain
by Amazon